SANTA ANA PUBLIC LIBRARY

D0758109

BLOOD ON THE SNOW

BLOOD ON THE SNOW

The Carpathian Winter War of 1915

Graydon A. Tunstall

University Press of Kansas

Published by the University Press of Kansas (Lawrence, Kansas 66045),
which was organized by the Kansas Board of Regents and is operated
and funded by Emporia State University, Fort Hays State University,
Kansas State University, Pittsburg State University, the University of
Kansas, and Wichita State University

Library of Congress Cataloging-in-Publication Data

Tunstall, Graydon A. (Graydon Allen)
Blood on the snow : the Carpathian winter war of 1915 / Graydon A. Tunstall.
p.   cm. — (Modern war studies)
Includes bibliographical references and index.
ISBN 978-0-7006-1720-3 (cloth : alk. paper)
ISBN 978-0-7006-1858-3 (pbk : alk. paper)
1. World War, 1914–1918—Campaigns—Carpathian Mountains. 2. Austro-
Hungarian Monarchy. Heer—History—World War, 1914–1918. 3. Russia.
Armiia—History—World War, 1914–1918. 4. Winter—Carpathian
Mountains—History—20th century. 5. Carpathian Mountains—
History, Military—20th century. I. Title.
D556.T86 2010
940.4'25—dc22   2009052229

British Library Cataloguing-in-Publication Data is available.

Printed in the United States of America

10 9 8 7 6 5 4 3

TO WENDY, MY WIFE AND SOUL MATE

CONTENTS

A photograph section appears following page 106.

ACKNOWLEDGMENTS

MANY PEOPLE HAVE BEEN of inestimable assistance throughout this multiyear project. Among them is Peter Broucek, retired head of the Austrian War Archives World War I Section, who first suggested the topic to me years ago. My utmost gratitude goes to Dennis Showalter, a constant mentor, for encouraging me to complete this work. I thank my editor, Michael Briggs, for his enduring support throughout this book's long gestational period. Special mention is also due Vannina Wurm in Vienna for her diligence and keen eye; and Ferenc Pollmann, in Budapest, who brought to my attention key holdings in the Budapest War Archives on the Honvéd participation in the war, and to the memory of Leopold Moser, a true friend and former librarian in the Vienna War Archives.

I am especially grateful to Carolyn Pointer Lowry and Brittany Vosler for their pleasant demeanor in the face of innumerable manuscript revisions, and to Jessica Magro for her valuable assistance in the early stages of this work. I thank my good friend and colleague, Kazimierz Robak, for helping to locate and translate relevant Polish sources, and the University of South Florida for its support of my research.

. . . and to those who fought and died in the Carpathian Mountains in the winter of 1915, may your sacrifice finally be recognized.

BLOOD ON
THE SNOW

Introduction

There is no enemy more formidable than nature.   Anonymous

THE CARPATHIAN WINTER WAR of 1915 presents one of the most significant—and, in terms of human sacrifice, most tragic—chapters of World War I military history. The winter mountain battle that pitted allied Austro-Hungarian and German armies against Russian troops was unprecedented in the age of total war. The *Karpathenkrieg* comprised three separate campaigns launched by the Habsburg Supreme Command from mid-January to April 1915. The Eastern front operation, which ultimately engaged more than one million men on each side, could hardly have been conducted under worse conditions. The Carpathian theater lacked the railways, roads, communication lines, and other important resources necessary for maneuvering mass armies. Moreover, the contenders soon found themselves ensnared in an inhospitable mountain environment in wintertime. The three-month campaign, which ended in spring 1915, left the Austro-Hungarian Army under chief of the General Staff, Conrad von Hötzendorf, in shambles. The Russians did not fare much better. Casualties on both sides surpassed those of the so-called blood pump battles of Verdun and Somme in 1916, earning the Carpathian Winter War the dubious title of the Stalingrad of World War I.[1]

Historically significant, though little known (in the United States, virtually unknown), the *Karpathenkrieg* served as the background to the Gorlice-Tarnor offensive, the Central Powers' greatest victory of World War I. The months-long campaign saw some of the most brutal combat of the war. Before the last rifle fell silent, the blood of some one million Austro-Hungarian, Russian, and German soldiers soaked the snowy Carpathian terrain. Countless others lost limbs to frostbite or suffered similar debilitating fates. Exhaustive archival research has unearthed detailed eyewitness accounts of the battles that raged on the Eastern front. Major primary sources are deposited in the *Feldakten* and *Nachlaß* (private donation) collections of the Vienna War Archives, others in the Budapest War Archives. These archival documents, many written in *Kurrentschrift,* oftentimes contradict the official Austrian historiography on World War I, *Österreich-Ungarns letzter Krieg*.[2]

Of particular importance to this study is the extensive manuscript collection of the Vienna War Archives. Several manuscripts detail the events of key participants in the Carpathian Winter War, including those of the South Army, a combined Austro-Hungarian and German entity deployed to support the buckling Habsburg front lines. The conditions encountered by Hungarian troops, particularly Group Szurmay, are recorded and housed in the Budapest War Archives.[3] Interestingly enough, the personal diaries, telegrams, and other communiqués of commanders situated a safe distance from the front at Habsburg Supreme Headquarters offer a diverse account of Carpathian Winter War events. The daily logbooks (*Tagebücher*) of Conrad von Hötzendorf's personal adjutant, Rudolf Kundmann, are particularly enlightening, as are those of Colonel Karl Schneller, section head of the "I" (Italian) Group in the General Staff.[4]

Personal accounts of participants in this tragic chapter of World War I history offer additional relevant source materials. A detailed chronicle by Kralowetz von Hohenrecht Gottlieb, chief of staff of the Habsburg Third Army X Corps, describes the hardships the corps encountered. The corps, one of the main offensive units deployed in all three Carpathian campaigns, was ill-prepared for the winter weather and terrain conditions. Habsburg Colonel Georg Veith, another key witness, describes in gut-wrenching detail the adversity his men encountered battling the Russian armies in the Carpathian hellhole. Veith is cited in numerous important sources, including the Austrian official history of the world war.

Before World War I, potential battle zones were classified as either a *Manoverierzone*, suitable for conducting a war of maneuver using mass armies, or a *Durchzugzone*, through which armies would march to reach the major battle site, but not conducive for a major military operation. Though Russian, Habsburg, and German military strategists designated the Carpathian region a pass-through zone, the territory would provide the setting for the largest confrontation in the world war to date, and one of the largest in modern warfare. Hundreds of thousands of Habsburg infantry were subjected to extreme deprivation in their simultaneous struggle against overpowering Russian forces and the harsh winter mountain environment. Blizzard conditions alternated with periods of thaw, wreaking havoc on military and supply operations. The challenge to provide the front lines with a steady stream of food, supplies, ammunition, and artillery proved insurmountable.

The defense of Galicia presented a special challenge for the Dual

Monarchy's military. The Galician province extended beyond the Carpathian Mountains, and its northern and eastern frontiers were indefensible. Though three major rivers traversed the province, the Dniester, the Moldova, and the Ceremuș, none provided an effective defensive barrier. Thus, invading forces could attack from three directions. The extremely limited road and rail access to inner Austria posed another major problem in securing the monarchy. Entrée to the region required navigating five major Carpathian passes, a time-consuming undertaking.

In winter 1915, moving troops and supplies into the Carpathian Mountains proved a serious challenge, one that Habsburg Supreme Command failed to overcome during the Carpathian campaign. Roads that were easy to traverse in the summer months required several hours, often days, to navigate in winter. However, of all the Habsburg military's missteps, its blind adherence to the short war dogma is perhaps most noteworthy. Despite indications to the contrary, Habsburg Supreme Command remained in a state of denial. The conflict would not endure; therefore, making provisions for a winter battle was superfluous. Conrad's decision to launch a major military operation in the densely wooded mountain region in the winter of 1915 seemed even more far-fetched. Habsburg shortsightedness and Conrad von Hötzendorf's determination to conduct a major offensive in a pass-through zone cost hundreds of thousands of *k.u.k.* (*kaiserlich und königlich*, "imperial and royal") soldiers their lives. In the three months spanning the Carpathian Winter War, Habsburg Supreme Command deployed infantry masses into the mountainous theater with no provision for winter uniforms or suitable equipment. The men's boots, with soles constructed of cardboard, quickly disintegrated in the wet and snowy conditions. The more fortunate received winter clothing from home. Icy mountain slopes caused many to lose their footing—and their lives—slipping into the path of Russian sniper fire. Contrary to official Austro-Hungarian military reports, the majority of Carpathian war casualties were not related to combat. Hundreds of thousands of Habsburg troops fell victim to *der Weisse Tod* (the White Death) lying in the open in subfreezing temperatures with no shelter. How could soldiers, deployed in a region where timber was plentiful, freeze to death? The answer lies in Habsburg Supreme Command's stubborn refusal to acknowledge the possibility that the war would extend into the winter months. Conrad's troops were sent to the Carpathian war theater without the most rudimentary winter provisions, including warm clothes, winter boots, and saws with which to fell trees for firewood.

All three Habsburg offensives relied heavily on the element of surprise—a factor all too often compromised by poor weather and terrain conditions, which gave the Russians ample time to initiate countermeasures. Conrad's armies became easy targets for czarist troops situated on well-fortified positions on dominating terrain in late December 1914 and early January 1915. The Habsburg attackers were forced to strike uphill amid a volley of Russian gunfire. Moreover, czarist troops were better acclimated to the cold and adept at exploiting the winter weather conditions to their advantage, oftentimes attacking unsuspecting Habsburg troops during a snowstorm.

The Carpathian Mountain range, stretching in an arc from the Czech Republic in the northwest to Slovakia, Poland, Hungary, Ukraine, and Romania in the east and Serbia in the south, evokes legendary tales of werewolves and vampires, particularly the region of Transylvania. For participants in the Carpathian Winter War, life in the mountains became a terrifying ordeal, particularly at night. Wolves howled, wind whistled through the trees, and ominous shadows rattled the nerves of the most daring souls. While lying in the open with no shelter during the long winter nights, soldiers' fears of an enemy ambush intensified. Survival required the utmost physical and mental fortitude. In many respects, survival meant leaving the civilized world behind and relying on primal instinct. Veterans of the Carpathian Winter War later recalled feeling surrounded by death and a lingering sense of impending doom. Many were unable to cope and committed suicide.

Mountain warfare as characterized by the Carpathian winter offensives produced a combat experience vastly different from the trench warfare of the west. Heavy rainfall and blinding snowstorms left little time for rest or relaxation. Discomfort became the order of the day as troops became susceptible to lung disease, exposure, hypothermia, and frostbite. Snow, ice, and the rugged mountain terrain made large-scale troop movement difficult. The Carpathian Mountain terrain, which was considered unsuitable for large unit warfare even in the summer months, complicated military operations and supply efforts, and it placed increased physical demands and risks on the soldiers. The physically demanding daily routine of maintaining roads and reconstructing positions damaged by enemy action left Habsburg troops physically and morally weakened.

Readers of this investigation will note the frequent depiction of Habsburg troops as utterly exhausted and increasingly apathetic. At the risk of sounding repetitive, the mental and physical condition of Habsburg troops is critical to understanding the Carpathian Winter War. The exhaustion experienced in combat under winter conditions is incomprehensible to those who have not suffered under such circumstances. Reading the daily logbooks of Habsburg units participating in the Carpathian Winter War, one would be hard-pressed to find an entry that did not include the words *ganz erschöpft* ("utterly exhausted"). The men's physical and mental exhaustion was exacerbated by hunger. Food supplies often did not reach the front, and those that did were often frozen solid. The men began to hallucinate about food, driving them to near insanity. In the winter of 1915, not only did Habsburg Supreme Command decide to deploy massive armies into a region unfit for a major combat operation, but also, it did so with no provision for the most basic of necessities—food, clothing, and shelter.

Combat exhaustion became even more widespread when a shortage of reinforcements forced soldiers to man the front lines for months at a time with no rehabilitation. Such was the fate of hundreds of thousands of Austro-Hungarian soldiers in the Carpathian winter campaign. Few conflicts, including World War I and World War II, have recorded such debilitating experiences. As a recent study on the psychological effects of war explains, "in war there's perhaps no general condition that is more likely to produce a large crop of nervous and mental disorders."[5]

The cumulative effects of exhaustion, hunger, and combat on a soldier are multifold. One is the physiological effect of battle stress on the human body. Sleep deprivation and too little food compound the effect, which natural elements, including rain, snow, cold, and the dark of night, then exacerbate. These factors in combination create "a state of prolonged and great fatigue."[6] Combat-induced stress causes the nervous system to alter its inner survival instinct. Bodily functions are similarly affected, often after the fighting has ended and the soldiers become weary.[7] During combat, soldiers' emotions rise and fall in dramatic sequence. That the soldiers could not escape their fate or overcome the violence during fighting periods pushed them into states of profound emotional and physical exhaustion. The men often drew inside themselves, finding it extremely difficult to communicate with anyone who had not suffered the same experience. Soldiers in this state usually collapsed as a result of nervous exhaustion.

The profound lack of sleep produced further psychological damage. The lack of food, or the few unappetizing rations, compounded their mental injuries and had a tremendous impact on the troops' effectiveness in battle. In combat, soldiers were at the mercy of the weather, which caused further torment. The worst conditions were experienced during winter months. Weary soldiers spent the long winter nights struggling to stay awake to avoid frostbite or freezing to death. Emotional fatigue set in, compounded by the impact of the elements and the lack of food and sleep. Compasses malfunctioned, leading units, some as large as regiments, to march blindly in circles in dense woods during blizzards. Water jackets froze, leading machine guns to misfire or fail to fire. The troops often had to resort to warming their rifles over fires so the weapons functioned properly.

Sadly, much of the pain and suffering experienced by *k.u.k.* troops during the Carpathian Winter War could have been reduced, if not avoided, had Habsburg Supreme Command made provisions for the conflict enduring into winter. Command's blind faith in offensive doctrine obscured the need for any serious training in defensive warfare. For the Carpathian Winter War, this signified that no precautionary measures were initiated or retreat plans determined until much too late. Most importantly for the planned major offensive actions, Habsburg Supreme Command failed to adequately consider the inherent terrain limitations, which restricted freedom of movement and logistical support for large troop formations. Unfortunately, except the November and December 1914 mountain campaigns, no practical experiences existed to study or review in preparation for the campaign. A fateful cynicism grew among the soldiers who were compelled to suffer the consequences of their leaders' shortsightedness.

What, then, drew Habsburg Supreme Command to the Carpathian Mountain region? A garrison of 120,000 men in Fortress Przemyśl was under siege by Russian troops and in danger of surrendering. Time was of the essence, and the Carpathian Mountains offered the shortest route to the beleaguered fortress. Conrad von Hötzendorf convinced the Habsburg military leadership to launch a major offensive before the terrible summer and fall campaign losses had been replaced. The San River fortress became a metaphor for the very existence of the Dual Monarchy and a driving influence over Habsburg military strategy on the Eastern front.

As the events of the Carpathian Winter War unfolded, a tragic fact became strikingly clear. Conrad's dogged assertion, or gamble, that a Carpathian campaign would be short and swift proved wrong, at the cost of hundreds of thousands of lives. From the moment the first Habsburg soldier disembarked from his train en route to the front, numerous signs challenged Conrad's claim. On the eve of battle, a fierce snowstorm struck the Carpathian Mountain theater. The attack order was given even though poor weather and terrain conditions had delayed the arrival of all the intended troops. Consequently, too few soldiers were deployed on too broad a front. Many attack units were ordered to provide flank security, thus fielding more troops than necessary for that purpose, and thereby weakening the main offensive thrust.

The Carpathian Mountain range measures 120 kilometers at its greatest width and 100 kilometers at its most narrow. Its median elevation of 1,100 meters stretches in a 1,500-kilometer arc encompassing 190,000 square kilometers. At the outbreak of war, only a few mountain passes provided road and rail access through the mountains to the Hungarian Plains or, in the opposite direction, onto the Galician plateau. During the 1915 Carpathian winter campaign, transporting supplies was limited to the five major Carpathian Mountain passes: the Wyszkov, Lupkov, Beskid, Uzsok, and Dukla. Owing to its accessibility and proximity to the Hungarian Plains, the Dukla Pass was of primary interest to the Russian military, and thus it became the site of particularly fierce fighting. (Of the five major mountain passes, the Uzsok, Dukla, and Lupkov were the most strategically important.)

The major Carpathian Mountain passes remained covered in snow from November 1914 through April 1915. A sudden rise in temperatures turned snow to rain, resulting in widespread flooding in the valleys. The forested mountain terrain forced the separation of advancing battle formations, producing uncoordinated and sporadic small-unit combat. Units frequently became lost and were unable to rejoin their formations.

The Uzsok Pass, some forty-five kilometers southeast of the Lupkov Pass, featured steep roads and cavernous mountain ravines that provided access to the Dniester and Stryj valleys, which were strategically important to the Habsburg Carpathian offensive. The Uzsok Pass, at a higher elevation than the Lupkov, possessed numerous bridges spanning its deep canyons. A railroad had recently been constructed in the area as an alternative to the difficult terrain and had a mile-long tunnel. Dense forests covered the mountainside in and around Uzsok Pass. In a major setback on 1 January 1915, Habsburg armies lost control of the pass to the Russians. Regaining possession of the area was crucial for Habsburg troops to seize the main Russian railroad centers, particularly those at Ustrzyki Dolne, Sanok, and Lisko. These remained primary objectives for Habsburg arms throughout the Carpathian campaign. With the Uzsok Pass under Habsburg control, the Russians would be forced to flee the mountain ridges south of the Ustrzyki Dolne railroad junction.

The two San River towns of Sanok and Lisko, strategically located to defend the river valley, became the objectives of the first two Carpathian offensives. Sanok, situated high on the mountainside overlooking the San River, was the region's major cultural, industrial, and transportation center. Steep slopes in the *Altstadt* section of the city swept down to the San River. Lisko, situated in the rolling hillside of the Carpathians, overlooked the San River. Their railroads made Sanok and Lisko key military objectives.

The Dukla Pass, forty kilometers wide and sixty kilometers long, provided the Russian armies the most advantageous attack route for an invasion of Hungary. The pass was relatively broad and not much higher than the adjacent countryside. Straight roads in good condition and with easy grades connecting Hungary and Galicia traversed the pass. However, the Dukla was the most difficult of all the Carpathian passes on which to establish defensive positions, and furthermore, there was no railroad access. Early in the Carpathian winter campaign, the Russians had seized the two minor passes on either side of the Dukla and designated the pass a major jumping-off point for counterattacks once the Habsburg offensive commenced. Behind the Dukla depression, a railroad line led to Mezölaborcz, a major communication center possessing the only double-track railroad into that key area. Thus, Mezölaborcz became the brass ring both sides fought fiercely to possess, particularly when Russian general Ivanov launched a counterattack three days after the start of the first Habsburg offensive.

The Lupkov was the highest and largest of the five main Carpathian Mountain passes. Located some twenty kilometers southeast of the Dukla Pass, its access to both Fortress Przemyśl and Hungary made the route strategically important. The Lupkov had a good road that crossed the crest three or four miles to the northwest, but zigzagged as a result of the steep slopes and ridges on both sides. The thinly forested pass featured no dominating heights. In early November 1914, Fortress Przemyśl was besieged by Russian troops for the second time in as many months. They used the area as a staging ground for an invasion of Hungary. After wrenching the Uzsok Pass from Habsburg troops on 1 January 1915, the Russians began their advance, first toward the Dukla and then the easier-to-navigate Lupkov Pass. At the approaches to the Lupkov Pass, attacking army units would have to defile for several miles along its single road, making them vulnerable to defending troop gunfire. The railroad traversing the pass lacked long bridges and thus could not be disrupted for long periods of time; however, it had sharp, narrow curves and a steep grade.

In the final days of 1914, General Conrad faced two serious challenges. A Russian invasion of Hungary must be prevented at all costs and the besieged 120,000-man garrison at Fortress Przemyśl rescued. Under mounting military and political pressure, liberating the fortress became a major objective. Indeed, Emperor Franz Joseph made personal appeals for the garrison's rescue and wept openly upon its final surrender on 22 March 1915.[8] The tense situation at Fortress Przemyśl worsened as food stores declined and the Russian noose tightened. At the beginning of the New Year, estimates had food provisions lasting only until mid-March 1915.[9] The Russians sought to take Fortress Przemyśl, but not by the brute force of the

September–October 1914 siege. Instead, with the Przemyśl front now a secondary theater, the Russians sought to starve the garrison into submission.

General Conrad's September 1914 through March 1915 operational planning placed the liberation of Fortress Przemyśl as its primary military objective. By the end of the Carpathian winter campaign in mid-April 1915, two-thirds of the Habsburg army, several German corps, and four Russian armies participated in the bloody contest. Significantly, each of the three campaigns in winter 1915 used similar tactics and targeted the same objectives as the fall 1914 endeavor. However, Conrad's latest endeavor differed in one very important aspect: weather in the Carpathian Mountains had worsened significantly. Considering the extraordinary challenges the Austro-Hungarian armies encountered in the fall battles, how could Habsburg Supreme Command possibly ignore the obvious risks involved in a winter campaign?

Nonetheless, for seven months, beginning in October 1914 and ending in April 1915, the Habsburg chief of the General Staff remained fixated on liberating Fortress Przemyśl. Ironically, Conrad had opposed the construction of additional fortresses during the prewar era. He argued that too many field army soldiers would have to occupy the citadels and they cost too much to build. Fortress Przemyśl had itself suffered from decades of neglect, and most of its armaments were considered antiquated. In the immediate prewar period, small sums appropriated to fortresses went to construction at the Italian frontier.[10] During the alarm period, defensive positions were hurriedly constructed around Fortress Przemyśl's perimeter over a forty-two-day period.[11] The San River bastion remained susceptible to heavy artillery fire; thus, its defensive capabilities were underrated. However, the fortress was strategically located near the gap between the marshes of the San–Dniester River line, a major travel route between central and southeastern Europe. More importantly, Fortress Przemyśl stood as the bulwark against a Russian invasion onto the Hungarian Plains, where the Dukla Pass and the lower San River basin granted the easiest access. The fortification would halt, or at least detain, invading czarist troops in their quest to invade Hungary, a key Russian objective in the defeat of Austria-Hungary.

Fortress Przemyśl came to symbolize Austro-Hungarian military prestige and in time excessively influenced Habsburg Eastern front strategy, particularly after the monarchy's embarrassing Balkan defeat to Serbia in early December 1914. Conrad, intent on breaking the Russians' stranglehold on the fortress, placed his armies in grave danger, ordering attacks along the shortest route to liberate the garrison. In each of the winter campaigns,

Habsburg troops were ordered to launch uphill frontal assaults. Disregarding the fact that Habsburg troops had yet to recover from the severe bloodletting of the summer and fall 1914 campaigns, Conrad now ordered his badly shaken armies to undertake what amounted to a suicide mission.

Not surprisingly, the Austro-Hungarian army incurred horrendous casualties and reduced the Habsburg army of 1914 to a militia (*Miliz*) or skeleton army. The severe loss of professional officers and soldiers in the early campaigns led to its designation as a *Landsturm* army. The astounding casualties early in the war necessitated the reorganization of the Austro-Hungarian army in October 1914 and again before the Carpathian Winter War. By fall 1914, the *k.u.k.* army deployed when war was declared had largely been destroyed. The destruction of the Dual Monarchy's professional officer corps forced the need for retired and replacement officers to return to duty. These reserves and older soldiers were physically incapable of withstanding the rigors of mountain warfare, were unfamiliar with modern military techniques, and lacked the professional officer corps' leadership and language skills, critical for maintaining cohesiveness in a multinational army. Such deficiencies significantly influenced the monarchy's Eastern front military operations. During the 1915 Carpathian campaign, the replacement of professional soldiers with inexperienced officers along with poor strategic planning led to ongoing battlefield defeat.

The Carpathian Winter War proved significant for many reasons. It would be the final campaign for the once revered *k.u.k.* army. In the chaos of the opening battles, the Habsburg army sacrificed 40 percent (420,000 men) of its mobilized combat troops (100,000 dead, 220,000 wounded, 100,000 prisoners of war). Only 404,000 professional officers, noncommissioned officers, and soldiers of the million-man army fought in the initial August–September campaigns. Thus, well over half of the Habsburg army was now made up of reservists or *Landsturm* troops (comparable to the U.S. pre–Iraq War national guard). Tons of war matériel, weaponry, food, 216 artillery pieces, and 15,000 railroad rolling stock and hundreds of kilometers of railroad tracks and locomotives were also forfeited in battle and subsequent retreat.[12] Furthermore, in sacrificing Galicia, grain warehouses and important manpower were also lost. How could these be replaced?

From a tactical standpoint, the Habsburg military leaders failed to incorporate the lessons of modern warfare and instead continued launching sacrificial uncoordinated infantry attacks without sufficient artillery support. Officer corps training was inconsistent, and candidates were not appropriately trained for the 1914 war conditions. Many were unable to meet the demands of modern war and lacked the necessary strong will. By the time the Habsburg military used more modern warfare tactics and updated its arsenal of weaponry at the behest of its German ally, it was almost too late. Waning confidence in Austro-Hungarian military leadership incited the Germans to increasingly impose their command influence on Habsburg Eastern front operations. Major squabbles over command issues first arose during the Carpathian winter campaign, not the Brusilov offensive, as many have suggested.

In retrospect, Austria-Hungary's calamitous defeat in the Carpathian Winter War can justifiably be attributed to the missteps of the Habsburg Supreme Command. Not once during the entire campaign did Conrad (or any member of his Operations Bureau, for that matter) visit the front to assess the true situation. Instead, Habsburg military leaders remained oblivious to the harsh battlefield realities, frequently basing their plans on faulty or incorrect assumptions. In Conrad's mind, pushpins on his battle maps represented divisions, when they actually had been reduced to brigade- or regiment-size units. As the Habsburg military situation steadily deteriorated, scores of field commanders ignored or delayed following orders, waiting for neighboring units to act. Those that launched an attack often found themselves in an untenable position when nearby units balked. The men soon lost confidence in their commanders and in the success of their mission.

Aside from the nebulous goals to free Fortress Przemyśl and prevent an invasion of Hungary, Habsburg Supreme Command drew criticism from the rank and file for its failure to set clearly defined objectives. It became increasingly difficult for the *k.u.k.* army to achieve a decisive victory once the initial Carpathian campaign was launched without the requisite troop strength. During the first Carpathian offensive launched in late January 1915, the Habsburg 175,000-man attack force (Third and South Army), with 1,000 artillery pieces, clearly lacked the troop numbers to fulfill its challenging multiple missions. So why did Conrad insist on undertaking a grandiose military operation without the necessary troop mass? Had additional units been deployed for the initial offensive, as they would be later on, perhaps the campaign could have succeeded. This is discussed in greater detail in Chapter 2. In the second Carpathian offensive Conrad's armies did in fact outnumber Russian troops, at least initially. However, this advantage was soon negated as Chapter 3 will explain.

The Winter War campaigns had two primary objectives: to encircle the extreme left flank enemy positions to end the enemy pressure on this front, and to free the besieged Fortress Przemyśl. The question arose of determining a military strategy that was based on a fixed defensive position: Fortress Przemyśl. In Conrad's defense, he was not alone in underestimating the effects of winter weather and mountain terrain on his troops. General Nikolai Yudovich Ivanov (1851–1919), commander of the Russian Southwest front, pushed his armies until they became so deeply entrenched in the Carpathian Mountain theater that they were barely able to extricate themselves. They did so at great human cost, when the Germans launched their relieving Gorlice–Tarnov offensive in early May 1915. Ivanov was determined to push through the Carpathian Mountains and invade Hungary, despite his seeming acceptance of the *Stavka*'s decision to make Germany the main enemy that must be eliminated first. His successes extended into April 1915, when czarist troops reached the last ridges protecting Hungary. This forced the Germans to launch the May Gorlice–Tarnov offensive to prevent the collapse and annihilation of their Austro-Hungarian allies. Meanwhile, the majority of Russian troops remained motionless on the German front.

The Carpathian campaign produced an unprecedented loss of men and material. Austria-Hungary lost 800,000 troops, six times the number of the garrison troops in Fortress Przemyśl that they had set out to free. Russia sustained well over 1,000,000 casualties. Losses to the Austro-Hungarian officer corps far exceeded those of any other major combatant. During the first five months of the war, the army suffered 3,200 officers dead and 7,000 wounded—at least one-third of the entire officer corps.

By the end of 1914, the Habsburg army had sacrificed 1.25 million troops. Pressing problems faced the army, among them widening gaps in the front lines and persistent shell shortages. *Ersatz* (replacement) troops could not replace the enormous losses, nor were they useful in major offensives. Valuable Habsburg manpower was unbelievably squandered. On average, a soldier fighting in the Carpathian Winter War lasted from between five to six weeks before he was killed, wounded, or captured. Suicides became a common occurrence.

In fairness to the two commanders, engaging in winter mountain warfare on such a scale had no precedent in the annals of military history. In addition, no suitable means existed to gather accurate and timely situation reports. In the first offensive, launched 23 January 1915, the attack front proved too wide for the troop numbers, and in the second, on 27 February, too narrow. The chronic shortage of reserve formations also proved a major deterrent to success.

During mobilization, all excess manpower lacking training and equipment were ordered into *Ersatz* units. The original role of these basically third-line troops was to provide tactical reinforcements for the front. Because of the multiple battlefield defeats, massive casualties, and lack of reserve units, already during September 1914, such *Ersatz* units often found themselves hurled into the front lines as self-sufficient combat units, in defiance of Habsburg Supreme Command orders.[13] The enormous influx of new, inexperienced recruits in August 1914 comprised the first monthly allotment of March Brigades, as well as *Ersatz* units. Later they consisted of wounded officers and men returning to duty, as well as *Landsturm* troops.

Often, *Ersatz* soldiers did not receive rifles until they arrived at the front lines, and therefore, they had little if any marksman training. Both Austro-Hungarian and Russian wounded troops abandoned their weapons on the battlefield, leading to significant shortages. At the beginning of the war, Habsburg units received eight weeks of basic training, but the unanticipated scale of casualties and the widening gaps in the front lines curtailed future unit training time to four weeks, and later two weeks, as replacements had to be rapidly deployed to the front lines. In addition, the shortage of rifles slowed down the formation of the March units. In fact, the war minister lamented, if rifles were available, he could ship an additional 200,000 soldiers to the front.

Four March Brigades containing 469,000 troops had to replace the 82 percent infantry losses by the end of 1914.[14] This resulted in multitudes of inexperienced and inadequately trained soldiers being rushed into battle, which resulted in incredible numbers of troops perishing. There were many problems with such March Brigades, or *Ersatz* units. Most importantly, they often lacked professional officers, and, if supplied with it, their artillery was antiquated. The units possessed no machine guns or signal or technical equipment. As the Carpathian Winter War approached, the question of the reliability of particular replacement troops such as Czech, Romanian, Italian, and Ruthenian became a major factor as anti-Habsburg and anti-military propaganda from specific areas of the Dual Monarchy increasingly appeared at the front. Often, reserve officers helped carry this propaganda to the front lines.

The nationality problem came to the forefront before the war, but some signs appeared even during mobilization. One problem was that the national groups listed above made unwilling soldiers. In particular, the Ruthenians (Ukrainians) resented that they were fighting the Russians, because they shared the same religion as Russians and understood the Russian language. The fact that two-thirds of the officers in the army at mobilization were German made matters worse. Slavic troops did not understand why they should fight their fellow Slavs, the Serbs and Russians. Desertions began fairly quickly, and in 1915, Czech desertions became quite frequent. Slavic troops grew increasingly unreliable, which caused the army structure to break down. The Germans feared that the Austro-Hungarian army was on the verge of collapse and could only be maintained if they intervened. Italian, Romanian, and Czech upper classes shunned military service before the war. A combination of national and social unrest was matched by military mismanagement on the other side, a major factor in the unreliability of various troops.

Moreover, Austria-Hungary was the only major power without a reserve army. Consequently, inexperienced *Landsturm* reserves comprised some two-thirds of its troops deployed in August 1914, the majority having undergone little basic training long before the war erupted. The unsuspecting new soldiers became cannon fodder in the desperate attempts to halt the overpowering Russian attacks. However, the practice raised another problem. How would field commanders fill the ever-widening gaps in the front lines?

Furthermore, *Ersatz* troops proved undisciplined and lacked physical fortitude. They arrived completely unprepared for the physical and mental demands of a winter mountain campaign. Desertion developed as a major problem, and it became obvious that replacement units should not enter the front lines without additional training. The early shortage of replacement troops forced the sick and wounded to return more rapidly to the front lines. At the beginning of 1915, 90 percent of the ailing soldiers, reputedly recovered, were deployed into *Ersatz* units.

No investigation of the Carpathian Winter War would be complete without providing insight into its mastermind, Conrad von Hötzendorf. The tremendous suffering endured by troops he commanded stemmed partly from Conrad's inability to accurately assess his army's capabilities. Throughout his tenure as chief of the General Staff of Austro-Hungarian forces on the Eastern front from 1914 to 1917, Conrad devoted much of his time to his mistress, and later his wife, Gina von Reininghaus. A self-proclaimed avid mountain climber, Conrad failed to consider important terrain features such as rivers, mountains, and swamps, as well as weather conditions, in his offensive plans. His shortsightedness and wishful thinking persisted into the latter years of the war, including his ill-fated spring 1916 Italian *Straf* campaign.

At this juncture, a retrospective look into the events leading up to the Carpathian Winter campaign is critical to understanding this tragic chapter in military history. When the Central Powers declared war in July and August 1914, Austria-Hungary represented the least militarily prepared European great power. In the decades following the 1867 *Ausgleich* (compromise), the Dual Monarchy's two parliaments in Budapest and Vienna consistently proved parsimonious in allocating funds for the military, particularly Budapest. Until 1913, army recruiting remained low and below the other great powers, although the empire's population had increased 40 percent.

The Habsburg Common Army drew its recruits from all regions of the multiethnic empire. Professional officers, versed in several languages, provided a cohesive force among the various nationalities. The ability to communicate with their troops gained the soldiers' trust and respect. When enemy efforts devastated the professional officer corps and reserve officers replaced them, communication faltered as did confidence in the new replacements. Often, sergeants had to "translate" a commander's orders to the troops.

The Habsburg army lacked the strength to launch two offensives in 1914; thus, no concentration of forces could oppose either Serbia or Russia. When Conrad decided to change the original deployment ordered on 1 July, in Galicia against Russia, back to the San–Dniester River line (the so-called *Rückverlegung*), the troops had to march from their railroad unloading areas to the originally designated deployment line in the August heat. Conrad's sudden change of mobilization and deployment plans resulted from his decision to launch a major offensive to crush Serbia before the reputedly slower-deploying Russians presented a major military danger to Habsburg troops. This proved to be a major mistake, which later led to devastating battlefield defeats.

As a result, 40 percent (or twenty divisions) of the Austro-Hungarian army originally deployed against Serbia. Thus, the two designated offensive armies on the czarist front, the First and Fourth, originally consisted of nine divisions rather than the twelve designated for a War Case "Russia." First Army advanced north, the Fourth to the northeast commencing concentric advances. Third Army, designated to protect the attacking armies' right flank positions, launched a disastrous late August seven-division offensive against twenty-one Russian divisions that attacked almost simultaneously. Meanwhile, Second Army had deployed most of its forces to defeat Serbia in War Case "Balkan," when in a War Case "Russia" it had been designated to protect the Habsburg extreme right flank positions. Thus, in 1914, only one corps (XII) deployed in that important area.

Numerically superior Russian forces rapidly penetrated into the gaps between the Habsburg armies. The Habsburg Second and Third armies' offensive proved indecisive, and Fourth Army's rear echelon became seriously threatened when the Russians smashed into the gap between First and Fourth armies. Lacking reserve formations to halt the strong enemy advances, Habsburg forces retreated on 2 September after the overwhelming first Battle of Lemberg defeat. The three Austro-Hungarian armies then launched a second offensive once their fronts had finally been consolidated, but they suffered a further devastating defeat. To save the Habsburg armies from annihilation, they retreated on 11 September after the second Battle of Lemberg. The Third Army's retreat during 13 and 14 September produced chaos, partly because the fall rainy season washed away the rain-soaked roads, and the destruction of bridges and railroads seriously retarded all movement.

The lack of a retreat plan led to panic within the Habsburg ranks, though less experienced soldiers also reacted out of fear and mistrust of their "foreign" brothers in arms. The hasty retreat resulted in the costly loss of matériel. The fact that the army was untrained in defensive warfare methods compounded the chaotic situation. Initially, the San River line appeared to present a suitably strong defensive position against the pursuing Russians. However, the army proved too exhausted to establish a viable defensive along the river. Thus, it continued to retreat further west on the treacherous, waterlogged Galician roads. Second Army deployed into the Carpathian Mountains between the Uzsok and Dukla passes.

The debilitating situation forced Conrad to seek the assistance of their powerful German ally—a bitter pill considering their early and increasingly persistent efforts to influence Habsburg military operations. A period of interallied squabbles commenced, preventing the establishment of a unified command structure and undermining chances for a Central Powers victory. The inability to establish a cohesive allied strategy partially resulted from a personality conflict between Conrad and his German counterpart, Erich von Falkenhayn. Their opposing viewpoints polarized portions of the military establishment into the "Westerners" camp, led by Falkenhayn, and the "Easterners," represented by Conrad and Falkenhayn's nemeses, the German Eastern front commanders, Hindenburg and Ludendorff. The Westerners believed that ultimate victory could only occur on the Western front, but during December 1914, that front settled into trench warfare, with massive troop concentrations opposing each other along the lengthy battlefront, which stretched hundreds of kilometers. Citing the Western front stalemate, Conrad argued that the Eastern front presented the greatest promise for a decisive victory and that, with German support, allied forces could prevail over the Russian colossus and then the Germans could return to the Western front to end the war.

By the end of September 1914, the Russians had conquered the greater part of Galicia and planned to defeat Germany by unleashing a "steam-roller" offensive across the Vistula River, with four armies advancing into

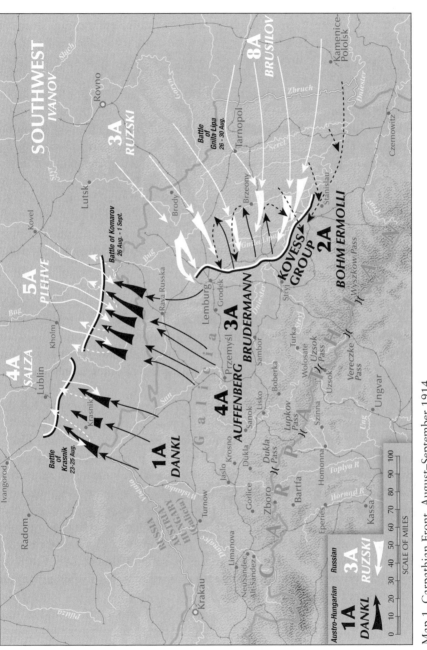

Map 1. Carpathian Front, August–September 1914

Silesia and toward Berlin. As early as October, czarist general Ivanov made plans to launch an offensive through the Carpathian Mountains to invade Hungary to force Austria-Hungary out of the war. Such a campaign faced difficulties, particularly because *Stavka,* the czarist supreme headquarters, had selected Germany as the next major military objective. In addition, Russian strategists had to protect their flanks between the Northwest and Southwest fronts before attempting to attack the Carpathian Mountains or invade Germany.

The Carpathian Mountain region initially became the focus of attention when the Habsburg army retreated in mid-September 1914. Both General Conrad and General Ivanov soon discovered that the Carpathian Mountain region had correctly been designated as ill-suited for prolonged large troop maneuvers. Though both ultimately lacked the necessary troop strengths to achieve a decisive victory, each feared the other intended to envelop their respective extreme flank positions in the far reaches of the Carpathian Mountains. Insufficiently prepared for a winter mountain campaign but unwilling to yield to their opponent, both armies sustained enormous casualties in the world's first total war mountain campaign. Both also rushed to launch an offensive in the inhospitable mountains because Conrad and Ivanov believed that the first who seized the opportunity to launch an offensive would gain a critical advantage. But there was a major determinant of the Carpathian campaign: the remaining area of the Southwest front had equivalent opposing troop numbers, so an offensive north of the mountain range offered little chance of success.

The Russian fall Vistula River campaign failed to capture Berlin, but the invasion routes to Vienna and Budapest remained exposed and nearly defenseless at various Carpathian Mountain crossings. The September Habsburg retreat caught the attention of Cossack troops roaming the Carpathian Mountain range and introduced small unit warfare to the vast mountain theater, but did not yet threaten Hungary. The Carpathian Mountains developed into the main Eastern front battleground for the 1914–1915 winter campaign because both the extreme czarist left flank and Habsburg right flank positions invited opposing envelopment movements. With the exception of the German Second Battle of the Masurian Lakes in early February 1915, the crucial Eastern front battles developed primarily in the Carpathian Mountain campaign.

The Habsburg Third Army retreated mid-September 1914, and Fortress Przemyśl fell to the Russians. The October Habsburg offensive later liberated the fortress. Mountain weather conditions were a major concern: a great amount of snow fell at Uzsok Pass as early as 28 September 1914. The three October-through-December monthly Habsburg campaigns offered the first glimpse into the difficulties inherent in waging war on winter mountainous terrain and produced some of the highest casualties of the entire war.

The early October Habsburg offensive objective, in conjunction with German support, was to free Fortress Przemyśl and regain the San River line. Conrad launched a hasty offensive because he feared that the fortress could not repulse a massed enemy attack. The allied campaigns forced the Germans to shift considerable troop numbers to that front to save the Habsburg army from catastrophe. During the October campaign, the fortress withstood multiple czarist mass attacks between 3 and 8 October in a Russian attempt to storm the citadel before a Habsburg counteroffensive could relieve it. The Third and Fourth armies, after advancing eighty kilometers, could not cross the San River because of strong czarist defensive positions.

As the Third Army approached Fortress Przemyśl, the flooded roadways along the seventy-eight miles rearward to the railroad supply head could not maintain the logistical support for the army. Thus, the Third Army plundered the fortress' food supplies upon reaching it. In the interim, six days of resupply efforts replaced some of the food and ammunition the field armies had confiscated. Destroyed bridges had to be rebuilt after the recent czarist retreat, so the available time for resupply proved short, but it did not restore the fortress food provisions ransacked by the Third and Second armies.

The Second Army cooperated with the Third Army relief effort at Fortress Przemyśl by attempting to roll up the Russian extreme left flank positions. On 6 October, Second Army's VII Corps advanced along the major Mezölaborcz-Lisko-Rostocki-Baligrod road to seize the Uzsok Pass and then the enemy-held major railroad junctions at Turka, Stary Sambor, and Lutoviska, which remained important offensive objectives during the further fall and 1915 Carpathian Mountain campaigns. On 7 October, the first serious mountain snowstorm introduced initial severe weather and terrain conditions to the advancing Habsburg troops. By 13 October, Habsburg armies had advanced the eighty kilometers to the San River. This area between the Dukla and Uzsok passes developed into the fulcrum for the 1915 Carpathian Winter War campaigns.

The Habsburg October offensive, which recaptured Fortress Przemyśl between 10 October and the first week in November, eventually failed for many reasons, including frontal attacks launched against extremely well-prepared Russian mountain positions, which reoccurred as a major factor during the 1915 Carpathian campaigns. Vital mountain artillery batteries had been deployed on the Balkan front; they were thus unavailable for the major Russian theater. Weather remained a major factor throughout fall and winter 1915. Heavy fall rains intermittently produced a muddy morass, retarding logistical and troop movement, including heavy ammunition wagons, artillery, and general supplies. Icy, snow-covered high-elevation roads proved difficult, if not futile, for transport. Supply efforts had to halt overnight until the roadways' icy cover had melted by midday the next day.

Russia dealt the Habsburg army a stunning blow in its three fall 1914 campaigns, as well as in the subsequent 1915 Carpathian offensives. A successful offensive depended on speed and coordinated regular transport of troops, supplies, ammunition, artillery pieces, and shells, but only four narrow-gauge Habsburg railroad lines provided access to the 400-kilometer-wide Carpathian Mountain front. One major two-track line extended from Budapest to Mezölaborcz in the Laborcz Valley, making the latter a primary objective for Russian action during the first Carpathian campaign. Its early February 1915 surrender precluded use of this important railroad hub for offensive purposes to recapture Fortress Przemyśl and interrupted the Third Army's right flank supply efforts for the offensive forces.

Austria-Hungary's sparse railroad network posed a tremendous military and logistical disadvantage throughout the war. Extending like a spider-web from Budapest, the Hungarian railroad system provided limited access to the main Habsburg operational area. Furthermore, it could not satisfy the various requirements of such large military forces. The huge number of troop transports overtaxed the low capacity rail lines, delaying the arrival of troop units, reinforcements, and war matériel, as well as transporting the wounded homeward. Internal political bickering between Austria and Hungary had for decades led to political impasse. Consequently, few railroads, stations, or ramps had been constructed from Budapest to the Carpathian Mountain region—a severe military handicap during the Carpathian campaign.

Nor could the poorly constructed and dilapidated Galician roads meet the sudden enormous increase in demand. Other passageways through the sparsely populated forested mountains were too few and primitive for military use. For each increase in rail troop transport intensity, there came a corresponding disturbance of *Ersatz,* supply, and war matériel traffic. These factors disrupted the maximum technically feasible Habsburg rail traffic intensity, delaying all transport movement.

Four Habsburg armies and forty-two divisions were ultimately transported into the wintry abyss. In early 1915, many units transferred from the Balkan and Galician fronts, the *Hinterland* and the German Eastern and Western fronts for the offensive undertakings. A total of 4,952 trains transported 168,080 sick and 26,240 wounded POWs from the Russian front to the *Hinterland*. The train traffic between January and the end of March 1915 totaled 2,752 trains, which transported 14,404 officers, 643,081 troops, and 13,783 wagons and artillery pieces to the front. This encompassed one army commander, ten corps commanders, and forty-two divisions through 116 days and 2,547 trains. On average, twenty-three trains traveled per day, and sometimes up to fifty-four.

The majority of units transferred to the Carpathian theater arrived from the Russian front north of the mountains. These included five corps commanders (X, XVIII, V, IV, XI) and twenty-one divisions on 1,288 trains. Three corps commanders (XIX, XIII, VIII) and seven infantry divisions were transported from the Balkan front in 615 trains. In addition, the German ally sent two corps commanders (XXIV and II) and six infantry divisions on 471 trains and two infantry and four Habsburg cavalry divisions from the homeland to the front in 173 transport trainloads.

Transport from the Russian front to the homeland during the same period included 346,829 sick and wounded, and 92,600 prisoners of war.[15] Tragically, Conrad could not replace the catastrophic 1.25 million losses incurred during the 1914 campaigns. By the end of December 1914, only 303,000 Habsburg troops remained between the Vistula River and the Romanian frontier to oppose the Russians.

The San River Fortress Przemyśl citadel served as a guiding, or more appropriately, misguiding light for Conrad's Eastern front strategy between October 1914 and April 1915. "Rescue Przemyśl!" became the Habsburg call to arms—for the Russians, "March to Budapest!" The fortress had proven beneficial during the chaotic September Habsburg retreat, when it slowed the Russian pursuit at the fortress environs, preventing the Russians from invading Hungary and enabling the battered army to retreat unscathed from the San River line. Meanwhile, San River bridgeheads, hastily constructed to protect the northern flank of the fortress, surrendered, enabling the enemy to approach the fortress unimpeded. Conrad feared its loss, which he thought would represent the defeat of the army and the Dual Monarchy.

Because of the lack of funding to upgrade the fortress before the war, all supply and building activities to make the citadel defensible occurred during the alarm and mobilization periods. Not until August 1914 did 27,000 workers provide preliminary preparations for the fortress mission to secure it against a preemptive Russian attack. That process terminated forty-two days later. The fortress initially had to be protected against an anticipated mass czarist cavalry attack and then secured against a possible siege. Prewar planning had anticipated weeks, even months, to prepare the fortress for war, but by 1914, only a few weeks remained. Between 14 and 18 August 1914, the workers constructed new defensive lines, artillery positions, ammunition supply depots, and additional structures to plug the gaps between the various interval positions. By the time the Russians reached the fortress environs on 15 September, seven new zones and twenty-four defensive positions spanned a fifty-kilometer area.[16]

The fortress commander, General Kusmanek, received his assignment just months before the declaration of war. The decision to deploy Habsburg Supreme Command headquarters within the fortress compounded his myriad problems, which interfered with fortress preparations and greatly increased its security problems. A series of three defensive lines consisting of concentric rings formed by nineteen permanent and twenty-three smaller forts protected the fortress, which was forty-eight kilometers in circumference. The main citadel zones were completed, but secondary ones were only partially finished. The citadel's main weakness remained that it could not withstand modern heavy artillery fire. Fortunately, the Russians' heaviest artillery received priority for the German, not Austro-Hungarian, front. Once besieged in September 1914, the fortress bound nine czarist infantry and two cavalry divisions. After its second siege commencing on 4 November, the fortress became a secondary theater, tying down fewer enemy troops (six infantry and one cavalry division).

A German October offensive attempt to seize Warsaw at the lower Vistula River front initially relieved the pressure on the gravely threatened Austro-Hungarian lines. The German drive forced the Russians to retreat on the Southwest front to the San River and Chyróv area to protect their flank positions between the Northwest and Southwest fronts. Later in November, when the Germans had to retreat before superior czarist numbers, they resumed their westward advance against the Habsburg army and encircled Fortress Przemyśl for the second time on 8 November. The Russians utilized inclement weather conditions to sever all rail and road access to the fortress. The besieging Eleventh Army consisted of six infantry divisions and one cavalry division, representing half the troops deployed during the first siege.

The fortress mission remained to repel any enemy offensive efforts and disrupt its rearward communication lines by binding as many czarist troops as possible. The second loss of the fortress represented a major blow to Habsburg prestige. Fortress Cracow became the target of major Russian attacks as the enemy sought to press the Habsburgs from their normal retreat routes to Vienna and force the main Carpathian passes to protect their west

Galician positions. The Russian Tenth Army launched a major offensive from the Vistula River valley into Germany, while the Southwest front attempted to maintain East Galicia and the left Vistula River front crossing points. This forced the Habsburg armies rearward from the San River line. The German retreat from Warsaw in late November exposed the Austro-Hungarian armies' northern flank; First Army retreated from its San River positions at Ivangorod, suffering a major defeat; and Third Army moved to the Dukla Pass and Second Army through the Uzsok and Lupkov passes, creating an eighty-kilometer gap between the Third and Fourth armies.

Meanwhile, Habsburg Fourth Army right flank units had deployed between the Fortress Cracow perimeter and northern Vistula River bank. Third Army front extended from the Carpathian forelands to the upper Dunajec River because Second Army had been transferred to the German Northwest front to defend Silesia, a major industrial area threatened by the czarist Vistula River front activity. The Russians discovered the serious weakness on the Habsburg front southeast of Cracow, where the Habsburg Second Army troops had been deployed. The czarist Third and Eighth armies launched an assault against the entire Habsburg front, but particularly Fortress Cracow. During November, defense of the Carpathian Mountain front, spanning hundreds of kilometers, rested on the exhausted eleven-division Third Army and Army Group Pflanzer-Baltin's irregular territorial forces. Conrad now encountered two problems: he must defeat the Russians pressing Fortress Cracow and restore the Carpathian Mountain situation. He ordered Fourth Army units deployed north of Fortress Cracow to intercept and halt the advancing czarist army. When Fourth Army failed, the army rapidly rail-transferred south of the fortress environs to counter the menacing flank threat emanating from that area.

During the first half of November, while major battles extended to Fortress Cracow, the Russian Third Army advanced through the Dukla Pass area. Then on 19 November, heavy snow and frigid conditions settled into the mountains. At the end of the month, the Russian Eighth Army advanced along the shortest route at the upper San River, then pressed further westward. The Russians seized the Lupkov Pass, then the Dukla, to provide easy access to the Hungarian Plains. Meanwhile, the situation south of Fortress Cracow worsened as the Russian Third Army repulsed the weak Habsburg covering troops forcing them back into the mountain regions. Then on 26 November, the czarist army shifted north toward Cracow to attempt to turn the Austro-Hungarian right flank positions and sever the Habsburg retreat route. This also isolated Fortress Przemyśl, where the besieging czarist 12th and 19th Infantry Divisions had transferred to the Carpathian battlefield, signifying that the siege army now consisted almost entirely of reserve formations.

The Austro-Hungarian army found itself in a critical situation during early December. It had to launch an offensive to prevent neutral Italy and Romania entering the war, as well as halt the steady Russian military advance westward. Repeated battlefield defeats on the Russian front had created an unfavorable military situation, and the embarrassing Serbian debacle early in the month caused a major loss of Habsburg prestige, specifically in the Balkans. Germany pressed the Habsburgs to retrieve their military honor by launching an offensive against Serbia, and to prevent Italy and Romania from seeking irredentist aims in the Dual Monarchy. The early December battle, with a Limanova-Lapanov victory, proved welcome after so many defeats. The Russians retreated fifty kilometers, their Eighth Army losing 70 percent of its manpower. The success temporarily prevented the Russians from invading Hungary, ended the threat to Fortress Cracow—and, because of their threatened flank positions, it forced them to abandon a major campaign into Germany.

At the height of battle in mid-December, the Third Army attacked the open Russian flank in the Carpathian Mountains. The assault forced czarist formations to retreat from the area and from the Fortress Cracow front, resulting in the Limanova-Lapanov victory, the first in the war for Austria-Hungary. At the same time, General Ivanov determined to transfer the mass of his armies into the Carpathian Mountain area as a prelude to an invasion of Hungary, because "the road to Berlin lies through Austria-Hungary." During the ensuing late December campaign, the Russians secured their extreme left flank positions. After Limanova-Lapanov, Conrad ordered his depleted troops to pursue the retreating Russians, but that ended quickly on 17 December, mainly because of high casualties and an enemy counteroffensive that hurled Habsburg forces rearward into the Carpathian Mountains toward the main ridges.

General Falkenhayn's goal remained to push the Russians behind the San–Vistula River line to reduce the enemy's offensive capabilities. The early December Habsburg Third Army December mission entailed binding the Russian Eighth Army and severing the last major czarist supply and transportation artery, as well as blocking the Russian retreat route.[17] In late December, when the Russians seized the critical Dukla Pass and created a defensive line extending from the Uzsok Pass, they placed the Habsburg army at a great disadvantage. After Limanova-Lapanov, battle reports emphasized the enormous casualties and the extraordinarily strenuous physical efforts required to survive the inclement weather and harsh terrain conditions. In addition, Habsburg troops lacked cover as well as regular food and supplies. Many active duty officers, noncommissioned officers, and soldiers fell in combat, which resulted in slackened discipline and battle effectiveness, while combat battle fatigue produced troop apathy.

In early December, the Russians had penetrated key Carpathian passes leading to Budapest, but Habsburg troop numbers proved insufficient to halt them. Galician roads remained in terrible shape, with only one route suitable for logistical support and troop reinforcements, seriously hindering operations. The troops had been engaged in combat for months, during which division numbers had sunk sharply. In addition, serious deficiencies, particularly of artillery shells, prevailed, further lessening battle effectiveness. The 1914 casualties had been so enormous that replacement troops could not fill the ensuing gaps in the front lines.

General Ivanov was confident his troops could now garner a decisive victory over the Habsburg armies. However, reinforcements were needed between the Uzsok Pass and Romanian frontier, his most threatened strategic area, where only four czarist divisions stood. Ivanov insisted that Fortress Przemyśl was encircled by only weak forces—quite an exaggeration—and that a mere two cavalry divisions defended the key terrain between the Uzsok Pass and Baligrod. Czarist reinforcements would have to transfer from the German Northwest front where the major Russian offensive had been scheduled. Ivanov planned for his troops to traverse the Carpathian Mountains to invade Hungary, now that his flank positions had been secured. Intending to strike at the point of least resistance, he concentrated troops near Mezőlaborcz to occupy the main Carpathian Mountain crossings.

At the end of December, the Austro-Hungarian military situation appeared bleak, especially when considering the loss of professional soldiers. The army desperately needed time to recover from its ordeal and replace its enormous casualties. It also had to defend the major Carpathian Mountain crossings against Russian advances, in particular because the Third Army had retreated far into the region and the Russians threatened to invade Hungary in early 1915. Thus, Conrad determined to launch a Carpathian Mountain offensive early in the New Year, although he lacked reserve formations, and his rapidly diminishing troop numbers would face superior Russian numbers. Both Conrad and Ivanov looked to the Carpathian theater as the weather caused a weeks-long pause in the fighting.

Chapter 1 traces Habsburg army preparations to launch the first Carpathian offensive from early January 1915. Serious questions arise relative to the army's preparedness for a major military operation in such adverse winter mountain weather and terrain conditions. Further problems included

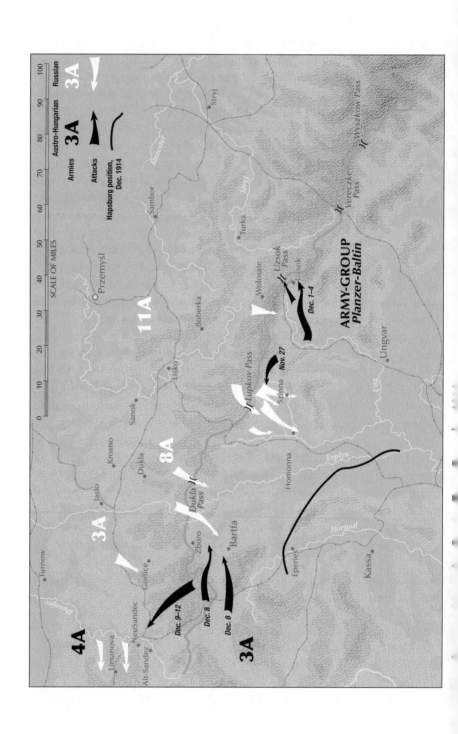

	Armies		Attacks	Hapsburg position, Dec. 1914
	Austro-Hungarian	**Russian**		
	3A	**3A**		

SCALE OF MILES

0 10 20 30 40 50 60 70 80 90 100

Turnow

Gorlice **3A**

Neusandez **4A**

Limanova

Alt-Sandez

Dunajec

Krosno

Jaslo

Dukla

Zboro

Bartfa **8A**

Dukla Pass

Dec. 9–12

Dec. 8

Dec. 8 **3A**

Eperies

Kassa

Hornad

Homonna

Toplya

Sanok

Lisko

Boberka

11A

Przemysl

Sambor

Dniester

Turka

Stryj

Stryj

Wolosate

Uzsok Pass

Uzsok

Lupkov Pass

Nov. 27

Szinna

Dec. 1–4

ARMY-GROUP
Planzer-Baltin

Ungvar

Ung

Vereczke Pass

Wyszkow Pass

the lack of artillery shells and difficulties deploying artillery on the rugged terrain, compounded by the difficult and unresolved logistical problems.

Chapter 2 highlights the first Carpathian offensive, launched on 23 January 1915, and its catastrophic outcome. Chapter 3 describes the second Carpathian effort, launched on 27 February 1915. For the first time during the war, Habsburg forces initially outnumbered czarist troops. The chapter details their struggles to overcome two fierce adversaries: the overwhelming Russian forces and the terrible mountain conditions.

Chapter 4 discusses the third and final Carpathian offensive in late March, scheduled to coincide with a breakout attempt from Fortress Przemyśl, an objective of all three offensives, and the bloody April Easter Battle. With Russian troops on the verge of breaking through the battered Habsburg Carpathian Mountain defensive positions, an invasion of Hungary appeared imminent. The chapter concludes with the Gorlice–Tarnov offensive, the Central Powers' greatest victory of World War I, which spared the Habsburg army from final defeat and possible annihilation in the Carpathian war theater.

1

Background to the Battles

Those who do not know the conditions of mountains and forests, hazardous defiles, marshes and swamps, cannot conduct the march of an army.

Sun Tzu, *The Art of War*

BY JANUARY 1915 their Carpathian Mountain exertions had left Russian and Austro-Hungarian troops exhausted.[1] Weather conditions forced a pause in major operations, allowing both sides to rehabilitate. Localized isolated battles erupted when each sought to improve front-line positions, particularly those between Gorlice and the Uzsok Pass.

Despite the relative quiet, neither side could rest, keenly aware of the considerable preparations necessary for upcoming battle. Habsburg troops prepared new defensive positions as they awaited the arrival of reinforcements. Air and cavalry reconnaissance monitored the location and concentration of Russian units while simultaneously identifying potential sites for positioning additional troops and artillery. Convinced of Russian intent to invade the region, Conrad planned a preemptive strike, and accurate intelligence was critical to the operation's success.

Amid alarming diplomatic reports emanating out of Italy and Romania, Conrad staunchly advocated launching a Carpathian Mountain offensive. The region held the greatest promise for victory over the Russians; a win that would persuade Italy, Romania, and Bulgaria to remain neutral. Conrad's plan resurrected two of his earlier 1914 objectives—one defensive (preventing the invasion of Hungary), the other offensive (liberating Fortress Przemyśl). The Dukla hollow area thus became a key battleground for the operation. Habsburg Third Army eastern flank units, the major attack force, would strike in echelon formation toward the Lisko–Sanok railroads to sever the Russians from their major transportation centers.

Initially, General Boroević left flank forces and neighboring Fourth Army southern flank units were to assume a defensive stance. The success of the Third Army's operations hinged on regained control of Uzsok Pass and capturing the major railroads supporting the Russian troops along the San River. Deployed between the Romanian frontier and Wyszkov ridges, Army Group Pflanzer-Baltin's mission was to protect the Third Army's extreme right flank. South army troops, primarily Habsburg units, deployed into the *Waldkarpathen* region east of Uzsok Pass between Third Army and Army Group Pflanzer-Baltin. From there, they had to traverse the Verecke Pass and Wyszkov ridges and advance to the Stryj River. If successful, South Army troops would either join the Third Army offensive or continue advancing eastward. Conrad's plan depended entirely on timing, surprise, and total cooperation among all participating armies. Under no circumstances should the operation falter and afford the Russians time to transfer in reinforcements. If everything went as planned, the battle would be short, and Habsburg troops would then be free to cross the Carpathian Mountains into Galicia. However, several aspects of Conrad's plan were flawed. The shortage of railroads in the Carpathian Mountain region slowed the mobilization and deployment of troop masses. Habsburg military strategists underestimated or simply ignored the significant demands placed on the troops. The severe weather conditions and rugged terrain left Habsburg troops exhausted and demoralized, making them ideal targets for insidious national propaganda. Reports of mass desertions among certain ethnic groups, most notably the Czechs, unnerved Habsburg Supreme Command.

Conrad committed grave, though perhaps unintentional, errors in planning his Carpathian campaign. The first late January 1915 offensive failed to adequately address the formidable logistical challenges inherent in winter mountain warfare. When the intended swift victory gave way to a prolonged winter confrontation, Habsburg troops had to battle superior Russian numbers without the benefit of a reliable support system. Positioned on higher ground, czarist sharpshooters gunned down Conrad's troops one by one as they slowly navigated through the deep snow, jokingly comparing it to a rabbit hunt.[2] Many Habsburg soldiers took their own lives to escape the nightmare.

Habsburg Third Army daily logbooks provide disturbing eyewitness accounts of the dreadful battle conditions, many of which diverge significantly from official postwar publications. Field commanders' pleas for additional rest and rehabilitation from the 1914 campaigns before the offensive's launch date went unanswered by Habsburg Supreme Command. Urgent requests for ammunition and additional troops can be found throughout the various *Tagebücher.*

Habsburg military strategy focused on preventing a Russian offensive in the Carpathians for some time, with the notion that victory in that theater would release some Habsburg forces for deployment elsewhere. The plan proposed that the Third and South armies encircle czarist extreme left flank positions and then push them behind the San–Vistula River line, liberating Fortress Przemyśl in the process. A Russian offensive could potentially neutralize Habsburg efforts and return the initiative to the enemy. In what would become the Second Battle of the Masurian Lakes, in February 1915, the German Ninth Army attacked enemy forces over the Narev River, pressing the Russians behind the Vistula River. The resulting gigantic pincer maneuver, launched from widely separated allied flanks, reincarnated Conrad's 1914 grandiose plan. This did little to endear Conrad to the Germans, who increasingly began to question his leadership abilities and the viability of the Austro-Hungarian armies. Mounting casualties, declining morale, desertion, and waning resistance power seemed to justify the Germans' concerns.

Fearing the collapse of his ally's front, General Falkenhayn begrudgingly accepted Emperor Wilhelm's decision to utilize the four newly trained German corps for a February East Prussian campaign (the Second Battle of the Masurian Lakes) to coincide with the Carpathian offensive.[3] Nevertheless, Falkenhayn was convinced that Conrad's Carpathian offensive would not render a decisive victory because he lacked the troops necessary to envelop and overpower Russian extreme flank positions dispersed over hundreds of kilometers.

The South Army's need for mountain equipment for the upcoming offensive sparked yet another episode of allied friction. In a 15 January telegram, General Ludendorff warned Conrad that he would withhold German assistance unless Habsburg Supreme Command agreed to provide the much-needed equipment.[4] Ludendorff revealed that a number of German generals preferred that the South Army be deployed on more favorable terrain.

Habsburg reconnaissance efforts intensified despite inclement weather conditions. Intelligence reports indicated that Russian troops had constructed blocking positions all along their front to compensate for their fewer numbers. Deteriorating weather conditions increased the demand for road maintenance to facilitate the movement of troops and supplies.

Conrad opposed creating a Central Power Supreme Command, citing national, dynastic, political, and military considerations. Nonetheless, he continuously demanded that the Germans provide reinforcements for his Eastern front operations. He argued that, with the failure of German military efforts in the West, the time had come to focus on the East. Conrad insisted that victory had thus far eluded his troops because the Germans refused to provide the necessary reinforcements.

The Carpathian Winter War further illuminated the need for a unified allied command, and the issue remained a bone of allied contention until the war's end. German High Command outwardly questioned General Conrad's leadership capabilities, and clashes between Conrad and Falkenhayn aggravated the issue.[5] The two military leaders were as dissimilar in stature as in their strategic beliefs. The taller Falkenhayn commanded a greater presence, in contrast to Conrad, who was relatively short in stature and grandfatherly in appearance. The two rarely communicated by telephone, interacting instead at impromptu meetings that Falkenhayn dominated. Inevitably, days later, Falkenhayn received a communiqué from Conrad contradicting or questioning any agreement the two had reached.

Falkenhayn reminded Conrad that in the West, Anglo-French troops outnumbered the Germans two to one. Therefore, he could spare no troops to support Conrad's Carpathian operation. Conrad insisted that only an additional six German infantry divisions could produce a military victory and that by transferring three to four German divisions to the Habsburg Third Army's eastern flank positions, Russian troops could be encircled. He added that defeating the Russians would persuade Italy and Romania to remain neutral. During their most recent exchange, Falkenhayn was surprised to learn that the Habsburg Third Army had been forced to retreat fifty kilometers into the mountains. When asked whether he could assure that the Habsburg armies deployed in the Carpathian Mountains could maintain their current positions, Conrad replied that he could not.[6]

Pressure to launch an offensive in the Carpathians also partially stemmed from bleak reports emanating from Fortress Przemyśl. In early January 1915, Habsburg Supreme Command ordered the designation of a fortress minimal defending force, with the remaining garrison troops providing offensive punch for a future major breakout effort. The minimal defending force received orders to destroy important military objects within the fortress before joining any successful breakout effort. During the latter half of January, garrison forces reorganized in preparation for that breakout attempt. According to a 17 December situation report, the fortress could only hold out until 15 January; horse feed would be depleted by 10 January. However, a later 1 January 1915 report estimated that the garrison could hold out until 18 February if 7,000 horses were slaughtered for their meat. Despite the reprieve, Conrad remained under intense pressure to take the initiative and rescue the fortress. The decision to slaughter horses to extend the fortress food supply naturally reduced the number of pack animals available for moving supplies and ammunition as needed, as well as transporting the sick and wounded to and from fortress perimeter positions. A 15 January report stated that slaughtering an additional 3,500 horses would extend the garrison's food supply to 7 March. When czarist siege troops learned of the butchering occurring behind the fortress walls, they began to mimic the sound of horses whinnying. The Russians jokingly compared Fortress Przemyśl to the Trojan horse: in the Greek legend, the warriors rode inside the belly of a horse, while in Fortress Przemyśl, the horses rode inside the bellies of the warriors.[7]

The Habsburg armies deployed in the Carpathian Mountains bore little resemblance to the fighting force mobilized in July 1914. Having lost much of its professional and noncommissioned officers and experienced soldiers in the initial campaigns, the *k.u.k.* army of January 1915 more closely resembled a *Miliz* (militia) force, now reduced to "more or less an improvised army of reserves."[8] The severe bloodletting in the opening and fall campaigns necessitated the Habsburg army's reorganization in October 1914 and again in January 1915.

Österreich-Ungarns letzter Krieg describes the 1915 Habsburg army as a *Volksheer,* a military force far inferior to its once-proud legacy, while Austrian historiography acknowledges the Russians' superior ability to adapt to the winter mountain environment.[9] Perhaps most damning, however, was Habsburg Supreme Command's failure to learn from its November 1914 to early January campaigns. Instead, the 1915 Carpathian Winter War became more a question of what Conrad *wanted* to do (*wollen*), as opposed to what he *was able* to do (*können*).

It is impossible to accurately assess the total losses incurred during the 1915 winter offensive. Recording losses was a complicated task, particularly considering the transfer of nearly every small infantry unit to another at some point during the campaign. Wounded, sick, and frostbitten soldiers continually transferred from the front. Soldiers from the Balkan and Galician fronts and hundreds of thousands of *Ersatz* (replacement troops) later transferred to the Carpathian Mountains. Austrian official sources estimate the winter offensives produced some 800,000 casualties, but the number is likely far greater. Though the high casualty rate alone is astounding, the fact that most were not related to combat (something *Austria-Hungary's Last War* and other official reports fail to reveal) is even more mind-boggling.

On 1 January 1915, Conrad and Falkenhayn exchanged views about Habsburg Carpathian offensive plans and sparred over who should command the new South Army set to deploy in the Carpathian theater.[10] Falkenhayn made numerous valid arguments against Conrad's plan, including the fact that a 375-kilometer expanse separated the flanks of the German and Austro-Hungarian strike forces.[11] Furthermore, the mountain region lacked the necessary roadways and higher-capacity rail lines, and presented serious communication and logistical challenges. With Russian defenders firmly entrenched on higher ground, Conrad's plan might yield a few local-ized military gains at best, not the highly touted decisive victory. Falken-hayn further explained that deploying additional German troops in the east meant compromising his Western front operations—something he was not willing to do.

Emperor Wilhelm interceded, assuring Conrad of German support for the undertaking. Vienna's urgent appeals, the threat of Italian and Romanian intervention, and growing concern that the Habsburg army's continuing battlefield defeats might cause it to collapse persuaded the German emperor to accede to Conrad's request for reinforcements. In a letter to the emper-or's military chancellery and foreign minister, Conrad justified the need for a major Carpathian offensive, citing growing Russian military presence in the region and the crisis at Fortress Przemyśl. He assured the Germans that the Balkan front was not in imminent danger. The Save and Danube rivers had frozen over, and sufficient Habsburg troops were in position to repel a Serbian attack. To underscore his assertions, Conrad transferred three of his own divisions from the Balkan front to the Carpathian Mountains in early January 1915.

The issue of Italian neutrality became a lightning rod for the allied com-manders' diametrically opposed viewpoints. Conrad refused to consider Italian territorial demands, insisting that the Russian front held the greatest opportunity for victory.[12] German diplomatic and military leaders increas-ingly pressured Vienna to relinquish territory to Italy to at least ensure its neutrality.[13]

The ongoing Fortress Przemyśl crisis limited Conrad's military options. Taking its cue from Conrad, the German Eastern front command (*Oberost*) expressed grave concern over the situation hoping to divert Falkenhayn's attention to the Eastern front. *Oberost* punctuated its argument by remind-ing Falkenhayn of the severe criticism he received for his failed Western front Ypres campaign in late 1914.

General Falkenhayn remained nonplussed and held fast to the assessment that action be taken on the Serbian, not Russian, front. Victory against Ser-bia would open the Danube River for the delivery of much-needed arms and ammunition to Turkey, a Central Powers ally since November 1914. Citing growing concern over the neutral states, Falkenhayn suggested that Conrad crush Serbia with the troops intended for his Carpathian campaign because the weakened Serbian army suffered from severe losses, privation, disease, and a critical shortage of matériel. A Habsburg victory over Serbia would also restore prestige the empire had forfeited earlier at the hands of its tiny Balkan foe.[14] Arguing that a Balkan campaign was not feasible, Conrad repeated his demand for the transfer of all available German troops to the Carpathian front.[15]

The bickering finally ended on 8 January, when Falkenhayn begrudgingly informed Conrad of Emperor Wilhelm's decision to supply German troops for his Carpathian offensives. He promised to provide two and a half divisions if Conrad agreed to two conditions. The Habsburg units should comprise the majority of the newly created army, and it should be commanded by a German general, von Linsingen.

On 11 January generals Conrad, Falkenhayn, Ludendorff, and Linsingen met in Breslau to discuss allied Eastern front operations. Conrad seized the opportunity to promote his Carpathian operation as the surest means to keep Rome from entering the war.[16] Falkenhayn disagreed, arguing that Italy's neutrality could best be secured by Austro-Hungarian territorial concessions.

Another serious challenge facing Habsburg Supreme Command surfaced during the winter of 1914–1915. Growing numbers of politically unreliable Czechoslovakian, Ruthenian, and Romanian replacement troops were deployed on the Eastern front. Their arrival coincided with an increase in antimilitary, antidynastic propaganda. Troops deserted in increasing numbers, a problem that continued throughout the Carpathian winter offensives. Among the most notorious defections was that of Czech Infantry Regiment 28. The regiment, recruited from industrialized Prague, reputedly crossed over to the enemy en masse "without a single shot being fired from a Russian battalion."[17] At no other time during the war, with the possible exceptions of the summer 1916 Brusilov offensive and the late October 1918 final battles of the war, had Slavic soldiers so brazenly shirked their duty as in the Carpathian Winter War.

Exacerbating the problem, the Carpathian Mountain region was home to a large Ruthenian population, many of whom were Russian sympathizers who shared similar religious beliefs and language, and who provided the Habsburg enemy with valuable intelligence information. Not surprisingly, Austro-Hungarian troops deployed in the hostile region grew increasingly paranoid. Episodes of "spy mania" led to hundreds of civilians being charged with espionage and hanged.

General Conrad concluded that only a swift and decisive action would prevent an enemy breakthrough of his thinning front lines. The Russian threat to the Dukla Valley and Uzsok Pass, gateway to Hungary, also must be neutralized. Conrad proposed launching an attack from Mezőlaborcz in the Laborcz Valley toward Lisko–Ustrzyki Dolne–Sanok. The objective was to seize the key rail connections located behind enemy lines and advance along the shortest route to Fortress Przemyśl.

In December 1914, Russian control of key Carpathian Mountain pass positions gave czarist troops an important strategic advantage, one they utilized to deter advancing Habsburg troops. Efforts to outflank czarist positions required Conrad's troops to undertake long and strenuous maneuvers. Even so, the Russians skillfully avoided encirclement, retreating at the last possible moment to reestablish solid defensive positions.

Few examples of major winter mountain battle existed before the Carpathian Winter War. Nonetheless, the problems Conrad encountered in the November and December 1914 campaigns should have remained fresh in his mind. Without exact timing, luck, and an efficient supply system, the Carpathian winter offensive was doomed to fail. Without any of them, it collapsed.

On the Eastern front in early January 1915, strong indications existed that Russia was increasing its Carpathian military presence. In the West, the Germans had settled into protracted trench warfare against the English and French after the first battle at Ypres. Turkey established a front in the Russian Caucasus in late December and on the Middle Eastern front. Its December victory left the Serbian army decimated and incapable of any large-scale operations.

Russian military strategists, particularly General Ivanov, anticipated that an immediate attack could deal a deathblow to Habsburg troops, which would persuade Italy and Romania to join the Entente. Situated close to railroad lines and on more traversable terrain, Russian troops were in an excellent position to carry out the plan. If needed, significant reinforcements could rapidly deploy into the mountains.

General Ivanov obviously believed that a rapid offensive could best be launched against Austria-Hungary rather than Germany. This, however, raised a serious question: once Russian forces broke through to the Hungarian plains, would they then be able to extricate themselves fast enough to avoid a possible major counteroffensive on their northern German flank?

A campaign against Germany, *Stavka* acknowledged, presented a serious military challenge. German Eastern front troop numbers had tripled since war was declared, and the efficient Prussian rail system permitted the transfer of large contingents to any battle zone. Russian maneuverability was much more limited on that front. Furthermore, if czarist troops deployed along the Vistula River attempted to invade German territory, their flanks would become exposed. General Ivanov's strategy in winter 1915 aimed to neutralize the threat to his extreme left flank Carpathian Mountain positions before any attempt at invading Germany.[18] Consequently, intense enemy attacks targeted Conrad's Third Army and endangered the neighboring Fourth Army to the north. Enemy action also threatened to isolate Army Group Pflanzer-Baltin in the East Carpathian region.

At a meeting in Siedlice on 17 January 1915, Russian military leaders decided to launch a major offensive against Germany as a logical continuation of their 1914 Vistula River campaigns. A significant advantage of the plan was that many Northwest front rivers, lakes, and swamps would be frozen this time of year, facilitating troop movement. However, as was so often the case, *Stavka* had divided council. The impasse led General Ivanov to focus on preparing for a Carpathian Mountain offensive, disregarding the decision that had made Germany Russia's primary target in early 1915.[19] He began initiating steps to invade Hungary. Ivanov calculated that the action required only fourteen to eighteen days of preparation, including the transfer of troops and equipment. Maintaining a steady flow of supplies was critical.

On 13 November 1914, *Stavka*'s General Danilov requested that Ivanov prepare a detailed assessment of the Carpathian front situation. Ivanov's chief of staff, General Alexejev, responded to the request by offering explanations for the urgent need to transfer reinforcements to the Southwest front. These included that Fortress Przemyśl siege troops were too weak to sustain a forceful Habsburg attack, thereby requiring an additional four to five divisions' worth of reinforcements. Alexejev also noted that a mere two cavalry divisions defended key Uzsok Pass and Baligrod positions and that an invasion of Hungary necessitated additional manpower. He further insisted that mountain artillery was critical in view of the Carpathian terrain and weather, and he assured that, given the proper resources, the Southwest front armies could garner important victories and thereby gain important political influence vis-à-vis the neutrals. In his closing argument, Alexejev warned of a new German threat to the Southwest front even though, other than a 17 January telegram reporting the capture of a few Germans in the area, no evidence supported the assertion. The report, however, convinced *Stavka* to transfer XXII Corps and six mountain artillery batteries to the Southwest front, which impaired czarist Tenth Army's efforts against the Germans at the Second Battle of the Masurian Lakes.[20]

When the war ended, Russian generals blamed General Ivanov's machinations for spoiling any chance of an early 1915 victory on the German front. *Stavka*'s eventual support for Ivanov's plan attested to its weakness by allowing a front commander to interfere in major command decisions.

Inconsistent decisions regarding the division of forces and deployment of reserves further illuminated the Russian High Command's proclivity for allowing personal interests and prestige to influence military decisions. In the final analysis, czarist Carpathian operations led to defeat on both fronts. *Stavka*'s decision to pursue a Carpathian operation signified Russian awareness of the serious threat the Germans posed to czarist right flank positions. General Ivanov claimed that reinforcements were necessary because his insufficient forces could not withstand a Habsburg attack. He must launch an offensive to encircle Habsburg right flank positions in order to invade Hungary. Ivanov further demanded first-class troops, not unseasoned reserve formations, because of the excessive demands of mountain warfare.

By 11 January, General Ivanov had deployed large troop concentrations near the Dukla Pass area, where Russian control of Uzsok Pass helped further his intentions.[21] On 20 January final plans for a Russian invasion of Hungary determined that a frontal assault through the Carpathian Mountains toward Hungary would neutralize any Habsburg threat in the region. An unanticipated drawback of the plan was that it would draw Russian armies deep into the 250-kilometer Carpathian Mountain front, making a rapid retreat difficult and increasing the threat to the Northwest (German) front flank positions.

In early January 1915, thirty-five Habsburg divisions faced twenty-nine czarist entities on the mountain front. South of Fortress Przemyśl, along a 140-kilometer line extending to east of Uzsok Pass, nine and a half Habsburg divisions opposed nine enemy divisions. Along the 250-kilometer-long mountain ranges extending from Uzsok Pass to the Romanian frontier, four and a half improvised second- and third-line Army Group Pflanzer-Baltin units countered five Russian national guard divisions. At Fortress Przemyśl, three and a half divisions countered four infantry and two cavalry besieging divisions.

Like their Habsburg counterparts, Russian troops deployed in the Carpathian Mountains could also be described as a trained militia force; they had encountered equally difficult weather and terrain conditions.[22] This meant that by early 1915, two peasant armies deployed in the Carpathian war theater sought in vain to defeat the other. Battlefield disease resulted in serious losses to both sides. Intestinal typhus led to an order for Habsburg troops to boil all drinking water and milk.[23] Implementation of an immunization program and the onset of colder weather helped contain the illness.

On 1 January 1915 Conrad ordered that all wounded soldiers keep their rifles with them so they could later be given to replacement troops. As an added incentive, Fourth Army offered to pay any wounded soldier who carried his rifle and bayonet to field hospitals.[24] For supply columns, smaller *Panja* wagons and sturdy horses had replaced the more cumbersome military-issued wagons and larger draft animals. Hay proved difficult to transport into the mountains and was replaced by alternative feed sources. A feed shortage led to the starvation death of tens of thousands of horses.[25]

Battle raged at the Fourth Army southern flank at Gorlice, and on 1 January Russian forces captured Uzsok Pass. The serious setback endangered Third and Fourth Army inner flank positions.[26] The ensuing struggle forced the Third Army to retreat, exposing its flank positions as well as those of Army Group Pflanzer-Baltin. Between 1 and 15 January, 2,300 Habsburg officers, 121,000 troops, 20,000 horses, and 3,300 wagons dispatched to the Carpathian front. During the month of January 1915 alone, more than 1,000 trains transported 5,500 officers, 260,000 soldiers, 39,400 horses, and 7,500 supply wagons and artillery pieces. Simultaneously, 62,000 sick and wounded Habsburg soldiers and 38,000 Russian prisoners were transported from the front lines. South Army consisted of some 350 officers and 24,500 soldiers.[27]

The troops defending Uzsok Pass suffered extreme exhaustion and lacked shelter from the harsh elements.[28] General Pflanzer-Baltin could not prevent his battle-weary troops from abandoning their Uzsok Pass positions. Conrad sought to reinforce the Army Group, but the severe rail limitations to that theater prevented rapid action. The situation stabilized when arriving reinforcements launched a counterattack.[29] The three infantry and one *Honvéd* (Hungarian) Cavalry Division that comprised Army Group Pflanzer-Baltin had received inadequate training and were commanded by inexperienced officers. Rain interrupted supply efforts as the badly needed reinforcements were in transport to the front.[30] On New Year's Day, Russian troops attacked Uzsok Pass under cover of night.[31] The surprised Habsburg troops withdrew in chaos to the Ung Valley, allowing Russian troops to advance against Third Army flank and rear echelons. Army Group Pflanzer-Baltin received orders to attack the advancing czarist flank, but the troops proved too exhausted and were only capable of fulfilling defensive missions.[32] The only serious in early January 1915 engaged Army Group Pflanzer-Baltin's flanks.

Russian occupation of much of the province of Bukovina near the Romanian frontier demanded immediate countermeasures to prevent a collapse of the thinly manned Hungarian front. The First Army V Corps, under the command of General Paul Puhallo von Brlog, transferred from the northern front to secure the Third Army's endangered right flank area and participate

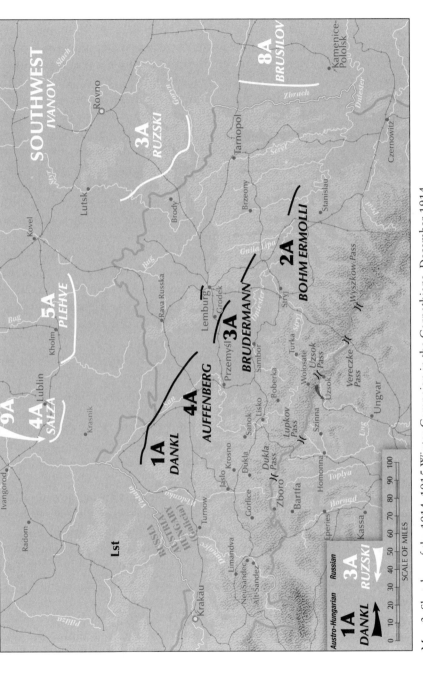

Map 3. Sketches of the 1914–1915 Winter Campaign in the Carpathians, December 1914

in the upcoming operation. The corps participated in all three Carpathian winter campaigns as a significant attack element. Its transport into the Carpathian Mountain theater commenced on 3 January. As Habsburg forces commenced preparations for the upcoming offensive, Russian Third Army forces struck the inner flanks of the Fourth and Third Army and at Gorlice, where the two czarist fronts intersected. Third Army III Corps and a newly formed four-cavalry division force received orders to close the gap that had formed between the two armies. That breach continued to be a hot spot throughout the Carpathian campaigns.[33]

In early January 1915, little hope existed for the timely liberation of Fortress Przemyśl. A 1 January muster report estimated that the garrison housed 128,000 soldiers and 14,500 horses, though their physical condition was rapidly declining. Russian siege troops utilized the pause in battle to construct a railroad around the fortress perimeter, which would allow them to more easily vanquish any breakout attempt.

Flooded roads and dense fog slowed troop and supply movement as steady rainfall transformed the ground into a vast sea of mud.[34] Sleds utilized to transport supplies in higher elevations and roads increasingly required maintenance. The effective use of artillery became extremely limited. Overall, the situation proved a harbinger of things to come.

The constant stream of Fourth Army units being transferred to the Carpathian Mountain theater produced an unsettling situation. Furthermore, many of the new arrivals' homes were situated behind enemy lines. Paranoia and the threat of desertion, particularly among Ruthenian troops, increased.

The Russians continued to fortify their positions, while the Habsburg Third Army remained too weak to resist a major attack. On 2 January General Boroević received orders to prepare his eastern flank forces for a powerful strike against the czarist-controlled Lisko–Sanok railroad and communication centers, which had fallen to the Russians at the end of December 1914. Third Army west flank units would join the eastern flank attack force once it had gained momentum. General Boroević planned to seize several critical railroad junctions. If Ustrzyki Dolne could initially be seized, the target railroad trunk lines at Lisko–Sanok would buckle, also threatening Russian positions near Fortress Przemyśl. This strategy basically rehatched Conrad's December 1914 campaign plan.[35]

The same day, Conrad ordered Army Group Pflanzer-Baltin to retake Uzsok Pass, but heavy snowfall disrupted the effort as hazardous road conditions and the snow drastically slowed troop and supply movement. Much-needed mountain artillery remained on the Balkan front.[36] The X Corps situation remained static in the Laborcz Valley, a hot spot of the first two Carpathian offensives. The exhausted 2nd Infantry Division reported a severe loss of officers and horses.[37] Habsburg command ordered all units to maintain their positions and utilize the time to clear obstructed roads.[38] The 2nd Infantry Division engaged czarist troops at Jasiel, doorway to the strategic rail junction at Mezölaborcz, which fell to the Russians after fierce battle in early February 1915. Only four X Corps artillery pieces supported the Habsburg infantry in days-long battle against czarist troops. The inexperienced X Corps troops received orders to defend the key battleground. Their prolonged and difficult approach to the front forfeited the element of surprise, permitting the enemy time to institute countermeasures. Jasiel, defended by the Habsburg 2nd Infantry Division, again fell to the Russians on 7 January.

Poor visibility and harsh weather conditions did not deter Russian activity around Fortress Przemyśl.[39] Numerous Habsburg communiqués complained of the shortage of professional officers available for the upcoming offensive.[40] A prevalence of less experienced reserve officers serving as field commanders would have serious repercussions for the military operation. On 3 January an XVIII Corps report revealed that the persistent harsh conditions were having a demoralizing effect on the troops. To make matters worse, corps artillery batteries had not arrived. XVIII Corps, under the command of General Heinrich Tschurtschentthaler, nonetheless succeeded in taking the high ground northeast of the Baligrod communication center without serious battle.[41] Tschurtschentthaler had commanded the Habsburg 44th Infantry Division until December 1914, at which time he became commander of the XVIII Corps, a position he held until March 1915. He later served on the Italian front in the Tyrol.

Habsburg Supreme Command ordered intense reconnaissance missions in preparation for the approaching offensive. It was imperative that preventative attacks bind enemy troops to keep them from being transferred to areas designated for the upcoming offensive.[42] Enemy pressure forced Army Group Pflanzer-Baltin's left flank and Fourth Army units rearward. The recent loss of Uzsok Pass forced Army Group Pflanzer-Baltin's Corps Hofmann to retreat between 3 to 5 January.[43] Significant reinforcements were needed to retake the pass, future site of major battle. Habsburg III Corps received orders to close the dangerous gap between the Third and Fourth Army inner flanks by attacking at these positions.[44] Conrad anticipated that the addition of three V Corps infantry divisions and units from other fronts would be sufficient to produce a swift and decisive victory. Additionally, a Habsburg show of force in the Carpathian Mountains would keep the neutrals from entering the conflict.[45] Amid growing concern over the crisis at Fortress Przemyśl, Conrad ordered fort commander General

Kusmanek to devise a breakout plan by mid-February.[46] At least three czarist reserve infantry and two cavalry divisions supported by numerous third-line units now besieged the fortress.[47] The New Year brought strict food rationing at the fortress, with bread servings reduced by one quarter and animal feed being prepared for human consumption. The slaughter of horses had two positive effects: it provided additional meat to sustain the garrison and increased the supply of oats for human consumption. On the other hand, fewer horses were now available to perform heavy tasks, including moving artillery shells and ammunition, as well as transporting the wounded. Habsburg intelligence reports indicated that eleven infantry and two cavalry divisions of the Russian Third Army were deployed southeast of Gorlice, twelve infantry and five cavalry divisions of the czarist Eighth Army further southeast. Three regular and two Cossack and third-line national guard divisions had reportedly been deployed between the Uzsok and Verecke passes.

X Corps received orders to prevent enemy excursions into the Laborcz Valley and to expand its reconnaissance efforts. Ensuing skirmishes with enemy troops reduced X Corps numbers as the launch date for the major offensive loomed. Significantly, control of the frontier ridges gave the Russians easier access to Mezőlaborcz, where General Ivanov intended to mass czarist troops for his own offensive, set for three days after the 23 January Habsburg initiative. On 4 January work began to improve and restore the supply transport routes and to construct a small-gauge railroad for V Corps supply trains.[48] The following day, Conrad issued an order to all field officers forbidding the insertion of March Brigade replacement troops into combat as self-standing units and to transport artillery into the mountains.[49] V Corps troops began taking position on the high terrain at the Third Army extreme right flank. While Russian forces remained mainly passive, both sides reinforced and improved their positions. General Boroević requested that Conrad supply him with additional troops to reinforce his army's right flank to spearhead the offensive.[50] In the days leading up to the offensive, heavy rains and mud made it difficult for troops to remain in position and severely limited supply and reconnaissance efforts.[51]

General Conrad again admonished X Corps 2nd Infantry Division to prevent Russian troops from infiltrating the Laborcz Valley. It was imperative that the division seize the higher ground to the west and intensify its reconnaissance efforts.[52] Upon Conrad's request, German general Hindenburg agreed to transfer two and a half Ninth Army divisions to the Carpathian front. The move, approved by Emperor Wilhelm on 8 January, created the new South Army under German command and expanded allied influence to the Habsburg front.[53] South Army German troops experienced delays in their estimated nine-day travel time, particularly after transfer to the low-capacity Hungarian railroads. German troops finally arrived thirty hours late, delaying the South Army's offensive by one day.[54] Though Third Army's III Corps attacked toward Banica near Gorlice on 5 January, the isolated attacks lacked crucial coordination between the armies' inner flanks. The rugged terrain produced numerous isolated and uncoordinated attacks throughout the Carpathian campaigns, which proved damaging to both the Habsburg Third and Fourth armies.[55] On 5 January czarist troops temporarily postponed a planned attack at Gorlice on the Fourth Army front, using the time to construct stationary fortified positions.[56] The lull prompted Conrad to order the transfer of three Fourth Army divisions to the Third and South armies as reinforcements for the offensive.[57] A day earlier, Army Group Pflanzer-Baltin's Corps Hofmann, still recovering from engaging czarist troops earlier at Uzsok Pass, came under enemy attack. General Peter Freiherr von Hofmann commanded the corps bearing his name until February 1917. For his later success in forcing czarist troops out of Uzsok Pass, Hofmann was sometimes referred to as the savior of Hungary, for preventing its invasion. Units had to cancel reconnaissance patrols because of flooding, while corps reports cited widespread disease and frostbite within the ranks.

As a counter to the late December 1914 Russian gains, VII Corps deployed at the Dukla Pass southwest of Baligrod. A main objective was to keep the pass roads open.[58] Indicative of the serious casualties sustained in recent military actions, a 5 January VII Corps report listed 95 dead, 227 sick, 235 wounded, 37 captured, and 36 missing in action as of 3 January 1915.[59]

Reinforcements were desperately needed for the upcoming offensive. The crisis persuaded Balkan theater commander, Archduke Karl, to transfer seven divisions to the Carpathian front, including the three-division XIX Corps. General Ignaz Trollmann Freiherr von Loucenberg served as commander of the XIX Corps in January 1915. He served under Attack Group Puhallo during the Carpathian campaigns. General Trollmann, like his fellow field commander, General Sandor Szurmay, acquired a tremendous amount of combat experience in the three Carpathian winter campaigns. Embarrassment over the monarchy's December 1914 Serbian defeat still lingered, but the additional seven divisions could produce victory on the Russian front.

The Habsburg Third Army lost a third of its troops during its most recent engagement with the enemy. This prompted Conrad to request another two divisions from the Germans to support his Carpathian operation. Given the shortage of his own reserve troops, Conrad insisted that he needed seven additional German divisions, four to protect the Italian frontier and three for the Romanian frontier.

As Habsburg–Italian diplomatic negotiations dragged on, Conrad maintained that Rome's *irredentist* demands pointed to its intention to wage war against the Dual Monarchy, but he insisted that territorial concessions were out of the question. The Germans kept pressure on Habsburg leaders to accede to Italian territorial demands, further straining already tense allied relations. Conrad asserted that the monarchy's erstwhile ally merely awaited a Habsburg defeat to justify entering the conflict. Thus, a swift and decisive victory over Russia would preclude a three-front war.

On 6 January inclement weather conditions continued to wreak havoc on offensive preparations. Flooding conditions continued while labor crews worked feverishly to repair damaged roads. Snowfall continued in the higher elevations, where the lack of alternative supply routes created severe problems.[60] The need for road repairs reached a critical stage as the transport and placement of artillery pieces presented serious challenges.[61] General Szurmay discovered that his intended approach route was not suitable for transporting artillery and bridges in the region desperately needed repair. Regardless of the enormous logistical difficulties, the threat to Habsburg flank positions must be neutralized.

Regaining control of the Uzsok Pass was critical for Third Army success. It remained quiet on 6 January; however, there were sightings of enemy reinforcements shifting to opposite Third Army's right flank positions. The Third Army III Corps and Fourth Army IX Corps inner flank situation continued to raise security concerns. Uncoordinated efforts at the corps' inner flanks were the source of many problems in the coming months. General Rudolph Kralicek commanded the Fourth Army IX Corps for two years beginning in November 1914.

The previous loss of professional soldiers severely reduced the Habsburg army's combat effectiveness. Most units were now comprised of reserve officers and officer candidates. The Fourth Army had sacrificed much of its offensive power, having relinquished numerous divisions to Third Army.[62] Continued Russian occupation of the Bukovina intensified the need to immediately reinforce Army Group Pflanzer-Baltin's front to rectify the situation. Enemy gains had also increased the potential for Romanian interest in the province of Transylvania.

Group Puhallo, mainly V and XVIII Corps, comprised the Habsburg Third Army main offensive. Group Joseph, essentially VII Corps, received orders to hold the Dukla Pass, while Group Szurmay was assigned to safe-guard Uzsok Pass and adjacent Borynia. Strong Russian forces occupied the intended Group Szurmay and XVIII Corps attack sites.

Main roadways became closed to vehicular traffic, prompting the need for makeshift sleds. Preparing artillery firing positions continued to pose an increasingly difficult challenge. An important railway leading to the Cisna depot would soon be operational, and the single narrow-gage forest railway was now operational for V Corps utilization.

Horses collapsed from overexertion, and combat troops had to assist in road repairs. The operation came to rely heavily on pack animals, particu-larly at higher elevations, creating an urgent need for straw and hay to feed them.[63] The animals had become easy targets for enemy snipers, who rec-ognized their importance. Injured horses were shot to put them out of their misery; others died from starvation or exhaustion. The starving animals gnawed on tree bark but later died when, after drinking water, their bloated stomachs burst. Many lost their footing and broke their legs attempting to navigate the icy mountain passes. On 7 January VII Corps repulsed a czarist attack, while nearby, the X Corps 2nd Infantry Division battled the enemy. General Conrad threatened the Germans with transferring his Second Army from the Polish front back to the Carpathian theater, but he abandoned the idea as too time-consuming. However, Conrad used the threat to pressure German High Command into agreeing to supply additional troops to his Carpathian operation. As German Ninth Army troops prepared to deploy into the Carpathian Mountains to join Habsburg units, forming the new South Army, General Freytag-Loringhoven, the ranking German military liaison to Habsburg Supreme Command, voiced grave concerns over the hazardous terrain chosen for the German troop deployment. German sol-diers were unaccustomed and ill-prepared for the rigors of winter moun-tain warfare and did not possess the proper equipment. Though General Freytag-Loringhoven's arguments proved justified, tragically, they fell on deaf ears. Conrad, meanwhile, assured Falkenhayn that two good roads and a railroad line were located in the South Army deployment zone and that he would supply light wagons and draft animals for German use. When asked whether his Third Army would be able to hold the Carpathian ridge-lines for the next several weeks, Conrad could not say for certain.

On 8 January, Third Army's main mission encompassed ensuring the safe arrival of reinforcements by securing the travel route between Mezőlaborcz and Takcsany. Third Army left flank forces (III and VII Corps) must thwart any Russian offensive effort directed against the vulnerable Fourth Army southern flank.[64] The gap between Third and Fourth Army remained a major concern, particularly near Gorlice. Fourth Army nonetheless had to surrender two additional divisions to the Third Army.[65] Snowdrifts obstructed the few traversable areas of the front; many roadways were completely blocked. Situation reports indicated increasing losses due to illness and frostbite.

An order to conserve artillery shells confirmed a persistent ammunition shortage that continued to plague Habsburg military operations. Numerous corps logbook entries bemoaned the urgent need for shelter and ammunition, particularly artillery shells. Artillery pieces, many of which had been lost or become irreparable, remained in short supply. A ten-day period of Russian passivity beginning on 8 January offered Habsburg troops welcome relief. Frantic preparations for the upcoming offensive continued, but reconnaissance missions frequently had to be canceled as a result of dense fog and snow in the mountains.[66] En route from the Balkan front, XIX Corps' three infantry divisions and a cavalry division received orders to secure the Mezőlaborcz–Takcsany–Nagypolany rail line upon their arrival at Third Army's eastern flank. Once all V Corps troops assembled, it would support the effort to regain Uzsok Pass. A major offensive launched in the direction of Uzsok, Turka, and Lutoviska was scheduled for 20 January. The XVIII, XIX, and a portion of the X Corps would seize the main objective of Lisko–Sanok. A preliminary attack the day before aimed to seize Uzsok Pass and secure that flank area.[67] However, this required Group Szurmay's flank units to first advance forward. Army Group Pflanzer-Baltin would support the Third and South Army offensive by striking Russian positions.[68]

South Army consisted of five infantry and two cavalry divisions, which included two- and three-quarter German infantry and one cavalry division (half the 3rd Garde Division, the 1st Infantry Division, the 48th Reserve Infantry Division, and the 5th Cavalry Division). Two infantry divisions, two separate brigades, and one cavalry division (19th and 55th Infantry divisions, 12th and 131st *Landsturm* brigades, and 10th Cavalry Division) represented the Habsburg portion. Of the army's 45,700 soldiers, 19,645 were German and 26,055 Austro-Hungarian.

Returning to the burning issue of Italy's demands, Conrad advised Foreign Minister Berchtold that surrendering territory would be construed as a sign of weakness and would only prompt greater demands. Thus, concessions to Rome must be avoided.[69] On the other hand, Conrad supported negotiating a separate peace treaty with Russia to allow him to focus on defeating Italy if war ensued between them.

On the Carpathian front, XVIII Corps advanced from its assembly area to its new deployment area with no serious enemy interference. Its progress slowed, however, as it encountered unfavorable terrain and weather conditions.[70] Labor and technical units continued efforts to maintain supply and troop traffic flow, while overburdened railroad lines experienced multiple delays.[71] Clearing snow-blocked supply routes received priority, but a shortage of labor crews hampered the effort. Enlisting the aid of combat units to maintain the roads became commonplace.

Though it became increasingly critical for Habsburg forces to regain control of Uzsok Pass before the main offensive, prevailing conditions guaranteed that the planned two-pronged advance required Herculean effort. Meanwhile, Army Group Pflanzer-Baltin struggled to traverse the mountain ridges on its front, retarded by two meters of snow.

This study will focus on Hungarian Group Szurmay, whose initial mission was to retake Uzsok Pass, and the Habsburg army X Corps' bloody defense of the strategically important Laborcz Valley and railroad center at Mezölaborcz. General Sandor Szurmay commanded his eponymous corps from November 1914 until February 1917. He also commanded the 38th Infantry Division beginning in December 1914. Corps Szurmay engaged in fierce battle in all three Carpathian winter campaigns.

Army Group Szurmay and other units, such as Archduke Joseph's VII Corps, fought to defend against an invasion of their homeland. As the Carpathian campaign continued, many Hungarian soldiers placed a handful of their home soil in a knapsack before they deployed to the battlefield. Should they die in this foreign land, at least the dirt from their homeland could be placed on their grave. Though often outnumbered, these troops fought stubbornly and bravely; however, their efforts were retarded by the many years of an official *Magyarization* policy, which declared Hungarian the official language of the country and forced the indoctrination of Romanians, Slovaks, and other ethnic minorities to ensure Hungarian dominance. This did not improve any Romanian, Slovak, Croatian, or Slovenian patriotic feelings. These troops, serving as unwilling combatants, often proved unreliable in combat.

Russian troops threatened to advance into Laborcz Valley to seize Mezölaborcz, their chief objective. If successful, the move would cripple any Habsburg operation to rescue Fortress Przemyśl.[72] On 8 and 9 January general instructions for the offensive now targeted 22 January as the launch date. Army Group Pflanzer-Baltin was already engaged in battle. On 9 January continued difficulties hampered preparations for the approaching action. VII Corps' 17th Infantry Division reported it had completely depleted its supply of artillery shells, leaving the infantry without artillery support for ten days. One corps cannon regiment had been in repair for days.

Table 1. Austro-Hungarian Troops Transported to the Carpathian Front

Recovered Troops Sent to the Field

Year	Officers	Men
1914	6,182	133,683
January–June 1915	16,444	459,256
Totals	22,626	592,939

Total 1914 Replacement Troops

	Officers	Men	Total
Reserves	12,000	639,000	651,000
New Formations	5,000	292,000	297,000
Total	17,000	931,000	948,000

Source: Franek, "*Die Entwicklung des österreich-ungarischen Wehrmacht*," 11; see ÖULK, Ergänzungsheft, 5; *Probleme der organization im ersten Kriegsjahre*, 25. Franek's numbers differ in the two sources.

Most remaining operable artillery pieces had been pulled out of their positions, and it would require several days to emplace them again because of the prevailing conditions. Reconnaissance efforts continued to be hampered by bad weather.[73] Maps for reconnaissance purposes proved useless thanks to poor visibility. X Corps' patrols advanced at a rate of one kilometer an hour. Alternating periods of light rain and snow exacerbated conditions in the valleys. The severe conditions placed an added burden on pack animals, which did not receive proper veterinary care.

The threat of the Fourth Army coming under attack at Gorlice resurfaced. A reported nine czarist divisions were in position to strike Fourth Army right flank positions. This raised concern about the possibility of Fourth Army receiving orders to transfer more units to Third Army.

Army Group Pflanzer-Baltin's left flank forces received orders to attack, while its right flank units must block any enemy advance. The army group must initially support the main offensive effort and then shift to assist the South Army in battling its way out of the mountains. If Pflanzer-Baltin's troops encountered no significant Russian resistance, they would then launch an offensive. On 20 January South Army should attack, while its cavalry units destroyed railroads behind enemy positions. Transport of the 6th and 19th Infantry divisions to reinforce Army Group Pflanzer-Baltin received confirmation.[74]

Returning to the major offensive force, Third Army, once its eastern units advanced, its western units would also attack. Fourth Army southern flank units would then thrust toward Jaslo to protect the offensive force's northern flank.[75] The immediate mission of the army's designated eastern flank offensive group was to secure the new V and XVIII Corps' major supply center and reconnoiter forward, while XVIII Corps seized the railroad junction at Ustrzyki Górne.[76] Reports emanating from Fortress Przemyśl, meanwhile, warned that enemy troops were being shifted from Uzsok Pass and that portions of two divisions were now positioned in the designated V and XVIII Corps and Group Szurmay deployment area.[77] Sorties were called off as a result of the declining health of the fortress inhabitants.

The two-pronged attack to recapture Uzsok Pass consisted of V Corps 33rd Infantry Division assaulting czarist positions at the pass with the support of South Army forces. Simultaneously, XIX Corps troops would advance to Mezölaborcz.[78] As the launch date neared, preparations to retake the strategically important pass intensified.

A X Corps manuscript deposited in the Vienna War Archives detailed the prevailing weather conditions (frequent snowfall alternating with rain) harassing Habsburg troops. Many supply routes remained in poor condition, while labor crews constructed serpentine approaches on steeper high-elevation ridges through deep snow. This would assist the movement of heavy ammunition and artillery wagons that could not be easily moved forward.[79] Reports of lung and intestinal disease had become widespread. Transporting the wounded through the deep snow proved a daunting task. The drifting snow required skis and sled runners for supply wagons, but none were readily available.[80] Deep snow, frigid temperatures, high winds, and fog blanketed the entire front, while frost and ice covered the few mountain passageways. Huge mounds of shoveled snow framed the roadways.[81] Oftentimes visibility was limited to 50 meters. Unit logbooks continued to emphasize the lack of troop shelter and the necessity for engineering units to assist in the construction of defensive positions.[82]

Meanwhile, a foreboding silence pervaded the Galician and Carpathian fronts. Major supply depots continued to be prepared, while technical troops proved unsuccessful in maintaining major passageway traffic flow because of insufficient troop numbers. On 10 January XVIII Corps secured the area for construction of its main supply center and then attempted to seize the Ustrzyki Górne area.[83] Continued Russian passivity on 9 and 10 January provided the Third Army the additional opportunity to recuperate and continue making preparations for the offensive.[84] Railroad transport became limited to ten trains a day, while its escalating usage severely overtaxed the few existing lines and produced further serious delays that hampered timely troop deployments and the commencement of operations.[85]

Habsburg Supreme Command's attention remained focused on the vital Mezőlaborcz communication and transport center.[86] Only two field howitzers and one field cannon battery were assigned per division.[87] Entire Third Army artillery batteries remained behind the main mountain ridges when it was critical that as many as possible be positioned rapidly to support the offensive. The designated Third Army portion of the offensive toward the Lisko–Sanok–Lutoviska railroad junctions would end the enemy's ability to rapidly shift troops or reinforcements to any threatened front areas.

On 11 January the strategy for "one of the most difficult campaigns an army ever faced" neared completion.[88] The Austrian official history, however, described the approaching offensive operation as a "cruel folly." Undertaking a major offensive on snow and ice covered mountain terrain in −20°C to −30°C temperatures, if not an act of desperation, certainly did not represent sound military planning. The November and December 1914 Carpathian Mountain experiences indicated that more realistic planning was appropriate. The proposed Third Army eastern flank attack in the densely forested *Waldkarpathen,* a region possessing few traversable routes for supply or reinforcement transit, was questionable. Moreover, during all three Carpathian offensive efforts, deadly frontal assaults were launched. General Conrad claimed that his actions were dictated by the time pressure to relieve Fortress Przemyśl. The Habsburg Supreme Commander's hasty planning and failure to achieve critical mass at key attack areas led to disaster. It should be recalled that Conrad's strategy relied heavily on luck, surprise, and mild weather, none of which worked in his favor.

X Corps, for example, was ordered to attack as one of its divisions approached the front, producing a chaotic and deadly situation. On 11 January, the Corps was ordered to advance over hazardous terrain, a move that exposed its 2nd Infantry Division's northern flank positions and further exhausted the already battle-weary troops.[89] The same day, XVIII Corps command learned that its artillery units had been transferred behind the forward ridgelines, while its supplies arrived on makeshift sled columns. Available Group Szurmay troops prepared roadways for wagon traffic; nevertheless, they remained impassible, even when oxen were used.

Already on 13 November 1914 czarist general Danilov requested an exact description of the Carpathian Mountain situation in the area of Sanok–Sambor–Stryj from General Alexejev, the Southwest front's chief of staff. General Alexejev presented arguments for the necessity of reinforcements for that front, emphasizing that only weak czarist forces besieged Fortress Przemyśl. Thus, an energetic attack from the fort could endanger his position. He argued further that just two cavalry divisions occupied the critical area between Uzsok Pass and Baligrod, and therefore, reinforcements were crucial there as well. However, the Southwest front would have to be reinforced at the expense of the German Northwest front, chosen by *Stavka* as the main campaign area. General Ivanov requested four to five divisions to strengthen the siege of Fortress Przemyśl and answered a question posed by *Stavka* by stating that German strength in the Carpathian Mountains could only be determined by battle. Finally, in order to continue exploiting any success against the enemy, the main Carpathian passes must be held solidly to secure Galicia. On 16 November, the argument changed to the fact that Southwest front troops must attack Fortress Cracow and secure the Southwest front's left flank area by seizing the Carpathian Mountain passes. The major Vistula River crossing points, in any case, must be kept in Russian hands.

On 11 January General Ivanov reported the significance of a possible Habsburg offensive to *Stavka*. Claiming to ensure maintaining possession of East Galicia, Ivanov deployed reinforcements to the Dukla Pass region as he chose the Mezőlaborcz area for his main assault. He utilized the reputed threat to the czarist extreme left flank positions to justify the increased troop concentrations. Thus, he requested reinforcements to launch his own frontal offensive to encircle the Habsburg extreme right flank mountain positions and then proceed to invade the Hungarian plains.[90] This, he claimed, would also thwart any Habsburg offensive efforts. Both General Conrad and General Ivanov viewed the Carpathian Mountain region as a viable setting to launch a major decisive offensive and prepared for such an action.

We will now examine the activities of an Army Group Pflanzer-Baltin division to gain insight into the prevailing battle conditions on that isolated front. The 54th Infantry Division consisted of nine mostly Transylvanian supply battalions, primarily older soldiers with some battalions composed of mainly Romanians. Staff officers, transferred from militia-level support services, had little if any combat experience. Furthermore, the division lacked almost all necessary basic equipment. Because they lacked uniforms, some officers wore civilian clothes, with a star placed on their sleeve designating them as military personnel. The troops received a variety of obsolete rifles as armaments but few machine guns. Division troop morale and fighting value had sunk so low that Hungarian *gendarme* units enforced discipline. The division had sustained severe casualties in the earlier Bukovina struggles.

Between 10 and 15 January smaller division infantry units, such as the Meszoly battalion, experienced enormously exhausting marches. They then launched attacks against Kirlibaba, a key position situated on top

of a rock formation, where one machine gun emplacement easily blocked
the approach road. The ensuing division assault occurred without artillery
support, while the advance march required constant shoveling. Movement
remained greatly restricted by the deep snow, and a path had to be shoveled
to the front before the attack. Thus the battalion units advanced one and
a half kilometers, not the ordered eight. On 12 January the forward attack
group was repulsed by heavy enemy fire, while on 13 January the deep
snow hindered launching a full-scale assault. The attacking *Landsturm*
troops' obsolete dark uniforms (regular troops wore a more suitable color)
made them easy targets against the stark white snow backdrop; they thus
sustained numerous casualties before being forced to retreat. Early on 14
January the Meszoly battalion recaptured some positions.[91]

Since October 1914 Pflanzer-Baltin's forces had been conducting guerilla
warfare and small-scale actions against third-line Russian cavalry divisions
to prevent an enemy incursion into Hungary. At the advent of the New
Year, the Russians seized control of some of the main Carpathian Mountain
passes, and with the czarist invasion of the Bukovina, their troops had to
be halted because of the threat of Romania entering the war. Thus, during
early 1915, the Army Group received a few well-equipped units, the XI
and XIII Corps, to enable it to participate in offensive operations. However, throughout the Carpathian campaign, Army Group Pflanzer-Baltin remained handicapped by the minimal railroad capacity to its theater, which
limited the rapid transport of significant troop numbers. This inadequate
railroad network had negatively affected the 1914 mobilization and deployment, and during the ensuing campaigns, they could not be utilized to the
extent Habsburg Supreme Command desired.

Newly issued orders emphasized that if the Third Army's initial offensive effort succeeded, Fourth Army must immediately attack the retreating
enemy. In addition, on 22 January, a Group Szurmay brigade must assist
V Corps 33rd Infantry Division in recapturing Uzsok Pass and then jointly
advance to Turka. Group Szurmay's units maneuvered through meter-deep
snow, which took a physical toll on its troops.

General Boroević's revised Third Army offensive mission called for the
seizure of the strategically important Ustrzyki Dolne transportation center
to prevent the enemy from accessing its major Lisko and Sanok transportation hubs. Habsburg control of the Lutoviska–Baligrod area would also
threaten Russian Eighth Army flank positions. A Habsburg offensive force
composed of ten infantry and two cavalry divisions would either advance
north to seize the Uzsok Pass–Turka–Stary Sambor area, or northeast toward the Solinka and San rivers. Success of the Third Army's operation

hinged on close cooperation of the neighboring South and Fourth Army southern flank efforts.[92]

In the meantime, intelligence reports indicated that the Russians would be receiving a reinforcing corps in East Galicia and another in the Bukovina. Habsburg Fourth Army, although facing strong enemy positions and constantly transferring units to participate in the approaching offensive, received orders to block the transfer of enemy troops to Third Army's front. Artillery shells must be conserved for the forthcoming offensive and thus should be utilized only to defend against an enemy attack.[93]

On 12 January X Corps advancing artillery units proceeding into the mountains halted for an extended period along a stretch of mountain road. Additional batteries received orders to move forward to supplement the few already in position.[94] Six men of Infantry Regiment 29 had frozen to death, while fifty more suffered severe frostbite—an ominous harbinger for the forthcoming campaign. A partial mission of the main Attack Group Puhallo in conjunction with Pflanzer-Baltin's Corps Hofmann was to reconquer Uzsok Pass by launching the mentioned two-pronged attack. V Corps troops must be deployed by 12 January in preparation for the operation. The other major offensive force, Group Krautwald (2nd, 24th, 34th, and 43rd Infantry divisions), must seize Baligrod, then strike toward the Lisko–Sanok railroad centers as soon as Group Puhallo had established adequate flank security. X Corps 2nd Infantry Division would provide that security. General Josef Freiherr Krautwald von Annaue began the war as commander of the 34th Infantry Division, but in January 1915 he became the commander of the Third Army X Corps, which fought in the major battle at Mezölaborcz. His command included the 2nd, 24th, and 34th Infantry divisions. Krautwald was promoted to general of the infantry on 1 May 1917. Meanwhile, Group Joseph (essentially VII Corp's 17th and 20th *Honvéd* Infantry and 1st Cavalry divisions) must seize and hold the entrance to the Dukla and Jasliska Passes to prevent the transfer of significant enemy troop numbers against the Third Army attack groups. Group Colerus (III Corps' 22nd and 28th Infantry and 4th Cavalry divisions) initially must block the approaches to Zmigrod and later join the attack. Groups Colerus and Joseph (Third Army left flank units) would advance when the Third Army right flank forces forced the enemy's withdrawal from the vital transportation centers.[95]

A high-ranking Habsburg Operations Bureau General Staff officer warned that the proposed main Attack Group San River offensive would be "methodical mass murder." He further complained about the "headlessness" in the command chain and the obvious inferiority of Habsburg artillery in comparison to that of the Russians.[96]

Transfer of XIX Corps from the Balkan theater to the Carpathian front commenced on 22 January and continued as the corps mission evolved into neutralizing any enemy advance toward Czeremcha in the key Ung Valley.[97] Third Army numbers presently were too weak to engage in any decisive undertaking; nevertheless, it must prevent further Russian territorial gains. Numerous units requisitioned additional food rations and heavy sleds because of the problems created by poor road conditions.[98]

Army maps, critical for both planning operations and position orientation, were often obsolete and also did not present such important new features as railroad lines or their extensions. The failure of bridges and roads to be listed resulted from civilian authorities failing to inform the military of their existence. Maps of Hungary proved particularly misleading because general-purpose and special editions did not coincide. Town names and various locations varied depending on the particular map. The prewar *Magyarization* process resulted in many German and Slavic names being replaced with their Hungarian versions on more recent renderings.

Habsburg units continued to encounter numerous obstacles completing troop deployments and other preparations for the impending offensive. For example, on 13 January X Corps reported that its few natural valley passageways had flooded and all movement had slowed to one kilometer per hour. On higher terrain, snow obscured gigantic potholes, requiring that horse march columns first test sections of roadways before bringing artillery and ammunition columns forward. Road surfaces were in continual need of shoveling, and the loss of horses continued.

Many artillery pieces had to be disassembled for transport into the mountains. The few guns placed into firing positions had to be pulled by multiharnessed pack animal teams interspersed among ammunition columns. The transport of crucial artillery became increasingly difficult on the treacherous terrain. To their dismay, arriving V Corps divisions discovered that their artillery batteries had not been ordered forward.

On 13 January, a major reconnaissance mission reconfirmed that only two enemy cavalry divisions defended the crucial area between Uzsok Pass and Baligrod. General Ivanov had requested reinforcements because of the recognized czarist numerical weakness between the two locations, but also planned to puncture Habsburg lines defending the Dukla Pass and seize Mezölaborcz, crippling Habsburg offensive efforts to rescue Fortress Przemyśl. In addition to General Conrad's obvious multiple problems, Foreign Minister Berchtold insisted that the recent enemy seizure of the Bukovina province and resultant threat to Transylvania signified that Romania would enter the war if it appeared advantageous to seize its *irredenta* goals.[99] Berchtold insisted that something had to be done on that front! During the night 13 to 14 January, South and Third Army received orders for their units to cooperate and advance to seize Uzsok Pass, although some units designated to participate in the operation had just begun their transport to the front. Both armies must bind opposing enemy troops while completing preparations for the offensive.[100] The rugged mountain terrain selected for South Army deployment forced it to be divided into three attack groups to achieve its mission by launching envelopment movements against the enemy. South Army's terrain proved much more challenging compared to Third Army's. The revised 14 January Third Army offensive plan included V Corps' 33rd Infantry Division rapidly advancing to the Uzsok Pass to strike Russian flank and rear positions. XVIII Corps' primary mission remained to advance to Ustrzyki Górne while a separate detachment supported neighboring South Army efforts. Four divisions of Attack Group Krautwald must advance through Baligrod and then its left flank units swing toward Lisko–Sanok once main Attack Group Puhallo achieved success. The army's left flank Group Joseph's (VII Corps) and Group Colerus' (III Corps) missions remained the same. Two divisions served as a reserve pool (7th and 29th Infantry Divisions). Conserving artillery shells must continue while the Russian penchant for night attacks made night security a high priority.

The 14 January intelligence reports indicated that the Russians intended to launch an offensive at the Fourth Army Gorlice area.[101] Little could be expected at this front area because of small troop numbers and Fourth Army having to transfer numerous divisions to the Carpathian theater to avoid having to attack particularly strong czarist positions. Meanwhile, the winter weather intensified: heavy frost deposited a thick coat of ice on roadways, while a further meter and a half of snow accumulated. Skis and wagons on sled runners became the necessary mode of artillery and supply transport. Blizzard conditions severely curtailed the pace of preparations for the forthcoming offensive undertaking. The resultant poor travel conditions caused XIX Corps to arrive twelve hours behind schedule. XVIII Corps troops shoveled drifted snow on the ridges.[102] Lightly wounded soldiers assisted.

Inclement weather conditions, termed "a good indication of things to come" during the bitterest cold winter months, promised to produce a difficult campaign unprecedented in military history.[103] The opening of a small-gauge forest railroad line for supply purposes presented its own unique problems, while regular railroad lines required constant shoveling. Group

Szurmay (40th Infantry and 8th Cavalry divisions, 75th and 128th Infantry brigades, and 1st Hussar Cavalry Brigade) must cooperate in the effort to recapture Uzsok Pass and then advance to Turka and Stary Sambor to participate in main Attack Group Puhallo's mission. Strong Russian resistance could be anticipated in the areas of Patakujfalu and Dvernik in the Ung Valley leading to the strategic Laborcz Valley.[104]

The necessity of a Fourth Army southern flank attack to support the approaching Third Army offensive received increasing attention. IX Corps flank units must prevent the Russians from attacking the Third Army's northern III Corps at all costs. Fourth Army's present mission included unconditionally maintaining its positions and launching a frontal assault against well-fortified enemy defensive positions at Gorlice. The operation's success depended on the close cooperation of the inner flank III and IX Corps. However, terrain features separating the two corps made this an extremely difficult task.[105] In addition to providing the main offensive thrust, Third Army must also support Fourth Army's flank positions.

Conrad became agitated at an 11 January allied conference in Breslau when he realized that he faced a fait accompli. General Falkenhayn had made the decisions, and thus there would be no discussion. Meanwhile, 29th Infantry Division, one of the two reserve divisions, arrived in Mezölaborcz after a seventy-two-hour railroad transport during a snowstorm.

Hungarian premier Tisza joined Foreign Minister Berchtold's earlier chastisement of Conrad for the recent evacuation of the Bukovina. If the Russians invaded Transylvania, Tisza predicted that Romania would enter the war.[106] Conrad ordered Army Group Pflanzer-Baltin to launch an attack to roll up the enemy's extreme flank positions to relieve pressure on the Bukovina front.

Meanwhile, by mid-January 1915, enemy pressure forced Third Army left flank units to retreat as czarist troops continued to infiltrate the Dukla Pass. Near Uzsok Pass, Habsburg units retreated from Verecke Ridge and Wyszkov Pass, where the South Army would soon launch its offensive. Russian activity had intensified where Habsburg forces intended to launch their attack; however, significant Habsburg Third Army reinforcements would not arrive until mid-January at the earliest.

During the night to 15 January critical road improvements were completed during heavy snowfall and fog conditions. Reconnaissance patrols shoveled their way through snowdrifts. The troops found themselves increasingly unprepared for the demanding circumstances. The proliferation of Slavic national propaganda produced an increasingly negative effect on troop morale, discipline, and the cohesion of certain units, particularly Czech.

Troop units ranging from engineering to infantry performed critical road repairs and maintenance. XVIII Corps utilized 700 hand-pulled sleds for supply transport, while V Corps possessed none.[107] Snowdrifts blocked roadways, and dry wood for building sleds was in short supply, a problem made worse by the fact that labor crews had not been issued saws.[108]

Field officers complained that senior commanders, such as Conrad, were unaware of the situation at the front because they never visited it. Meanwhile, Conrad's offensive plans would prevent Russian troops from advancing into Transylvania from the Bukovina and preclude unnecessary compromise with Italy.[109] Relative to Fortress Przemyśl, a report indicated that if 3,500 horses were slaughtered immediately, the garrison could hold out until 7 March. General Kusmanek, citing dwindling food reserves, inquired whether the fortress would be relieved in the near future or whether he should attempt a breakout effort. Conrad delayed his reply to the query. Foraging efforts before the fortress perimeter provided sufficient food for the garrison to survive another week.[110] In the interim, VII Corps, commanded by Archduke Joseph August von Alcsut, buttressed its security preparations for defending the Laborcz Valley while V Corps units advanced into the Solinka Valley. The Archduke commanded VII Corps from November 1914 for two years. He became notorious as the commander of the devastated Hungarian Fourth Army at the onset of the Brusilov offensive. Two V Corps divisions must occupy Ustrzyki Górne and the nearby heights while the third established positions in the Ondava Valley. XIII Corps, scheduled to arrive on 28 January, would provide the impetus for Army Group Pflanzer-Baltin's offensive into the Bukovina and protection of the neighboring South Army flank position.[111]

On 23 January, part of the South Army mission was to advance east of Uzsok Pass in unison with Third Army Group Szurmay. Allied friction continued over provisioning concerns for the South Army German units. On 15 January, General Ludendorff threatened Conrad that unless German troops received the proper mountain equipment, he should not expect their assistance. Conrad meanwhile assured General Falkenhayn that the maximum number of forces had been designated for the rapidly approaching major offensive—a gross exaggeration.

Significant Russian pressure continued against the Dukla Pass, the most favorable terrain to puncture the thin Austro-Hungarian lines defending Hungary. No significant czarist reinforcements had been detected in the

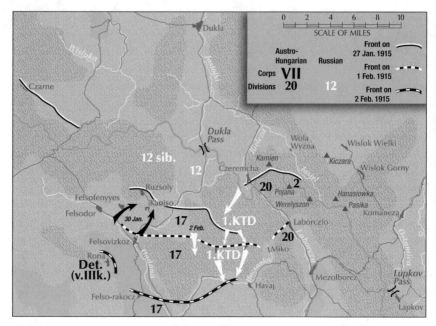

Map 4. Habsburg VII Corps, 27 January 1915

Uzsok Pass region destined for a major assault effort.[112] However, the Russians had reportedly begun creating an army composed of four to five reserve divisions with 110,000 to 120,000 troops in preparation to invade either Transylvania or Hungary. This threatened South Army and Army Group Pflanzer-Baltin offensive efforts because only *Landsturm* troops could deflect the new threat.

On 16 January a X Corps daily logbook entry stated that "deficient preparations [for the offensive] are unavoidable."[113] Additional corps logbooks frequently noted the insurmountable difficulties encountered in attempting to maintain supply and troop movement through drifting snow. Less than a week before the launching of the offensive, important supply routes remained unusable; X Corps must conduct a long detour to provide the much-needed goods. Hand-pulled sleds and reserve draft animal columns transported the most crucial necessities over the steep mountain slopes. The thirty toboggans provided per division assisted such efforts.[114] The troops' physical and moral conditions continued to decline as incidents of frostbite increased dramatically.

One strategic supply route was reported only passable for individual sled columns, but multiple sections required special caution during usage. Crucial road stretches still required constant maintenance services. The steep inclines and drifting snow made movement dangerous. Futile efforts continued to maintain the passageways for troop and supply purposes.

The East Carpathian Mountain region had been quiescent during the last half of December 1914, but in early January 1915 the Russians launched the mentioned offensive into the Bukovina, threatening Pflanzer-Baltin's western group rear echelon area. Russian occupation of the Bukovina continued to provide an imminent threat of a czarist invasion of Transylvania and Romanian intervention against the Dual Monarchy. The unfavorable Habsburg military situation, combined with the deficient railroads leading to that theater, still prohibited transfer of large troop numbers to that area. The late arrival of XIII Corps, however, forced a delay in the Group Pflanzer-Baltin offensive undertaking.

General Adolf Freiherr Rhemen zu Bärensfeld commanded the Habsburg XIII Corps from 12 October 1912 until July 1916. During the Carpathian Winter War, XIII Corps first defended against a stronger Russian Dniester Group and later the Russian Ninth Army.

Group Puhallo must advance on 20 January to seize the Ustrzyki Górne area. Third Army's northernmost III Corps must cooperate with the Fourth Army IX Corps flank positions to neutralize any enemy attack at their inner flanks, while a seven-mile gap separated Third Army's III and VII Corps.[115]

On 17 January, night security measures increased while much work remained to improve present positions. Instructions were issued to spare horses and wagons.[116] Third Army reconnaissance missions confirmed deployment of additional enemy infantry and artillery units before their lines. XIX Corps troops finally began arriving in strength, as corps reports described the multiple difficulties resulting from the unfavorable conditions. X Corps reported chest-deep snow, enormous snowdrifts, and blocked passageways. Modifying sleds for use with ammunition wagons required extensive improvisation. XVIII Corps prepared bridge equipment for its attempted crossing of the San River, but blizzard conditions severely handicapped all efforts. Ice-coated wires disrupted telephone communication. Fatefully, multiple troop formations designated for the offensive had still not arrived. The X Corps three divisions (2nd, 24th, and 34th) possessed only three mountain artillery pieces. Conrad ordered additional artillery units transferred to the front lines regardless of prevailing conditions, but to no avail.

V Corps command requested a delay in launching the offensive because snow masses blocked mountain passages and such difficulties would negate the vital element of surprise. Also, the chances of an early military success would rapidly dissipate if the enemy gained time to initiate effective countermeasures, which is precisely what occurred during the three Carpathian offensives. Other corps commanders also requested a delay in the operation until conditions improved. Then temperatures suddenly rose, hovering around freezing. Thawing conditions descended on the northern Fourth Army front, but heavy snowfall continued in higher elevations. However, by 21 January, the mercury again plummeted, and an additional meter of fresh snow further hindered movement.

A Group Szurmay *Honvéd* Infantry Division arrived and immediately began establishing security positions.[117] The 38th *Honvéd* Infantry Division reported only two functional field cannons and requested additional machine guns. Responding to the supply chaos, V Corps command ordered two cavalry squadrons to regulate and assist traffic flow between the major Takcsany and Cisna supply centers. Troops had to improvise sleds for an entire supply column and requested the necessary tools. X and XVIII Corps also began improvising sled columns, while the latter awaited the opening of a forest rail line. All the while, troops continued arriving.[118]

Confusion reigned as Attack Group Krautwald prepared for its offensive. X Corps' 2nd Infantry Division received the order to protect the group's left flank positions while keeping strong enemy forces at bay. Obviously, X Corps 34th Infantry Division's 6,500 men could not effectively resist the opposing 14,000 Russian troops, and thus the reserve 29th Infantry Division was rushed to the front.[119] VII Corps troops, deployed to assist X Corps' efforts to halt Russian incursions, could not fulfill that mission. Preparations continued amid last-minute change of plans. Additional artillery units received orders to move to the front while reconnaissance missions continued despite the difficult conditions. Habsburg troops trained to march with full field packs after their long battle pause.[120]

Pflanzer-Baltin, whose talent for battlefield improvisation became Habsburg legend, planned to launch a two-pronged offensive buttressed by XIII Corps' three regular army divisions. A left flank group would advance while right flank forces defended against a potential Russian attack. Pflanzer-Baltin's basic concept, determined by the inhospitable winter mountain terrain, called for assault units to advance in separate columns, seize an objective, and then continue the advance. However, positions lay buried under two meters of snow, and travel remained a slow and hazardous undertaking. Ammunition columns could not reach some front sectors. Meanwhile, conserving artillery shells, particularly high explosives, remained an important priority. One column required seven hours to advance three kilometers.

Intercepted Russian radio transmissions indicated that an enemy attack was imminent.

On 17 January General Falkenhayn reaffirmed to Conrad his intention to deploy the four new German reserve corps on the Eastern front, barring an unforeseen Western front emergency. It pleased Conrad to learn of Germany's forthcoming second Masurian Lakes battle, and he replied that the campaign assured a "great success."[121] The German effort would coincide with Conrad's Carpathian operation, a replay of his 1914 envelopment attack strategy.

Five days before the offensive, a blizzard enveloped the battlefield. Habsburg troops had little protection from the elements and received only an irregular supply of ice-cold rations. Once the attack commenced, V Corps troops must advance quickly to support Group Szurmay efforts to seize Uzsok Pass. The 7th Infantry Division, the last reserve division, was transferred to Group Szurmay. Despite Habsburg gains at Uzsok Pass, the December 1914 battles demonstrated that controlling the key Uzsok–Turka road became difficult once the enemy received reinforcements.[122] Prevailing conditions did not bode well for a rapid Habsburg success. Cooperation between Third and South armies remained crucial. While a Third Army V Corps detachment assisted South Army's seizure of Uzsok Pass, the enemy must also be expelled from Turka, the heights at Borynia, and the Stryj Valley, the latter the site of a December battle. The right flank of the South Army German XXIV Corps would attempt a double envelopment of enemy positions by seizing major pass roads and blocking the Russian retreat route.

South Army prepared to launch a surprise attack before the enemy received reinforcements. However, railroad transport difficulties delayed the arrival of the division intended to assist in recapturing Uzsok Pass. As troops prepared for the encirclement maneuver, the enemy extended its positions. Moreover, the Russians retreated at the last possible moment, forcing the attackers to undertake long, laborious countermaneuvers.

Habsburg infantry units could expect little artillery support because only a few batteries had reached the war zone, partly because only draft animal columns transporting light loads could traverse the inhospitable terrain. XVIII Corps' 44th Infantry Division reported that it required three days to place one cannon squad into position.[123] As Russian reinforcements reportedly approached the Uzsok Pass area, Third Army received orders to launch its offensive on 23 January and the preliminary strike against the pass the day before.

Troops began assembling for the operation on 19 January despite prevailing blizzard conditions. Critical supplies had not reached the VII Corps front although urgent requests for additional labor units had been dispatched to keep supply routes functioning. Three XVIII Corps munitions columns remained bivouacked behind the mountain ridges because of lack of shelter for troops and pack animals. Reconnaissance reports confirmed enemy troop concentrations, particularly in the San River region between the main offensive objectives, Lisko and Sanok.[124]

Fortress Przemyśl's time was running out, explaining why South Army must launch a deadly frontal assault. Conrad again allowed the fortress to dictate his strategy. Upon arrival, XIX Corps vanguard units must seize Baligrod and then bind the opposing troops. If V Corps seized key road sections, XIX Corps could achieve its mission. However, because they lacked warm food or shelter, V and XVIII Corp soldiers could not adequately prepare for their missions.[125] The seriously unprepared and ill-equipped Habsburg armies found themselves forced to improvise while assisting labor units in keeping supply lines operational.

Serious battle did not erupt until 20 January, but enemy presence stymied all reconnaissance efforts on 21 and 22 January. For most troops, the ascent into the Carpathian Mountains provided a new and unnerving experience; for others, it was a deadly one.[126] Regretfully, many of the Habsburg's finest mountain troops had spilled their blood on the Galician plains during the August–September opening campaign. The increased railroad traffic continued to overburden the few Habsburg railroads.[127] Thus, the shortage of South Army troop units forced a one-day delay in launching its offensive. Third Army Attack Groups Puhallo (V and XVIII Corps) and Krautwald (X Corps) missions remained unchanged. After seizing Uzsok Pass, Attack Group Puhallo must advance to Lutoviska. Inner flank cooperation between Third and Fourth Army remained critical, particularly once the Fourth Army launched its frontal attack because dominating mountain heights separated it from Third Army's III Corps.[128]

Despite deteriorating conditions on 21 January, twelve Third Army divisions, deployed on a 100-kilometer front extending from the Dukla Pass depression to east of Uzsok Pass, poised to attack. Troops positioned on the forested ridges south of the Upper San River area remained only sixty kilometers from Fortress Przemyśl. The stage had been set for the first example of massive protracted mountain warfare in the age of total war.

Meanwhile, on 20 January, General Ivanov continued planning for his invasion of Hungary. Similar to Conrad, he envisioned a frontal attack to seize the remaining Carpathian Mountain ridges before an advance onto the Hungarian plains, knocking that country out of the war. Ivanov persisted with his plan, despite *Stavka*'s determination that Germany be the early

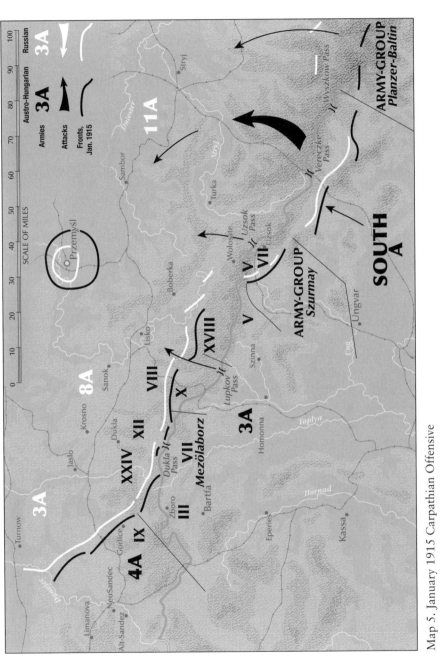

Map 5. January 1915 Carpathian Offensive

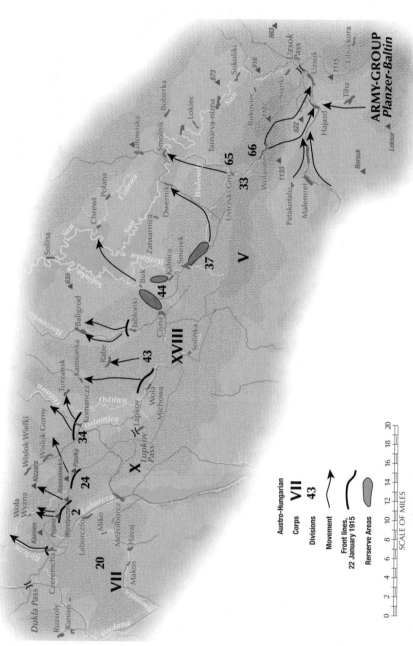

Map 6. Concept for January Offensive

Austro-Hungarian

Corps   **VII**

Divisions   **43**

Movement

Front lines,
22 January 1915

Reserve Areas

SCALE OF MILES

0 2 4 6 8 10 12 14 16 18 20

ARMY-GROUP
Planzer-Baltin

VII

20

X

Lupkov
Pass

XVIII

V

33

65

66

Dukla Pass

Ruzsoly
Kaniso
Makos
Havaj
Mezolborcz
Miko
Czeremcha
Kamien
Poljana
Werehiszoz
Wola
Wyzna
Hanasiowka
Pasika
Rzczara
Wislok Wielki
Wislok Gorny
Turzansk
Kamionka
Rabe
Okomancza
Lupkov
Wola
Michowa
Solinka
Cisna
Jablonki
Buk
Kalnica
Smerek
Dwernik
Zatwarnica
Smolnik
Boberka
Lokiec
Tarnarva-nizna
Sokoliki
Uzsok
Pass
Uzsok
Tiha
Libuickora
Stanki
Bukoviec
Wolasate
Patakofalu
Malemret
Hajasd
Borsuk
Loksar
Ustrzyki Grn
Chrewt
Polana
Lutowiska
Solina
Baligrod
Sol25
635
873
916
863
1115
1107
822
1133

2
24
34
43
37
44

San
Czarna
San
San
Wetlinka
Wolosa
Hoczewka
Solinka
Ostawa
Ostarnica
Laborcza
Udava
Ondana

1915 military priority. He initially sought to neutralize regional Habsburg offensive pressure. Again like Conrad, Ivanov remained obstinate in pursuing his grand scheme, disregarding the human cost and danger it posed of drawing major Russian forces deep into the frigid Carpathian hellhole. He failed to consider, or chose to ignore, the grave threat that would emerge on his northern flank if his massed troops suddenly had to be extricated from the mountain theater, as occurred during May (Gorlice–Tarnov offensive).

It is important to note that the larger Russian troop numbers were insignificant at the outset of the Habsburg offensive. The Habsburgs possessed more divisions, but Romanov units contained more troops. An equal number of troops deployed on both sides of the front north of the Carpathian Mountain region.

On 21 January XVIII Corps reported that its shortage of artillery prevented it from either achieving artillery superiority or effectively supporting its infantry. On 22 January a Group Szurmay brigade received orders to advance from the Uzsok Pass area to liaison with V Corps 33rd Infantry Division to attack toward the Uzsok–Turka line. Inhospitable terrain and meter-deep snow created many problems for the endeavor. Considering the czarist ability to transport reinforcements rapidly, swift control of the Uzsok–Turka line would be an extremely important, yet immensely difficult, mission. Thus, the Third Army right flank attack group (V Corps and Group Szurmay) must seize Turka.

Pressured to relieve Fortress Przemyśl, Conrad ordered a Third Army frontal attack along the shortest route to the fortress along the Lupkov Pass saddle to force the Russians to mass strong defensive forces in that region. South Army eastern flank positions must deflect any enemy threat to Army Group Pflanzer-Baltin. South Army mission remained to traverse the remaining mountain ridges to reach the Galician plains, where it would initiate maneuver warfare.

The lack of railroad unloading ramps impeded attack preparations and slowed the movement of supplies. Losses from illness continued to rise as a result of the extreme climatic conditions. The enormous preoffensive difficulties ultimately proved insurmountable.[129]

The Russian and Habsburg armies each prepared to launch their own offensive over the Carpathian mountain walls. Eventually, two-thirds of the Habsburg army and four Russian armies became embroiled in the battle. In only three and a half months, more than two million casualties were sustained. Was it possible for the Habsburg winter mountain campaign to succeed despite Conrad's hastily prepared plan?

2

The First Carpathian Offensive
January–February 1915

Religious souls visualize hell as a blazing inferno with burning embers and intense heat. The soldiers fighting in the Carpathian Mountains during that first winter of the war know otherwise.   Colonel Georg Veith

COLONEL GEORG VEITH recorded:

On 23 January we rushed forward into the icy hell of the Carpathian battlefield. We stormed the Uzsok, Verecke and Wyszkov Passes, but on the northern slope of the mountains, the troops encountered a blizzard. The reports from these days are shocking. Everyday hundreds froze to death. The wounded that were unable to drag themselves forward were left behind to die. Entire ranks were reduced to tears in the face of the terrible agony.

Each night, the 21. Infantry Regiment dug in until the last man was found frozen to death at daybreak. Pack animals could not advance through the deep snow. The men had to carry their own supplies on foot. The soldiers went without food for days. At $-25\,°$C, food rations froze solid. For seven days straight, the 43. Infantry Division battled overpowering Russian troops with no warm food to sustain them. For a full thirty days, not one single man had any shelter. Hardly a battalion on the Habsburg front consisted of 200 men as lines grew thinner and thinner. Battle-weary front line troops were continuously being wrenched from one position to another to plug a newly-formed gap. Medics and those not seriously ill or injured were called into service. A constant state of mass confusion reigned; a tremendous detriment to any military command. Apathy and indifference were gaining a foothold and could not be contained.[1]

Conrad's armies faced an unfavorable tactical situation from the outset.[2] The Germans grew increasingly alarmed over the rapid deterioration of Habsburg combat strength. A decline in morale, discipline, and physical

Table 2. *k.u.k.* Troops Transferred into the Carpathians

Units	Number of Trains	Russian Front	Railroad Line
XVIII Corps 43rd + 44th IDs	271	December 20–28, 1914	Mezölaborcz & Ungvar,
X Corps 2nd + 24th IDs		January 11–12, 1915	Sianka
V Corps 33rd + 37th IDs	149	January 3–12, 1915	Mezölaborcz
Landsturm Brigade	14	January 10–14, 1915	Borgo
XIX Corps 7th, 29th, 40th IDs	230	January 13–21, 1915	Mezölaborcz + Ungvar,
XIII Corps 36th + 42nd IDs	92, 104	January 22– February 3, 1915	Sianka
VIII Corps 9th + 21st IDs	189	January 25– February 5, 1915	Körösmezö
		February 6–16	Mezölaborcz + Ungvar, Sianka
3 *k.u.k.* IDs	615	December 20, 1915– February 16, 1916	

Source: Ratzenhofer, "*Aufmarsch hinter den Karpathen.*"

stamina followed. Adamant that no time be lost, Conrad refused to post-pone the attack, gambling that the current break in the weather would last. It was a gamble he would lose, for just as the operation got underway, a blizzard struck along the front. Now Conrad's armies became engaged in a life-and-death struggle against the czarist military foe and the forces of nature. In order to advance, Habsburg troops had to first clear a path through the deep snow or hack their way step by step along the icy moun-tain passes.

Third Army right flank Group Szurmay's preoffensive attack on 22 Janu-ary failed to achieve its main objective despite having captured some impor-tant positions. Terrain conditions wreaked havoc on Szurmay's operational timetables, critical for the mission's success. Some units came to a complete standstill; pack animals were useless on the slippery ground. At an alarm-ing rate, frostbite and exposure claimed the lives of more Habsburg soldiers than enemy action.

The Third Army, expanded to fifteen infantry and four cavalry divisions and supported at its right flank by the South Army, struggled to execute Conrad's orders. The 175,000-man attack force was too weak to launch a frontal assault along the 160-kilometer-wide front intended to envelop the enemy's extreme left flank positions and roll up its front. Insufficient troop strength combined with the expansive front resulted in units attacking in single file. Not surprisingly, the daring endeavor produced catastrophic losses. In all, twenty and a half divisions participated in the Carpathian offensive commencing on 23 January 1915. On the Galician front, forty-one infantry and eight cavalry divisions opposed thirty-eight czarist infantry and fifteen cavalry divisions.[3] The Third Army's front extended from Uzsok Pass to Gladyszóv, South Army's from Uzsok Pass to Army Group Pflanzer-Baltin's front. The operation extended from the Dukla depression to east of Uzsok Pass.

Group Szurmay eventually seized Uzsok Pass, and the South Army, Verecke Pass. Szurmay then focused on his next objective, advancing to Turka and Sambor. At the extreme right flank, Army Group Pflanzer-Baltin's ragtag forces advanced through deep snow into the Bukovina province, aiming to strike the enemy communication centers. Once Habsburg troops regained the Bukovina, Pflanzer-Baltin's troops would assist the South Army in its efforts to debouch onto the Galician maneuver zone.

Four low-capacity railroad lines extended from Budapest into the mountains. Moving large military formations, reinforcements, and supplies into the Carpathian Mountain theater presented a logistical nightmare. Excessive, unavoidable delays in launching the offensive gave the Russians ample time to initiate countermeasures. The attack on czarist positions on the northern slopes of the Carpathian Mountains under blizzard conditions became an exercise in futility and made excessive demands on the ill-prepared soldiers. Conrad's highly anticipated swift victory soon vanished when his armies were forced to halt at the mountain ridgelines. Habsburg Supreme Command expressed its extreme displeasure over the lack of progress, which did not bode well for future endeavors.

The atmosphere on the home front and on the battlefield grew tense when the ill-fated first offensive commenced. Attention focused on the Carpathian Mountains, where the vast battlefront made it difficult to maintain control. The operation occurred in stages, commencing with first the Third Army's eastern, then western, flank. The terrain and inclement weather conditions precipitated isolated and uncoordinated battles. Mountain slopes and ridgelines separated units from other columns, frustrating unified action. Third Army could not advance if the neighboring Fourth and South armies failed to make progress, leading to major difficulties.

Such circumstances raised serious concerns among field commanders, who held little confidence in the operation's success. As Conrad continued to order repeated attacks, field officers attempted to pass their orders to neighboring units, convinced the effort was futile and would only result in additional unnecessary bloodshed. In January 1915, for example, General Boroević tried to shift responsibility for the main offensive effort to nearby General Pflanzer-Baltin. General Böhm-Ermolli, commander of the second offensive in February, also made attempts to pass his mission onto Army Group Pflanzer-Baltin. Both generals recognized that the plan lacked several critical prerequisites required for success. In view of troop shortages, the time factor, and severe weather and terrain conditions, the plan was unrealistic. Because of his obsession with liberating Fortress Przemyśl, Conrad violated a fundamental rule of military leadership: a commander must know the capabilities of his fighting instrument. Such ineptitude helps explain the German High Command's refusal to allow its troops to be subordinated to Austria-Hungary. Increasing unrealistic demands on field commanders and their troops led to the growing lack of confidence in the Habsburg Supreme Command itself.

Battalion and brigade commanders wasted no time expressing their serious concerns about the operation. Numerical inferiority disrupted the attack momentum and forfeited the essential element of surprise. In addition, Habsburg field commanders warned that the mountain terrain frustrated cooperation between neighboring units, aggravated further by unreliable wire communication as a result of snow and ice on telephone lines. Moreover, heavy snowfall impeded troop movement and caused soldiers to abandon artillery batteries behind the high mountain ridges rather than transport them to the front. With little and often no artillery support, advancing Habsburg infantry bore the full force of Russian firepower. Third Army sacrificed over two-thirds of its soldiers in its failed initial Carpathian offensive, many of whom succumbed to illness or froze to death.

Separated attack groups often lost their bearing in the blinding snowstorms. The soldiers suffered from frostbite; their weapons jammed from the bitter cold. Nevertheless, Conrad's soldiers continued their attacks.[4] Troops were expected to undertake exhausting marches through meter-deep snow to reach the battlefield, only to find no shelter awaiting them. In a cruel twist of fate, frigid conditions interspersed with sudden periods of rising temperatures and thaw. Steady rain and melting snow turned the valley terrain into a pit of mud as troops, artillery, ammunition, animals, and supply wagons sank into the mire. Rising floodwaters swept away bridges, and soldiers were forced to lie in their waterlogged positions.

A Habsburg artillery officer's diary offers a vivid portrayal of the disorder and dismay that characterized the opening campaign. His entries describe repeated, swift, unproductive, and exhausting marches and detail the deplorable conditions along the mountain roadways and in gun positions, dubbed *Strafstellungen* (penalty positions) by the men. Supply wagons sank to their axles as heavy traffic flow on the poorly constructed roads produced quagmires. Adding to their misery, soldiers often had to help move heavy equipment. Even horse-drawn wagons with ten to fourteen harnesses could not navigate the muddy passageways.[5] Troops gathered fallen branches and tossed them into the mud in an effort to stabilize road surfaces. Countless horse carcasses blocked the roadways and were likewise heaved into the muck.

South Army German troops were unfamiliar with mountain environs. Their inexperience and general unsuitability for mountain warfare became a major disadvantage. Because they lacked the most basic winter attire and equipment, hundreds of troops suffered frostbite every day, and many succumbed to the White Death (*der weisse Tod*). Weather and terrain conditions took a heavy toll on horses and other draft animals. Though map keys designated the Carpathian Mountain region as maneuverable terrain, many mountain slopes proved too steep for the animals to traverse. German artillery units, arriving late at the front, likewise had no experience in mountain warfare. The few artillery pieces that actually arrived were limited to off-road passages and ineffective firing positions.

Returning to the offensive undertaking, the attacking troops advanced slowly through man-high drifted snow, which exacerbated the terrain conditions. Forward movement of artillery and supplies proved time-consuming and tedious. The troops' physical condition had already deteriorated because of their prolonged stay in the trenches commencing in December.[6] As twenty Habsburg divisions advanced toward the Dukla, Lupkov, and Uzsok passes, they became exposed to the difficult Carpathian conditions. The attackers advanced in line formation with no reserve formations to continue if the attack proved successful. As losses mounted, the front lines became too extended for even the surviving troop units to defend.

Major Attack Group Puhallo advanced northward to seize the terrain north of the Russian major railroad and supply center at Ustrzyki Dolne, encompassing the conquest of important czarist railroad and road connections. Its right middle flank advanced along both sides of Lutoviska and its valuable railroad connection, while its 43rd Infantry Division advanced toward Baligrod to connect with Attack Group Krautwald. General Puhallo's paltry three-division force would advance into a critical forty-kilometer gap in the Russian lines south of Fortress Przemyśl toward the Lisko–Sanok railroad lines. A weak defensive force of two Russian cavalry divisions defended this portion of the front, which offered the most rapid egress to Fortress Przemyśl.

There were many problems with the Third Army offensive action. The first day's mission was to reach enemy artillery positions, which proved elusive. The operation also lacked thorough planning and preparation. In an obvious blunder, artillery did not advance with the attacking forces because the snow-enveloped terrain hindered movement, making guns difficult to place into new positions. Conrad, having seized the initiative, envisioned a swift victory, and with the element of surprise, he attempted to preempt a long winter mountain campaign. He intended to neutralize any Russian offensive plans on this weakly held portion of the front. This caused the near annihilation of the attacking troops in the three disastrous Carpathian efforts.

It proved impossible for troop units to cooperate in battle because they failed to achieve a significant advantage against the enemy or overcome the adverse conditions. Thus, attempts to outflank individual enemy positions failed as the enemy simply extended their flank positions when attacked. The resultant Habsburg frontal attacks produced enormous casualties because the mountain terrain was unsuitable for maneuvering major troop formations. This resulted in partial attacks, with the advancing units often forced to separate, which exacerbated the pressure to relieve Fortress Przemyśl. One problem was the lack of sufficient manpower to accomplish the missions. Group Puhallo transferred an entire brigade to neighboring Group Szurmay for an assault against Uzsok Pass after the operation commenced. Group Puhallo now consisted of two and a half divisions to cover its forty-kilometer-wide front along the upper San River. The area contained important roads and railroads providing egress to the lower mountains north of Uzsok Pass. The group advanced twenty kilometers north of the pass in a short time, but faltered as it sustained heavy losses. It possessed no reserves to maintain the attack momentum. An excessive number of troops deployed for flank protection left too few for the attack formations. In addition, the inadequate reinforcements entered battle piecemeal.

Moreover, when the VII Corps defended key positions near Dukla Pass, it affected the mission to encircle czarist positions elsewhere. Thus, the 20th *Honvéd* Infantry Division could not support X Corps' 2nd Infantry Division efforts against the opposing mountain heights. Both divisions became outflanked, creating a major predicament. In hindsight, if two additional divisions had deployed at Group Puhallo's front, the mission might have succeeded, particularly by capturing the railroad junction at Ustrzyki Dolne, from which the Russians transferred troops and reinforcements to any threatened front sector. If General Puhallo had been able to maintain his attack momentum, the ensuing enemy counterattacks on 26 January might have been prevented. Soon, however, the enemy severed the important Chyróv–Sambor railroad line at Dukla Pass.

In effect, Group Puhallo's efforts created an isolated battle zone, in which progress became increasingly limited as the casualties escalated. This, combined with admirable czarist defensive efforts, destroyed any chance for additional success. Again in hindsight, the operation would have been better served by launching a rapid thrust with additional manpower and firepower, which would have greatly increased the chances for success.

Nevertheless, the group advanced the twenty kilometers and with Group Szurmay crossed the San River on 26 January. The mentioned transfer of one of Group Puhallo's brigades to Group Szurmay, however, introduced the practice of transferring military units for other purposes than the major offensive. In doing so, Habsburg leaders lost sight of the military axiom of massing forces at the main portion of the attack front. The surrender of an entire brigade seriously weakened General Puhallo's middle and left flank positions, removing forces required to successfully complete the mission.

As Attack Groups Puhallo and Krautwald advanced a dangerous twenty-kilometer gap soon separated them. Although reserve formations could have neutralized the problem, none was available, with Puhallo's flanks suddenly badly exposed. This weakness did not go unnoticed by czarist military leadership, and the result became obvious on 26 January 1915, when they launched a major counterattack.

Meanwhile, Group Krautwald's mission was to strike the Russian Eighth Army's eastern flank positions. X Corps (2nd, 24th, and 34th Infantry Divisions) must advance through Baligrod. The group's heavyweight left flank would then advance toward Lisko–Sanok, but instead, it encountered strong enemy resistance. The X Corps' 2nd Infantry Division mission became to protect the group's left flank, then advance to the northeast, where the Russians had assembled troops. The VII Corps' 20th *Honvéd* Infantry Division, ordered first to envelop the czarist positions in cooperation with the 2nd Infantry Division, failed. Yet the entire Carpathian offensive effort relied on 2nd Infantry Division's success.

On 23 January, General Krautwald's forces encountered heavy resistance, which forced its left flank units to retreat to their original positions. By 25 January, the group received orders to hold those positions and, if possible, expand its right flank success. The army's left flank groups Joseph and Colerus must prevent enemy egress over the main ridges on their front or prevent czarist troops from intervening against the army right flank offensive efforts. The VII Corps (Group Joseph) must block the invasion route through the Czeremcha saddle area, most important for the defense of Dukla Pass.[7] Group Colerus (III Corps) retained the important mission to protect the neighboring Fourth Army's southern flank (inner flank of the two armies).

Third Army's overall mission remained to envelop the enemy's extreme left flank positions from the Habsburg right flank, then advance northward into the Sanok–Rymanov–Krosno–Jaslo basin area. Groups Puhallo and Szurmay would perform the flanking maneuver because General Szurmay's mission remained to seize Uzsok Pass and then advance to Turka and Sambor, the site of an important enemy road and railroad line. Group Szurmay's forces proved inadequate to seize the pass or prevent the enemy from transferring reinforcements from the pass area.

On 22 January, three infantry and one and a half cavalry divisions advanced toward the pass. A neighboring South Army left-flank column was to advance and bind the anticipated opposing enemy forces to minimize the danger to Group Szurmay's right flank as it advanced. The area's importance emanated from the threat of a Russian breakthrough at the Third and Fourth armies' inner flanks.

South Army transport delays retarded its launch date to 24 January, except for Corps Hofmann, which advanced on 23 January. Hofmann's troops encountered stiff enemy resistance as a column advanced toward Uzsok Pass, while its remaining troops pressed south to southeasterly through the wooded Carpathian Mountains toward Fortress Przemyśl. However, they achieved little progress because of the terrible conditions.[8] The same fate neutralized Third Army's Group Szurmay's efforts to advance from Uzsok Pass to Turka and Sambor.

In the East Carpathian range, General Pflanzer-Baltin deployed his troops in echelon formation to advance toward his multiple objectives. Some forces must recapture the Bukovina province, while others helped South Army to escape its mountain prison, but the army group lacked sufficient numbers to accomplish all its missions. Yet Pflanzer-Baltin's ragtag forces garnered the only major victory of the entire Carpathian campaign. Only insufficient railroad capacity prevented their achieving further significant gains by receiving reinforcements.

Conditions along the few roadways leading to the various army fronts had not improved. The night of 22 January was quiet, clear, and cold, and icy road conditions delayed the arrival of an XVIII Corps supply column.[9] Critical routes remained in such poor condition that additional labor crews became necessary to keep them open. Numerous *Landsturm* units performed such road maintenance duty.

When Third Army advanced, Fourth Army southern-flank units would join it, depending on the conditions.[10] Its right flank IX Corps would co-operate with the Third Army III Corps to launch an encircling maneuver toward Banica, near the critical Gorlice intersections.[11] Close cooperation between the two army flanks would neutralize the Russian threat from the area of Uzsok Pass, but deep snow and the distance to traverse made this difficult to accomplish.

Blizzard conditions, including deep snow and man-high drifts, exacer-bated the advance, left Habsburg troops cold and exhausted, and made fu-tile the attempts to move artillery pieces and supplies into the mountains.[12] Units reported increasing illness and frostbite cases. Attempts to open snow-bound railroad stretches failed because of labor unit unavailability; thus, inadequate supplies and ammunition stores reached the front lines.[13]

Group Szurmay troops advanced twenty-five kilometers before the main Attack Group Puhallo. Third Army right flank's small numerical advantage was eleven infantry and two and a half cavalry divisions against nine in-fantry and four cavalry divisions. In the area west of the Czeremcha roads, Group Joseph's (VII Corps) four infantry and two cavalry divisions op-posed five Russian infantry and one cavalry division. The enormous logisti-cal problems of moving large troop formations by rail into the mountains became a serious deterrent to Habsburg success. Railroad delays allowed the enemy time to initiate effective countermeasures.

Meanwhile, between 20 to 26 January, Group Szurmay's right flank units had the additional task of maintaining its supply artery despite enormous obstacles. To avoid a bloody frontal attack against strong enemy-blocking positions, Szurmay dispatched strong side columns through the crucial Ung Valley, also a protective area for Laborcz Valley. This, however, increased the threat to his now-exposed flanks. Szurmay achieved partial success by sacrificing the element of surprise. The group required five hours to seize key Ung Valley positions (four kilometers' distance) through the inclement conditions. Troops had to shovel their way through an icy storm, many ultimately suffering from frostbite.[14] The inhospitable terrain and blizzard conditions wreaked havoc with operational timetables, and Third Army advanced just three to four kilometers per day. Its slow progress caused Fourth Army to launch an attack from the southern flank to assist Third Army efforts.[15]

Meanwhile, Conrad planned to commence a new attack impulse.[16] VII Corps must continue to block the potential major enemy invasion route through Dukla Pass, protect X Corps' flank positions, and attack any en-emy troop concentrations. The 17th Infantry Division commander General LeBeau reported that artillery units were not in their ordered positions; his troops were endangered by their own artillery fire, and he faced an unfavorable tactical situation. The failure of the 20th *Honvéd* Infantry Division to seize high terrain positions left both flank positions exposed.[17] VII Corps' inability to achieve notable progress against well-defended and entrenched czarist defensive lines between 23 and 29 January continued to threaten the 17th Infantry Division's flank position. Further success became unlikely, given the multiple adverse circumstances. XIX Corps' 34th Infantry Division, for example, lost 5,000 men in one day, while frostbite continued to plague the weary troops.[18]

On 24 January Third Army again attempted to advance and recapture Carpathian passes, but in the early morning hours, fog and heavy snow prevented significant progress.[19] Group Puhallo's XVIII Corps' 44th Infantry Division advanced in column formation, its progress interrupted by weak enemy forces on 23 and 24 January, but the Russians retreated after a short battle.[20] Although supply conditions remained unfavorable, the corps regrouped to renew its attack on 25 January through a gap between the Russian Eighth Army and its Group Uzsok.

X Corps reported that the increasing necessity to provide Third Army left flank security drained the main attack force. Numerous artillery units had just begun to arrive at the front while corps ammunition train columns stretched far back into the rear echelons. Forward movement remained a tedious job on the snow-draped terrain. The corps advanced twenty-two kilometers to attack the well-defended enemy but found itself in danger of getting lost in the thick fog and deep snow. Even with all available reserves inserted into the thinning lines, it failed to seize the opposing enemy positions. If X Corps retreated, it would endanger the entire offensive operation. Moreover, the shortage of officers, insufficient artillery support, the inclement weather, and disrupted communications hindered their effectiveness.[21]

On 24 January X Corps' 2nd Infantry Division fought pitched battles to seize high terrain, with both sides suffering severe casualties. The division received no artillery support because of the snowstorm and dense fog, while having to shovel its way into attack position. Without reinforcements to replace the mounting casualties, X Corps witnessed ever-extended lines until available reserves moved into the forward battle area to assure their maintenance.[22]

When the adjacent VII Corps 20th *Honvéd* Infantry Division retreated to its 22 January positions, it freed enemy troops for deployment elsewhere. A powerful czarist surprise attack launched in dense fog pummeled X Corps' 2nd Infantry Division. A delay in X Corps action compromised the crucial element of surprise.[23] Meanwhile, 2nd Infantry Division's multiple missions far exceeded its capabilities (while it occupied a vital position on the front).

V and XVIII Corps and Group Szurmay deployed along the upper San River line with the objective to drive the Russians from the San River valley area to neutralize any threat to its rear and flank areas. On 23 January, the V Corps' 37th *Honvéd* Infantry Division, its troops exhausted from a difficult advance, failed to attain its objective.[24] Front-line unit reports detailed the debilitating effects of the blizzard conditions on offensive efforts. XVIII Corps' 43rd Infantry Division indicated that one to two meters of snow delayed its marches. In valleys, washed-out roads had turned into a sea of mud. Enemy troops barricaded the slopes along the valley leading to Baligrod, the division attack column's goal and a major objective throughout the Carpathian offensives.[25]

The Russians initially withdrew a short distance along a major portion of their upper San River front. However, inconclusive Habsburg successes reversed when they coincided with a wave of severe winter storms and a powerful enemy counterattack on 26 January. As Habsburg casualties reached crisis levels, the front lines became overextended. This dangerous cycle forced surviving combatants to brave the harsh conditions for weeks while awaiting reinforcements, which often failed to arrive. Repeated orders to resume attacks resulted in the meager reinforcements being hurled piecemeal into battle to fill the appearing gaps. Overpowering Russian counterattacks later added to the troops' misery.

X Corps' 34th Infantry Division reported severe losses, including numerous frostbite cases, while Infantry Regiment 90 suffered when it attacked strong enemy positions. One infantry regiment lost 700 to 800 men during a czarist counterattack. Foggy conditions and close proximity of front positions (200 to 300 paces) prevented artillery support. Troops had to shovel snow for supply traffic.[26]

On 24 January, General Ivanov reported to Russian High Command (*Stavka*) that reinforced Habsburg troops had attacked some of his weak positions and requested four to five infantry divisions be transferred as reinforcements as soon as possible. He claimed that enemy troops intended to retake Fortress Przemyśl. The two czarist fronts (Germany and Austria-Hungary) resulted in the two front commanders squabbling over requests for troops, reserve formations, and additional supplies. General Ivanov pursued his cherished Carpathian offensive even though the *Stavka* had determined that the Russian 1915 priority was the German front. He would launch an overpowering counteroffensive against the unsavory Habsburg attackers on 26 January. Its major objective, Mezőlaborcz, a key Habsburg communication center and railroad hub, witnessed bloody battle for the next two weeks.

Meanwhile, the Habsburg Third Army left flank III Corps would launch an enveloping attack to the northwest to block enemy approach routes and protect Fourth Army's southern flank IX Corps (inner army flanks). But III Corps must await further Third Army right flank success to advance, which did not occur. This forced Fourth Army to attack at the two armies' inner flanks to assist Third Army forward momentum.[27]

Heavy snowfall and dense fog early on 24 January made it difficult to prepare for the next day's operation; terrain difficulties continued to retard progress and exhausted the troops; thus, forward momentum and operational success could not be restored.[28] V Corps launched reconnaissance missions to ascertain suitable advance routes. Meanwhile, intelligence reports revealed that the Russians had strengthened their positions, including deploying heavy artillery at Borynia critical for an advance from Uzsok Pass and where a Habsburg assault had been planned.

General Szurmay's efforts had already failed, and each rearward move threatened Third Army's right flank positions. Nevertheless, Habsburg troops continued their futile efforts to retake the main ridgelines lost in December 1914. The unfavorable conditions continued to cause a critical time loss and lack of artillery support for the unfortunate infantry.[29]

When VII Corps' 20th *Honvéd* Infantry Division did not launch its designated attack, the enemy hurled a surprise five- to six-battalion counterattack against the understrength neighboring 17th Infantry Division west of the Dukla roads. Two infantry companies surrendered, and heavy enemy machine gun fire caused serious losses, creating apprehension about the operation.[30] At only twenty paces from the enemy, Habsburg troops failed to advance further, while a serious threat to the corps' right flank positions occurred west of the Dukla road.

Meanwhile, Third and South Army cooperative efforts faltered, partly because of the difficult mountainous terrain separating them. Neither army gained a significant tactical advantage nor overcame the wretched conditions. South Army attack units had advanced just ten kilometers from their original positions. Shoveling snow off roadways, particularly for new artillery positions, retarded swift movement. Soldiers sank chest-deep into the snow, while snowstorms halted all supportive artillery efforts. Troop exhaustion and darkness ended all progress. Major clashes stayed confined to areas closest to the few natural traversable routes through the valleys, but in as close a proximity to a railroad line as possible. Limited frontal attacks resulted in excessive bloodshed.[31] Numerous assaults, often aimed at isolated enemy positions, allowed the Russians to shift reserves to thwart any momentary threat. Habsburg commanders often delayed obeying attack orders, preferring to await a neighboring units' victory, which often never materialized.

From the beginning, General Boroević expressed apprehension regarding the potential for success in the campaign, correctly predicting that the enemy would strike his battle-weary soldiers as soon as his forces committed to battle.[32] Many Habsburg division commanders realized that any chance of success had ended. Meanwhile, on 25 January, unbeknownst to the Habsburg military, the Russians assembled substantial forces to launch a major counteroffensive, while Army Group Pflanzer-Baltin failed to succeed in its efforts on the eastern flank front. Casualties escalated as the weather conditions deteriorated. The Army Group attacked in −20°C temperatures in two meters of snow. It required three hours to advance just 1,000 paces, while the horrific conditions killed an enormous number of horses.[33] As General Boroević unsuccessfully attempted to expand his right flank, heavy enemy contingents attacked his left flank forces, forcing them back to their original positions. Attacking Third Army middle units encountered strong Russian defensive positions.

Group Szurmay, meanwhile, finally forced the enemy from Uzsok Pass as the snow turned to torrential rain, soaking the attacking troops. Many suffered from frostbite and other ailments, leading Szurmay to request a one- to two-day break from further offensive undertakings for his battered troops to find shelter. Meanwhile, the heavy rains transformed the single corps supply route into a terrible mess.[34] The senior 66th Infantry Brigade physician reported that he encountered numerous cases of frostbite, overexertion, and hunger; having lost half its troop stand, the brigade required rest and rehabilitation.[35] A 34th Infantry Division report (X Corps) emphasized that troop physical depression had reached epidemic proportions.[36] The lack of adequate troop training and physical preparedness for winter mountain warfare exacerbated the crisis. Supply columns had to travel nearly thirty kilometers, with multiple delays.[37] Loss of its supply route could prove disastrous to Szurmay's forces.

The V Corps at last attained its previous day's objective, but with almost all reserve troops already committed to battle and those remaining considered unfit for front-line duty. However, to neutralize any threat to the Habsburg flank area, they must keep the Russians from the San River region. On 25 January Lutoviska and its railroad station capitulated, allowing the famished troops to advance further. Anticipating a clash with enemy vanguard units on 26 January, they actually attacked strong Russian positions.

Significant terrain difficulties again prevented attaining the corps march goals of Ustrzyki Dolne. When Third Army failed to achieve its decisive success, it received orders to "hold to the last man" and avoid unnecessary losses.[38] Unbeknownst to Habsburg Supreme Command, the battle raging between the Dukla and Uzsok passes had reached a turning point because the Habsburgs achieved no significant military success. Attack Group Puhallo (V and XVIII Corps) had attained the Upper San River region, but its insufficient troop numbers and the lack of reserve forces prevented further progress on this front. Nearby, XVIII Corps encountered unexpected resistance as it attempted to advance with no hope of a timely deployment of reinforcements.[39] Some XVIII Corps troop units successfully crossed the San River, but during the process, the units became intertwined. When Conrad ordered the rapid movement of supply trains forward, food resources for the starving troops received priority over artillery shells and ammunition.[40] Enemy counterattacks along the Dukla roads forced the VII Corps to retreat, creating a threatening gap between it and III Corps that introduced the danger of the enemy piercing the thin, overextended division lines, while also threatening the main Habsburg retreat route.[41]

X Corps' attack efforts resulted in fierce, bloody encounters with the enemy, but successful enemy flanking maneuvers and heavy frontal fire forced a corps retreat. Deep snow and low-lying fog curtailed progress and left the benumbed Habsburg troops without artillery support. They endured four days with no protection from the elements as uniforms froze to their bodies. As significant czarist reinforcements deployed on the battlefield to launch a major counterattack, the condition of Habsburg troops had reached a critical point. During battle between 22 and 25 January, X Corps' three divisions incurred enormous casualties but still continued their attack.[42] The corps finally received orders to terminate its offensive on 25 January, to dig in, and to hold its forward positions. Having depleted all its reserve troops, X Corps awaited the insertion of the 29th Infantry Division, currently in transit, into Third Army's weakening eastern flank attack in the Lupkov Pass area. Conrad ordered X Corps to regroup as the enemy increased its pressure against VII Corps' denuded forces along the Dukla Pass road.[43]

Telephone equipment continued to malfunction, exacerbating command functions, and as the wintry conditions intensified, X Corps reported that it could no longer resist the powerful enemy.[44] Artillery and supply train columns had to be transported on sleds, and troops often had to hack frozen ground under enemy fire in order to create a path to advance.

General Ivanov now attacked in an attempt to destroy the mauled Habsburg army. This, he reasoned, would sway Romania to join the Entente.

Russian Third and Eighth armies would support the weaker czarist contingents already defending the 300-kilometer front extending from Uzsok Pass to the Romanian frontier. On 26 January Ivanov received the XXII Corps as reinforcements from the German front, which enabled him to unleash a major counteroffensive against Third Army's left flank and middle positions (VII and X Corps). The weakened Third Army could not halt the ferocious onslaught and quickly sustained heavy casualties. As fierce battle erupted between the Dukla and Uzsok passes, the Russians focused their main attention on Dukla Pass, particularly the Mezölaborcz railroad and communication hub in the Laborcz Valley. These events resulted in intense, bitter fighting, which provided the deathblow to the Third Army offensive. Ivanov targeted the area between the Ondava and Laborcz valleys, where the mountains posed the least impediment for the shortest, most direct route to their objective: Budapest, Hungary.

Ice storms and wintry weather conditions enveloped the mountains, while the evolving attrition battle produced enormous casualties. Group Szurmay reported that the heavy snow masses behind its main forward ridgelines posed a serious danger should its troops be forced to retreat and its rear echelon supply columns be unable to move forward.[45] On 30 January, Szurmay requested additional labor units to keep the serpentine road to Uzsok Pass open.[46]

The Russians exacted a heavy human toll on the Third Army positions situated between the Dukla and Lupkov passes.[47] Three corps protected this obvious invasion route into Hungary along the seventy-seven-kilometer front extending through the Ondava and Laborcz valleys. Meanwhile, South Army engaged in a three-day battle through 27 January, but its winter equipment and armaments proved inadequate for the task. Hundreds of soldiers suffered frostbite, and many draft animals succumbed to the unbearable conditions. The South Army front fluctuated along the ice- and snow-covered ridges. Artillery positions, often too distant from the front lines, could not support the infantry, and German artillery had been trained for flat terrain deployment, which proved of little worth in the elevated terrain. Third Army command, in the meantime, ordered its battered troops to maintain their positions, but it lacked the reserve units necessary to halt the enemy onslaught. V Corps had attained its objectives when the Russians counterattacked their right flank positions, but Conrad ordered that the offensive be continued. XVIII Corps' 43rd Infantry Division advanced north of Baligrod, but the reinforced enemy forces soon halted their retreat and put up ferocious resistance. Diminished troop numbers and the distended thirty-kilometer corps front ensured that the troops could not be relieved from front-line duty. The excessive demands and terrible conditions often resulted in attack orders failing to reach the front. The condition of South Army troops had also deteriorated. By mid-March, daily sick call fluctuated between 400 to 700 soldiers, while later, between 11 and 23 March, the army lost 6,758 men to illness alone.[48]

The Russians launched their counterattacks along the critical Dukla roads in the most effective direction to devastate Habsburg troops. VII Corps bore the brunt of the initial czarist thrust as the enemy penetrated into the defensive lines west of the Dukla roads.[49] Eight to twelve battalions smashed into the 20th *Honvéd* Infantry Division positions several times before advancing toward the sensitive Third and Fourth Army inner flank positions. Meanwhile, eight to ten battalions (8,000 troops) launched ten attacks against the 17th Infantry Division front, forcing it to retreat or face annihilation.[50]

VII Corps sustained heavy casualties as the Russians repeatedly broke through its front. Without reserve troops, the corps situation rapidly became critical.[51] Insufficient troop numbers and difficult terrain forced the left flank units to retreat. Further powerful enemy actions against the VII Corps front widened the gap between it and the III Corps. Russian prisoners of war alerted their interrogators to an impending strike against the reeling Habsburg lines, resulting in Corps Command ordering its troops to halt the looming enemy onslaught. After many days of marching over rough terrain, the few remaining reserves arrived at the front just as three Russian divisions launched an attack.[52] Unable to resist, Habsburg troops withdrew.

A 25 January South Army Corps Gerok report blamed the battlefront conditions for its lack of success. In addition to the normal difficulties, the pathless terrain traversed a primeval forest enveloped by at least a meter of snow. The temperature dropped to −23 °C, further hampering supply efforts and causing an agonizing state for the troops. Many, on the verge of physical collapse, went without warm rations for days. The culmination of these circumstances reduced several Habsburg units to 30 to 40 percent of their original numbers.

On the Third Army front, the enemy unleashed mass assaults during an ice storm. The Russians constantly deployed new forces toward the vital Mezőlaborcz rail center; they also attempted to conquer the entire Dukla basin region. The czarist assaults, which endured until 10 February, forced Third Army to retreat to its initial attack positions. When the Russians smashed into X Corps lines defending Mezőlaborcz, it immediately created

Table 3. Habsburg Losses During the First Offensive

Corps/Group	Troop Stand	Reinforcements	Losses	Troop Stand
	23 January 1915		6 February 1915	
III.	17,070	4,000	9,000	12,070
V.	17,660	5,500	16,600	16,500
VII.	13,250	7,200	13,080	7,370
X.	25,440	7,000	22,220	10,220
XVIII.	19,530	1,500	8,010	13,020
Group Szurmay	30,880	3,000	14,490	19,390
XIX (29 ID)	10,940	2,500	5,440	7,900
Total	134,770	30,700	88,900	76,570

a serious crisis. The czarist forces intended to sever the major Homonna–Mezölaborcz rail connection and separate the Habsburg armies, which would neutralize main Attack Group Puhallo's successful advance.

The czarist assault against VII Corps in the strategic Mezölaborcz–Lupkov–Cisna area followed parallel mountain heights to conquer the Mezölaborcz railroad junction and extend the ten-kilometer gap between it and III Corps. Habsburg defenders also suffered defeat and retreated from the Lupkov Pass area.[53] Freezing temperatures, deep snow, and windy conditions prevailed in the mountains. The snow-packed roads, blanketed by a meter of fresh snow, proved almost impassable, resulting in multiple supply traffic stoppages. Civilians and troops alike labored on the most important road stretches.[54] Commanders made frantic requests for the deployment of March company reserve troops to the front as soon as possible, despite the long, difficult marches to get there.

The ensuing days witnessed further serious reversals along the III, VII, and X Corps' fronts.[55] The Russian attack against Third Army west flank corps also disrupted the right flank offensive operations. X Corps retreated again after being pummeled by two overpowering enemy assaults, as VII Corps established new defensive positions while launching futile counterattacks against the superior enemy forces. This consumed the troops' last vestige of strength.[56] Half the troop stands consisted of inadequately trained and prepared *Landsturm* units, further decreasing Habsburg combat worthiness. XVIII Corps' 43rd Infantry Division's offensive capabilities disappeared in just five days, while its troops became apathetic. The division commander described his unit as defenseless.[57] Immediately upon arrival at the front, the 29th Infantry Division deployed to rectify the deteriorating III and VII Corps military predicament. The threatening loss of the Cisna depot and railroad junction had to be prevented at all costs because it would sever V and XVIII Corps' supply route. In one day, X Corps 24th Infantry Division recorded 174 cases of frostbite and a fatality as well as numerous lung-related illnesses.[58]

Unfavorable battlefield conditions also continued to affect South Army offensive efforts. Exhausted soldiers advanced through deep snow that blanketed the wooded terrain and ridges without artillery support.[59] The Russians gave no indication that they intended to surrender their favorable positions; therefore, they continued to attack.[60] Meanwhile, the enemy gained valuable time to improve their defensive positions against South Army, which had lost five precious days.[61] The czarist troops rapidly organized effective defensive resistance just a few kilometers behind evacuated front-line formations.

Having sacrificed 2,800 VII Corps soldiers since 25 January, a surprise enemy assault captured the key Ung Valley Czeremcha position. The corps possessed no troops to regain the lost terrain.[62] Archduke Joseph noted on 27 January:

A new enemy arrived today, but a rather fair one because it hampers both the Russians and us. This is the enormous snow and terrible cold. Terrible reports have already been arriving (especially from the 20. *Honvéd* Infantry Division) about the numbers of frostbite cases, many of which are serious. In the evening, it started snowing heavily, which may be good for us because the Russian supply, advanced far forward, would be difficult.[63]

The critical battle situation and unrelenting winter storms that intensified after 26 January exacted a tremendous human toll. In three days, VII Corps' 17th Infantry Division lost 1,700 men and the 20th *Honvéd* Infantry Division 2,000 on the first battle day. Sickness and frostbite continued to account for more casualties than combat.[64] The night of 27 January witnessed further heavy snowstorms, strong winds, and subzero temperatures. Ill-prepared replacement troops, pressed into the front lines in a futile effort to stem the enemy tide, sustained serious losses.[65] Artillery shell shortages exacerbated the Habsburg crisis, and some batteries withdrew from the battle zone when their shell supplies expired.[66] The unrelenting Russian pressure in the Dukla Pass and Mezőlaborcz areas forced a Habsburg retreat to the Hungarian frontier, while battle continued to rage at the upper San River Valley region and the Cisna supply depot.

A letter by General Erich Ludendorff written to General Moltke on 27

January 1915 bemoaned the Carpathian Mountain military situation and complained that the terrain difficulties had been anticipated. Ludendorff lamented the fact that the "Austrians" retreated at the mere appearance of a "superior" enemy force on the battlefield. Under the mistaken impression that Fortress Przemyśl could only resist until 7 March, he believed they could not save the fortress.[67] The German High Command, as mentioned, had earlier opposed the South Army deployment in the difficult terrain east of Uzsok Pass; in hindsight, such arguments seem justified.

The conditions described above, combined with a lack of feed, led to the sacrifice of animals, so crucial for maintaining a steady flow of supplies. Increasing numbers of damaged supply wagons and animal carcasses blocked the supply routes. Train commanders received orders not to abandon supplies in the rear echelon areas.[68] Herculean efforts proved necessary to sustain supply movement from the distant rearward railroad unloading stations to the front lines. Almost the entire Third Army front had now been forced onto the defensive.[69]

In retrospect, Attack Group Puhallo obviously lacked sufficient troop numbers for its ambitious mission and most likely needed twice its allotted strength to attain the objective, Lisko–Ustrzyki Dolne. With greater numbers, Group Puhallo may have forced the Russians back to protect their main railroad supply lines instead of launching their successful 26 January counterattack.[70] Regardless, the excessive demands placed on Puhallo's numbed soldiers left little hope for a decisive Habsburg success any time soon as troop apathy and battle fatigue became universal.[71] As prolonged exposure to the harsh conditions caused mental breakdowns, the troops retreated to their original positions. However, information surfaced that the Russian fighting machine was also faltering as entire czarist units surrendered. The Austrian official history of the war concedes that the initial Habsburg territorial gains did not justify the tremendous bloodletting or the troops' physical and moral suffering. The first Carpathian campaign cost the Third Army almost 80 percent of its manpower, the majority attributable to noncombat causes such as frostbite.

Major battle now focused around Baligrod and the Dukla Pass region. The overwhelming enemy assault against XVIII Corps' 43rd Infantry Division almost destroyed its battle worthiness.[72] It is remarkable that General Borević even maintained his lines because as his troop numbers declined, the enemy received reinforcements to launch further attacks. Third Army would not receive major reinforcements before mid-February. Could the Russians be kept at bay that long?

Only 55,000 III, VII, and X Corps soldiers now defended the major

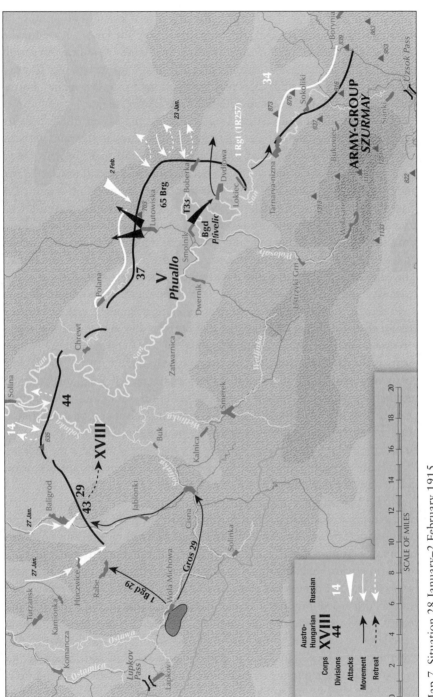

Map 7. Situation 28 January–2 February 1915

invasion route through the Ondava and Laborcz valleys into Hungary. The inadequate numbers, the extended front areas, and the lack of hope for the timely deployment of reinforcements made the Habsburg military situation untenable. Some units had sustained sacrificial bloodlettings, yet Conrad ordered his troops to hold their present positions to the last man.[73] Fortunately for the troops, the enemy did not press its advantage.[74]

On 28 January Group Szurmay encountered increasing difficulties. Its 71st Infantry Brigade lost some of its reserve forces and supply trains without battle. General Boroević, meanwhile, notified Conrad that his army could no longer undertake offensive action because of the horrendous conditions and escalating casualties.[75] The inclement weather limited military action to brief flurries of activity. Escalating shortages of draft animals forced infantry sections to assist transporting ammunition, artillery, machine guns, food provisions, and battle baggage. Before battle, soldiers warmed their hands and weapons over fires to remove ice and snow to make them functional. The end of battle did not signify rest for the suffering troops. Casualties escalated as the surviving soldiers' mental and physical capabilities declined.

III Corps engaged in major combat extending from the end of January until well into February. On 28 January both its divisions (22nd and 28th) retreated. Further Russian assaults against the corps endangered the Fourth Army inner flank situation, but its retreat removed the basis for any Fourth Army offensive action to assist it.[76] On 29 January the Russians launched another major assault against the critical Laborcz Valley railroad junction at Mezőlaborcz. The attack continued until it capitulated on 6 February. Unrelenting czarist attacks in the Dukla hollow and Laborcz Valley consumed the reeling Third Army's offensive capabilities. As the army's means of resistance evaporated, the seemingly endless Russian onslaught continued against the defending III, VII, and X Corps.

Blizzard conditions continued to exacerbate the Habsburg supply situation. Supply trains halted when drifting snow obstructed their movement, but no labor crews were available to restore service. Group Szurmay's 8th Cavalry Division required eight hours to transfer its battle trains four kilometers rearward, exhausting its pack animals. Telephone service interruptions caused by frozen wires continued to delay transmission of orders, and soldiers discarded important material and equipment during their repeated retreat movements. Enormous snowdrifts forced troops to move along treacherous secondary paths and road shoulders to skirt the worst sections. Even the local light Polish *Ponja* wagons required four to six horses to move. The steepness of roads and their concomitant icy conditions made them almost impossible to utilize, often forcing single-file movement through meter-deep snow. Even adding civilian workers to assist the road maintenance proved inadequate.[77]

Conversely, the consistently severe weather conditions facilitated czarist defensive efforts and provided valuable time to implement necessary countermeasures as the attackers exhausted themselves. Persistent unfulfilled requests for reinforcements exacerbated the apathy spreading through Habsburg ranks. Many soldiers succumbed to the White Death, while others chose to end their suffering by standing up in their position to receive a Russian sniper's bullet. Nightfall brought no rest because of the fear of freezing to death or being attacked by wolves.[78] The repeated collapse of Habsburg defensive lines forced the constant removal of weary soldiers from a nonthreatened area to march them to the threatened section. They could not replace the escalating losses, but units still received the standing order to "hold positions to the last man"—an order that in the present circumstances held little meaning.[79] Lacking sufficient manpower, counterattacks proved futile.

VII Corps' 17th Infantry Division reported that thirty men in one company suffered from frostbitten feet. Two other companies listed ninety-six cases of frostbite and numerous other casualties. All field units presented wrenching accounts of the debilitating conditions and horrific demands placed on their soldiers.[80] Nonetheless, division command ordered that they hold all positions and launch a counterattack on 30 January.[81]

The deepening crisis necessitated deploying additional inadequately trained replacement units into battle without any combat-experienced officers. They served as cannon fodder against the enemy's superior numbers, but no other troops were available to attempt to halt the enemy drive. Artillery support often failed to neutralize Russian positions because the guns were positioned too far behind the front, while the snow masses stymied attempts to move them forward.[82] Division commanders realized that any chance of successful offensive action had vanished and their flank positions would be threatened if neighboring units failed to join their attack or retreat movement, a frequent occurrence.[83] Group Szurmay reported that many of its troops had fallen ill or collapsed from sheer exhaustion, and requested that every effort be made to bring food supplies forward. A XIX Corps' 34th Infantry Division report revealed that "along the entire road lay numerous exhausted men affected by the cold, snow and difficult terrain." Such conditions had reached epidemic dimensions.

Meanwhile, Group Szurmay's 40th *Honvéd* Infantry Division battled colossal snow masses as it endeavored to maintain liaison with its extended left flank positions. Cold-related illnesses and hunger rendered many troops incapable of performing their duties. Combat boots were of inferior quality. Their soles, consisting of a cardboardlike material, became saturated and shredded, causing the poor-quality leather to rip. Combat boots disintegrated, and if new ones did not arrive soon, the number of incapacitated soldiers would increase significantly. Adding to their misery, the troops had not received regular nourishment for two days. When it finally arrived, each platoon received an allotment of five pieces of bread per soldier.[84] In addition to insufficient supplies, severe deficiencies in weaponry greatly inhibited the Habsburg army. The increasing scarcity of rifles, the result of loss on the battlefield, proved an insurmountable problem that affected the battlefield situation and the training of March Brigade replacement troops, who entered combat having only practiced with sticks. To diminish the shortage, special troop details collected the weapons of dead and wounded Habsburg and Russian soldiers; however, their efforts often proved futile.[85] A persistent shortage of artillery shells also hindered the army's efforts by hampering artillery effectiveness, while the extreme effort required to transport them into the mountains compounded the situation. In fact, lacking transportation means, the recently arrived 29th Infantry Division had no ammunition column.[86] Thus, the army paid particular attention to preventing the loss of artillery during the many retreat movements.

On 30 January, as persistent enemy pressure forced a rapid Third Army retreat, General Boroević requested replacement troops to supplement the poorly prepared VI March Battalion troops scheduled to arrive soon. He claimed that this would enable him to halt the unrelenting Russian attacks.[87] As his situation deteriorated, Boroević requested a full-strength infantry division to alleviate the V and VII Corps' dire situation.[88] Conrad ordered Fourth Army to either transfer another infantry division to the reeling Third Army or launch its own offensive to support its neighbor. The recent transfer of numerous Fourth Army divisions to the Carpathian front signified that its own offensive endeavors must be launched with far fewer numbers against strong Russian defensive positions. As the Fourth Army *Tagebuch* repeatedly recorded, any offensive endeavor would be an act of human sacrifice for "the common good," as no chance existed of achieving success.[89] A brigade, formed from Fourth Army Infantry Regiments 81 and 88, transferred to the VII Corps to buttress its wavering front lines in that strategic area.

In the meantime, enemy forces continued to pummel X Corps positions in the vicinity of the Mezölaborcz railroad junction, while VII Corps' twenty-four-kilometer front at Dukla Pass successfully resisted repeated enemy attacks.[90] The presence of significant czarist reinforcements in the Dukla Pass area indicated that the enemy's major offensive effort remained in the critical Mezőlaborcz area.[91]

As inclement weather conditions persisted, countless soldiers, too weak to complete strenuous marches, simply vanished in the frozen abyss.[92] The heavy snowfall made travel on the few secondary roadways difficult and continued to affect the use of artillery in battle.[93] A 30 January 8th Cavalry Division report indicated that dismounted cavalry troopers, prisoners of war, and civilians performed roadwork and maintained and repaired communication lines.[94] General Szurmay placed priority on ammunition and food echelon deliveries along the Uzsok Pass serpentine roadway, forbidding train column stoppages except to feed horses.[95] A Group Szurmay 66th Infantry Brigade report provides insight into troop morale. It described its troops as famished and exhausted, its numbers as seriously diminished. The brigade requested wagons to transport wounded to the rear echelons and reported that its artillery units ran out of shells![96] The 7th Infantry Division commander reported that Infantry Regiment 68 troops could perform only limited military action.

In the eastern Carpathian Mountain region a meter of fresh snow covered Army Group Pflanzer-Baltin's positions, requiring ski patrols for reconnaissance missions. Gusty winds and blowing snow blinded the troops. Many units lost their way maneuvering, and additional troops froze to death or suffered frostbite.[97] Compasses proved worthless in the densely forested and snow-covered terrain. Similar conditions also affected Third Army's V Corps and Group Szurmay.[98]

Even Fourth Army troops further north had to shovel through almost two meters of snow to advance. The Third Army situation continued to worsen, partly because General Boroević inaccurately assumed that the Russians' offensive objective was only to neutralize his right flank offensive efforts.[99] Snow masses also hindered czarist attacks, which often collapsed at the defensive barbed-wire entanglements.[100]

South Army continued its slow, painstaking attacks toward multiple objectives. Its German troops now better understood Habsburg tribulations in this winter hell, but after seven days of steady combat, all troops required rest. Artillery pieces sank into the deep snow once moved off the roadways and often became irretrievable. A shortage of draft animals forced troops to continue to assist moving equipment, as well as shoveling passageways and secondary routes.[101] Individual soldiers often did not return from assigned missions. A succinct description of battlefield conditions:

At the end of January, a sudden thaw and rain set in. Everyone was drenched to the bone, with no chance to dry off. Adding to this, the men's clothing froze to their bodies overnight like an icy suit of armor. Those that didn't have nerves of steel broke down. Then, the Russian counterattack struck. The soldiers, already half mad before the ordeal, retreated in apathetic resignation to their original positions. By now, even the enemy had enough of the fighting. On their side too, entire units surrendered. Finally, the killing subsided. There we were, where we had begun in mid-January; but in the time that had passed, yet another army had perished.[102]

Night temperatures sank to −20°C and often times lower. Prevailing conditions prohibited the placement of machine guns off the roadways, while icy slopes had to be hacked step by step under enemy fire. Ice-covered roadbeds continued to prevent nighttime travel or delivery of supplies.[103]

General Conrad planned to launch a Fourth Army southern flank counterattack, which he originally scheduled for 7 February, to alleviate the Third Army's crisis.[104] Five divisions (10th, 11th, 13th, 26th, and 45th) and the 11th *Honvéd* Cavalry Division would strike southward to relieve pressure on Third Army III Corps positions. In the interim, the Russians continued buttressing their troop strengths between the Uzsok and Dukla passes. As Habsburg losses escalated, an impending collapse of the VII and X Corps fronts appeared imminent.[105] Because of the desperate need for reinforcements, the 23,000-man VIII Corps transferred from the Balkan theater to Boroević's front in an attempt to provide momentum to his stalled offensive efforts. Limited railroad capacity, however, produced delays in the transfer of the corps. Conrad stipulated that VIII Corps be deployed as a single entity, rather than being inserted piecemeal as so often occurred. Meanwhile, Infantry Regiments 81 and 88 continued their travel to the hard-pressed VII Corps to participate in a counterattack.[106]

Increasing attention focused on the threatened Mezölaborcz area, one so critical for troop and supply movement to the Third Army eastern flank. Conrad determined that once reinforcements provided security for that area, they would launch an offensive. The question remained whether sufficient troop numbers could be assembled for defensive purposes until adequate relief arrived. March Brigade replacement troops of 2,000 men possessing, at most, eight weeks' basic training deployed to the front. As the military situation worsened, training time for these *Ersatz* troops lessened. VI March Battalion soldiers, like their predecessors, lacked sufficient preparation for the rigors of mountain battle and extreme conditions.[107]

A VII and X Corps retreat endangered the entire army front, which had become increasingly incapable of offering effective resistance. General Boroević ordered the two endangered right flank corps to maintain their positions, regardless of the cost. With just 15,800 soldiers on its twenty-eight kilometer, three-division front, the battered X Corps nevertheless launched an attack to relieve pressure on the decimated III Corps.[108] On South Army's front, Russian tactics continued to retard offensive endeavors and forced Habsburg commanders to constantly react to the enemy's astute countermeasures.[109]

On 1 February, General Conrad ordered the transfer of a further Fourth Army division to the Third Army front, while two and a half additional divisions redeployed to the critical Mezölaborcz area to buttress Third Army's buckling flank. VIII Corps, currently en route, would launch a decisive counterattack on 7 or 8 February. Until then, Third Army had the unenviable mission to maintain their increasingly threatened positions, which would also serve to protect the exposed South Army left flank. The Mezölaborcz–Lupkov railroad line, where the enemy concentrated its offensive efforts, was vital for the success of any offensive action launched to relieve Fortress Przemyśl. The depleted VII and X Corps, however, could offer little resistance to the enemy efforts.[110] Fierce fighting continued on this front throughout the first week of February. A report aptly described the dwindling Habsburg troop stands as the *k.u.k. Stakettenzaun* (picket fence) army. Efforts to fill front-line gaps with the few available troops failed to reverse the deteriorating situation. Only significant reinforcements could change the momentum of battle.[111]

Hungarian Premier Istvan Tisza increasingly pressured Conrad to prevent an invasion of Hungary. In turn, Conrad exhorted General Boroević that his fifteen-division army encountered "a mere twelve-division enemy force."[112] Ignoring the debilitation of the Third Army, Conrad demanded that Mezölaborcz be held, while the Russians continued to deploy a seemingly endless flow of reinforcements.[113] Meanwhile, a new wave of subzero temperatures caused the proliferation of frostbite, with some infantry regiments sustaining 50 percent casualties.[114] The Third Army situation had become so perilous that in defiance of direct orders, Boroević hurled arriving reinforcements into battle piecemeal. On 1 February Army Group Pflanzer-Baltin, delayed by XIII Corps' late arrival, finally joined the ill-fated offensive. The Army Group divided into two groups: one marched west and the other east along the existing railroad lines. The meter-and-a-half-high snow halted the western column forward movement on its second operation day.[115]

In the meantime, the Russians counterattacked the Habsburg positions in the Baligrod area during a driving snowstorm with temperatures of −21°C. The assault threatened V Corps' rear echelon areas, and after days of fierce fighting, it widened the gap between V and XVIII Corps. This substantially increased the threat of a breakthrough of the defensive line and Habsburg defeat. When Russian troops crossed the San and Stryj rivers, it required prompt and immediate action to reconquer Stryj Valley to prevent the encirclement of South Army's suddenly exposed flanks.[116] Orders to maintain present positions at any price received the reply: "We will hold, cost what it will!"[117] Poor visibility conditions made South Army frontal assaults against fortified Russian entrenchments risky, and they achieved little.[118]

Displeased with Third Army's VII and X Corps' constant retreat movements, Conrad warned that the entire Habsburg military situation would be compromised if the corps failed to hold their positions. Generals Conrad and Boroević's divergent perceptions on strategy and tactics produced growing personal discord, inflamed by disagreement on how best to utilize in-transit reinforcements.[119] Boroević argued that heavy snowfall had wreaked havoc on his battlefront and obstructed critical supply routes, while his undermanned *Landsturm* labor units simply could not maintain the supply roads. He also reported that he required another 6,000 troops just to maintain steady supply movements.[120]

The 37th *Honvéd* Infantry Division again reported that severe losses left its front lines untenable. In just four days, the V Corps unit sustained almost 80 percent casualties (10,500 troops to 2,000), while on average 500 soldiers a day either froze to death or succumbed to frostbite.[121] Also, in a matter of days, another *Honvéd* regiment reported 2 officers and 500 men dead or missing, 10 officers and 203 soldiers wounded, and 630 sick (many from frostbite and hypothermia). Because of the acute situation, medics, the wounded, and noncombat personnel had to charge into the front to stem the enemy tide.[122] On 3 February, deep snow limited all travel to skis. On 4 February, the regiment endured a third day of marching over the difficult terrain, with the demanding exertions leaving the troops exhausted and incapable of action. The loss of thirty-two front-line officers further diminished the unit's fighting capabilities.[123] The division retreated without any apparent serious enemy pressure. To prevent a catastrophe on this portion of the front, 33rd Infantry Division was ordered to support the decimated division.[124]

X Corps' 2nd Infantry Division now defended a five-kilometer snow-covered, densely wooded front with just 1,000 soldiers. On 22 January the division numbered 8,150 troops. The 2nd and 24th Infantry Divisions together had declined to far less than half a full-stand division.[125] The 2nd division encountered fierce battle in six different defensive positions around Mezölaborcz. Division commanders warned corps headquarters that as a result of the twelve days of battle, their troops could not resist another Russian night attack. Only retreating and allowing the troops time for rest and rehabilitation could prevent military disaster. When the 2nd Infantry Division retreated overnight to 1 February, it exposed the neighboring 24th and 34th Infantry Division positions, forcing them to withdraw also, followed shortly by the 29th Infantry Division.[126] Exhausted troops, many having marched through deep snow during the night, were hurled into battle at daybreak.[127] Feeble attempts at launching counterattacks failed because of inadequate troop numbers and extreme troop fatigue.

Group Szurmay also sustained heavy battle losses (three battalions reduced to 130, 150, and 300 men, respectively). Troop fatigue prevented Infantry Regiment 68 from launching an attack.[128] General Szurmay requested better mountain equipment, while his infantry received little artillery support and multiple shells sank unexploded into the deep snow. When the 7th Infantry Division supported a frontal assault toward its objective, the Turka roads, it collapsed when the troops encountered intense enemy fire. Infantry regiments 19 and 79 sustained devastating losses, some attributed to frostbite.[129] Two infantry brigades halted by huge snow masses and fatigue had to withdraw.[130] Even after receiving replacement troops, they numbered just 1,300 men. Severe weather conditions continued to claim as many lives as combat.[131] Numerous frozen corpses lying across the landscape presented a gruesome sight.

Also, on 1 February an aircraft landed in Fortress Przemyśl conveying an order to form combat-ready units from garrison troops to prepare for a possible breakout attempt. In a worst-case scenario, a skeleton force would remain in the fortress to destroy infantry weapons, artillery, and fortress gun turrets, while the remaining garrison attempted to pierce enemy siege lines to join the field armies.[132] Intercepted Russian radio transmissions regularly revealed enemy intentions, which prevented disaster. XVIII Corps again reported its *Landsturm* troops to be unreliable because some simply abandoned their positions while others refused to reoccupy those lost. Some infantry companies had been reduced to thirty or forty men.[133]

Although III Corps had been specifically ordered to maintain its current frontier ridge positions, the lack of numbers prevented it. On 2 February, Fourth Army commenced assembling its designated forces for its 7 February attack to relieve enemy pressure on the Mezölaborcz area. Meanwhile, III Corps' left flank troops retreated. After sustaining grievous losses, its two divisions numbered half their normal stand. VII Corps' 17th Infantry Division also lost almost half of its troops, many to frostbite.[134] As battle continued to rage at Mezőlaborcz, the Russians launched further storm attacks. Infantry regiments 81 and 88 finally prepared to launch a counterattack on 6 February, but the continuing VII and X Corps retreats jeopardized the overall situation.[135] The few arriving reinforcements were dispatched piecemeal into the numerous front-line gaps.[136]

Meanwhile, as Italian demands for territorial compensation to maintain its neutrality increased, rumor had it that Rome would declare war by the end of April if its demands remained unsatisfied.[137] Conrad again insisted that the diplomats await improvement in the Carpathian military situation before complying with Italian demands.[138] On 2 February, a joint ministerial council meeting in Vienna discussed the matter. On the same day, Group Szurmay's demanding mission resulted in heavy casualties and halted attack efforts, terminating in an evening retreat. If the group retreated much further, the Russians could invade Hungary. German general Ludendorff charged that Szurmay's unnecessary retreat endangered neighboring South Army's 3rd Garde (German) Infantry Division.[139] While battle raged, snowbound areas remained impassable. VII, X, and XVIII Corps could barely defend their positions.[140] On 3 February, Group Szurmay again received orders to maintain its positions at any cost, while the Russians continued their vicious attacks. Habsburg soldiers could not even attack weak enemy positions because of the wintry conditions and steep icy approaches. This forced them to fire their weapons while standing upright, making them sitting ducks to the defenders.

Conrad informed the emperor's military chancellery that the unfavorable Carpathian conditions, combined with tenacious Russian defensive efforts, precluded his achieving the anticipated victory, but he also criticized Germany's lack of cooperation, brutal egotism, and ruthlessness.[141] He claimed they minimized their own battlefield failures and exaggerated even the slightest victory while trivializing any Habsburg achievements. Berlin's persistent diplomatic and military pressure to cede territory to Italy to assure its neutrality galled Conrad, considering that he transferred his Second Army to the German front in November 1914 to assist in the protection of the industrial province of Silesia from invasion.

On 2 February numerous V Corps' 37th *Honvéd* Infantry Division staff officers reported to sick call. Corps numbers had declined precipitously, and despite protective measures, frostbite cases continued to increase.[142] XVIII Corps also reported numerous cases of frostbite. A neighboring brigade's failure to launch an ordered attack forced a V Corps division to retreat, creating a major breach between it and Group Szurmay positions and inviting an enemy breakthrough. The V Corps main supply depot, located seventy-eight kilometers away, entailed traversing two particularly difficult mountain passes. On one desolate cart path, it required three hours to travel one kilometer. An enemy attack appeared imminent, threatening the corps flank and rear echelon positions.[143]

XIX Corps received orders to launch an attack toward Baligrod on 3 February, but the 29th Infantry Division commander considered it a hopeless endeavor. General Zanantoni suggested delaying the attack until the situation improved.[144] Fortress Przemyśl witnessed a further rations reduction and slaughtered an additional 7,200 horses. The deteriorating physical condition of man and beast dashed any hopes for a successful breakout attempt. A minimum of 3,500 horses would be required just to reposition artillery to any threatened areas and maintain regular delivery of shells and ammunition. At night, troops foraged for food outside the fortress perimeter.[145] A citadel provisions report indicated that food supplies would last until 7 March, horse feed until 4 March. On 3 February, air reconnaissance reported a seven-kilometer column of Russian artillery and infantry approaching Sanok, another twenty-kilometer-long column moving southward.

The Russians unleashed artillery barrages against the fortress' northwest and southwest walls. Harassing enemy fire became constant, ending a period of relative calm. Enemy assaults launched on 12, 13, and 18 February sought to tighten III District defensive perimeter lines. On 19 February a further Russian assault failed, but on 13 March, czarist forces captured a Habsburg stronghold at Na Garoch-Batyce.[146] Disaster threatened when the enemy again broke through VII Corps 20th *Honvéd* Infantry Division lines, forcing a retreat that increased the threat to Mezölaborcz from the northwest and exposed X Corps' 2nd Infantry Division's flank position. An attack by at least six Russian battalions and devastating heavy enemy artillery forced the division's retreat.[147] The artillery fire particularly threatened division battle trains, prompting 2nd and 24th Divisions to rush theirs rearward. After hand-to-hand combat, a portion of the 2nd Division front collapsed.[148]

On 3 February the Third Army crisis worsened even further when the Russians hurled massive waves of troops against the battered VII and X Corps north of Mezölaborcz, intensifying the friction between Conrad and Boroević.[149] On that fateful day, XVIII and X Corps surrendered additional territory. Strong enemy pressure also extended the gap between III and VII Corps, providing the Russians an excellent opportunity to exploit.[150] Meager reinforcements attempted to thwart an enemy breakthrough at this vulnerable position. Because of the deteriorating situation, the earlier plan to deploy combined infantry regiments 81 and 88 and the 106th *Landsturm* Brigade to launch an attack had to be abandoned. General Boroević ordered his left flank corps units to defend their positions at any cost while contemplating inserting the in-transit VIII Corps at his right flank to launch a powerful counterattack. However, the new crisis situation made this unfeasible.[151]

The transfer of the VIII Corps ten days after the launch of the offensive raises the question why it was not utilized earlier to achieve better mass for the original attack. Meanwhile, overpowering enemy attacks threatened the entire Mezőlaborcz area, which also endangered the abysmal Third Army supply situation.[152] Even if the weather improved, it would require three to five days to reopen key transport arteries.[153] Supply train stoppages continued unabated while extensive snow drifting made the Lupkov forest railroad line inoperable. Overnight, fresh snowfall required further troop energy for shoveling paths before commencing any movement.[154]

Infantry regiments 81 and 88, participants in key future battles, experienced difficult approach marches to the front. On 3 February the troops marched six and the next day twelve and a half hours through dense woods, to enter battle the next day. For three days the exhausted and inexperienced Infantry Regiment 81 soldiers suffered from hunger, exposure, and frostbite. March Brigade units returned both regiments (81 and 88) to full strength before they entered battle, but both retreated after enduring fierce battle and sustaining excessive casualties. The Russians, contrary to their usual practice, proved relentless in their pursuit of the retreating troops, capturing many prisoners of war as entire units were cut off from escape routes.[155]

Also on 3 February, XIX Corps Infantry Regiment 33 dwindled to 300 troops, having sacrificed 1,500.[156] Corps troops must defend their positions, otherwise the Cisna transportation hub would become exposed to attack. The deteriorating Third Army troop conditions concerned army command because they could not anticipate any immediate improvement in the overall situation. General Boroević rushed any available replacement troops into his collapsing lines.[157] He preferred to surrender terrain to avoid further unnecessary casualties while awaiting the arrival of reinforcements, but Conrad ordered that all lines be held whatever the cost because he remained deeply concerned about VII and X Corps' retreat movements and the widening gap between III and VII Corps.

Major obstacles continued to hobble South Army in its offensive efforts, while complaints multiplied about the lack of artillery support. The rugged mountain terrain favored the defenders. German artillery batteries still remained too far from the front to be effective.[158] The overall situation required that South Army continue its efforts to encircle the enemy's main retreat route as the Russians continued to threaten Habsburg positions in the San River Valley, specifically the single road connection to the V Corps rear echelon area. The few available reserve troops consisted of very young or older soldiers, many recovered from wounds or sickness.[159]

Under mounting pressure, Conrad ordered a gradual retreat until the Fourth Army attack could assuage the Third Army's desperate plight. Meanwhile, heavy czarist artillery barrages drove X Corps battle trains away from the Mezölaborcz area.[160] The Habsburg military crisis had plateaued! As dense fog continued hindering Third Army artillery fire, enemy troops pierced X Corps defensive lines while exhausted 2nd Infantry Division soldiers fought hand to hand along their five-kilometer defensive line during a driving snowstorm.[161] When forced to retreat, the division began the movement under terrible conditions. Czarist troops smashed through the stunned Habsburg troops, which sustained additional casualties they could ill afford.[162] An XVIII Corps retreat jeopardized the earlier V Corps gains.

On Army Group Pflanzer-Baltin's front, heavy snowfall sabotaged the 6th Infantry Division attack. Of 1,000 casualties, half resulted from illness, a quarter from frostbite.[163] Sickness or frostbite struck one hundred troops per day. On 4 February, the Russian assault on Mezölaborcz halted rail traffic to Lupkov, the main Third Army eastern flank supply line. Only the czarist failure to immediately pursue retreating Habsburg troops prevented a cataclysmic defeat. When Mezölaborcz finally fell during the night to 5 February, the victors paused to celebrate their bloody victory.[164]

On Group Szurmay's front, 66th Infantry Brigade lost half its stand to frostbite and physical overexertion in less than a week. One XVIII Corps unit dwindled to fifty to sixty men and three machine guns; nevertheless, it received orders to hold its extended positions. The lingering transportation difficulties resulted in half of necessary supplies reaching the front.[165] Essential railroad traffic became even more congested.[166] The Russians also assaulted the defenders' flank and rear positions on the high terrain they had just conquered at Borynia near Uzsok Pass.[167] Czarist units, some neck-deep in snow, extended their attack at the San River area, forcing the hapless defending units across the river on 6 February. All able-bodied soldiers were thrust into battle in a desperate attempt to stem the enemy onslaught.

The appearance of sunshine allowed Habsburg units to finally receive much-needed artillery support, while the enemy hurled additional reinforcements against the Third and South armies.[168] General Boroević again implored Conrad to spare his troops from further suffering by terminating the present operations until weather conditions improved. Pressured by the dire situation at Fortress Przemyśl, Conrad denied the request, planning to renew the offensive in the same area as the recent failed effort, but this time on a more compressed front.[169] He did not want to have to accept responsibility for the loss of Fortress Przemyśl. However, by early February Third Army had proved not only incapable of achieving its multiple missions but even of maintaining its positions. It must be recalled that its offensive had been launched with insufficient troop numbers and little consideration for the ramifications of a winter mountain campaign. Field commanders too often received orders that they could not expedite under the grueling circumstances.

The attrition of professional officers and noncommissioned officers continued to demoralize the troops as their faith in Habsburg Supreme Command dissipated.[170] Most corps troop numbers now equaled that of a division while their front lines extended twenty-eight to thirty kilometers (XIX Corps' 29th Infantry Division front alone encompassed sixteen kilometers).[171]

Artillery pieces increasingly required repair while enemy action destroyed many others. An hour of strenuous troop effort might gain 1,000 paces, while night brought renewed snowstorms and biting icy winds.[172] Too often, disoriented troops marched in circles until exhausted for no gain, and many stragglers collapsed in the snow and froze to death.[173] Many wounded did not survive the jarring cart rides down the mountain pathways, while others were abandoned to die on the battlefield. The 42nd *Honvéd* Infantry Division's *Landwehr* Infantry Regiment 28 lost 26 officers and 1,800 enlisted men within two days, many of whom froze to death.[174]

Fourth Army finally launched its long-overdue attack on 10 February, but its belated efforts proved too late to save Mezőlaborcz.[175] After fifteen days of combat, X and VII Corps surrendered the crucial territory and retreated, the corps missions far exceeding the troops' capabilities.[176] Plans to launch a counterattack to recapture Mezőlaborcz never materialized because of continued Russian military success.[177] Battle-weary troops hurriedly marched from adjacent nonthreatened areas to endangered positions, but they often arrived too late to affect the outcome of battle. Meanwhile, Group Szurmay failed to seize the enemy stronghold of Borynia at the doorstep of Uzsok Pass, while its troop strengths dwindled by half in less than a week, the majority a result of frostbite and exhaustion. Many soldiers collapsed while shoveling snow along the roadways. Some of the few available reinforcements had to assist in maintaining supply-route traffic.[178]

Third Army's desperate situation and the disagreements between Conrad and Boroević prompted Conrad to transfer his more pliable Second Army commander, General Böhm-Ermolli, from the German northern front back to the Carpathian theater. It would deploy between the Third and South armies. Conrad claimed that Third Army (eighteen infantry and three and a half cavalry divisions) had become too large and unmanageable, so he must divide the army's front into two segments. He planned to transfer six additional divisions to Second Army, while General Böhm-Ermolli would assume command on 15 February and, soon thereafter, launch a new offensive to relieve Fortress Przemyśl.[179]

South Army must continue its efforts, but its meager successes cost almost 10,000 men.[180] Efforts to envelop opposing positions resulted in the enemy merely extending its flanks, which absorbed the few remaining South Army reserves.[181] Three to four rows of barbed wire protected numerous czarist rear echelon positions as well. The opposing front lines were often in such close proximity that it prevented artillery support for the attacking infantry. A newly created XVII Corps had its divisions transferred from Fourth Army to Third Army to assist efforts to recapture Mezőlaborcz and halt enemy progress against Third Army. The intervening rugged mountain terrain continued to prevent South Army and Third Army from assisting each other's efforts. The frozen ground made it impossible to dig trenches, while troops that waded through mountain streams had their wet uniforms freeze on them.[182]

Third Army launched its ill-fated offensive on 23 January 1915 with a 135,000-man complement. Two weeks later, on 5 February, official Habsburg sources reported a loss of 89,000 men, a significant number of which suffered from severe frostbite and exposure. Some 30,000 replacement troops reinforced the army during the operation. Individual corps losses proved disturbing. An example of smaller unit casualties, *Schutzen* Regiment 20 sank from 60 officers and 3,400 men to 9 officers and 250 men after many froze to death. A *Landwehr* infantry regiment reported a mere 130 troops available for duty. The 2nd Infantry Division incurred 90 percent casualties, sinking to 1,000 men after multiday battle against superior enemy numbers.[183] In two weeks, Third Army had sacrificed most its strength (at least half to sickness and frostbite), overextended its front lines, and fatigued its soldiers. Table 3 provides corps troop numbers on 23 January, the number of replacement troops, losses sustained between 23 January and 6 February, and the troop stands on 6 February 1915.[184]

V Corps lost most of its men to sickness and frostbite. The 37th *Honvéd* Infantry Division now numbered 2,000 troops, while X Corps' 24th Infantry

Division sustained 40 percent casualties. The majority of Infantry Regiment 81 casualties were listed as missing in action or captured. The deployment of inexperienced and inadequately trained March Brigade recruits momentarily returned many units to near full strength, but this most recent allotment of cannon fodder, as with their predecessors, proved unprepared for the arduous physical tasks that confronted them. The condition of Infantry Regiment 101 was depicted as "deathlike." By midnight one night, blowing snow reduced visibility to such an extent that Russian troops approached the regiment lines undetected and launched a bayonet attack against the unsuspecting defenders. Entire companies simply vanished, forcing the meager available reserves to rush forward, but fortunately the Russians again failed to press their advantage. Conrad ordered his battered troops to maintain their positions until the 7 February Fourth Army offensive, which after multiple postponements did not occur until 10 February.[185]

As conditions continued deteriorating, Army Group Pflanzer-Baltin's officers openly complained of war weariness, a clear indication of the seriousness of the situation.[186] The Army Group troops could not find shelter in the deep snow and frostbite cases became rampant. No longer able to defend themselves, many soldiers surrendered to the enemy. As much as 90 percent of the Army Group troops had resided in mild climate regions before the war and thus were not acclimated to the harsh winter weather. Worse, most had not been issued suitable winter uniforms or equipment.

An interesting letter from General Krautwald (X Corps commander) to Conrad emphasized that corps troop numbers had sunk to a dangerous level during the brutal Mezölaborcz battle. The troops had no shelter to protect themselves from the elements, while officer casualties increased troop apathy and reduced unit battle effectiveness. Krautwald warned Conrad that his troops could no longer resist enemy attacks, and he further cautioned that the situation could only worsen if they did not retreat and rehabilitate. However, if the corps continued its present retreat, neighboring units would be threatened with encirclement. He also reported that many of his troops surrendered to the enemy.[187]

Between 6 and 16 February, inclement weather conditions continued to negatively affect military operations, and thus no major success occurred at Uzsok Pass. During this time the 106th *Landsturm* Brigade and VIII Corps' 21st Infantry Division arrived at the front after several railroad delays. Third Army intended to utilize these troops to launch a counterattack against the enemy. VII Corps had sustained grave losses, while on one front sector, two *Honvéd* regiments opposed nine enemy units.[188] The worsening situation raised the pressing question of where to deploy in-transit VIII Corps troops to produce the most advantage.[189]

Anticipating that enemy efforts would continue, Conrad remained adamant that Habsburg attacks continue, regardless of the enemy's seemingly endless supply of reinforcements. XVII Corps received orders to attack supported by III and VII Corps. For the effort to succeed, XVIII Corps must maintain its positions, even though it had previously been unable to do so. Meanwhile, VIII Corps endured a forty-eight-hour railroad transport with multiple delays to reach the front.[190]

Third Army reported further alarming losses and the danger of its front collapsing as XIX and VII Corps continued their bloody retreats. The meager available reserves could not be brought into action quickly.[191] On 8 February VIII Corps' 21st Infantry Division at last launched a counterattack against the enemy troops mauling the VII Corps.[192] The Corps' twenty-five-kilometer front made it difficult for units to maintain liaison in the inhospitable, forested, and snowbound region. Any Russian attack could garner easy success.[193] Rising temperatures and melting snow produced flooding in lower elevations. Third Army eastern flank units received orders to assume a defensive posture until the reinforced Second Army deployed and launched a renewed offensive in the near future. Additional divisions should arrive in midmonth, but railroad troop transport continued to experience major delays and stoppages.[194]

Artillery shell shortages combined with the lack of regular logistical movement resulted in an order to spare shells. Many batteries simply ran out of them, particularly badly needed high explosive shells, as deliveries faltered on the icy routes.[195] This required artillery to fire the far less effective shrapnel shells against the entrenched enemy positions. Numerous inoperable guns continued to be shipped to the rear echelon for repair and returned still malfunctioning, while the extensive use of available weapons led to normal wear and tear to many of them. V Corps command reported fourteen of forty-five pieces defective, while renewed snowfall halted all traffic to the front.[196]

On Army Group Pflanzer-Baltin's front temperatures dipped to −29°C in the Bukovina while deep snow continued to retard all attempts at movement. Telephone connections to its various units were almost nonexistent, and the Army Group's few available, but obsolete, artillery pieces could not be placed into position. Lacking reserves or reinforcements, the Group's *Landsturm* battalions melted away. The worsening situation also produced treasonous behavior among war-weary troops. For example, a Bosnian-

Herzegovinian regiment, Infantry Regiment 1, had to be withdrawn from the front lines to be disciplined while the brigade commander refused to accept responsibility for the regiment. Although combat fatigue partially explained the incident of surrendering to the enemy after seven days of constant battle, the regiment nevertheless was transferred out of Pflanzer-Baltin's ranks.[197]

A report relative to the earlier Bosnian-Herzegovinian Infantry Regiment 2's serious losses in battle cited professional officer losses, replaced by un-qualified reserve officers, to explain the serious casualty rates. Numerous self-inflicted wounds and the unit's debilitated state prompted a request for ten to twelve competent officers to restore its combat effectiveness.[198] On 9 February, warmer temperatures caused mud to replace ice as the main obstacle on supply routes. Two additional Fourth Army divisions were transferred to the Carpathian front as XVII Corps prepared to launch an attack on 10 February. Also, South Army German troops at long last captured the Zvinin heights objective on 9 February, then repulsed a strong Russian counterattack, both sides sustaining considerable losses. One Habsburg regiment counted just 175 survivors.[199]

The threat of an Entente naval campaign against the Turks at the Dardanelles also affected the situation. German diplomatic and military pressure on the Habsburgs increased to maintain the neutrality of Romania, Bulgaria, and Italy, even at the cost of surrendering territory to ensure Italy's neutrality. Conrad, however, maintained his position that no territory should be surrendered to Italy pending the successful conclusion of the Carpathian campaign.

On 10 February XVII Corps' belated attack encountered strong Russian resistance after achieving initial slow, painful progress. The failure of adjoining units to provide adequate support for the attack caused the corps to incur heavy casualties as it engaged the enemy in isolated skirmishes between 10 and 14 February. Simultaneously, fierce czarist counterattacks wracked the V, XVIII, and XIX Corps, which resulted in the acceleration of IV Corps' 31st and 32nd Infantry Divisions' timetable for the Second Army offensive rail transport.[200]

When the X Corps' 2nd Infantry Division flank again suddenly retreated, it exposed the VII Corps flank and rear areas. Many of these exhausted soldiers remained in their positions to await capture by the enemy.[201] The Russians pursued the reeling Habsburg troops, an unusual occurrence, capturing many who became cut off or surrounded. These famished troops received no food, and many suffered from severe frostbite.[202]

Continued czarist battlefield successes negated any Habsburg Third Army efforts to rectify its situation before Second Army's offensive operation scheduled for late February. South Army and Army Group Pflanzer-Baltin, however, continued their efforts to wear down Russian resistance power.[203] The enemy's supply of manpower appeared inexhaustible as czarist troops launched incessant mass assaults against the hapless defenders.[204]

Three thousand exhausted XVIII Corps troops were nearly surrounded while defending a critical fourteen-kilometer front, forcing them to join the retreat. XVIII Corps lacked any reserve formations necessary to counterattack, but Conrad ordered the rattled III and IX Corps troops (Third and Fourth Army inner flanks) to launch an attack on 15 February to support a renewed XVII Corps offensive effort.[205] A questionable assumption remained whether Third Army's reeling eastern flank troops could maintain their positions much longer.

After XVIII Corps right flank position units had retreated, V Corps surrendered its main supply center, seriously compounding its logistical woes and relinquished some of its San River positions. Renewed enemy pressure at its flank and rear echelon positions threatened to envelop them, and after an overnight retreat, the corps' supply trains withdrew further rearward. It was essential for the overall military situation that V Corps maintain its positions, but when enemy troops successfully encircled its flank, it also caused the center to buckle. The troops' resistance capabilities had been so weakened that any enemy attack forced the defenders to recoil before it.

As Russian artillery fire continued to batter Habsburg defensive positions, they requested the immediate dispatch of any available March Battalion replacement troops. Renewed heavy battle at the Uzsok Pass area underscored the necessity for reinforcements. On 10 February General Kusmanek reported that, if they slaughtered an additional 3,500 horses, the fortress garrison could hold out until 13 March. Approval was granted, but with the proviso that the fortress maintain its offensive capabilities. By 11 February, however, just 600 of the remaining horses could be harnessed to pull artillery, sufficient for just four batteries. The fortress requisition commission seized any hidden provisions it could discover, while foraging outside the fortress perimeter yielded another 10,000 grams of sugar beets, 2,000 grams of root vegetables, and 100 grams of cabbage and other edibles.[206]

With Fortress Przemyśl's situation deteriorating, Second Army's mission became to liberate the fortress with 52,000 of its soldiers attacking an estimated 37,000 Russians. Seven divisions, four from Fourth Army, bolstered the Third and South armies' inner flanks while Fourth Army's mission remained to bind opposing enemy forces. Conrad expected Army

Group Pflanzer-Baltin to launch a major offensive, but without receiving sufficient reinforcements. Despite the importance of the army group's mission, it received just one machine gun and one artillery battery for support. Commanders would have to make do; improvisation ruled![207]

On 12 February, General Böhm-Ermolli arrived at his new headquarters. A day later, Russian forces hurled the hapless V, XVIII, and XIX Corps even further back.[208] Lacking any reinforcements, the troops suffered from frostbite, exposure, and other cold-related illnesses resulting in additional significant losses.[209] Also, Conrad informed the emperor's military chancellery that liberating Fortress Przemyśl would be almost impossible, although every effort would be made to accomplish it. Three days later, Franz Joseph urged Conrad to do whatever necessary to prevent the garrison's surrender. The emperor's directive reaffirmed Conrad's decision to launch the second Carpathian offensive.[210]

After three weeks of continuous battle, enormous gaps existed in the front lines. Meanwhile, any earlier South Army lust for battle and expectations of victory had dissipated.[211] X Corps' 2nd and 24th Infantry Divisions now numbered less than a full-strength regiment. The continued setbacks necessitated the immediate deployment of VIII Corps' 9th Infantry Division into the endangered V Corps sector, while its 21st Infantry Division transferred into the X Corps' front to stabilize the enemy threat in the Laborcz Valley, which weakened the planned Second Army offensive force by an entire corps.

A sudden onset of warming temperatures again transformed the ground to mud and further delayed all supply movement. By 14 February only the most necessary supplies could be transported. The perpetual shortage of labor detachments aggravated the situation and prompted pleas for assistance. VII Corps Commander Archduke Joseph complained: "Caused by the sudden very mild weather, a huge amount of snow began to thaw. The Ondava River has flooded the entire valley. In the trenches water is one meter deep."[212]

Between 31 January and 20 February Army Group Pflanzer-Baltin's polyglot group advanced through its snow-shrouded mountain battle zone, surprisingly emerging victorious onto the Galician plains. On 20 February, after the capture of Stanislau, a two infantry and one cavalry division group advanced to relieve enemy pressure against the South Army's rear echelon areas and assist its escape from its mountain entrapment. However, intelligence reports indicated that the enemy was transferring substantial reinforcements, indicating preparations to launch a strong counterattack against the Army Group.[213]

On 14 February, as poor terrain conditions persisted, XIX Corps rebuffed another fierce enemy attack. The Russians now hurled six to seven infantry divisions, supported by a number of rifle regiments, against the weak corps positions. Battle-weary V and XVIII Corps troops defending the San River line were outnumbered four to one, while further Russian reinforcements worsened the situation.[214]

In retrospect, General Conrad's first Carpathian offensive was doomed to fail. Many warnings about the problems of such an operation had reached Conrad; however, he refused to heed advice from other generals. This included General Falkenhayn, to whom he would be forced to turn when disaster struck. Aside from the unfavorable general conditions, Conrad failed to mass adequate troop strength necessary to succeed. The 175,000-man Third and South Army force proved inadequate to accomplish its mission. Furthermore the Russians, in addition to advantageous defensive positions, possessed more favorable road and railroad connections, thus enabling the rapid deployment of reinforcements. Czarist troops maintained a significant numerical advantage throughout much of the Carpathian Winter War.

The Russian army also maintained a tactical advantage and utilized inclement weather to its advantage. Czarist commanders waited for a weak moment in a Habsburg assault to launch a counterattack. Moreover, Habsburg operations suffered from a serious lack of coordination between its attacking forces, partially as a result of the terrain features. Many sources claimed that the adverse weather conditions explain the primary reason for the first Habsburg offensive's failure. These assertions provided a convenient explanation for many command blunders.

Surrendering the critical railroad Mezölaborcz–Lupkov junction represented a severe setback to the Habsburg objective to rescue Fortress Przemyśl. Any attempts to liberate the fortress were contingent on controlling the major Mezölaborcz two-track transport connections. Thus Conrad must launch an immediate counterattack to regain it, partially as a result of increasing pressure to protect Hungary from invasion and liberate Fortress Przemyśl.

Another reason for the failure resulted from Habsburg Supreme Command's negligence and inadequate planning. Its armies had not been provided the necessary equipment or preparation time for such a daunting mission. For example, when Group Puhallo advanced into the forty-kilometer gap in enemy lines, defended only by weak cavalry units, it advanced twenty-five kilometers. However, as its lines extended, the group became far too weak to accomplish its mission. Nonetheless, Conrad ordered Puhallo to relinquish a brigade to Group Szurmay to assist its effort to seize Uzsok Pass.

An envelopment maneuver might have succeeded, but the Fortress Przemyśl crisis necessitated the attack assume a more direct, frontal approach, and Puhallo lacked the troop strength for such an ambitious mission.

The shortage of reserve forces placed a tremendous strain on surviving troops. Inadequate artillery support and multiple batteries left behind the mountains in the rear echelons helped increase casualty lists. The shortage of artillery shells and lack of mountain artillery pieces, because they had been deployed on the Serbian front, further hampered operations. The enemy's numerical advantage and more effective artillery arm exacerbated the problem. Apathy, rising frostbite casualties, and the White Death eroded the men's confidence in their higher commanders.

While attacks were launched in haste, logistical challenges remained insurmountable. The intense physical demands on Habsburg soldiers are incomprehensible. Before reaching the front, the men had to first perform long and exhausting marches under the constant threat of frostbite and the White Death. Lacking food and sleep, and in near-constant battle with both the elements and a forceful enemy, Habsburg troops suffered severe psychological and physical stress.

With the devastation wrought by the first Carpathian offensive fresh in our memory, we now turn to Conrad's second undertaking in late February 1915.

Chief of the Austro-Hungarian General Staff Conrad von Hötzendorf (left) with his adjutant, Rudolf Kundmann. Imgano/Hulton Archive/Getty Images

Austro-Hungarian troops positioned in the *Waldkarpathen*. Hulton-Deutsch Collection/CORBIS

Habsburg troops advancing on the Carpathian front. Courtesy of Photos of the Great War. http://www.gwpda.org/photos/

Habsburg infantry resting at a Carpathian Mountain pass. Courtesy of Photos of the Great War. http://www.gwpda.org/photos/

Habsburg troops on the firing line in the Bukovina. Courtesy of Photos of the Great War. http://www.gwpda.org/photos/

Russian artillery on the Eastern front. Hulton Archive /Getty Images

Austro-Hungarian ski patrol positioned along a Carpathian Mountain pass.
Courtesy of Photos of the Great War. http://www.gwpda.org/photos/

Russian infantry lying in wait on the Carpathian front. Hulton Archive/Getty Images

Troops transporting a machine gun by sled on the Habsburg Carpathian front.
Courtesy of Photos of the Great War. http://www.gwpda.org/photos/

Habsburg troops on the snowy Carpathian mountainside. Courtesy of Photos of the Great War. http://www.gwpda.org/photos/

Austro-Hungarian troops take aim on the Carpathian front. Courtesy of Photos of the Great War. http://www.gwpda.org/photos/

Russian General Nikolai Ivanov. Ridpath's *History of the World*, vol. 10, Cincinnati, 1921. Reproduced by permission.

3

The Second Carpathian Offensive
Late February–Mid-March 1915

Every mile is two in winter.   Emily Dickinson

THE RECENT FAILURE OF THIRD ARMY offensive efforts should have cautioned Habsburg Supreme Command against renewing its Carpathian Mountain winter campaign.[1] By all indications, continuing the operation would further debilitate its already weakened army.[2] Persistent adverse weather conditions assured that maneuvering in the mountains would be dangerous and reduce troop morale. Despite the dreadful outcome of Habsburg military operations in December 1914 through mid-February 1915, General Conrad insisted on pursuing another Carpathian offensive. What justification did the Habsburg chief of the General Staff offer for his lofty plan? Was it the threat of a Russian invasion into Hungary, the liberation of Fortress Przemyśl, or mounting political pressure to prevent Italian and Romanian intervention? In actuality, all three factors led to Conrad's fateful decision to launch a second offensive on some of the same terrain, though on a much more limited front. The ill-fated effort would bring the *k.u.k.* army closer to the brink of annihilation.

In early February 1915, severe winter weather continued to wreak havoc on Habsburg military operations. In a cruel twist of fate, blizzard conditions alternated with periods of sudden thaw, leading one exasperated Habsburg field commander to remark, "It's as if the heavens are against us!"[3] Habsburg army orders and daily corps log entries describe the deplorable travel conditions that prevailed throughout the month of February 1915. Heavy snowfall in the higher elevations blocked key mountain passes. From 20 to 25 February, snow mixed with rain, creating hazardous travel conditions. Numerous major roadways were completely washed away or transformed into pits of mud. Circumstances did not bode well for the movement of troops, supplies, and ammunition—basic requirements for any military operation's success.

As the launch date for the second offensive approached, the severe weather and terrain conditions became greater causes for concern. Trenches filled with stagnant rainwater and melted snow became the perfect breeding ground for disease. Infantry columns struggled to make their way forward through the mire. Horse-drawn supply trains sank to their axles, and horse cadavers and broken-down wagons blocked the travel routes. Oftentimes, conditions forced entire supply columns to a complete standstill. The entire Habsburg supply system had collapsed before the Second Army received its orders to attack.

In the valleys, unseasonably warm daytime temperatures often fell to below freezing overnight. The extreme temperature fluctuations took their toll on the single-lane roads and trails. The four mountain railroad lines and inadequate Galician roads further slowed the movement of supplies to the troops. In one area of the front, a solitary transport artery was to supply four corps. This shortcoming would have a decisive impact on the outcome of the Habsburg second offensive. Supply routes required constant maintenance. Enormous snowbanks lined both sides of the mountain roads, which prevented the use of side columns for movement. Roads turned to sheets of ice overnight, making travel risky for pack animals and infantry units. The dire conditions forced Habsburg Supreme Command to postpone launching the Second Army offensive for a few days. The delay cost the Habsburg army the crucial element of surprise and granted sufficient time for an effective Russian counterstroke.

The Second Army commander, General Eduard Böhm-Ermolli, disagreed with Conrad's decision to launch the offensive without delay. Like his predecessor, General Boroević, he favored postponing the attack until weather conditions improved. General Boroević had also advised against taking further offensive action until the critical need for reinforcements had been met and the required troop numbers systematically assembled. This, Boroević explained to Conrad, would prevent unnecessary casualties, something the Habsburg cause could ill afford. It would also provide additional time to improve logistical preparations. Despite these valid arguments, General Conrad insisted the offensive continue as planned. He simply could not risk denuding other war theaters in order to provide additional troops for his offensive endeavor.

General Boroević's doubts about Conrad's operational plan were evident from the outset. Experience had taught the wily army commander that if neighboring armies did not advance simultaneously with the main attack force, the outcome would be limited to transitory territorial gains. With the Second Army offensive looming, daily South and Third Army situation reports warned that under the present adverse conditions, military action would be severely impeded.

Artillery support for the infantry attacks, the Achilles' heel of all three Habsburg Carpathian offensives, remained inadequate and was further hampered by gross transportation and terrain limitations. Improper transport means and poor positioning further reduced the effectiveness of artillery support during the January offensive, while the lack of sufficient artillery batteries had a decisive and negative impact on the outcome of battle. At the very least, greater artillery presence would have had a positive psychological effect on attacking Habsburg troops. However, transporting artillery and ammunition into the mountains became a near-futile effort, leading some field commanders to question whether it was worthwhile. Soon numerous unit commanders would opt to leave some artillery batteries behind the mountain ridges in favor of transporting shells for the available guns. The shortage of suitable wagons and harnesses further limited artillery use. Increased heavy traffic left roadbeds a bottomless pit of mud. Artillery batteries that reached the front lines often remained idle for a long time because poor visibility rendered them useless. To make matters worse, shell supplies often ran out.

On one particular day, a wounded Russian soldier fluent in German was taken prisoner. During interrogation, he was asked his opinion of Habsburg artillery. The Russian POW replied, "Pretty awful! Our artillerists are always joking about how the famous Austrian artillery is only being used as a shield because that's all it's good for!"[4]

The Habsburg army's inability to rapidly maneuver artillery once it was placed into firing position further stymied efforts to support the infantry, and increased the danger of batteries being overrun if retreat suddenly became necessary. Moreover, Habsburg artillery often proved unreliable and in need of constant repair. Many guns that presumably had been repaired were returned to service still unworkable. Habsburg Supreme Command continued to receive disconcerting reports regarding the poor combat performance of replacement March Brigade units. In critical battle moments, the fighting and resistance power of these ill-prepared troops too often melted away. Meanwhile, once critical reinforcements arrived, Second Army would assume command of present Third Army right flank units for the second offensive campaign.[5]

The tenuous military situation led to growing concern over the reliability of certain nationalities in the Habsburg ranks. As a consequence of the growing demand for replacement troops, soldiers were now being transferred out of their normal regimental territorial districts to other front-line units. Entities that once shared a common ethnicity became mixed with troops of diverse nationalities. This had a progressively harmful effect on Habsburg army morale and cohesiveness. The myriad of languages spoken at and below the regimental level reduced communication among the officers and their men. This became particularly evident with the arrival of reserve officers, who lacked the language skills of the professional officers they replaced. This often created a volatile atmosphere of mutual mistrust and disrespect. Habsburg Supreme Command received reports of the increasing unreliable performance of once-trustworthy *Landsturm* units on the battlefield. In growing numbers, battalions and regiments began deserting en masse to the enemy.[6] Czech soldiers were particularly suspect, especially to General Conrad. Czech deserters now serving in Russian intelligence units encouraged fellow nationals to desert.[7]

Adverse weather conditions did not bode well for Conrad's second offensive effort. Torrential rains on 18 February produced rapid melting of snow and ice. Deteriorating roads and bridges prompted an urgent call for repairs. Field cannon regiments, unable to be positioned behind their respective units, were transferred to rear areas. Valiant efforts to provide field armies with a continuous flow of supplies failed.

Extended periods of heavy rainfall caused rivers to overflow their banks. At some river crossings, high water levels forced troops to cross at bridge overpasses under the threat of enemy fire. Major terrain obstructions caused infantry formations to maneuver at greater distances. At the lifeline of the arriving IV Corps, artillery units and supply trains became stuck in the mud. A twelve-kilometer section of the key supply route was rendered impassable. Similar conditions were soon reported along other connecting routes. Supply trains could no longer advance on a regular basis. On many valley road surfaces, already damaged from previous heavy usage, traffic was reduced to a trickle. On the eve of the second offensive, the danger of all movement coming to a complete halt threatened the launching of the operation.

On 19 February, sections of the bridge connecting the key supply depots and roads leading to the span became impassable. All available cavalry horses and troops formed an improvised supply line that provided front-lines troops with half of the required daily rations. Supplies for XVIII Corps had to be transported by horseback over more challenging terrain, while V Corps supply efforts remained problematic, having to now replace the route lost earlier to the enemy with the loss of Mezölaborcz. Transporting the sick and wounded to rear echelon areas came to a near standstill. Many critically wounded did not survive the jarring ride down the mountains. Many froze to death, if they did not succumb to blood loss first.

Unit reports to Habsburg Supreme Command through 20 February described the enormous time and effort given to rectifying the supply crisis. More than 7,000 civilian workers and prisoners of war assisted in repairing major roads to keep traffic moving. Field commanders cautioned that the offensive should be postponed until the weather conditions improved. Their warnings fell on deaf ears—the liberation of Fortress Przemyśl demanded immediate action!

On 23 February an artillery officer observed, "There is no apparent railroad organization and no preparation. . . . troops are starving and continue to be mistreated. Trains are not where they are supposed to be, indicative of the constant senseless shifting of rail cars."[8] Simultaneously, surprising Army Group Pflanzer-Baltin victories prompted General Conrad to consider transferring substantial reinforcements to this extreme right flank area to expand the successful advance. However, a single low-capacity railroad line led to this portion of the front with a daily limit of twelve trains. Assembling sufficient troop numbers there would be time-consuming and would require long, exhausting marches through deep snow. Throughout the night into the morning of 21 February, heavy rains fell again, prompting new orders to restore the roads to operating condition.[9] The main road to the Cisna area was in particularly poor condition and endangered provisioning for the 27 February offensive undertaking.

Returning to Second Army planning, General Böhm-Ermolli determined to launch his offensive with Third Army units placed under his command. The Second and Third Army's offensive objective was to recapture Lupkov, thereby regaining access to its narrow-gauge railroad to expedite supply movements and to recapture the transport and communication junction of Mezölaborcz. The main offensive thrust would be launched northward toward Baligrod by an attack group under the command of a Hungarian general, Tersztyánsky. The Second Army offensive direction must coincide with Third Army attempts to recapture Mezölaborcz.[10] Until the offensive launch date, newly designated Second Army units (the former Third Army right flank troops) remained in their positions, while six and a half additional divisions received orders to move behind the present front lines. Once combined, these forces would launch a frontal attack against the well-fortified and well-positioned czarist defensive positions, preventing egress to the most direct route to Fortress Przemyśl.[11]

Increasing reports that the Fortress Przemyśl garrison resistance was on the verge of collapse helped spur the decision to launch the second offensive along the shortest route to the fortress. Once the offensive commenced, not a day could be sacrificed. Despite the unfavorable conditions, the besieged garrison must be freed.

What little progress Third Army's VII and X Corps achieved toward regaining Mezölaborcz between 15 to 18 February came to an end when XVII Corps' offensive efforts failed and the corps was forced to assume a defensive posture. Meanwhile, Army Group Pflanzer-Baltin's inadequately armed and trained second- and third-line military units surprised the weak opposing Russian forces in the Bukovina and in southeastern Galicia. In the process, Kolomea fell on 16 February; Czernovitz, the capital city of Bukovina, followed on 17 February; Stanislau on 20 February.[12]

After capturing Stanislau, Pflanzer-Baltin's left flank group shifted to relieve enemy pressure against the South Army's rear area and to assist its escape from the mountains. Indications abounded, however, of the enemy assembling strong forces nearby, signaling the preparation of a czarist counterattack. The enemy quickly reacted to the military threat posed by Army Group Pflanzer-Baltin's successes by assembling a new Ninth Army to retaliate. The superior czarist railroad lines enabled the rapid transfer of significant troop numbers to reinforce threatened Russian positions. The Habsburg's limited railroad situation and extreme time pressure relative to Fortress Przemyśl forced General Conrad to transfer troops to the Third Army right flank area, rather than Pflanzer-Baltin. One of their offensive missions involved drawing additional Russian forces into the mountains to enable Pflanzer-Baltin's successful efforts to continue.

Second Army headquarters requested the attack set for 22 February toward Lupkov be postponed because deteriorating roads interfered with the Third Army's assault toward Mezölaborcz.[13] On 22 February, instructions to Attack Group Tersztyánsky emphasized that the threat to Fortress Przemyśl made a military success imperative. Second Army must attack and cooperate with a simultaneous fortress breakout effort toward it.[14] The serious time constraints forced the launching of the offensive before all designated units had assembled. The Habsburg army would have neither the matériel nor the manpower necessary to accomplish its mission. Severe weather warnings went unheeded, causing undue suffering for the war-weary soldiers. Not until 24 February would heavy artillery batteries be ordered forward, but few were actually moved to the high mountain front.

On 22 February a key half-kilometer stretch of road was washed away, preventing the 27th Infantry Division units from reaching their designated deployment area. The following day the road to Takcsany, a major supply depot, closed, forcing the 41st *Honvéd* Infantry Division to utilize a detour march route.[15] Horses sank in the mud; many died from exhaustion while attempting to extricate themselves. Carts and wagons bogged down to their axles. Constant stoppages forced units to halt for long periods of time. In preparation for the impending attack, ultimately postponed until 27 February, new infantry units advanced only six kilometers on 22 February, followed by twelve over the next two days. Some units received orders to leave supply wagons in rear echelon areas except those transporting food provisions.

In view of the calamitous supply situation, the General Staff Railroad Bureau commenced closely monitoring supply train movement along the routes most crucial for the impending offensive. One meter of new snow fell in higher elevations. Then on 24 February a Railroad Bureau expositor report warned that the Takcsany–Zemplenoroszi supply route, particularly at a serpentine section of the road, was impassable and would be unusable for days. The Railroad Bureau complained that the number of road maintenance crews were inadequate to perform the Herculean task. If additional workers were not available soon, combat units would be utilized to perform emergency road maintenance. The success of the campaign hinged on the maintenance of supply routes.[16]

Meanwhile, the Germans planned their own preemptive strike against the massed Romanov armies on the Northwest front. The entire German strategic reserve consisted of three reserve and one regular army corps transferred from the Western front. By the end of January 1915, the Teutonic Eighth and Ninth Armies had established defensive positions in Poland. The ensuing Second Battle of the Masurian Lakes commenced during an intense day-long blizzard. Meter-deep, wind-whipped snow created man-sized snowdrifts. As with the Carpathian campaign, most German supplies and reserve ammunition remained rearward, snowbound at railroad depots. Yet because of the severe weather conditions, it proved a perfect time to launch the attack, as it caught the Russians by surprise. The ongoing Habsburg military crisis prompted the German decision to concentrate their strategic reserve in the east for a major offensive against the Russians to relieve the pressure on their ally.

Intercepted Russian communications alerted German Eastern Command of the enemy's intention to invade Prussia and create a new army somewhat further south. The Germans thus advanced their timetable to disrupt the czarist intentions. The immediate German objective became to neutralize the Russian Tenth Army, presently deployed forward of the Angerapp Lake line, which had become isolated from its neighboring units. Between 6 and 7 February, czarist Tenth Army forces, oblivious to the impending attack, shoveled snow from their positions. On 7 February, a German Tenth Army hammer blow drove the startled Russian covering forces rearward, threatening its potential retreat route to the Augustov forest. The Germans then struck the czarist flank.

The Second Battle of the Masurian Lakes attained its primary objective of purging East Prussia of enemy presence. Another Russian army had almost been destroyed and significant troop numbers taken prisoner. The military success, though a tactical one, did not produce the required strategic victory and depleted the German strategic reserve. German forces, bogged down by the weather conditions, terminated the offensive effort because of the breakdown in communications, the serious supply problems, and general troop exhaustion. The troops had reached the end of human endurance.[17]

In the following month, Grand Duke Nicholas and The Russian High Command (*Stavka*) would support launching a renewed czarist offensive in the Carpathian Mountains under pressure from General Ivanov, the front commander. The failure to gain a military decision on the German front partly influenced the Russian decision. Also influencing their decision making was the fact that a major victory over the Dual Monarchy might incite Italy and Romania to join the Entente war effort. The factor of neutral states was also a major determinant in Conrad's Carpathian Mountain adventures.

Returning to the Carpathian Mountain theater, Habsburg Supreme Command anticipated that the Russians planned to launch an offensive through the mountains to invade Hungary, which placed the Habsburg Second Army commander in a daunting situation. The present successful Russian advance had to be halted. The XVII Corps, its capabilities and numbers diminished by earlier fruitless attacks, received orders to defend its positions on 16 February and then prepare to resume its attack the next day in cooperation with the Third Army offensive. A fierce enemy attack, however, forced the corps to retreat instead. In the meantime, the warmer temperatures created swollen waterways and impaired movement on the washed-out roadbeds.

Meanwhile, well before the Second Army offensive commenced, the escalating Third Army left-flank crisis forced the diversion of in transit Second Army reinforcements to that hard-pressed front. At the extreme western left flank, 16,900 XIX Corps soldiers countered 28,000 enemy troops.[18] These unfavorable numbers necessitated a speedy redirection of two infantry divisions from the Second Army front, the 41st *Honvéd* (20 February) and the 27th Division (23 February), to the endangered sector.

Renewed enemy assaults in the Cisna–Baligrod vicinity resulted in further serious battle. The enemy continued its onslaught against the XIX

Corps along both sides of the vital Baligrod–Cisna roads, steadily intensifying its desperate tactical situation. The corps became incapable of warding
off further czarist attacks. Its divisions retreated without any serious enemy
pressure.[19] Between 12 and 14 February the corps reported 27 officers and
1,138 troops sick or wounded. 43rd Infantry Division reported only 2,820
troops remaining, and the 34th, 3,200.[20] General Böhm-Ermolli's first order
exhorted the faltering XIX Corps and Group Szurmay to maintain their
positions; he then ordered V and XVIII Corps to retake their previously occupied positions south of the San River, once sufficient reinforcements had
arrived.[21]

On 15 February a Corps Hofmann (Army Group Pflanzer-Baltin) report
relative to the condition of its troops emphasized their constant close contact with the enemy and their having reached the extreme parameters of
their physical capacities. Furthermore, casualties from illness, frostbite, and
battle had reduced the battle stands to a minimum and negatively affected
morale.[22] Officer and noncommissioned officer losses led to their lesser presence at the front. Many *Landsturm* and reserve troop units lacked effective
leadership, and some were no longer capable of offensive action.

By 16 February General Böhm-Ermolli concentrated on consolidating
his battlefront and avoiding piecemeal insertion of reinforcements into the
front lines.[23] March (replacement) formations received transport priority
over new troop entities. General Böhm-Ermolli, in an attempt to rectify the
serious numerical deficiency in artillery, ordered the numerous batteries behind the main mountain ridgelines be brought forward. He set 19 February
as his offensive launch date.

Russian heavy artillery began firing on the sensitive Wola Michova
transportation area. The defending corps sustained an additional 10 percent casualties, while the X and XVII Corps also reported serious losses.[24]
An enemy attack pierced the front between V Corps and Group Szurmay,
forcing the V and XVIII Corps to retreat. Fourth Army must, if necessary,
launch a relieving attack to assist its neighboring army.[25] Its IX Corps was
ordered to launch an attack on 17 February despite the weather and terrain
difficulties.[26] Serious problems had occurred already in the approach march
as high water levels dogged the troops as they crossed numerous water lines.
Attack routes were turned into pits of mud.

The unfavorable troop conditions were well documented. On 17 February, numerous corps commanders reported their troops were exhausted and
apathetic. The adverse conditions that existed in early February persisted,
further diminishing troop numbers. The Carpathian mountain terrain limited observation in the forward areas. Casualties increased as ammunition

supplies became depleted. Additional howitzer shells and heavy howitzers were desperately needed.[27]

Poor communication and lack of liaison between units produced battlefield confusion and numerous uncoordinated counterattacks, which the Russians easily rebuffed. The few arriving reinforcements, hurled into the melee under no artillery support, failed to stem the Russian tide. Repeated enemy blows forced a XIX Corps retreat, creating a ripple effect along the entire front. Only significant reinforcements could stabilize the reeling Habsburg front. However, the last available troops had been inserted into the front lines, and Habsburg resistance verged on collapse.[28]

The multiple communication problems supported the argument to reduce the scope of the Second Army offensive to both sides of the Baligrod roads. Narrowing the width of the attack front also provided the advantage of the San and Solinka rivers, forming protective flank barriers for the advancing troops. It also appeared to offer more favorable ridgeline objectives for the advance. Yet potential danger existed at the Second Army right flank area. The addition of three recently arrived infantry divisions would assist in reconquering the Lupkov small-gauge railroad line.

Again, as early as 16 February, General Böhm-Ermolli ordered all available artillery batteries to the front. Meanwhile, various batteries that already arrived had not been positioned where ordered. Only Group Szurmay found most of its assigned artillery properly positioned before the offensive, partly because its terrain was more favorable for gun placement. However, most batteries remained several days' march behind the main mountain ridges. The repeated argument that heavy howitzer artillery placement in mountain terrain was difficult, if not impossible, was later contradicted under far worse conditions in the Italian Alps, where successful placement of artillery was accomplished, albeit with tremendous effort.

General Conrad pressured Böhm-Ermolli to launch a decisive offensive along the shortest route to the beleaguered fortress. This frontal attack had neither adequate material preparation nor all of its divisions inserted into the battle line. Missing artillery batteries would not be ordered to the front until 24 February, some arriving on 27 February.

XIX Corps, its left flank now reinforced by the 41st *Honvéd* Infantry Division, would initiate the Second Army offensive. Its attack direction toward Lupkov was perceived to be the enemy's most vulnerable position. The 19 February launch date was postponed to the next day. The corps' objective became to regain the dominant terrain, where it offered the Russians little advantage, then attack Mezőlaborcz.[29] Meanwhile, the corps received a brief respite when the enemy halted its attacks to recuperate from its own severe losses. X Corps' 24th and 34th Infantry Divisions received orders to support the XIX Corps' offensive effort.[30] Wary of the escalating danger of an enemy breakthrough between the V Corps and Group Szurmay's northern flank, VII Corps must continue to bind enemy forces and attack to seize terrain, but the corps failed to advance (X and VII Corps had the mission to seize the Lupkov area). III Corps must demonstrate to draw enemy attention from the main battle area. As the 27th, 32nd, and 38th Infantry Divisions arrived to reinforce Second Army efforts, Fourth Army's IX Corps (13th and 26th Infantry Divisions) planned attack achieved slow, insignificant gains against strong enemy positions.[31] Multiple units requisitioned additional artillery and shells, requesting that their attack await proper artillery support. Numerous batteries reported that many guns had ceased to function and that howitzer shells were necessary to neutralize enemy defensive positions.

Conrad ordered that reserve forces be utilized to maintain attack momentum once the offensive was launched and that Second Army should not await the late arrival of supporting infantry division units before launching its effort. Such pressure stemmed partially from intelligence reports that indicated that four czarist siege divisions had been transferred from the Fortress Przemyśl arena to the Carpathian front. Further slaughter of fortress horses extended food rations a few more days. Any additional decrease in food portions would not only endanger the troops' physical well-being, but further reduce their ability to perform their duties—and, as a result of the horse slaughter, lessen the fortress's remaining maneuver capabilities. Early February witnessed a sharp decline in garrison combat worthiness. Sickness had become rampant, and deaths caused by severe exhaustion escalated. Fortress food supplies would last until 16 March, a fact that increased the pressure to launch a relieving offensive as soon as possible.[32] However, the time of year was obviously not conducive for such a military endeavor.

General Metzger, chief of the Habsburg Operations Bureau, discussed the approaching offensive via field radio with the Second Army chief of staff, General Bardolff. Metzger claimed that pressure to attack did not result from the critical Fortress Przemyśl situation, but nevertheless, the offensive should be launched as soon as possible. Above all, Second Army should not await the arrival of the 31st Infantry Division, but rather redesignate it a reserve unit.[33]

The Second Army offensive launch date depended on the military situation at Lupkov; therefore, its attack front was extended to include the XVIII Corps middle and right flank forces and even V Corps.[34] Argument held that if the offensive did not also include Lisko–Ustrzyki Dolne and Fortress

Przemyśl, the enemy could attack the isolated South Army and Army Group Pflanzer-Baltin. The obsession to liberate Fortress Przemyśl bestowed on the Second Army the formidable task of launching an offensive on a constricted twelve-kilometer front and attempting to seize the enemy's most developed defensive positions on the dominating terrain at Zebrak and Chrysczczata.

Bitterly cold nights, combined with wet conditions, took a heavy toll on the troops' health. Every day thousands fell ill, suffered from frostbite, or succumbed to exposure; losses to illness doubled. The problem of maintaining an adequate flow of supplies also remained unresolved. Labor crews had to maintain the main supply route, Nagypolany–Zemplenoroszi–Cisna.[35] Draft animals, 1,650 in all, were transported into the mountains to assist in restoring the disabled supply system. The terrible road conditions led to confrontations between the multiple units seeking to utilize the same routes. The 31st, 32nd, and 38th Infantry Divisions were delayed in reaching the Second Army front and were unavailable to participate in the initial phase of the campaign.[36] Meanwhile, the enemy extended powerful attacks to the Third Army front and Beskid ridges. Reinforcements were a dire necessity, but why had they not been dispatched earlier?

On 19 February South Army's 19th Infantry Division reputedly could not conduct offensive operations. Low troop morale resulted from soldiers suffering from extreme exhaustion verging on physical collapse. Casualties, illness, and frostbite cases had taken a heavy toll after six days of uninterrupted battle. The division's capabilities had declined so disastrously that it could not repel a serious enemy attack.

The order to launch the 20 February offensive emphasized that Third Army must participate for Second Army to succeed. Third Army's mission remained unchanged while the main Second Army offensive forces would attack along the Baligrod roads toward Lisko. The initial military objective remained the area of Lisko–Ustrzyki Dolne to interrupt the crucial Russian east–west railroad line. Advancing Habsburg forces should draw numerous czarist troops, preventing increased Russian numbers from being deployed against South Army and Army Group Pflanzer-Baltin. These two armies would join the offensive action once they had received adequate reinforcements. Fourth Army's XI Corps (15th and 30th Infantry Divisions) and First Army's 5th Infantry Division were transferred to Army Group Pflanzer-Baltin, whereupon the group commander shifted two infantry and one cavalry division to assist South Army efforts to extricate itself from the mountains.[37] The Russians, perceiving Habsburg intentions, hurled significant formations against South Army, while the new Russian Ninth Army deployed against Army Group Pflanzer-Baltin to halt its victory train. South

Army remained entrapped in the mountains and the Army Group's efforts soon became crippled by strong enemy countermeasures.

The Second Army offensive, now postponed until 22 February, would drive a wedge deep into the enemy front. However, a major disadvantage appeared once progress had been achieved. Both flanks became more exposed to potential enemy activity, particularly in the Oslava Valley and Wola Michova area. Thus, a swift enemy counterstroke to cripple any progress must be expected.

Second Army priority remained to prevent a Fortress Przemyśl capitulation. XIX Corps must reconquer Lupkov by 22 February while 41st *Honvéd* Infantry Division defended the critical left flank area, where the enemy posed the greatest threat to the operation. The *Honvéd* division launched an attack without artillery support because of rain and poor visibility.[38] At the opposite Second Army flank, the gap between the V and XVIII Corps had been sealed. Coinciding with the arrival of replacement troops, a V Corps division (37th *Honvéd* Infantry Division) attained the San River and reestablished contact with XVIII Corps' right flank units.[39]

Any Third Army chance of reconquering the Mezölaborcz–Lupkov area disappeared when the enemy unexpectedly launched a general offensive against the army, again battering X Corps. If Third Army had no chance of regaining the crucial Mezölaborcz area, it served no purpose to launch a Second Army attack because it would invite swift enemy retaliation before Habsburg reinforcements could intervene in the battle. General Boroević informed Böhm-Ermolli on 20 February that he thought it doubtful that his forces could reach Mezölaborcz, partly because of the impassable conditions on the sole connecting road, whose side arteries had deteriorated so badly that his army could not launch its assault because it could not be resupplied. This upset Second Army command because Boroević's effort was vital for achieving military success.[40]

Böhm-Ermolli favored postponing the offensive until better weather conditions prevailed.[41] However, General Conrad, cognizant of Fortress Przemyśl's deteriorating situation, demanded that the offensive be launched without delay. Realizing that a Third Army attack was no longer feasible, he proposed to launch a left flank attack toward Chrysczczata to seize the railroad stretch north of Lupkov to threaten Russian rear echelon formations and force a czarist retreat. Unfavorable conditions continued on 21 February, as Second Army accelerated preparations for its offensive and XIX Corps commenced its advance.[42]

Second Army logbook entries revealed that on 21 February, Field Cannon Regiment 24's movement into the mountain terrain was hampered by the poor condition of the overused roads. XVIII Corps requested modern 15-centimeter howitzers or 10-centimeter cannons to counter the effects of "superior" enemy artillery, but, as with so many such requests for additional artillery units, they fell on deaf ears. The corps logbook also revealed that five artillery batteries and several major supply train sections remained below the mountain ridges.[43] Multiple corps logbooks continued to record complaints about the lack of sufficient artillery.

Excerpts from a X Corps manuscript in the Vienna War Archives provide a glimpse into the events leading up to the second Carpathian offensive. The author, the chief of staff of the Corps, wrote: "It is always the same events. In the beginning there is an attitude of 'hurray!' Then neighboring units balk, followed by the inevitable reversals, retreats and rehabilitation, demoralizing the neighboring units."[44] Meanwhile, the offensive timetable adjusted to coincide with the arrival of the IV Corps' 32nd Infantry Division into the area of Cisna (anticipated on 26 February), and in transit 27th and 32nd Infantry Divisions. On 23 February impassable conditions continued to plague the single supply route.[45]

A V Corps report complained about the inferior training and moral worth of arriving replacement troops—thus their limited battle worthiness.[46] Böhm-Ermolli, like Boroević, insisted that replacement troops fill the widening gaps in the lines because of excessive losses.[47] Third Army X Corps repelled renewed enemy breakthrough attempts in the blood-soaked Laborcz Valley.[48] Inclement weather conditions continued to frustrate Habsburg military efforts. Along the supply route, rising floodwaters threatened to wash out bridges, and the important Cisna road had become a vast expanse of mud. Close to half a kilometer of the route had been washed away; keeping supply lines functioning continued to be a futile effort.[49]

On 22 February, Attack Group Tersztyánsky received orders emphasizing that its achieving success was essential relative to Fortress Przemyśl.[50] The five-division XIX Corps (27th, 29th, 34th, 41st, and 43rd Infantry Divisions) transferred to General Tersztyánsky's command. As the offensive launch date fluctuated because of the horrendous overall conditions, the Russians remained ensconced in their strong defensive positions, posing a serious threat to the area of Wola Michova, which, if compromised, could cripple Second Army efforts.[51]

The lack of rifles attained crisis proportions as wounded soldiers abandoned their weapons on the battlefield. Emergency measures became necessary to conserve arms as IX March Brigade troops could not dispatch to the front before May because of the weapon shortage. Rifle training was often performed with wooden staffs, with actual weapons issued just before dispatch to the front. Wounded soldiers were ordered to retain their weapons, but many rifles disappeared on the way to the medical aid stations.[52]

Third Army command announced that its inadequate troop stands and the debilitated state of its men rendered them incapable of performing their ambitious missions. The 1914 Habsburg Imperial and Royal Army had long since perished on the battlefields of Lemberg, Ivangorod, Limanova-Lapanov, Serbia, and now the Carpathian Mountains. By early 1915 most front-line troops consisted of either older *Landsturm* or younger drafted soldiers. Possessing only the most rudimentary training, many conscripts soon met their fate. The escalating number of unseasoned soldiers in the front lines also catapulted the nationality problem into the foreground, threatening the cohesiveness of Habsburg fighting forces. Antidynastic and antimilitary propaganda spread through reserve officers, Czechs in particular.

A XVII Corps report depicted poorly executed marches that created serious delays in schedules. Many units, particularly March battalions, proved incapable of performing the demanding treks to the front. Rehabilitation of XIX Corps' 43rd Infantry Division had become a necessity.[53] Relative to the inadequate communication, telegrams arrived up to six hours after dispatch. Deciphering them lost further precious time.[54] The overexertion and undernourishment of pack animals further hampered transporting artillery over mountainous terrain, which remained ice-covered and slippery.

Only heavy-caliber guns could penetrate the well-dug-in Russian emplacements, so numerous batteries were ordered forward as fast as possible. Key road stretches continued to pose serious problems for efficient traffic flow. Some batteries arrived by 26 February, but too late to support the initial offensive action. In preoffensive planning, artillery preparation and gun emplacements had been scheduled for 25 February, with all batteries placed into firing position by the night of 26 February. Supporting barrages would begin at daybreak on 27 February when the offensive commenced.[55]

Arriving at the front just thirty-six hours before the operation, Attack Group Commander Tersztyánsky witnessed the supply roads' wretched conditions. Multiple supply train wagons were stuck in the mud; horse carcasses littered the long road. Thousands of exhausted laborers worked feverishly to maintain the ravaged roadway.[56] Many improvised methods were utilized in an effort to improve the dire situation.

The following day, a mixture of rain and snow further inundated the valleys. Sections of the Cisna roadway remained eroded or washed away. At one location, one and a half kilometers of roadway had been destroyed.[57] Multiple dispatches emphasized the critical supply situation. Meanwhile, the final offensive disposition was issued on 24 February. XIX Corps must attack toward Lupkov on 26 February, while the major Baligrod roads operation would commence on 27 February.[58]

On 23 February, Third Army issued directives that X Corps' 24th Infantry Division advance toward Mezölaborcz while its right flank units maintained liaison with Second Army's left flank 34th Infantry Division advancing toward Lupkov. Group Krautwald (X Corps, 2nd, 21st, and 45th Infantry Divisions), would attack on 25 February in the Laborcz Valley. Group Joseph (VII Corps) would advance while Group Kritek (11th Infantry Division and Group Berndt cavalry forces) and III Corps maintained their present positions.[59]

The Second Army numbered 99,852 rifles while anticipating the arrival of replacement formations within a few days. Its troops' physical condition, however, had deteriorated. Three times the number of veteran troops reported to sick call as just-arrived soldiers. Army health reports indicated the preponderance of bronchial and intestinal illness and frostbite cases.[60]

General Tersztyánsky's orders for the campaign provide an interesting insight into the mounting pressure to launch the offensive.[61] The urgency of liberating Fortress Przemyśl remained paramount, but the increasing threat of Italian intervention also demanded a rapid military victory over the Russians. Urged on by the battle cry "Free Przemyśl!" and unrelenting Habsburg Supreme Command pressure, the troops were driven to the limit of physical and mental endurance even before the campaign commenced. A swift offensive stroke must prevent the enemy from transferring reinforcements to the battlefront, while a Fortress Przemyśl report estimated that the fortress's food stores would last until 12 March, increasing the urgency for its immediate rescue.[62]

In addition, the surrender of Fortress Przemyśl would free Russian siege troops for transfer to the teetering Carpathian front, as well as representing a major military defeat. Numerous documents from the last two weeks of February 1915 emphasized that a military action must begin before the onset of the spring rainy season. The fortress remained 100 kilometers away, which explains initiating the offensive before assembly of the entire attack group had been completed. The northern Third Army front consisted of only 21,300 troops, of which 8,600 protected the vital Wola Michova area. Fresh troops, 9,400 in all, stretched across a twenty-kilometer front. Two in-transit divisions would reinforce these insufficient numbers.[63]

With the offensive launch date rapidly approaching, General Staff Railroad Bureau officials' priority was to transport the five infantry divisions designated to reinforce the main offensive group while facing the typical problems associated with maintaining a regular supply movement. The five divisions (13th, 27th, 31st, 32nd, and 38th Infantry Divisions), however, did not reach their deployment areas in time to participate in the operation. As the 13th and 38th Infantry Divisions detrained in their staging area, 32nd Infantry Division vanguard units began arriving while 27th Infantry Division remained in rail transit, with the 31st Infantry Division also arriving into its rear echelon area.[64] To compound preoffensive difficulties, the arrival of these divisions in the army's rear echelons created chaos. Meanwhile, intelligence reports indicated that significant enemy troop concentrations had deployed at the extreme Second Army left flank positions, while Pflanzer-Baltin reported that his group also encountered large enemy formations.

Weather conditions continued to delay offensive preparations, which were already two days behind the original scheduled jump-off. An additional meter of snow fell on high terrain.[65] Thus, launching the offensive on 24, 25, or 26 February proved impractical. These difficulties would have made any offensive attempt at that time a catastrophic sacrifice. A lack of engineering technical crews had a negative effect, and after fourteen days of deplorable road conditions, transport difficulties only worsened. An unimaginable number of horses collapsed from sheer exhaustion and starvation because hay supplies had been depleted; oats would soon follow.

The abominable conditions caused traffic directed toward the Takcsany depot to grind to a halt. The critical roadway segment between two villages remained impassable to the frontier ridges for days at a time, and the route to Cisna was barely usable. Combat troops had to transport ammunition and provisions. The offensive's success depended on regular traffic flow on the Takcsany–Baligrod roads.[66] Flooding and concomitant bridge damage continued to negatively affect operations in the Ondava and Laborcz valleys. Material preparations for the offensive were described as "downright pitiful."[67]

Emergency requests were repeatedly dispatched for additional labor detachments, partly to relieve exhausted work crews who worked ten- to twelve-hour days and often late into the night close to the front area.[68] Fatigue had long been the norm for such workers, causing a corresponding decline in health and physical conditions. Daily status reports indicated an average of 40 to 50 incapacitated men from a total of 320. Thousands of civilian workers and prisoners of war worked in nonendangered areas.[69]

A 24 February Takcsany Expositor report emphasized the impassable supply roads in a critical area for the offensive. In addition, IV Corps' 32nd Infantry Division vanguard train columns had been halted since 8:00 A.M. A forty-eight-hour pause must be granted to restore supply routes and service in the most deplorable state. During this two-day period, roads must remain closed to allow the emergency repair services.[70] Thus, combat units had to improvise ammunition and food supply transport.

Meanwhile, along the critical road stretch Takcsany–Nagypolany, the late-arriving 32nd Infantry Division supply train personnel toiled to keep that section open.[71] A report indicated that some improvements had been accomplished along the vital supply routes, which caused Conrad to urge launching the offensive as soon as possible. Attack Group Commander Tersztyánsky, however, insisted on testing his repaired supply apparatus for an additional day because of the recent supply difficulties and availability of a mere three-day accumulation of supplies.[72]

On 25 February, as the designated attack formations fine-tuned final adjustments for their mission, they still lacked three infantry divisions. Just the 13th, 31st, and 32nd Infantry Division vanguard units were available. XVII Corps' 45th Infantry Division's delay resulted from march difficulties.[73] At this optimal point, General Böhm-Ermolli discovered the absence of sufficient artillery battery emplacements for a successful offensive. At the last moment, he demanded that additional units be transported forward, particularly to the army's western flank positions. Thus, on 26 February several batteries were ordered to advance to Cisna by 1 and 2 March, but multiple batteries remained idle while a shell shortage persisted at the front.[74] Because heavy howitzer batteries remained in rear echelon areas, enemy artillery dominated the battlefield, and the solid czarist positions remained untouched.[75] Units had to continue to utilize their own means to transport ammunition supplies to their front.[76]

All activity on the major offensive supply thoroughfare ceased from 1800 hours on 26 February to 1800 hours the next day. Thus, when the roads could again handle two-way traffic on 27 February, the Second Army offensive was ordered to commence.[77] Meanwhile, on 26 February Third Army Commander Boroević announced that its attack must be delayed, and thus the main endeavor was rescheduled for 28 February. On 27 February, Third Army would demonstrate along its front. X and VII Corps with a XVII Corps division would launch an attack. Army reports indicated that 66 percent of the army's manpower and 75 percent of its horses remained without cover.[78] South Army launched a corps-size (XXIV) enveloping attack against strong opposing enemy positions, and the Fourth Army prepared to initiate a right flank advance.[79]

Also on 26 February, General Tersztyánsky assumed command of the XIX and XVIII Corps deployed in the Second Army right flank area at the Solinka River. A Third Army advance along the Beskid and Magura ridges

would have assisted Second Army left flank unit efforts to regain the Lupkov railroad line. The five-division XIX Corps must seize the heights of
the narrow Dzial ridges and Beskid Mountain crest,[80] with its initial efforts requiring close cooperation with Third Army X Corps. However, little
consideration was given to the fact that X Corps remained in a weakened
condition. Its 2nd Infantry Division numbered 1,778 men, and 24th Infantry Division, 2,884 troops; thus, the two equaled one third of a full-stand
division.[81]

Ultimately, Second Army's offensive failed because it lacked sufficient
numbers to assure success, although on 25 and 26 February March Brigade
replacement formations arrived, and half of the scheduled VII March Battalions was scheduled to arrive on 1 March.[82] The final offensive grouping
would be completed when much of the 27th Infantry Division and a portion
of the 32nd and 43rd Infantry Divisions moved into the front lines. Contingents from the 13th and 31st divisions arrived after multiple rail delays.
Their remaining units would arrive with the remainder of the 27th Infantry
Division on 1 March.[83]

Conrad pressured Fourth Army to launch an attack to relieve pressure
on the Third Army northern flank. But Fourth Army staff argued against
striking in the Gorlice area because the troops would encounter strong czarist fortified positions and sustain enormous casualties.[84] Then, during the
next two weeks, the Russians launched forays into the sensitive inner flank
area of Third and Fourth Army, which smashed those defensive lines until
they almost collapsed.

Both Second and Fourth Army commanders attempted to convince Conrad to transfer reinforcements to Army Group Pflanzer-Baltin's front to
supplement his heretofore successful campaign, thus transferring the onus
to achieve success to him. Conrad responded that the Army Group could
neither be reinforced nor advance quickly enough. In addition, the Russians
continued to reinforce their vulnerable flank area against the army group,
threatening its continued progress.

On 27 February a weak six-division assault force commenced its difficult mission. However, the return of warm temperatures again transformed
the single available supply line into a sea of mud, hampering normal supply efforts, and Second Army soon encountered strong enemy resistance.
Various units became separated in wooded valleys and along mountain
slopes, resulting in numerous uncoordinated and isolated battles. The terrain's narrow roadways hampered operational movement. Repeated orders
to press the attack despite the overwhelming obstacles indicated Fortress

Przemyśl's pervasive influence on field operations. Pressure to liberate the fortress shaped General Conrad's military planning until its surrender on 22 March 1915. He calculated that his momentary numerical superiority, the first in any major Habsburg campaign, countered thirty and a half czarist divisions. Russian numbers gradually increased until they equaled, then surpassed, Second Army troop stands.

XVIII Corps (adjacent to XIX Corps) undertook efforts to improve its positions. V Corps launched short assaults, while a detachment prepared to cross the swollen San River. They soon encountered strong enemy positions protected by several rows of barbed wire. The weakened VII Corps' 20th *Honvéd* Infantry Division, with 5,000 reinforcements, would attack. Group Szurmay (the Army's extreme right flank) must "unconditionally hold its lines."[85]

XIX Corps' assault produced unexpected gains: the 41st *Honvéd* Infantry Division, after traversing very difficult snow-covered terrain, seized a portion of the dominating Magurczyne position. Other Habsburg battlefield reports were far less encouraging. Little progress transpired along the Baligrod roads (the major offensive effort), and various attempts to advance created gaps between units.[86]

Corps Schmidt commenced its advance with only brigade-size units of the 27th and 32nd Infantry Divisions, insufficient to render a notable success. Third Army finally joined the Second Army offensive efforts. When XVII Corps' 45th Infantry Division advanced, fierce battle erupted. Artillery fire reverberated throughout the Laborcz Valley as VII Corps attempted to advance over the forward ridges.[87]

Attacks continued on 1 March where earlier battle had proven successful while inserting the few reserve troops. Because field commanders could not rely on receiving adequate reinforcements, they had to pin their hopes for victory on their present troop numbers. The tardy arrival of several divisions designated for the offensive signified that weaker forces launched the difficult missions.

In the meantime, the main XIX Corps attack force (29th, 34th, and 41st Infantry Divisions) continued its advance, while the Magurczyne position and surrounding high terrain received technical reinforcement, which proved difficult to overcome. Several rows of barbed wire made the approach to the Russian positions even more problematic because the enemy had entrenched itself in several reinforced lines. The 29th and 41st *Honvéd* Infantry Divisions encountered strong enemy positions. The 34th and portions of the 29th encountered lighter resistance. XIX Corps troops encircled

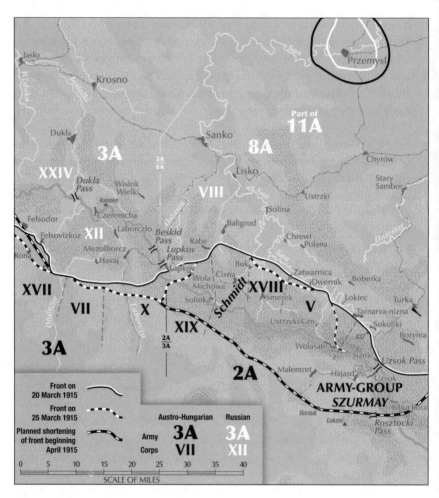

Map 8. Military Situation Second Half of March 1915

the enemy positions at Magurczyne, then 41st *Honvéd* Infantry Division
stormed the main position three times, each attempt halted by flanking enemy artillery fire.[88]

Overpowering the strong enemy defensive positions appeared unthink-
able, considering the battle-weakened condition of the attacking troops and
lack of effective artillery support. The available artillery batteries contained
a majority of light-caliber guns with limited stores of shells, but significant
artillery preparation against the strong enemy positions was imperative
for the Second Army to advance. Without it, the infantry again made the

Table 4. Artillery Pieces per Kilometer of Front

Units	Front (in km)	Guns	Guns per km
XIX Corps	8	50	6
Corps Schmidt	12	74	6
XVIII Corps	8	56	7
V Corps	20	38	1.8
Group Szurmay	28	220	8

Source: KAN, B/23, Mayern, 2. *Armee im Karpatenschlacht.*

ultimate sacrifice. XIX Corps, for example, counted just three cannon batteries in the combat area. Table 4 lists artillery pieces per kilometer of front, showing just how little support was available for the infantry.

Terrain and supply traffic difficulties continued to affect operations. The supply route between Rostocki Górne and Nagypolany finally became capable of two-way traffic, but this was negated in part by the pressing necessity to repair other supply route sections.[89] Nevertheless, the offensive continued. Second and Third Armies reported limited progress, while the Fourth Army's anticipated attack to relieve enemy pressure against Third Army's northern flank was canceled. Fourth Army launched a diversionary strike from the Second Army main effort on 6 March—over a week later than planned, and too late to affect Second Army efforts. One participant in the events explained, "On March 1 fog and heavy snow is falling. We are losing all sense of direction. Entire regiments are getting lost, resulting in tremendous casualties. On 6 March there was a complete change in the weather; clear skies, thaw during the day and −20°C overnight, causing the slopes to ice over."[90]

The Russian High Command had meanwhile ordered reinforcements to its threatened left flank area. On 1 March, the newly created Russian Ninth Army launched an overwhelming four-corps attack against Army Group Pflanzer-Baltin's right flank positions, forcing its troops to abandon them. The reinforcing XI Corps, set to arrive on 4 March, needed to cement a new defensive front. The enemy advanced into the northern Bukovina as far as the Pruth River. Thus, as Second Army launched its offensive, the previously victorious Army Group's success had been halted. When the enemy changed its *Chriffre* (decipher) key, the Army Group broke it and could ascertain czarist intentions beforehand and react accordingly.

The recently deployed XIII Corp on Pflanzer-Baltin's front discovered superior enemy numbers opposing it.[91] General Letschitzki's Ninth Army launched a general attack to protect its threatened extreme flank area and expedite a major attack launched further west. The Russians intended to sever General Pflanzer-Baltin's forces from the Carpathian Mountains and catch and destroy them. The czarist XVII and XXX Corps assaulted westward, while XI Corps advanced southward. Meanwhile, Habsburg XIII Corps northern flank positions were attacked as a major force struck the flank and rear of Corps Czibulka, threatening to cross the Dniester River.

General Pflanzer-Baltin prepared a middle group of two infantry and two cavalry divisions to disrupt czarist railroad lines, particularly in the Stryj River area, and prevent an enemy crossing of the Dniester River. On the opposite flank, the battered XIII Corps defended the Lomnica River line.[92] The newly formed Habsburg cavalry Group Marschall's intended offensive at the XIII Corps' northern flank was delayed on 27 February. Meanwhile, Russian pressure forced XIII Corps defenders north of Stanislau to retreat. Another enemy column crossed the Lomnica River and broke through Corps Czibulka and Group Marschall fronts on 28 February. Army Group Pflanzer-Baltin's situation had also become critical. Its commander doubled his efforts to prevent a Russian crossing of the Dniester River, although his defending troops' flank and rear positions were threatened. XI Corps vanguard troops would soon arrive, followed by the German 5th and Austro-Hungarian 6th Cavalry Divisions.

An example of problems encountered on the mountain front may be seen from the following artillery captain's diary excerpts. His guns had to be transported over mountain terrain blanketed by a meter of drifting snow. When snow melted, the few navigable roads became swampy.[93] Weakened and exhausted horses and artillerists traversed the wretched, inhospitable terrain. The steep snow-covered slopes raised the threat of possible avalanches. Multiple supply route segments were too narrow to allow artillery passage, while others traversed deep segmented brooks with ice-covered banks without bridges. Travel required ropes because wagon wheels became suspended over precipices. Fourteen horses were necessary to pull one gun or an ammunition wagon.[94]

When the artillery unit arrived in Lopienka, men and horses immediately collapsed. All sank into the snow and drifted into death-like sleep. It had required forty-eight hours to traverse forty kilometers (the first twelve hours entailed twenty-five kilometers to Cisna, the remaining nine, twenty-four hours). There had been no sleep for the men for ten hours.[95]

Company losses included three dead, nine wounded, twenty-seven with dysentery, twelve with typhus, fifty-seven with severe diarrhea, and three with frostbite. Yet the infantry suffered more than any other troops and remained barely battle worthy. The soldiers ate half-cooked meat and cold preserved canned food. They drank melted snow that trickled down from a cemetery above them, causing a sudden onset of intestinal sickness. From the original 4,000 men, 200 survived after a few days of battle. A large number of casualties resulted from frostbite cases.[96]

In one emotional passage, the author, a horse lover, described how few of the remaining animals could be utilized. At best, just one-third of the horses could march. Many fell ill, struggling against the daily adversities, and were shot when no longer able to perform their duties. The author then related his own personal tragic experience:

My horse, which so often saved my life, should neither be set free to die in misery from hunger along the roads, nor be sent to the so-called "recovery horse hospitals" to then be harnessed to a wagon and driven to death. The course of action that must be taken was quite obvious, but no shot fired in the entire campaign would be as difficult as this one. I readied my pistol; my hand wavered. My thoroughbred, a most noble creature, lay exhausted on the ground. He greeted me with a faint whinnying. . . . I dropped my pistol, but the horse whinnied again, so I raised my weapon and fired. Collapsing in the snow, for only the second time in the war, I wept.

Typical of his diary accounts is the following passage:

There were only 250 *Landsturm* troops and 70 horses remaining. We had to traverse to the next pass, about three kilometers away. Following ceaseless exertion, which brought us to the edge of collapse, the artillery battery arrived at Cisna. We were at the limit of our resistance capabilities and half starved. To our surprise there were neither quarters nor food available for us.[97]

The VII Corps commander, Archduke Joseph, wrote on 28 February:

From Nagyberzseny onwards, more than 1,000 workers are constructing a passable road. Along the way, we advance on the muddy soil very slowly. . . . [There is] extremely fierce machine gun and infantry fire. The 10:00 P.M. report relayed that my troops have entrenched themselves 50 to 200 paces from the enemy's position because they have sustained very serious casualties.[98]

Despite the unrelenting weather conditions, the Second Army offensive continued until 5 March. The 50,000-man assault force achieved little initial progress even though they possessed a numerical advantage. The effort soon appeared doomed, partly as a result of the chronic lack of artillery support. The enemy also sustained enormous losses, which led General Tersztyánsky to speculate that perhaps he could penetrate the Russian defensive lines. He later realized that the twelve-kilometer attack front was too confined to achieve a breakthrough because the enemy rapidly reinforced its front.

In addition to a lack of proper protective uniforms, including their cardboard-soled boots, a repeated complaint emphasized that field overcoats contained a substitute material that inadequately protected against cold, dampness, or wind. Soldiers' extremities became increasingly susceptible to frostbite while the White Death relentlessly claimed many additional lives. On 6 February, for example, Infantry Regiment 7 reported that more than half of its casualties had succumbed to cold-related illnesses. *Jäger* Battalion 9, with 490 infantry remaining, lost 510 men, 45 to frostbite and 115 reported missing, presumed frozen to death. Bosnian-Hercegovinian Regiment 2, with 2,750 soldiers, lost 530, including 100 to frostbite and 100 missing in action. Unit log book entries recorded widespread frostbite. In early February, frigid subzero temperatures claimed the lives of 26 officers and 1,800 men of the Croatian 42nd *Honvéd* Infantry Division in just two days. Half the losses resulted from frostbite, another 25 percent succumbed to the White Death or were listed as missing in action.[99] The 6th Infantry Division incurred 1,000 casualties between 30 January and 4 February, half of which succumbed to cold-related illnesses; others froze to death.[100] These conditions created escalating bitterness toward the *Hinterland,* except toward individual soldiers' families.

Many of the Second Army units (formerly the Third Army eastern flank) suffered from extreme battle fatigue. During the first offensive, Habsburg Third Army divisions had diminished to regiment size and smaller. X Corps continued its attempts to regain the critical Lupkov railroad station, but attacking along the steep, unforested southern slope ridges proved exceedingly difficult.[101]

With Fortress Przemyśl defenders on the verge of starvation, Viennese diplomats voiced concerns relative to Italy entering the war, which could spell disaster for Austria-Hungary. Early March czarist counterattacks forced General Conrad's attention to the Dukla Pass area. He ordered Third Army to seize the pass while Fourth and Third Army inner flank troops pressured the enemy.[102]

While reinforcements were necessary to sustain the Second Army attack on 1 March, multiple 13th and 31st Division units had not arrived on the front. Third Army efforts floundered when its X Corps attack encountered strong Russian positions on the Magura heights, where flanking enemy artillery and machine gun fire produced heavy casualties. Thick fog blanketed the battlefield until noon; then heavy snowfall buried valleys and higher elevations, with temperatures again plummeting to well below freezing.[103] The unrelenting weather conditions prevented effective artillery support for the troops, with the futile infantry attacks producing only additional bloodshed. VII Corps in particular sustained severe losses from launching uncoordinated attacks without adequate artillery support. Subsequent night attacks resulted in little success, but fierce battle erupted at daybreak. Corps casualties listed 271 dead, 805 wounded, and 100 missing in action.[104] The usual communication difficulties also hindered effective action. Group Szurmay, for example, reported that it required twice as long to have telegraph messages deciphered, requiring thirteen hours instead of the customary six![105]

Meanwhile, Army Group Pflanzer-Baltin's XIII Corps military debacle now threatened its rear echelon positions. A retreat order could not be dispatched immediately because corps troops were dispersed throughout the wooded mountain terrain and could not receive the order in time.[106] Reports that the czarist II Cavalry Corps, 11th Infantry Division, and the anticipated transfer of its XVII Corps (3rd and 35th Infantry Divisions) to its Ninth Army raised concern. The army battered open an eight-kilometer gap between Pflanzer-Baltin's two major battle groups. If the enemy successfully penetrated Pflanzer-Baltin's lines, it would force a retreat into the Carpathian Mountains. The arrival of XI Corps momentarily saved the situation, but a few hours later, the Russians again smashed into XIII Corps, forcing it into further retreat. The army group's western front area now became endangered. Second Army received the mission to draw as many czarist units as possible to its front to relieve the escalating enemy pressure on Pflanzer-Baltin's flank positions.

General Conrad warned that surrendering Fortress Przemyśl would have a serious demoralizing effect on the army and damage the monarchy's and its army's prestige. He goaded his freezing, combat-fatigued armies that their duty remained to liberate the fortress, and not one day could be lost in that effort. Because the estimated fortress food stores would be depleted by mid-March, the offensive must be continued at all cost.

Also, the Second Army's left flank VII, X, and XIX Corps reported additional serious casualties after launching uncoordinated attacks against entrenched enemy positions without sufficient artillery support.[107] Entire regiments again became disoriented in the dense fog and wind-driven heavy snow. Group Szurmay, for example, had to limit its efforts to patrol activities.

General Tersztyánsky continued his offensive efforts on the Baligrod front, attaining some cursory gains but no decisive advantage. The enemy's tenacious defensive efforts won the day, and additional reinforcements thus became necessary to even maintain the few hard-won territorial gains. Second Army nevertheless continued its offensive effort while still awaiting the arrival of the 13th and 31st Infantry Divisions.

A X Corps' 24th Infantry Division 1 March battle report cited the various difficulties aggravating accurate position orientation. Enemy fire from three directions on the condensed front produced severe losses. Troops became entrapped 100 paces before enemy defensive positions, with the attack collapsing before the second row of czarist barbed wire. A night retreat avoided further unnecessary losses and a possible debacle.[108] Worse, the division could not count on neighboring 34th Infantry Division support because it was presently fighting against the main enemy position at Lupkov and sustaining significant losses. Fortunately, the enemy did not press its advantage. Troops also suffered from frostbite and dysentery. The division fought on rugged terrain after the attack had commenced late because of dense fog. Its left flank forces sustained 233 dead and 922 bloody casualties.[109] Thus 41st *Honvéd* Infantry Division, bearing the brunt of an attack, had to retreat, sustaining heavy casualties partially as a result of effective enemy artillery fire.[110]

XVIII Corps suffered defeat south of Wetlina, its 101st *Landsturm* Infantry Brigade sacrificing 1,200 men.[111] The most recent replacement troops had insufficient training, proving unfamiliar with the basics of weaponry. Furthermore, the language difficulties encountered with Romanian and Ruthenian recruits combined with their lesser battle worth further exacerbated the brigade's situation while casualties mounted. Having participated in battle since 25 January also took its toll. Between 1 and 15 February, the brigade lost over 1,000 men. On 1 March alone 271 troops died, 805 were wounded, and 100 were reported missing in action. In view of battle reports citing troop demoralization, the brigade was almost disbanded.[112]

Nevertheless, Conrad and Böhm-Ermolli continued to seek a military decision, calculating that by early March, in-transit reinforcements would buttress the critical Second Army left flank area. However, losses also accelerated for the Third Army III, VII, and X Corps. VII Corps, involved in intermittent fierce battle, reported that between 1 and 4 March, 1,123 soldiers were dead, 2,167 wounded, and 602 missing in action.[113] Low morale became prevalent.

Fourth Army received orders to transfer an additional infantry division, the 14th, to Third Army and launch its own offensive along the Gorlice roads.[114] Further examples of casualties: XVII Corps sustained severe losses during sporadic night and day battle. Between 1 and 15 March, XIX Corps sacrificed about 1,000 men each day. The 32nd Infantry Division numbers sank to almost half. Infantry Regiment 41 combined its remaining five companies into one. The enemy also sustained frightful losses.[115]

By nightfall of 2 March it became evident that victory could not be achieved because each renewed effort was countered by powerful czarist counterattacks that sought to reconquer any lost territory. Meanwhile, the Russians struck both Second Army at the Baligrod roads and Third Army X and VII Corps in the Laborcz Valley, resulting in costly casualties.[116] Many commanders hoped that the Russians would wear themselves out with the repeated counterattacks, but enemy efforts continued until 10 March, although Habsburg forces launched another futile endeavor on 6 March.

While Second Army XIX and Corps Schmidt continued their offensive efforts on 3 March, the enemy struck the key position at Elevation 906 multiple times from three directions. All Second Army troops had been deployed, but the army had lost its numerical advantage. At its decisive left flank, 13,000 troops battled 21,000 to 28,000 fresh enemy troops. The Second Army had bled (and frozen) white.[117]

The weather remained a major factor.[118] Front-line troops had long recognized the futility of continuing the bloody effort. The following quote summarizes the feeling of innumerable officers concerning the offensive:

> The operation in East Galicia appears to have begun again without sufficient forces. Why can't we strike the Russians as Hindenburg did (overpower them right away at the onset) so they are given no time to reinforce and dig in. . . . What was needed most was not false geniuses, but simply well trained officers with human relations skills and good judgment—where are they?[119]

With the arrival of the 31st Infantry Division, Attack Group Tersztyánsky numbered 75,000 troops deployed on a thirty-four-kilometer front extending from the Beskids to the Solinka River. Nevertheless, no major Habsburg gains occurred once the Russians launched their fierce counterattacks along the Baligrod roads. On 3 March, the attack group nevertheless persevered in its attack efforts. In a clever tactical maneuver, czarist troops utilized the dense fog cover and a driving snowstorm to attack the 41st *Honvéd* Infantry Division (XIX Corps) at Manilova, but the division repulsed twenty-four enemy assaults. The 29th Infantry Division launched an uncoordinated attack, but extreme weather conditions soon halted an attempted flank advance. Having to cooperate with the 41st *Honvéd* Infantry Division robbed the division of freedom of movement north of the Oslava River. Overpowering czarist fire halted an eight-battalion assault against Elevation 704. The division commander recorded that this was another example of attempting to launch a coordinated thrust, but "too many cooks spoiled the soup."[120] The increasing number of Russian prisoners of war confirmed the enemy's continuing rapid transfer of significant reinforcements for their repeated counterattacks. Habsburg XVIII Corps failed to penetrate enemy lines and thus retreated, but the corps mission remained to bind enough enemy forces to assist Second Army offensive efforts.[121]

The Carpathian campaign was vicious; the struggle to conquer the Manilova heights proved no exception. An eyewitness account related that a *Honvéd* infantry regiment received an order to seize Manilova's key heights. Forty officers and 2,038 men with ten machine guns launched a surprise attack to seize the treacherous, steep slopes in a region heavily forested and shrouded with deep snow, retarding movement. *Honvéd* soldiers advanced to within 600 to 800 paces of enemy positions, to be halted by furious defensive gunfire. Once the soldiers overcame the initial shock, they advanced again. Because the Russians aimed their rifles too high, casualty numbers remained inconsequential. Four machine guns were inserted into the first infantry line to take enemy positions under fire.

The well-entrenched enemy received reinforcements as two separate Hungarian groups launched an attack. One group traversed a huge gorge to attack, while the other crossed steep and forested terrain. Fallen trees retarded the advance. When *Honvéd* troops came to within 300 paces of the main enemy positions, they encountered heavy defensive fire. However, the wooded terrain and deep snow camouflaged the attacking soldiers and again kept casualties to a minimum. The troops were difficult to observe when they advanced in a crouching position. The assault halted twenty paces from the main enemy lines as a result of enemy infantry fire and the attackers' physical exhaustion. When the fighting recommenced, it turned brutal. Russian soldiers refused to surrender even when *Honvéd* troops broke into their lines. The *Honvéd* order of the day emphasized that they must show no mercy and take no prisoners, which produced desperate battle. No orders could be dispatched in the melee; hand-to-hand combat determined the outcome. The enemy finally retreated from its main positions but then unleashed its customary counterattack against the most threatened *Honvéd* flank when they failed to solidify their newly captured positions. Nevertheless, the victors successfully warded off enemy attacks—but the situation remained critical. The Russians attempted to recapture Manilova at any cost, while the *Honvéd* troops could not continue their attack because of severe casualties and lack of reserves. Ammunition resupply occurred at night, and the wounded evacuated and new defensive positions prepared. A renewed Russian attack hurled the defenders out of their positions, followed by a general attack that surrounded the *Honvéd* positions. Bayonets halted the massed czarist troops during a heavy snowstorm. In the early morning, the enemy launched a partial attack that was repulsed.

Surviving soldiers performing reconnaissance missions encountered a horrific sight: mounds of fallen comrades blanketed the terrain. The troops had to remain on constant alert because enemy movement was observed. On 2 March, both sides attacked almost simultaneously, the Russians in mass formations. Both sides established well-positioned machine gun emplacements during the night, which produced enormous casualties. The *Honvéd* troops initially maintained their positions, although they sacrificed most of their officers—only three of forty survived the battle. Without sufficient leadership, the Magyar troops retreated, crushed by overwhelming czarist numbers. All available reserves hurled into battle could not halt the Russians. The *Honvéd* regiment suffered 939 dead and 430 wounded, including the officers. Prisoners of war stated that Russian Infantry Regiment 137 had been almost destroyed, and Regiments 49 and 50 had sustained such heavy losses that they had to be withdrawn from the front lines. Two additional regiments also sustained heavy casualties. The *Honvéd* postcombat battle report emphasized that determined, well-trained soldiers could attack and defeat a larger enemy force.

Elsewhere, Third Army X Corps continued fighting through the evening of 3 to 4 March to repulse alternating czarist counterattacks and storm attacks. The VII Corps, ensconced at close range to czarist forward lines, was ordered to continue its attack, but it lacked sufficient troop numbers. Only major reinforcements could sustain the attack.[122]

Further orders to continue the offensive were dispatched, as Conrad harangued his troops to exceed the small gains achieved because of the increasing time pressure relative to Fortress Przemyśl. Despite Herculean efforts and human sacrifice by many units, Second Army could not achieve significant progress. Because of the circumstances, Böhm-Ermolli requested that the attack be postponed until 5 March. Conrad, however, replied that the deteriorating Fortress Przemyśl situation allowed no delay in further action.

Meanwhile, South Army had to advance either to shift direction or intervene in Army Group Pflanzer-Baltin's battle. Heavy snowfall continued to create difficult conditions for the army.[123] Conrad considered Pflanzer-Baltin's recent retreat at Stanislau a tactical error. The group's mission, while still awaiting XI Corps' arrival, remained to bind enemy forces and assist South Army efforts by providing flank protection. It must also secure the Dniester River right flank area and prevent a czarist advance into Transylvania, but two meters of snow made it all but impossible to advance. Too few exhausted soldiers covered a vast frontage. A unit logbook entry explains, "The men simply remain lying down," and the enemy could easily break through the "spider web"–thin lines.[124] XIII Corps numbers dropped from 20,000 to 1,453 soldiers. The 42nd *Honvéd* Infantry Division provides examples: Infantry Regiment 26 had 178 troops available, and the 16th Infantry Brigade numbers sank from 1,900 to 500 men.[125] Further north, Third Army right flank forces must advance. A Fourth Army southern flank four-division assault force would attack toward Jaslo, while other units attempted to relieve enemy pressure on the Third Army northern flank.[126] Third Army left flank units must prevent enemy intervention against Fourth Army's efforts to seize the high ground at Gorlice, while in turn, Fourth Army must divert enemy troops from the Second Army front. On the southern portion of the German Northwest front, Habsburg First Army and German Army Group Woyrsch must prevent any significant czarist transferal of troops to the Second Army front.

General Conrad calculated that Fortress Przemyśl's garrison numbered 125,000 troops, of which 60,000 consisted of combat troops. Thirty-five thousand could launch a breakout attempt against the estimated siege army of two infantry, two cavalry, and various *Reichswehr* (third-line) divisions ensconced in multiple strong siege lines. Some czarist troops reportedly had been transferred to the Carpathian front to counter Habsburg operations. A fortress breakout attempt would coincide with Second Army offensive efforts, its details determined by Second Army progress. Even if Second Army efforts failed, the sortie must be launched, while a separate garrison force must destroy the citadel's works, defensive positions, and weaponry.[127]

The Habsburg military crisis persisted. Garrison provisions should now last until 19 March, adding a few days to earlier estimates. Seemingly disregarding the multitude of adverse conditions, General Conrad continued to expect more of his battle-weary troops. He intended to divert czarist attention from the middle Carpathian Mountain region to Army Group Pflanzer-Baltin's front south of the Dniester River.

On 4 March General Tersztyánsky renewed his offensive efforts after deploying the late-arriving 13th Infantry Division between the 27th and 31st divisions. Although the division was decimated rapidly, its action enabled Corps Schmidt to attack Manilova again. XIX and Corps Schmidt continued their efforts, while X and VII Corps regrouped in preparation for a further advance on 5 March.[128] V Corps and Group Szurmay continued attempts at the San River, but the bitter cold and new meter-deep snow continued to create poor visibility conditions, halting fighting because it proved impossible to advance.[129] Activity had to be suspended except for patrolling and shoveling paths to deliver ammunition, food, and replacement troops. The XVIII Corps, whose earlier supporting endeavors had failed, joined the San River undertaking.

On the Third Army front, X Corps continued to bear the brunt of fierce enemy attacks. Despite recent devastating losses, VII Corps was ordered to launch decisive attacks, which faltered because of czarist counter efforts, although all available troops had been inserted into the front lines. As a result of its losses, VII Corps had to rehabilitate its troops while simultaneously defending its positions. Fighting continued at close range to enemy lines, while the persistent blizzard conditions assured that the infantry received no artillery support. Group Szurmay troops sustained further substantial losses as a result of frostbite. The perpetual battlefield setbacks and concomitant heavy losses unnerved Third Army troops. VII and X Corps commanders realized that any attack against the strong enemy positions had little chance of success.[130]

Further examples of the substantial casualties abound: X Corps' 45th Infantry Division had 1,500 men, and Infantry Regiment 89 lost 1,200 between 28 February and 4 March. By 5 March, VII Corps had suffered 60 percent losses. At the San River front, V Corps surrendered terrain because of casualties and enemy numbers. On 6 March, accompanied by extreme weather change, casualties skyrocketed, and exhaustion and apathy became pervasive.[131]

Archduke Joseph, VII Corps Commander, commented:

General Boroević ordered the offensive continued "energetically." . . . Over the last two days, my *Honvéd* Division suffered terrible losses; its effective force numbers less than 2,000 . . . and tomorrow, despite the casualties, we have to attack again. My corps losses since 1 March: 12

officers, 1,121 men killed, 46 officers and 2,121 men wounded, 2 officers and 685 men missing. This is really terrible.

Further:

The attack . . . was halted by the enemy's horrific infantry and machine gun fire close to the Russian trenches, and collapsed with horrible losses . . . my artillery had to remain silent because there was wild hand-to-hand fighting in the forest. . . . My medical corpsmen were shot by the Russians as they ventured close to the wounded . . . of my own volition, I ordered that we remain in place. In the event we can advance, which is impossible under the circumstances . . . my right-flank neighbor was forced back. I could no longer take the responsibility for moving forward at such a high price of heavy losses, to make the X Corps's offensive possible . . . Yet the X Corps did not attack, but withdrew. . . . My right flank was undefended and hung in the air.

We counted up to 1,500 of our own dead, and how many didn't we find in the deep forest? The medical station treated 4000 wounded. If the Russians attack my completely exposed right flank, my brave corps . . . would be annihilated . . . during the last three days my losses were more than 60 percent! . . . my brave Infantry Regiment 46 lost more than 75 percent, and my *Honvéd* regiments lost 60 to 95 percent of last week's effective forces. . . . After nightfall my 39. Infantry Regiment was attacked by the Russians with superior numbers! The entire brave regiment consisted of only 450 men and yet they forced back the Russian masses, which, shot to pieces just in front of our trenches, mostly collapsed.[132]

Meanwhile, on 3 March General Ivanov informed *Stavka* that a powerful Austro-Hungarian–German effort launched toward Lisko–Sanok to relieve Fortress Przemyśl represented a dangerous attempt to unhinge czarist left flank positions and force the evacuation of Galicia. He insisted that halting the present Habsburg offensive could destroy his armies. His arguments convinced *Stavka* to assume the defensive on the German front because the main Russian offensive effort would now be launched on the czarist Southwest front. Ivanov's forces would smash through the last Carpathian Mountain ridges and invade Hungary, as the Russian general had intended since October and November 1914. On 19 March, Ivanov directed his left flank units to attack toward Budapest and outflank the Central Power lines between Cracow–Posen–Thorn. *Stavka*'s decision also involved political considerations because the collapse of Hungary would signify the defeat of the Dual Monarchy. Pressure would be placed on Italy, which might react to the British Dardanelles operation to attempt to open the straits, which in turn could also influence Romania's stance. Thus, on 20 March, czarist forces launched a series of short, powerful thrusts through the Carpathian valleys that continued into mid-April, when they finally ceased because of heavy casualties, troop exhaustion, and the adverse conditions. They also encountered more difficult supply conditions the further they progressed into the mountain imbroglio, reversing the earlier situation between the two opponents. Renewed heavy snowfall on 4 March brought a short period of relative calm to the Carpathian front.

The failure of the early March Habsburg Carpathian offensive forced military and diplomatic leaders to reconsider Italy's diplomatic and military position. Count Istvan Burian, Habsburg foreign minister since early January 1915, expressed growing concern over Italy's ultimate intentions. Meanwhile, General Falkenhayn again urged that an offensive be launched against Serbia to provide ammunition supplies to the Turks, allies since November 1914. General Conrad maintained his position that no Habsburg troops could be spared from the Russian front, and that a Serbian campaign would provide Rome an excuse to go to war.[133]

Before the 6 March Habsburg-renewed general offensive, no significant progress had been achieved after a week of effort. The critical element of surprise had again been compromised. Much time was squandered during the futile attempts to reinforce the threatened Cisna front. Constant interrupted heavy logistical traffic along the single supply roadway created sufficient delay, enabling the Russians to transfer reinforcements to counter any Habsburg offensive efforts.

All Habsburg units reported significant losses resulting from sickness and frostbite. V Corps' losses resulted from attempting to fulfill impossible multiple missions that included crossing the San River, binding enemy forces, and breaking through the enemy positions across the river. The corps suffered, as did so many others, from the combined effects of dwindling numbers and enemy numerical superiority.[134] Second Army lost 40,000 soldiers to frostbite alone in the first five days of March.

General Conrad dispatched a revealing letter to the emperor's military chancellery on 5 March to justify the 6 March renewal of the stalled Second Army offensive effort. Conrad reiterated that the Carpathian operation objective remained to liberate Fortress Przemyśl and drive the enemy from western and middle Galicia. Thus Second Army's sixteen divisions had attacked along the shortest, most direct route to the fortress toward Sanok–Lisko–Chyróv. The nine-division Third Army's mission had been to attack toward Krosno–Sanok, and Fourth Army's four-division southern flank toward Jaslo–Zmigrod. South Army's six and Pflanzer-Baltin's six (later seven) divisions must assist South Army escape from its mountain entrapment. Conrad claimed that every available division had been hurled into the Carpathian hellhole—a serious exaggeration.[135]

Conrad also raised the critical issue of neutral countries, especially Italy, because of the recent Habsburg battlefield failures. In addition, Fortress Przemyśl food stores reputedly would last until 23 March, adding four days to previous estimates. Thus, Conrad again reiterated that Rome's territorial demands for continued neutrality did not have to be met at this time.[136] He also criticized Germany's persistent military and diplomatic pressure to accede to Rome's demands for surrender of Habsburg territory. Denouncing his ally's brutal egotism, Conrad suggested negotiating a separate peace treaty with Russia and insisted that Berlin must participate in any territorial sacrifice to Italy.

He further urged that the "decisive" Carpathian military operation could still achieve a major victory. Herculean Habsburg efforts had failed (so far) because of fierce Russian resistance and the winter mountain weather conditions. Conrad lamented that previously victorious Army Group Pflanzer-Baltin had suffered a battlefield reversal, blaming the setback on South Army because it failed to attain its objectives after six weeks of battle. Second Army efforts terminated when they struck a solid, reinforced czarist defense line. Heavy frost and bitter cold continued at the front, and by 4 March, under mounting enemy pressure, Pflanzer-Baltin's right flank units were forced to retreat. Fierce, inconclusive battle raged against four czarist cavalry divisions and one *Schutzen* (rifle) brigade until 13 March.[137]

For Conrad, launching a breakout effort from Fortress Przemyśl became increasingly urgent. The perpetual inclement weather increased the number of sick and frostbitten troops; between 1 and 10 March the number of troops hospitalized increased. An additional 2,000 troops became designated as too exhausted for duty, and garrison morale reached new lows.

Returning to the 6 March Habsburg general offensive, while XVIII Corps left flank and V Corps right flank forces must advance, it remained crucial that the Fourth Army prevent Russian forces from being shifted against Second Army. The entire Habsburg front, stretching from the Vistula River to eastern Galicia, prepared for new decisive battle as time pressure relative to Fortress Przemyśl demanded frenetic activity.[138]

Stavka perceived the possible danger emanating from the Habsburg operation against their extreme left flank positions, the most sensitive portion of their front. Indications that Army Group Pflanzer-Baltin prepared to renew its advance raised serious concern about the threat to disrupt the major czarist transportation and communication links connecting eastern Galicia and Russia. This resulted in reinforcements being sent to counter the enemy threat. General Tersztyánsky, meanwhile, blamed the failure of his attack efforts on overall conditions and the fact that multiple artillery batteries remained behind the Carpathian ridgelines. However, he himself had left twenty-seven batteries in the rear echelon areas, and the Russians often utilized inclement weather conditions to launch attacks. Field commanders cautioned Conrad that no further progress was possible without significant reinforcements; the deteriorating battle worthiness of Habsburg units made even maintaining present lines questionable.

On the first day of the new Third Army offensive, severe casualties forced termination of the operation. Two potentially dangerous enemy tactical options threatened Habsburg efforts. The Russians could transfer troops from the Habsburg Second Army front to the Third Army theater. Also, if Third and Fourth Armies remained passive, additional czarist troops could be deployed against the hapless Second Army. The operation's success hinged on preventing the Russians from rapidly reinforcing their armies countering Second Army.[139]

Meanwhile, the beleaguered Third Army VII and X Corps faced insurmountable problems, while XVII Corps failed to crack Russian resistance. Once again, the weather conditions and close proximity of friendly forces to Russian forward positions prevented artillery support. Habsburg troops continued to sustain enormous casualties; nevertheless, the battered III and VII Corps received orders to launch another futile attack effort that produced further unnecessary bloodshed.[140] Despite the insertion of all available reserves, VII Corps defensive efforts against Russian attacks failed to halt enemy advances.

Third Army's inability to maintain attack momentum and Fourth Army's delay in launching a relieving offensive resulted in Second Army bearing the brunt of enemy assaults. Third Army at first repulsed attacks against its eastern flank positions, but once forced into a defensive stance, the stage was set for impending military disaster.[141] Meanwhile, Conrad prodded General Boroević to bind opposing enemy forces. However, Third Army's situation had deteriorated so quickly that it could not render serious opposition to the enemy. Aware of the Third Army situation, the enemy transferred numerous units against the battered Second Army—precisely what Conrad hoped to prevent!

The single Second Army's only battle success occurred when XIX Corps stormed the Magurczyne heights, enabling the corps to attain their crucial objective, the Lupkov railroad. The next day (7 March) they also conquered the bloodied position at Chrysczczata, securing General Tersztyánsky's right flank position.[142] XIX Corps troops repulsed seven renewed enemy night assaults while Corps Schmidt again advanced on Manilova.[143] Through its sacrificial efforts, Second Army succeeded in driving a sixteen-kilometer-wide wedge into enemy lines, but it was too weak to maintain momentum and garner a decisive victory. Meanwhile, the enemy reinforced its fronts against Group Tersztyánsky and the XVIII Corps. General Tersztyánsky ordered his officers to ruthlessly exert their authority over their battle-fatigued troops while division commanders must move their headquarters closer to the front for better control of their units (one was reported over forty kilometers from the battlefield).[144]

In the meantime, General Tersztyánsky's attack groups, Corps Lutgendorf and Schmidt, awaited an Army Group Pflanzer-Baltin feint attack to distract enemy attention from the critical Baligrod–San River line, where Second Army's offensive would be renewed along its entire front.[145] However, the steep ridgelines were so covered in ice that they proved difficult to traverse. A V Corps effort north of the San River failed to achieve the intended impetus for the Second Army endeavor. Heavy enemy artillery cross-fire and the futility of defending positions forced V Corps to surrender a key position. In spite of receiving reinforcements, the 41st *Honvéd* Infantry Division could not advance from Chrysczczata, and the offensive thus rapidly collapsed. Second Army success had been dashed by the same circumstances as the first endeavor, such as when adjacent armies launched attacks but failed to bind significant enemy units.[146] Meanwhile, four new czarist regiments (137th, 138th, 229th, and 230th) appeared on the Second Army front. The mission to rescue Fortress Przemyśl had become a Palladium for the Habsburg army.[147]

Nevertheless, General Conrad continued to anticipate a Second Army left flank success because it appeared to possess a relative numerical superiority over opposing troops. However, excessive losses brought the supporting XVIII Corps advance to a halt as extreme weather conditions made it impossible to prepare defensive positions on newly acquired terrain.[148] The offensive effort continued on 7 March, but urgent requests for additional artillery batteries to support V Corps' San River battle went unanswered because none was available.[149] Nevertheless, some infantry units successfully crossed the river in an attempt to pierce enemy positions and threaten czarist flank areas.

The Fourth Army's long-anticipated attack to relieve pressure on the northern Third Army flank was again postponed because of "unpredictable weather," although the operation was essential for Third and Second Army success. When finally launched, after achieving some inconsequential initial successes, it failed to penetrate the seemingly impregnable enemy lines because of insufficient troop numbers and artillery support.[150] General Conrad recognized that the Gorlice area represented the Achilles' heel of the czarist Northwest and Southwest front positions, where it formed the hinge that connected the two enemy fronts, but he lacked the necessary troops to take advantage of the situation. The Germans deployed the requisite troop strength in early May to launch an offensive that subsequently won the greatest Central Power victory of the war at the battle of Gorlice–Tarnov.

On the same day (7 March), South Army launched a new offensive effort along its entire front to envelop czarist positions. However, dense fog precluded artillery support for the infantry, who struggled as a Siberian cold wave struck the mountains, with temperatures plummeting to −23°C and more than two meters of snow falling.[151] The army's attempted double envelopment of Wyszkov and seizure of the dominating area heights failed to achieve significant progress. Battling the mountain blizzard conditions, all attacks ground to a halt.[152] Only the army's right flank XXIV Corps advanced, but it failed to achieve significant progress.[153]

Strong enemy forces attacked Third Army when it attempted to advance again. X Corps parried night attacks until 8 March, when it retreated; then multiple reports of enemy troop concentrations at the army right flank and III and XVII Corps fronts resulted in the order to hold all positions.[154] Blizzard conditions prevailed until midmonth, transforming mountain slopes into a treacherous glaze of ice and providing the enemy significant protection. The unbearable conditions wore down the soldiers' will to resist as they vainly sought shelter from the bone-jarring cold. This introduced an insidious disintegration process, which gradually spread among all Habsburg armies. Conrad had good reason to fear that the next serious military defeat could result in the total collapse of his army.[155]

Subzero temperatures caused machine gun water jackets to freeze, rendering many useless in battle. The exhausted and starving troops struggled to remain awake, fearing that sleep would bring the White Death, while frostbite cases continued to escalate.[156] Delivery of food to the front was only attempted at night, and thus the meager rations were frozen solid upon arrival. Often the food carriers succumbed to the horrible conditions. Interestingly, enemy snipers reportedly never shot at food servers; they often even knew their names. Front-line troops had to transport their own field kitchens.[157] Drifting snow halted movement near the front while the transport of wounded soldiers rearward came to a complete halt. Second Army sustained serious losses between 1 and 5 March. XIX Corps lost 5,400 men. In four days, the 32nd Infantry Division lost 50 percent of its manpower. Nevertheless, the corps received orders to maintain its gains and rehabilitate its badly shaken troops.[158] The 29th and 34th Infantry Divisions combined troop stands equaled one-third of a full infantry division.[159] V Corps also sustained severe losses: its 37th *Honvéd* Infantry Division lost an average of 250 soldiers a day.[160] After XIX Corps' seizure of the crucial heights at Chrysczczata during all night battle 7 to 8 March, a fierce enemy counterassault supported by overwhelming firepower forced its evacuation.[161] The high terrain became a field of corpses. The exhausted XVIII Corps meanwhile seized some territory at the Wetlina River, while V Corps and Group Szurmay reported severe losses of officers and horses at the flooded San River.[162]

The Habsburg military situation reached crisis proportions as Second Army exertions achieved little. As so often occurred, General Conrad had underestimated the Russian ability to swiftly and effectively neutralize his efforts; he'd also underestimated the difficulties posed by the rugged mountain winter conditions. It required three hours of extreme exertion to traverse just 1,000 paces on the Dzial ridges.[163] Despite the appearance of sunshine on 8 March, daytime temperatures hovered around −5°C and dropped to −20°C at night, accompanied by biting wind. Attempts to remove or rescue even lightly wounded men were hampered by the deep snow. Fallen soldiers near enemy lines could not be saved.[164] Physically and psychologically exhausted, the battered troops recognized the futility of assaulting the well-fortified enemy positions, particularly because they lacked reserve troops. The likelihood of Italy and Romania entering the war increased substantially with the continued Habsburg military setbacks.[165] Rome had not delineated its final demands for Dual Monarchy territory, but there was no doubt it would. In the meantime, General Falkenhayn pressured Conrad to encourage his foreign minister to conclude diplomatic negotiations with Italy because sufficient military concerns existed to avoid "trouble in the Balkans and Romania."

Böhm-Ermolli prodded his troops to continue their efforts to seize the Baligrod roads, while Conrad harangued his field commanders to obtain success because of the deteriorating Fortress Przemyśl situation. However, the enemy countered every Second Army effort by transferring reinforcements to any threatened area. After twenty-four hours of constant czarist attacks along the entire front, the Russian Third Army attempted to pierce the Habsburg Fourth and Third Army inner flank positions while, in addition, shifting significant troop numbers to the critical Homonna area in the vicinity of Mezölaborcz.[166]

An artillery officer described the cold, ice, and snowstorms, the critical need for night rest, and the possibility of an epidemic breakout during the 8 March attack. A shortage of drinking water led to the utilization of a source located beneath the burial site of twenty soldiers, resulting in sickness and disease. Some of this artillery battery suffered slow and purposeless deaths, further demoralizing the survivors.[167] The loss of more than half the battery's horses left barely thirty capable of duty while the regimental commander maintained his headquarters forty kilometers behind the front.[168] Targeting deep trenches and enemy strong points required heavy-caliber but also light shells to force the defenders to keep their heads down. With neither available, the infantry had to launch surprise attacks before daybreak. Available artillery shells were consumed rapidly, further compounding the existing shell shortages. Ignoring the generally unfavorable situation, 9 March army dispositions ordered the continuation of the attack. Corps Schmidt's troops must capture the dominating heights at Manilova and seize the area around the small village of Rabe. The shattered XIX Corps again prepared to repulse an enemy attack. All units reported the debilitating effect of the frigid overnight temperatures, which claimed numerous victims, while they achieved no significant forward progress. Blinded by his obsession to free Fortress Przemyśl under the time constraints, Conrad's failed frontal assaults sealed the offensive's fate. Conrad had somehow expected General Tersztyánsky to overcome the critical military situation. The steady arrival of czarist reinforcements indicated that the enemy had no intention of surrendering territory in any critical areas.

Because of its severe manpower shortage, XIX Corps requested that Infantry Regiment 33 labor detachments be utilized as combat troops, partially because its replacement troops proved unsuitable for it. The unrelenting pressure relative to Fortress Przemyśl produced the order to attack at the Dzial ridges, a somewhat constricted area not conducive to either maneuver or easy supply.[169] The difficult terrain between the Solinka brook and those Dzial ridges presented an almost impossible setting for launching a successful attack. Nevertheless, it was ordered.[170]

The Austrian official history confirms that the persistent fierce snowstorms caused rapid termination of any efforts to advance. Transport of ill soldiers from the front lines continued to be an exercise in futility, while the slick, icy ground proved impassable.[171] Second Army had reached to about fifty kilometers from Fortress Przemyśl's outer walls, but its units had been bled dry attempting to advance along the Baligrod roads, while the surviving troops suffered from extreme combat fatigue. Intelligence reports indicated that the enemy had constructed new defensive lines twenty-five to thirty kilometers behind the front, which did not bode well for the attempts to relieve Fortress Przemyśl.[172]

Weather conditions aided czarist counterassaults against XIX Corps' 29th Infantry Division positions. The enemy burst through division lines, forcing a retreat to earlier defensive positions. Because there were no reserves, the customary counterattack could not be launched. Man-high snow blanketed the XIX Corps front, where its 17,400 troops opposed 25,000 Russians. Losses steadily mounted; since 20 February, 41st *Honvéd* Infantry Division numbers sank from 12,000 to 2,110 men. Artillery support was rendered useless by wind-driven snow, while machine gun mechanisms continued to malfunction from the cold. Troops continued to starve while the anticipated daily order to "unconditionally maintain your positions" again remained in effect.[173]

Battle ensued between Third and Fourth Army inner flanks to bind enemy forces and prevent their transfer to counter Third Army offensive efforts. III Corps supported Fourth Army IX Corps efforts through artillery fire and demonstration activity, their locations separated by extremely rugged mountain terrain.[174] Meanwhile, Group Szurmay's sacrificial attack efforts on the afternoon of 9 March failed to jar the Russians from their domineering defensive positions. Despite rare effective artillery support, enemy crossfire halted all efforts to advance.[175] By the morning of 10 March the military situation had worsened, while blizzard conditions halted all military efforts.[176] The Russians finally attained equal numbers to the attacking Second Army forces on the decisive twelve-kilometer Baligrod front, and they continued to be more adept at fighting in winter conditions and utilizing the adverse winter conditions to their advantage, particularly during offensive operations.

The impending surrender of Fortress Przemyśl and sudden unfavorable Army Group Pflanzer-Baltin situation also affected Habsburg diplomacy. Disturbing news emanating from Rome brought additional German pressure on Vienna and Conrad to assume a more conciliatory position relative to Italy. General Falkenhayn pressured Conrad to negotiate with Rome because of the necessity of Italian and Romanian military support in the Balkans. But no Habsburg statesmen or military commander desired to surrender the Trentino to perfidious Italy.[177]

The Russians launched a counterattack that terminated any Habsburg efforts.[178] The fatigued Habsburg units retreated to their original positions, but entire battalions surrendered to the enemy to escape the inhuman conditions. Other soldiers continued to endure the torment in the frozen Carpathian hellhole.[179] Front-line troops desperately required rehabilitation and reinforcements to replace the enormous losses.

Artillery shells could no longer be fired within 800 meters of Habsburg lines because of increased short rounds, and its support of the infantry remained unsatisfactory.[180] Although numerous batteries left in rear echelon areas were ordered brought forward, significant numbers did not move. "Mountain" artillery batteries most suited for the campaign terrain remained stationed on the Balkan front. The enemy's successful rapid reinforcement of its positions on the Baligrod front made the Second Army's human sacrifice a wasted effort. Infantry divisions, which possessed regimental numbers of men or even fewer, manned three-kilometer or wider front lines.

By 10 March Habsburg military leadership had reached its nadir in effectiveness. Despite explicit orders to attack, no commander would take the initiative, waiting instead for adjacent units to act. A nervous atmosphere prevailed everywhere. Some field officers were cashiered and others transferred from the battlefront, destroying any remaining command stability and dissolving any remaining trust in the high command. Habsburg Supreme Command demonstrated a lack of empathy for the unbearable conditions under which its troops labored.

Four infantry divisions arrived to be inserted into Second Army front lines, but the prevailing situation neutralized the exploitation of any temporary advantage, and multiple problems were encountered in attempting to coordinate their insertion into front positions.

A 12th Infantry Division after battle report cited several factors to explain its unsuccessful early March offensive efforts at Gorlice on the Fourth Army front. Blizzard conditions prevented success as the troops reached enemy positions exhausted and stunned. Artillery preparation for the 9 March offensive should have commenced earlier, but the prevailing conditions delayed it until 8 March. The attacking troops encountered heavy flanking fire, producing numerous casualties.[181] When Habsburg artillery finally commenced firing, the enemy evacuated its front lines, negating its effect. After a half-hour advance to within 500 paces of the enemy's positions, heavy czarist infantry and machine gun fire halted further progress, and excessive losses halted the attack. Infantry Regiment 100 reported that of its 335 losses, 229 were missing in action.[182]

Archduke Joseph depicted the horrors encountered by his men:

On the terribly slippery slope . . . the *Honvéds* attacked with indescribable heroism and bravery. The horrifying casualties were caused partly by the unsuitable lower command. The shortage of officers had a negative effect because the charge was carried out piecemeal instead of unified.

The regiment's strength sank to 2,000 men. Both officers and men complained about Russian Infantry Regiment 73 brutality. They shot all our medical troops and the stretcher-bearers, even though they clearly saw them bending over the wounded . . . as well as moving wounded. All our dead lie unburied because we can't get close to them. I had respected the Russians as being a knightly rival, such things had never occurred before! Are they "wild Asians"?

After what happened, my *Honvéds* lost patience, there will be no mercy for captured Russians.[183]

Titular commander Archduke Friedrich, in a report to Emperor Franz Joseph's military chancellery, emphasized that the Second Army had attacked for nine days on its restricted attack front. Inclement weather conditions and well-fortified enemy positions prevented attaining victory while the enemy reinforced its numbers. Any available forces had to strike the enemy flank and rear areas in an attempt to prevent the establishment of new defensive positions and renewed resistance. Success depended upon maintaining the initiative and cooperation. But wasn't this advice a bit late?

On 11 March General Conrad pressured General Tersztyánsky that Fortress Przemyśl could survive for just one more week.[184] Even if they slaughtered additional horses and foraged foodstuffs and fodder, the garrison could only persevere until 24 March.[185] Only a successful major offensive had any chance of rescuing the fortress.

Second Army continued to encounter insurmountable odds attempting to maintain steady supply movement. General Tersztyánsky complained that supplies were not sufficient, while on 11 March, provision columns were in a holding position at Cisna. When supplies failed to reach the front, desperate appeals to maintain traffic on the roads increased. On the same day the Russians launched an anticipated counteroffensive against XIX Corps left flank positions, its assault toward Wola Michova threatening to neutralize Second Army offensive efforts. The only intact infantry division in that critical vicinity, the newly arrived 14th Infantry Division, had to be hurled into battle piecemeal. Although Second Army was now the brunt of major enemy counterattacks, it received orders to continue its offensive. However, once XIX Corps had to retreat, the army's offensive had been neutralized and the sole supply lifeline for the main attack group endangered.[186] How could enemy efforts be neutralized if steady czarist reinforcements hurled at the Baligrod front negated all Habsburg efforts?

The two-week campaign placed inhuman demands on the surviving combatants. In early March alone, there were 40,000 cases of frostbite reported because of blizzard conditions.[187] Coordination between units and communication breakdowns remained a common occurrence. When chances for a successful northern front offensive had dissipated, Attack Group Tersztyánsky received orders to prevent a Russian breakthrough at Wola Michova, but that proved impossible under the circumstances. The troops could accomplish nothing more,[188] and General Tersztyánsky finally admitted that success was unattainable.[189] However, was he not partially to blame for the situation? Russian troops could now easily smash through the thin, wavering Second Army lines; just maintaining the present positions required significant reinforcements. General Böhm-Ermolli reminded Tersztyánsky of the urgent necessity to liberate Fortress Przemyśl, as if such reminders were necessary! However, all approach routes remained covered in ice and snow, and the inclement weather conditions actually worsened.[190]

An interesting story in one officer's *Nachlaß* in the Vienna War Archives describes the exertions of Second Army troops in moving a supply column forward. One day, the troops encountered a particularly long stoppage. Hoping to discover the reason for the delay, the officer worked his way to the front of the line until troops told him to halt. When he inquired about the reason for the lengthy stoppage, he was informed that General Tersztyánsky did not wish to be disturbed during his afternoon nap. The general had ordered a halt to all military columns while he got some rest.[191]

For Second Army troops, noncombat casualties continued to outnumber battlefield losses. Indicative of this, one unit lost 150 men to enemy fire, 200 to frostbite.[192] Troops were forced to use snow for cover and protection, which increased the likelihood of frostbite.[193] The 27th Infantry Division found itself hampered by up to two meters of snow, while the strength of the XIX Corps dissipated drastically. With no relief in sight, troops became even more demoralized. Suicide remained a viable solution to some troops.[194]

On the Third Army front, a powerful enemy night attack against the inner flanks of the 21st and 45th Infantry Divisions was repulsed; then heavy snowfall ensured that the front remained quiescent throughout the remainder of the day. Efforts to strengthen positions and prepare a second defensive line behind the front were attempted, irrespective of current conditions.[195]

South Army reported some progress in its continued efforts despite heavy snowstorms, but achieved little success since it launched its effort on 7 March. The army, however, repulsed several enemy counterattacks.

Conrad's *Flügeladjutant*, Major Kundmann, observed, "it almost seems as though everything is working against us, even the weather," in relation to the impending demise of Fortress Przemyśl and the possibility of having to surrender the Trentino *irredenta* to Italy. Meanwhile, the next offensive effort planned for 12 March had to be postponed until 16 March because of the unrelenting weather conditions, although action was certainly imperative. Kundmann concluded that everyone had lost their nerve and could think only of retreat.[196]

General Tersztyánsky nevertheless contemplated continuing his Baligrod efforts on 12 March, indicative of the pervasive influence of Fortress Przemyśl. At Wola Michova, 21,000 czarist troops opposed 13,000 XIX Corps soldiers, bolstered by any reinforcements and reserve formations rushed to the threatened fourteen-kilometer front.[197] The enemy failed to exploit its numerical superiority, but the question remained unanswered of how to salvage the Second Army offensive. Russian troops then smashed through Group Tersztyánsky's defensive lines, producing substantial casualties and threatening to puncture his entire front. The threat of a XIX Corps collapse resulted in the transfer of all available reserve troops (five battalions) to the corps' western flank positions.[198]

On 10 and 12 March troop strength reports revealed additional serious troop losses. The 41st *Honvéd* Infantry Division was proclaimed incapable of undertaking offensive action, while 32nd Infantry Division had sustained 50 percent casualties. During four days, 27th Infantry Division sacrificed 3,290 soldiers, the 13th *Landwehr* Infantry Division 2,608.[199]

It proved fortunate that the enemy attacks eventually slackened, although Russian artillery fire continued its harassing fire. Indications of the deconstruction of Austro-Hungarian troop units multiplied. XIX Corps troops remained in a particularly precarious state, with 29th Infantry Division on the verge of collapse. Soldiers often endured exhausting marches to be immediately hurled into battle on unfamiliar terrain.[200] The 43rd *Landwehr* Infantry Division troops reputedly could no longer be relied on in battle, and 34th Infantry Division and XVIII Corps were at the extreme end of their physical capabilities; many V Corps troops suffering from frostbite could not attack.[201] Group Szurmay's efforts were neutralized by the same dire conditions, so he pulled his troops back to reduce the senseless loss of life, intending to regain any surrendered positions when weather conditions improved. A new wave of blizzard conditions signified that such relief would not be forthcoming soon. General Tersztyánsky concluded that his units could not undertake offensive action and that low troop numbers precluded launching counterattacks, so he was limited to defending his present positions.[202]

Continued Russian pressure on Manilova threatened Second Army's western flank positions, while X Corps supportive efforts failed to ease the battered XIX Corps' worsening plight. The shattered Second Army could not achieve its original missions. Various unit documents and logbooks emphasized that their troops had reached their physical limits. Tragically, Conrad appeared to ignore the extreme deprivations at the front, perhaps out of desperation with the rapidly deteriorating and seemingly hopeless situation.

A sudden thaw severely affected the single army supply route, but overnight freezing temperatures improved the road conditions somewhat. However, the problem of maintaining a steady flow of supplies and the care and feeding of horses remained unresolved. Army Group Pflanzer-Baltin's eastern corps wagons and field stoves remained marooned in their assembly area because of the extreme difficulties. The 15th Infantry Division possessed only five artillery pieces to support the next day's offensive—it required six hours to move a gun forward 500 meters.[203]

Conrad harangued Böhm-Ermolli again that Fortress Przemyśl food supplies would only last until 24 March, but he added that he did not want to increase pressure on the Second Army; rather, he was merely providing orientation for future decisions. The prevailing mood at Habsburg Supreme Command was described as pessimistic. Conrad accepted that Fortress Przemyśl's fate had been sealed, but nevertheless, he directed the fortress commander to launch a breakout attempt coordinated with Second Army offensive relief efforts.[204]

13 March witnessed numerous Russian attacks against Gorlice, though enemy efforts were repulsed with heavy losses between Lupkov, Cisna, and Wyszkov. The enemy did succeed in breaking through Second Army's extreme left flank 29th Infantry Division positions, crippling the army's offensive efforts. Further powerful Russian assaults forced XIX Corps to relinquish Magurczyne and Chryscczata, which had been conquered at the cost of tremendous human sacrifice. General Tersztyánsky now faced the unenviable task of conducting a comprehensive retreat.[205] Renewing offensive efforts would be impossible until the shattered XIX Corps recovered. Its present resistance power appeared almost nonexistent, its troops apathetic.

By 14 March the Russian numerical superiority had bled the defending Habsburg corps. Between 1 and 15 March Second Army sustained 51,086 casualties, more than one-third of its original 148,848-man complement. Attack Group Tersztyánsky incurred two-thirds of these losses (855 officers and 37,108 soldiers). Officially 54 percent of these (340 officers, 17,210 men) were killed or wounded, and an additional 451 officers and 11,098 men succumbed to sickness. In addition, 31 officers and 1,194 men became prisoners of war, while another 33 officers and 7,703 men were reported missing in action. Many wounded were presumed to have frozen to death.[206] The Second Army offensive drew five and a half enemy divisions into its imbroglio, relieving pressure against Army Group Pflanzer-Baltin's front.

The losses resulted primarily from launching repeated frontal attacks lacking artillery support against strong Russian defensive positions. Evidence of individual unit extreme human sacrifice proliferate the documents—one infantry regiment counted sixty-nine survivors, while only seventeen soldiers of *Jäger* Battalion 23 remained to fulfill their duties.

At midnight on 14 March the Russians achieved their only notable military success against Fortress Przemyśl by overpowering the perimeter sector at Na Garoch. No counterattack ensued because of the fortress reserve troops' weak physical condition. The appearance of enemy reinforcements prompted the order to evacuate all forefield positions. General Kusmanek persisted in his choice of potential breakout direction because he realized that his malnourished troops could not march, let alone fight on mountainous terrain.[207] He initiated necessary preparations for the garrison's breakout sortie to begin early on 19 March. The participating troops received the order to inflict maximum damage on enemy bridges, railroads, and ammunition depots as they advanced. Enemy food depots should be in close proximity—a real advantage to the advance direction. General Conrad informed General Falkenhayn of the failed second Carpathian operation, conceding that he had lacked sufficient manpower, but also blamed the overall unfavorable conditions for wreaking havoc on ammunition and food supply delivery, which also contributed to widespread illness, particularly frostbite. Conrad requested two to three German divisions be sent to buttress his collapsing Carpathian front.[208] In a letter to Foreign Minister Burian, General Conrad reiterated his explanation for the failure to rescue Fortress Przemyśl. Capitulation appeared to be imminent, restoring the question of neutral Italy and Romania.[209]

In examining the major causes of the failure of the second Carpathian offensive, one is first struck by the stark contrast between Habsburg Supreme Command's original high expectations and the tragic outcome of the operation. Conrad's failed effort had driven the Austro-Hungarian army to the brink of annihilation. The Second Army offensive, launched in haste before all the designated divisions had been deployed, lacked the necessary troop mass and adequate logistical preparations. Again, adequate military planning and preparation had not been accomplished.

Moreover, the direction of the offensive effort raises questions. A more realistic plan for liberating Fortress Przemyśl would have been to launch a flanking attack rather than the frontal assaults. However, Conrad's obsession to rescue the fortress and the associated time constraints sealed the fortress's fate. Conrad expected that hard-nosed General Tersztyánsky would overcome the enormous odds against operational success. Meanwhile, the arrival of significant czarist reinforcements between the Dzial ridges and Baligrod indicated that the enemy intended to maintain its regional dominance.

In reaction to the severe manpower shortages caused by enormous casualties, several corps inserted noncombat troops into the front lines. Because of time pressure, they decided to attack the Dzial ridges, a constricted area not suitable for maneuver or supply movement, while the terrain selected for the offensive between the Solinka Brook and Dzial ridges proved unfavorable for offensive action.

The transport of wounded and ill soldiers to rear echelon areas remained an exercise in futility. Even the lightly wounded often succumbed to the White Death. The front remained buried under deep snow, while the icy cover over the snow-laden landscape made movement impossible. Attacking troops advanced to the foot of enemy positions, where they could neither find cover nor prepare defensive positions, becoming easy targets for Russian infantry fire.

Second Army forward units advanced to within fifty kilometers of Fortress Przemyśl's outer walls, when the offensive was halted along the Baligrod roads. Intelligence sources indicated that the enemy had constructed a further powerful defensive line behind the present front, which did not bode well for relieving the beleaguered fortress even if Second Army managed to overcome enemy resistance at Baligrod.

Skillful Russian counterattacks, launched in terrible weather conditions, short-circuited multiple Second Army offensive efforts. Unit logbooks repeatedly bemoaned the number of artillery batteries languishing behind the mountain ridges and the constant problems encountered attempting to maintain steady supply delivery. On 4 March a Böhm-Ermolli request for additional field batteries was declined by his Attack Group commander, who had left twenty-seven batteries of his own artillery behind the forward ridges.

In a fateful repeat of the earlier Third Army offensive, Second Army efforts were launched frontally in the same direction as the earlier campaign against well-entrenched enemy positions, but this time on a more restricted front, producing similar tragic results. When severe muddy conditions delayed the Second Army operation, the element of surprise was sacrificed, again providing the Russians with sufficient time to reinforce their outnumbered troops in the anticipated attack area. Their more accessible supply routes and rail connections also ensured a steady flow of supplies and rapid movement of reinforcements.

The insurmountable problems encountered in maintaining supply movement remained unresolved. The single supply roadway for the operation, connecting Zemplenoroszi and Cisna, was continually subjected to the constant movement of troops, pack animals, and supply wagons. The enormous logistical demands combined with the extreme climate and terrain often made the route impassable for traffic.

Second Army efforts initially met with relative success, but the well-entrenched enemy troops repeatedly halted Habsburg efforts. Although the attack direction encompassed the eighteen-kilometer front extending between the Solinka River and the Dzial ridges, the actual attack frontage along the Baligrod roads involved only twelve kilometers, never the entire eighteen-kilometer frontage. Thus, the attack area proved too narrow, although it produced fierce fighting along the confines of the Baligrod roads. Limiting the attack front played a major role in the failure to gain the anticipated victory.

The deep winter mountain conditions called for experienced mountain troop units, but the monarchy's best alpine troops, such as the XV and XVI Corps, and mountain artillery batteries remained deployed on the Balkan theater. Weather and enemy artillery fire often interrupted battlefield communication, while blizzards aggravated efforts to maintain contact with forward units and supply efforts. Compasses malfunctioned, causing some units to march in circles. Corps, divisions, and Supreme Command maintained their headquarters far from the front, which exacerbated command functions. Such communication problems remained unresolved.

Now let us turn to a tragic, and perhaps preventable, chapter of the Carpathian campaign, the third Carpathian offensive, a miniature repeat of the earlier disastrous attempts, but just as disastrous for the participants. Only a major offensive had any chance to rescue Fortress Przemyśl. Could Conrad succeed?

4

The Third Offensive and Easter Battle
End of the Carpathian Winter War

If you know the enemy and know yourself, you need not fear the result of a hundred battles. If you know yourself but not the enemy, for every victory gained you will also suffer a defeat. If you know neither the enemy nor yourself, you will succumb in every battle.   Sun Tzu, *The Art of War*

DESPITE THE FAILURE of his previous two Carpathian winter offensives, Conrad von Hötzendorf pursued the same failed strategy for his third and final campaign. The last phase produced further pointless bloodshed and culminated in the surrender of Fortress Przemyśl on 22 March 1915. The new Habsburg offensive, which was delayed to garner additional artillery support, nevertheless proved inadequate against the well-fortified Russian positions. The plan's initial objective—to gain control of Loziov swiftly—faltered, and the additional time required to move artillery units forward provided the Russians ample opportunity to counterattack.

On 22 March 1915, the reinforced Habsburg V Corps prepared its assault; just three days before, a breakout attempt by the Fortress Przemyśl garrison had proved unsuccessful. The Habsburgs should have coordinated the two operations; instead, the isolated V Corps offensive, conducted by weak, recently defeated troops, proved a dismal failure. Once Fortress Przemyśl capitulated, Habsburg Supreme Command's focus should have shifted to creating a strong reserve force to meet new contingencies, but its failure to do so destroyed any chance for success.

As in the prior two offensives, Russian numerical superiority bled the attacking Habsburg V Corps white. The Second Army offensive terminated on 14 March, and the next day, the Russians attacked the Dzial ridges, a *Stutzpunkt*, or stronghold, on the Habsburg front. One after the other, XIX Corps relinquished positions seized earlier at tremendous sacrifice. General Tersztyánsky ordered his group to establish a strong defensive line while facing the daunting task of preventing an extensive retreat.

Conrad realized that his weak offensive troop strength, further diminished by weather-related illnesses such as frostbite, could not pierce enemy
lines.[1] The Second Army's new mission remained unchanged, despite its remote chance for success. Even Conrad's aide-de-camp noted that Habsburg
troops had reached the limit of their endurance and that further exertion
could only result in disaster. The Dual Monarchy must either persevere
or seek peace.[2] Conrad again rationalized the failure to relieve Fortress
Przemyśl to Foreign Minister Burian, stressing the problems caused by the
unexpected severe winter weather.[3] The unfavorable military situation made
further negotiations with Rome imperative, and Berlin pressured for their
immediate implementation.[4]

Group Tersztyánsky's troops grew apathetic, and Second Army reported
increasing physical and moral depression. Conrad's aide-de-camp reported
that Böhm-Ermolli also sank into a state of depression after losing 40,000 of
his 95,000 troops. Significantly, and contradicting official casualty sources,
only 6,000 of these losses resulted from battle; the rest were from frostbite
and sickness.[5] Many troops still lacked shelter, and squalid, unhygienic conditions abounded. V Corps recorded widespread intestinal illness among its
ranks, while 4 percent of Second Army troops reported to sick call. Frostbite permeated the ranks, and reports of typhus drastically increased.[6]

On 15 March Conrad reported to the emperor's military chancellery that
Fortress Przemyśl must surrender by 24 March, and again, he accused his
German ally of disloyal conduct in negotiations with Italy. Conrad blamed
South Army's battlefield failures for the sudden reversal of Army Group
Pflanzer-Baltin's initially successful offensive efforts.[7] Fortress Przemyśl
could not expect relief; nevertheless, the mobile fortress troops must launch
a breakout attempt to join the field army. With little confidence in the effort's success, Conrad nevertheless refused to surrender the fortress without
some honorable *k.u.k.* military effort.

Meanwhile, Böhm-Ermolli reported that his attack group could not attain its objective by 22 March. Thus, on 20 March, only V Corps and some
Group Szurmay troops (Second Army's extreme eastern flank) would be
available to continue the attempt to relieve the embattled fortress. Success
depended on simultaneous offensive action from neighboring units; however, Group Szurmay's left flank forces unexpectedly could not participate
in the new mission because of enemy attacks against it between 17 and
19 March. Group Tersztyánsky, in turn, would merely demonstrate on its
front.[8]

In a 15 March telegram, General Falkenhayn informed Conrad that he
would not be able to transfer the requested German troops to the Carpathian

front in time to affect the fate of Fortress Przemyśl. Nonetheless, Falkenhayn continued pressuring Conrad to use his influence in Vienna to encourage Habsburg diplomats to negotiate with Rome and Bucharest. The mood
at Habsburg Supreme Headquarters remained somber.[9] Foreign Minister
Burian had meanwhile decided to back off his hard-line stance toward Italy
and consider territorial concessions to Rome.

Between the termination of the Second Army's recent offensive efforts
on 14 March and Russia's unanticipated offensive on 20 March, preparations commenced for the V Corps' right flank attack to coincide with a
Fortress Przemyśl breakout attempt. Meanwhile, Second Army troops desperately required rehabilitation to restore their battle worth, but although
the second offensive effort had exacted a severe toll, Conrad ordered yet
another attack. Traversing the 100 kilometers of mountain terrain to Fortress Przemyśl would prove futile, partially because major Russian defensive
forces blocked the Habsburg attack route. Battered Habsburg forces had
to cross treacherous mountain terrain in harsh weather conditions against
a well-prepared foe. Citing the Fortress Przemyśl crisis, Conrad initially set
16 March for the new offensive launch date. The fortress garrison could
reputedly survive one more week, but given the severe time constraints, relieving the besieged fortress seemed impossible.

As melting snow exacerbated battlefield conditions, there was no rest
for Habsburg troops as the Russians continued to hurl superior numbers
against XIX Corps positions, forcing further retreat. An overwhelming
Russian counterattack compelled the 29th Infantry Division to surrender its
positions. On 16 March, Conrad summarized his failed Second Army offensive experience: sixteen and a half divisions (136,000 men), of which nine
(72,000 troops) comprised the main attack force, launched an unsuccessful
attempt to rescue Fortress Przemyśl. Conrad cited the deplorable conditions
as a main obstacle to success, reiterating that frostbite and other weather-
related illnesses caused the most losses. He also emphasized the enemy's
tenacity and admitted that if the forthcoming Fortress Przemyśl breakout
attempt failed, the fortress would have to surrender.[10]

For the next major operation, XIX Corps must consolidate the situation at Wola Michova and renew its offensive after receiving replacement
troops. Fourth and South armies needed to bind opposing enemy forces to
prevent the diversion of significant troop numbers against the weak Second
Army effort. Once Third Army recovered its strength, it must join the offensive endeavors, but it must maintain its present positions until then.[11] The
volatile nationality issue reappeared: captured Czech prisoners of war in
Habsburg uniforms that originally served with Infantry Regiment 36 (10th

Infantry Division) now served as czarist reconnaissance troops, wearing Habsburg uniforms to infiltrate their former front lines. Habsburg troops shot them when captured.

   Conrad deemed it essential not to surrender Fortress Przemyśl without a final heroic military action; therefore, the starving garrison must launch a breakout attempt "to maintain the honor of the army." The futile effort commenced on 19 March, utilizing as many garrison troops as possible. Even the Austrian official history conceded the remote chance of success for such an undertaking. Conrad insisted that an "honorable" military effort was necessary to maintain home front support for the war and soldier and civilian morale. Fearing the political and psychological repercussions of the fortress' capitulation, Habsburg military leaders made it a primary objective, "cost what it will."[12]

   Generals Conrad and Kusmanek exchanged telegrams concerning the fortress breakout direction. Considering the deteriorating garrison food situation and the troops' declining physical condition, General Kusmanek proposed launching the effort in a southeasterly direction. Conrad disagreed with Kusmanek and pressured him to reconsider his suggestion. Destruction of the fortress works and military equipment would commence on 21 March. The breakout force would consist of twelve to fifteen infantry battalions, each with 700 men.[13] Kusmanek initially acknowledged that the Russian deployment configuration would preclude a breakout effort in a southerly direction. On 16 March, however, he altered his decision and announced that he would launch his effort toward Lemberg, scene of the disastrous 1914 opening campaign. Conrad, however, continued to insist that Kusmanek support the forthcoming Second Army relieving offensive, but Kusmanek refused; his troops would advance toward Army Group Pflanzer-Baltin's positions in the eastern Carpathian Mountains.

   Conrad, in the interim, ordered the transfer of all possible troops from Second Army's battered western to its new eastern flank offensive positions. However, the final attack troop numbers proved too inconsequential to achieve battlefield success. Conrad emphasized the importance of coordinating this minioffensive effort with South Army, but an unanticipated Russian attack against XIX Corps prevented the transfer of more than its weakened 31st Infantry Division to V Corps for the offensive mission. The V Corps attack would advance toward the fortress in a northeasterly direction.

   On the eve of the fortress breakout attempt, the garrison troops' mood was somber, while health conditions continued to deteriorate. No one within the fortress believed that the effort could succeed. Instead, many participating troops hoped to become prisoners of war. Any chance for success required complete surprise, which the Habsburg armies had rarely achieved during the war. As they later learned, the Russians had broken the Habsburg cipher code and thus prepared for each effort.

The debilitated condition of Kusmanek's troops influenced his selection of advance direction. *Landsturm* Infantry Regiment 16 troops reported only 25 to 30 percent in good health. *Landsturm* Infantry Regiment 9 and only half of *Landsturm* Infantry Regiment 33 were deemed fit for duty. Given the troops' poor physical condition, Kusmanek ordered the breakout attempt toward the supposedly weakest sector of the siege front, reputedly defended by czarist third-line national guard units, rather than the difficult mountain terrain Conrad suggested.[14] The effort failed when Kusmanek's troops struck the enemy's fortified defensive positions.

With familiar tragic consequences, Fortress Przemyśl again influenced Second Army operations. Conrad realized that timely relief would not be forthcoming; nevertheless, he ordered the mobile fortress troops to launch an ill-fated breakout attempt. The promise of replenishing food supplies at enemy depots along the advance route motivated the famished troops. Attacking soldiers received an extra food ration as well as a rest day before the operation. Meanwhile, between 1 and 10 March, the number of fortress troops that reported to sick call had climbed to 12,140, lightly wounded to 6,900.[15] The enemy, aware of the proposed attack details, readjusted their troop and artillery positions accordingly. The ill-fated venture, launched with two infantry divisions and three infantry brigades, resulted in heavy human toll. The Russians later claimed to have captured 110 officers and 4,000 men during the failed attempt. The 23rd *Honvéd* Infantry Division and Waitzendorfer sacrificed 3,000 men, with the former sustaining an incredible 70 percent casualty rate. The 97th *Landsturm* Infantry Brigade suffered between 1,500 and 2,000 casualties, while *Honvéd* Infantry Regiment 2 lost 54 officers and 2,600 men.[16]

The Habsburgs publicly portrayed the military fiasco as a heroic deed; the publication of numerous self-serving congratulatory radiograms between the doomed fortress headquarters and the emperor's military chancellery followed to glorify the senseless sacrifice. Previous battle had already overtaxed fortress medical services before the 19 March endeavor. Now 1,500 wounded troops and 1,000 cholera patients received treatment, while the task of preventing epidemic outbreaks posed enormous burdens for the medical corps personnel. Cholera, typhus, and dysentery permeated the ranks.[17] Then the wounded from the failed breakout attempt arrived in dire need of medical attention. The fortress attempted no further missions after the seven-hour heroic battle because of the troops' utter exhaustion.

Meanwhile, the Russians pressed into the Solinka and Wetlinska valleys, whereupon Second Army's mission became to halt further enemy egress into those areas. The third Carpathian offensive's initial objective remained to seize the enemy position at Loziov, then advance further along the ridgelines.[18] In the interim, V Corps attempted to move its main defensive line to the high terrain extending from Polonina–Wetlinska. At these new positions, corps troops enjoyed improved food and supply delivery while gaining some relief from the previous inhospitable environment. The Polonina–Wetlinska position provided a panoramic view of the entire San River Valley with clear weather, contrary to the former Habsburg positions on the northern slope of the Dzial ridge, which lacked shelter and provided inadequate defensive conditions.

V Corps attack preparations required three days, mainly to transport supporting artillery into the mountains. On 17 March, the corps engaged in a moderate evening firefight while the 31st Infantry Division began assembling for the offensive endeavor.[19] Meanwhile, Group Tersztyánsky and XVIII Corps had to maintain their positions. The projected attack front proved too narrow to achieve a timely relief of the embattled fortress. Furthermore, no plans existed to reinforce neighboring Group Szurmay so it could participate in the operation or provide the necessary additional labor units to prepare and maintain roadways for the mission.

Fourth Army's reinforced southern flank forces must continue their offensive efforts along both sides of Gorlice–Jaslo. Troops had to transport artillery through deep snow, which retarded its movement.[20] After a twenty-four-hour delay, four Fourth Army infantry divisions (8th, 10th, 12th, and 39th Infantry Divisions) attacked at Gorlice, but the effort failed. Enemy defensive positions, as anticipated, proved too strong, and the failure to move artillery forward in a timely manner hindered the attacking infantry. Wasted effort and heavy casualties resulted.[21] Just six weeks later, on 2 May 1915, the Central Powers achieved their greatest victory of the war during the Gorlice–Tarnov campaign in the same area. A German army provided the manpower for that successful operation.[22]

Third Army's mission was to prevent the enemy from diverting significant numbers against Fourth Army. Once they assimilated the anticipated replacement troops into the ranks, Third Army would again launch an attack from its right flank positions. Second Army, meanwhile, must maintain its western flank positions until its replacement troops arrived while preparing its inadequate eastern flank forces to launch the attack. South Army would continue its offensive operations while Army Group Pflanzer-Baltin defended its western flank positions and its right flank units advanced to the

east.[23] Preparations for the new offensive included accelerated road maintenance efforts because of the unfavorable prevailing conditions and the
provision of available winter issue uniforms necessary to maintain battle
readiness. The operation commenced days after the fortress's 19 March
breakout effort had failed. Habsburg Supreme Command did not inform
Second Army or V Corps of the unsuccessful fortress attempt before their
own efforts.[24]

During 18 March, persistent melting conditions in the lower valley and
heavy snow in the higher elevations ensured that the transport of artillery
to the new attack positions remained a daunting task. The vital 1,200 pack
animals received inadequate care to keep them healthy. Delays in initiating
important operational measures, such as the proper positioning of artillery
and the necessity to establish telephone connections for reconnaissance missions, greatly assisted Russian counteractions.

On 17 March, seven-battalion-strong Group Lieb, assisted by the seven
additional artillery batteries, received the mission to attack Loziov, then secure the surrounding high terrain on 20 March.[25] Group Szurmay left flank
forces demonstrated to support the operation. A Group Felix, also consisting of seven infantry battalions, would follow Group Lieb, while V Corps'
33rd and 37th *Honvéd* Infantry Divisions attacked on their front areas.
On 19 March, General Conrad ordered strict adherence to the systematic
and careful preparations for the new Carpathian offensive. Army Group
Pflanzer-Baltin must be reinforced to continue both preventing the Russians
from advancing westward and supporting South Army attempts to traverse
the mountains.

On 20 March a glacier snowstorm struck, halting all forward movement. No wounded soldiers could be evacuated because an icy snow cover
again blanketed the entire front. A veteran colonel stationed on the front
described the situation:

> On 20 March a snowstorm breaks over us with a ferocity found only in
> glacial regions. All forward movement ceases; no wounded can be evacu-
> ated; entire lines of riflemen are covered as if by a white blanket. The icy
> ground, sanded smooth by storm, is impassible; digging in is impossible;
> the infantry stands without cover and unable to move in front of the en-
> emy's defensive works; the artillery is several days march behind.[26]

During the night to 20 March, Russian artillery unleashed a powerful
barrage against Third Army and attacked key positions using the weather to
their advantage. Ethnic differences compounded the problem as replacement

troops for XIX Corps' 41st *Honvéd* and 29th Infantry Divisions did not as-
similate easily. The threat of avalanches escalated; meanwhile, if snow continued to melt in the valleys, it threatened to uncover corpses, which would
create a "terrible stink."[27]

Austro-Hungarian officer casualties were highly disproportionate to
those incurred by the other major World War I combatants. They catego-
rized 48 percent as "missing and lost," an extraordinarily high number,
while the Germans listed only 16 percent and the Russians 25 percent. On
the other hand, only 8.7 percent of Habsburg officers died, while Germany
lost 16 to 18 percent and Russia 25 percent—another indication of Habsburg officers not fulfilling their duty in battle. Of the 19,296 Austro-
Hungarian officer casualties sustained in 1914, three out of four officers
killed, wounded, or missing were lieutenants, captains, or platoon and company commanders. Russian sharpshooters killed many, partly because they
made such easy targets in the suicidal frontal assaults.[28]

A Habsburg artillery officer recorded that constant enemy harassment
of nearby infantry troops denied them rest or rehabilitation; meanwhile,
strong indications abounded of an imminent major enemy offensive. The
infantry group commander ordered his soldiers to perform "busy work" to
convince his superiors of "intense activity." He depicted the situation at the
front as "the calm before the storm." The enemy apparently realized that it
opposed a handful of ill, unsupported troops. The officer described Russian
passivity as "eerie."[29]

Although seven artillery batteries had been designated to support the V
Corps undertaking, the number of guns proved far fewer. In one artillery
battery, one gun was inoperable and three were damaged. The only effective
artillery support emanated from neighboring Group Szurmay.[30] However,
the 20 March Russian general offensive that struck the Habsburg Third
Army eliminated any possibility of rescuing the fortress. The Carpathian
front remained in a state of constant flux between the 20 March czarist attack and mid-April 1915, as General Ivanov attempted to thrust through
the Carpathian Mountains onto the Hungarian plains to end the war. Simultaneously, a major Russian assault struck Second Army in the crucial
Lupkov Pass–Uzsok Pass areas.

The Russian attack resulted in the rapid seizure of key elevated terrain,
which prevented V Corps Attack Group Lieb from gaining egress to its assigned attack area. Troops attempting to retake lost positions merely regis-
tered casualties and further delay. The enemy blow struck the XVII Corps
and III Corps' 22nd Infantry Division positions, while the strategic Laborcz
Valley remained a major czarist objective. By 22 March, battle had extended

to the VII Corps. When Third Army reported that it could not maintain its positions with its outnumbered troops, Fourth Army had to transfer troop units to the hard-pressed army.[31]

The czarist objective was to penetrate the Habsburg Second and Third Army fronts to capture positions that protected important approaches onto the Hungarian plains. The czarist onslaught again threatened the remaining Habsburg positions in the critical Laborcz Valley while striking the cornerstone of the two-army fronts, the inner flank positions along the dominating Beskid ridges. Throughout the last week of March, relentless enemy pressure forced the reeling Habsburg defenders back toward the Hungarian plains. The simultaneous pressure on both armies foiled the normal procedure of wrenching exhausted troops from one endangered front sector to assist another. The resulting marches over the treacherous mountain terrain merely increased the troops' misery. Consequently, insufficient reinforcements reached the most threatened areas too late to make a difference. The enemy successes also threatened to disrupt the single supply route through Cisna to multiple Second Army corps.[32]

As Third Army commenced its retreat, enemy forces pummeled the III, VII, and X Corps in the Laborcz Valley. The Russians extended their attacks to the Fourth Army front. Despite sustaining enormous losses, the enemy attack momentum continued, bolstered by the arrival of further reinforcements. These Russian battlefield successes served as the background to the April 1915 Carpathian Easter Battle, General Ivanov's last attempt to defeat the Austro-Hungarian Army and bring Italy and Romania into the war on the Entente side. The elevated terrain south of Mezölaborcz provided the setting for fierce battle in March 1915.

Serious enemy attention also shifted to the Second Army western flank positions adjacent to Third Army's eastern area. Lacking reserve formations, Conrad considered transferring Second Army western flank forces to bolster the unstable neighboring Third Army front. This ignored the fact that neither army possessed sufficient troop numbers to close the threatening gap that now separated them. When General Ivanov extended his assault to the Second Army front, he concentrated on those weak inner army flanks to capture the main Beskid ridgelines running south of the Lupkov Pass, a major segment of the Habsburg front.

The czarist offensive also interrupted Conrad's intention to reinforce Army Group Pflanzer-Baltin, as his attention again became riveted on the threatened Third and Second army fronts. Fortunately, the Russians failed to utilize their superior numbers in the wooded mountain terrain between the Lupkov and Uzsok passes. Had czarist troops captured the Homonna

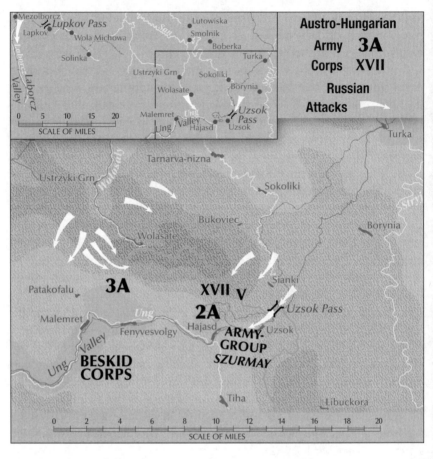

Map 9. Easter Battle, April 1915

railroad junction, it would have unhinged flank positions on the Ondava River and precluded the recapture of the Mezőlaborcz railroad junction, which was essential for any offensive effort to regain Fortress Przemyśl.

General Tersztyánsky's rapidly dwindling troop numbers and the renewed enemy attacks against the Baligrod front eliminated the possibility of transferring significant Second Army troop numbers to the threatened Third Army. Because of the increasing pressure on his own front, Tersztyánsky could transfer only 750 soldiers to the imperiled neighboring army.[33] During the next few days, Second Army front began to crumble as V and XVIII Corps fronts disintegrated. These corps needed to force the encroaching enemy back across the San River, but when the Russians pierced those corps' inner flank positions, it also eliminated any chance to rescue Fortress Przemyśl. The army had to recapture the surrendered terrain before they could again launch an attack toward the fortress.

Meanwhile, delayed preparations to launch V Corps' ill-fated offensive effort continued. The folly of the proposed rescue mission became obvious—the attacking troops numbered only 33,000, enough to seize the initial objectives, but not to gain any significant territory or advantage.[34] Also, V Corps command overestimated the protection against a surprise attack provided by its San River positions. Insufficient troop numbers existed merely to defend the overextended corps positions, and an icy snowstorm hindered troop movement. Exhausted, battle-weary troops comprised designated attack units, although they were no longer suitable for offensive purposes.[35]

In the interim, Russian forces crossed the San River undetected because of deplorable Habsburg security measures. Third Army command initially considered it insignificant that three companies of Slovak soldiers from the defending 37th *Honvéd* Infantry Division failed to perform effective security duty. However, the enemy quickly seized the blood-soaked Kiczera position as a direct result of the unpardonable negligence. The *Honvéd* Division received a belated order to hurl the enemy back across the river.[36]

When the Russians attacked the 37th *Honvéd* Infantry Division front, engineering and cavalry units moved into battle to halt the enemy. Most remaining division officers became casualties. The overextended V Corps defensive lines could no longer protect the San River front. The 37th *Honvéd* Infantry Division front finally crumbled when the enemy attacked the neighboring 33rd Infantry Division, its commander accused of "passive leadership" because his division retreated without pressing necessity. A poisoned bottle of soda water had reputedly incapacitated him. Division officers and troops who had reported to sick call in droves were returned to the front. Enemy efforts pressed back some division left flank units, partially because of the unreliability of Slovak troops. The badly mauled division surrendered eleven artillery pieces as the enemy rushed reinforcements to this vulnerable front sector.[37]

Any further V Corps retreat would seriously threaten XVIII Corps' right flank positions, but no reserve formations existed to support this endangered area. San River floodwaters temporarily protected against renewed surprise enemy attack as Russian artillery pounded Habsburg positions. In the unfortunate V Corps offensive effort, twelve battalions finally attacked the heights of Loziov during the night to 21 March. However, earlier Russian successes on the difficult terrain south of Dvernik made a defensive line untenable, forcing further retreat.[38] V Corps received an infantry division as reinforcement to rectify the 37th *Honvéd* Infantry Division's collapse. A serious problem of trust in the *Honvéd* division officers ensued.[39]

Meanwhile, V Corps could not place supporting artillery batteries until the night of 20 to 21 March, further delaying the attack.[40] The lack of reserve formations and sufficient troop numbers to maintain momentum negated any possibility of achieving success. The reinforced 31st Infantry Division and Infantry Regiment 76 finally launched the doomed offensive, with the support of the 33rd and 37th *Honvéd* Infantry Divisions. When the main attack division (the 31st) advanced to the northern slope of Loziov, it encountered enemy flanking fire. The solid Russian defensive positions repelled the frontal attacks. Infantry Regiments 73 and 76 advanced, but they completely exhausted themselves. The attack troops became apathetic, and their physical condition deteriorated.[41]

Böhm-Ermolli deplored the 37th *Honvéd* Infantry Division's failure, which had resulted in the unnecessary and premature surrender of important positions. Neglecting to support neighboring units produced a series of disasters. For example, the enemy struck XVIII Corps' Infantry Regiment 91 and captured numerous artillery pieces, precipitating its retreat just as czarist forces crossed the San River.[42] On 21 March, Group Lieb's attack units began retreating behind the river just as the enemy launched a strong attack. The Russians stormed the 33rd and portions of the 37th *Honvéd* Infantry Division positions after a night-long battle, forcing a retreat south of Dvernik.

Meanwhile, general conditions continued deteriorating as roadways remained in a wretched state, requiring constant maintenance and repair. The swollen San River swept away bridges, which required replacement and worsened the XVIII Corps situation. Stormy but thawing conditions during early 20 March reverted to frost and an icy snowstorm during the day. After a week of battle, Second Army no longer possessed any large intact combat units to halt the escalating enemy threat, thus neutralizing its offensive strength. The battered army retreated to its original jump-off positions. The enemy seized the dominating Zolobina heights and seriously threatened XVIII Corps' flank positions when they crossed the San River, because defending units could not delay the enemy advance. A meager half-battalion reserve force proved insufficient to restore the situation.

As heavy snow covered XIX Corps positions, czarist troops attacked its 29th and 41st *Honvéd* Infantry Divisions, forcing them to retreat. Simultaneously, the enemy forced X Corps' 24th Infantry Division's right flank units off the Beskid ridges, exposing 34th Infantry Division positions.[43] Because the Russians could easily hurl those units back, the order came to prepare a new rearward Habsburg defensive position. However, little progress occurred because they threw rear echelon labor units into battle to stem the enemy tide. The Russians also interrupted South Army's renewed offensive efforts by establishing new resistance lines immediately following a forced retreat. Meanwhile, if the enemy forced the Second Army further rearward, it would endanger South Army's left flank positions. The failure of Army Group Pflanzer-Baltin to achieve any further success finally forced South Army into a defensive posture.[44]

Meanwhile, the Fortress Przemyśl situation had become increasingly desperate: the garrison was on the verge of starvation, and the slaughtering of horses between 20 and 21 March left only enough animals to perform the most basic duties. Fortunately, the enemy did not launch serious attacks against the fortress on 19 to 20 March, but during the night, they assaulted defensive Sector VIII after a heavy artillery bombardment. During the next day, sustained Russian artillery barrages targeted the fortress's north front positions at the Siedliska group. The Russians then unleashed storm attacks against the northern, western, and northeastern citadel sectors and the Pod Mazurami defensive positions. On 20 March, fortress artillery fired their remaining shells. Habsburg troops dumped rifle ammunition into the San River, and preparations commenced for the destruction of all militarily useful objects.[45]

General Falkenhayn telegraphed Conrad that because the Carpathian operations held no hope for success, particularly in view of the imminent surrender of Fortress Przemyśl, Conrad should assume a defensive posture and launch an offensive against Serbia. South Army troops should participate in the Balkan campaign to secure transport of ammunition supplies to Turkey and perhaps influence Bulgaria, and possibly even Romania, to become allies.[46] By the end of March 1915, Foreign Minister Burian concluded that Russia could not be defeated in the near future. He thus urged

Conrad to take Falkenhayn's advice and launch an attack against Serbia. The renewed German pressure to initiate a Balkan campaign stemmed from the possible renewal of Entente attacks at Gallipoli and their continuing efforts to acquire Balkan allies.

A XVII Corps' 11th Infantry Division battle report reflected the situation of many Habsburg units during this battle phase. The division front extended more than ten kilometers. The 1st *Landsturm* Infantry Brigade defended a 4,000-pace front with its five remaining companies drawn from four different regiments, numbering approximately 700 rifles. Only two companies of reserve troops remained until fresh replacement troops arrived. Second and Third armies could not plug the multiple gaps that the Russians punched through their lines. Second Army possessed no reserves, but neither Conrad nor Third Army was aware of this dire situation, nor of the army's deteriorating situation. Third Army also could not maintain its forward lines when its numbers steadily declined, and thus the enemy threat to the two armies' inner flanks increased substantially.[47] Second Army received instructions to transfer any "dispensable manpower" to Third Army.[48] Meanwhile, the Russians pierced General Tersztyánsky's inner flank defensive position. Defending the Ung Valley roadways and rail line along the heights of the adjacent Uzsok Pass became critical as Group Szurmay's ability to defend its front with only one traversable communication line became increasingly questionable.[49] Second Army success required the possession of the Ung Valley.

A 21 March Second Army Command directive called attention to the embarrassing reports from the army front that created the impression that the officers', not the troops', attention now focused rearward. Thus during critical battle moments, field officers must master the dangerous situation regardless of the outcome. Böhm-Ermolli insinuated that Third Army, suffering greater losses and defending a wider front area, had halted night-long Russian storm attacks. He implored his army to maintain its positions at any cost, and he threatened that any commander that did not fulfill his duty would be relieved of command.[50]

Elsewhere, an enemy assault against the 20th *Honvéd* Infantry Division positions forced VII Corps to retreat, terminating its attack efforts as it sustained heavy casualties. The neighboring X Corps' 2nd Infantry Division, seriously weakened during the February Mezőlaborcz battles, again received the brunt of numerous Russian storm attacks. The 24th and 45th Infantry Divisions must hold their positions until reinforcements arrived.[51] Fourth Army would transfer its 26th Infantry Division, described as qualitatively and quantitatively inferior, to Third Army.[52]

XVIII Corps proved too weak to either delay or halt the encroaching enemy, while a meager reserve force could not restore its battered front. V Corps' 37th *Honvéd* Infantry Division received reinforcements to prevent an enemy breakthrough of its lines. Nevertheless, czarist forces tore the V Corps front asunder when its defenders could not fill the numerous gaps in its front lines. The 37th *Honvéd* Division's third defeat produced further demoralization, and its subsequent retreat raised the threat of enemy encirclement of V Corps Attack Group Lütgendorf, which launched the third offensive thrust toward Fortress Przemyśl. When the enemy repeatedly pierced XIX Corps' lines, the maelstrom consumed its few reserve troops as the battered survivors increasingly became apathetic. The Habsburg lines desperately needed reinforcements as division numbers swiftly sank, but where would they come from?

A 13 March battlefield report described Infantry Regiment 91 troops captured at the San River as apathetic, even confused. When the regiment received orders to attack, many men wept, while some threw themselves to the ground and let the snow bury them. Others sat in a dazed state and some intentionally exposed themselves to enemy fire. "Another man committed suicide, it appears that others have shot themselves out of sight, but this cannot be proven."[53] The XVIII Corps, its resistance capabilities also compromised, reputedly contained units in the same dire straits. Continuation of the "mini" offensive appeared senseless in light of the failed Fortress Przemyśl breakout attempt and the 37th *Honvéd* Infantry Division's lackluster performance. V Corps selected a new defensive line that its small numbers could maintain. The necessity to hold the 37th *Honvéd* Infantry Division positions caused V Corps Command to request more dependable troop replacements to prevent strong enemy forces from enveloping its eastern flank.[54] On 22 March, 37th *Honvéd* Division events forced 31st Infantry Division to terminate its offensive.

Second Army failed to prevent enemy egress into the gap between V and XVIII Corps as the Russians unleashed new assaults against V Corps. Enemy pressure increased against the inner defensive flanks on the high mountain ridges south of the Lupkov Pass, a keystone Second and Third Army position, but no intact units were available to halt it. Group Tersztyánsky's troops retreated to their original attack positions. While the exhausted Third Army proved incapable of launching counterattacks, the Second Army front reeled from czarist attacks during the next few days. Neither could counter the accurate and deadly czarist artillery fire, and supporting barrages proved woefully inadequate. However, the advancing Russians encountered increased terrain difficulties, and, as with the Habsburgs earlier in the campaign, they had to abandon multiple artillery batteries behind higher ridgelines. Thus, Russian formations discovered that their previous advantages dissipated as they moved deeper into the mountains.

General Ivanov's forces encountered additional serious material problems, such as ammunition shortages, which delayed launching some attacks. The unexpected lack of heavy artillery became a major hindrance as Russian troops moved into higher mountain terrain, where troops could only move such weapons with the utmost difficulty. The quality of czarist replacement troops also declined, which, combined with the concomitant heavy casualties and escalating troop exhaustion, negatively affected czarist troop morale. Increasingly, the unfavorable terrain conditions, delays in vital troop supplies, and multiplying communication difficulties took their toll.[55] Such negative factors assisted the retreating Habsburg troops, who previously had suffered the same dire disadvantages. Intercepted Russian communications detailed and confirmed the escalating enemy problems with conducting operations.

The often-hasty Habsburg retreats produced immeasurable suffering and additional casualties, accompanied by an enormous reduction in troop resistance power. Winter conditions replaced melting trench environments with a vengeance.[56] A 22 March operations order underscored the need to halt all enemy attacks against Third and Second armies. Habsburg commanders hoped that the enemy had finally expended its offensive strength. Fourth Army transferred its 26th Infantry Division to the imperiled Third Army while anticipating an attack against its own southern flank positions. Fourth Army must continue to "unconditionally" maintain its positions and counter an anticipated czarist attack to protect the critical Gorlice area.[57]

After the 22 March surrender of Fortress Przemyśl, the military situation turned further to Russia's favor. The besieging Eleventh Army transferred into the fierce Carpathian battle zone, enhancing the czarist numerical advantage. Russian Third and Eighth armies each received a reinforcing corps to deploy against the Habsburg Third Army. Politics also affected czarist strategy as decisive military action, in conjunction with the Entente's Dardanelles campaign, could bring Romania into the war against the Dual Monarchy.

General Ivanov finally attempted to smash into Hungary after crushing Habsburg resistance in the critical Homonna–Mezölaborcz area. The czarist advance concentrated on disrupting Habsburg railroad connections behind the Dniester River leading to the Habsburg *Hinterland*. The mission of General Brusilov's Eighth Army became to seize the major Homonna–Mezölaborcz road net and important connecting road between Wola

Michova and Homonna–Telepocz. With former czarist siege troops currently in transit, Ivanov would strike a deadly blow against the flank and rear of defending Habsburg units. The limited number of roads prevented a rapid fulfillment of the mission and forced utilization of deep column march formations over the terrain.

As the Russians smashed into the main Beskid ridges defensive positions, Habsburg Third Army northern flank forces suffered severe losses, and the army possessed inadequate reserve formations to counter the new onslaught. The staggering Second Army casualties forced the creation of a detachment of five March Battalion replacement troops designated Group Biffl, consisting of many recruits and replacement troops. The novice entity received three artillery batteries to assist its important mission of preventing a czarist breakthrough at the Second and Third armies' inner flanks on the Beskid ridges. These troops would arrive at the front between 22 and 24 March.[58]

On 22 March, an artillery officer noted that an enemy attack was imminent, but Habsburg troops were in no condition to resist. Indeed, a Habsburg retreat ensued over the main Carpathian ridges. In the meantime, the antagonists divided areas to gather straw and hay and forage for potatoes, causing the officer to remark that such sharing was only possible in an *ehrlicher* (honorable) war with the Russians. He wrote that one had the feeling that friend and foe agreed: "Don't bother me and I won't bother you."[59]

As for artillery, we had to learn new shooting techniques because this is the first time in the mountains. . . . It was difficult to observe the effectiveness of the artillery fire because of distance, snow and wooded areas, bushes and steep ridges all prevented observation. The snow cover, in particular, proved to be a major deterrent.

On 23 March, the day after the capitulation of Fortress Przemyśl, the field army's mission remained to repel enemy attacks. The day before, the fortress fired off heavy artillery shells, stuffed all gun tubes with explosives, and detonated them. They destroyed train installations. They took all the excess rifle ammunition and buried it or threw it into the San River, while demolishing all defensive works, slaughtering horses, and burning paper money.

Available reinforcements bolstered the threatened Second and Third armies fronts. V Corps transferred all dispensable forces to the more threatened neighboring XVIII Corps' Wetlina front, the recipient of incessant attacks throughout the night. These hurled stunned defenders behind the river, where they received orders to hold their positions until reinforcements arrived. The heaviest fighting, however, occurred against X Corps, survivors of the serious February battle at Mezőlaborcz.[60]

After the Fortress Przemyśl capitulation, the enemy threatened to break through both army fronts. Exhausted Third Army troops could not halt the czarist offensive by launching counterattacks as Second Army Command requested. Third Army right flank positions required immediate reinforcements, forcing the Fourth Army to relinquish further additional troops. When the Przemyśl garrison surrendered, Emperor Franz Joseph reputedly wept upon hearing the news. Some European historians have compared the fall of the fortress to the surrender of Stalingrad during World War II.[61] Three former siege divisions captured Dukla Pass during the April 1915 Easter Battle.

Meanwhile, the gap between Second and Third armies' inner flanks expanded. Group Biffl March battalion troops received orders to fill the breach because Second Army lacked the necessary troops. Though the Second Army's front began to buckle, it temporarily transferred some of its troops to the threatened Third Army X Corps. The unrelenting enemy successes against Third Army's critical right flank positions, however, also endangered Second Army positions north of the frontier ridges. The deteriorating Third Army situation prompted Böhm-Ermolli to request permission for a Second Army retreat.[62] Conrad, however, refused the request, citing morale and political considerations, particularly Hungarian leaders' fear of an invasion of their homeland.

V Corps continued to bear the brunt of ferocious enemy attacks as its situation grew increasingly desperate. Morale plummeted as troop numbers proved too weak to defend the corps' extended San River front.[63] Czarist counterstrokes neutralized all previous Habsburg offensive gains, forcing the thinning defensive lines to retreat further behind the main Carpathian ridgelines. However, the reeling armies came to enjoy an inherently stronger defensive advantage as they now forced the enemy to maneuver on higher mountain terrain.

The Russians hurled 100,000 troops against the Homonna railroad junction on 23 March, causing the Second Army defenders to buckle from the powerful attack. Conrad's customary order to defend all positions proved impossible to fulfill.[64] In one blow, Russia had established numerical preeminence and increased the threat of an invasion onto Hungarian soil. On Army Group Pflanzer-Baltin's front, the Russian Eighth Army struck the flank and rear of his forces battling the czarist Ninth Army on the Dniester River front. The enemy's objective became to encircle Pflanzer-Baltin's forces in the Styr River area, which, if successful, would threaten all north-west Carpathian Mountain crossings.[65] Major battle also erupted on III Corps' front. Earlier, three full-strength czarist regiments attacked the 22nd Infantry Division.[66] The corps lacked sufficient reserves to deflect an attack against its right flank position, where just one reserve battalion was available. Only 6,800 soldiers, many of them *Ersatz* troops, defended that portion of the front; therefore, the czarist action threatened to break through the entire corps' front.[67]

The Fourth Army chief of staff argued that another offensive effort by his army had absolutely no chance for success. He insisted that Fourth Army's 100,000 soldiers opposed 80,000 well-entrenched enemy troops, while its already limited offensive capabilities had been further compromised by the transfer of the 26th Infantry Division to Third Army. The army mission remained to prevent the diversion of opposing enemy troops to Third Army. In desperation, Conrad nevertheless insisted that Fourth Army launch an offensive action.[68]

Habsburg casualties continued to mount. VII Corps, for example, sustained 4,000 battle losses, including a significant number of officers. The same held true for III Corps, especially at its flank positions, where savage enemy attacks took their toll. X and XVIII Corps troops could barely maintain their front positions, partly because they also possessed few reserve formations. Reinforcements were desperately necessary to prevent further Russian penetration toward Wola Michova.[69] Examples of excessive smaller unit casualties included the decimated Infantry Regiment 12 and the 122nd Infantry Brigade, down to 400 soldiers, and 72nd Infantry Brigade to 100!

After two months of battle, South Army troop morale and battle effectiveness had decidedly diminished. Exhausted troops sometimes did not receive warm food for nine straight days. Unit strengths stood at best 30 to 40 percent of their original numbers. Hundreds of soldiers reported to sick call daily; by mid-March, that number climbed to 400 to 700 per day. Between 11 and 23 March, those classified as sick included 6,758 South Army troops. The army's offensive efforts ended on 23 March.[70] When Conrad ordered the South Army commander to transfer "dispensable" units to the embattled Third Army, he declined, stating that he required them for future operations.

The deteriorating Third Army situation raised the question of it retreating, which would endanger Fourth Army right and Second Army left flank positions. X Corps suffered four straight days of Russian storm attacks and concomitant severe casualties. For example, 24th Infantry Division absorbed five powerful attacks by as many as five czarist regiments. On the critical corps left flank, 2nd Infantry Division repulsed numerous enemy assaults. The unrelenting enemy pressure against X Corps and its subsequent retreats threatened the rear and flank positions of Second Army's Group Tersztyánsky. An enemy flanking maneuver forced a 24th Infantry Division retreat and the surrender of two important positions. The Russians entered the strategic eastern Laborcz Valley by overwhelming the defending 21st Infantry Division. Both sides sustained numerous casualties.[71] Third Army command frantically appealed for reinforcements, while Second Army shortened its front by a Group Tersztyánsky retreat to free up troops to assist Third Army. Conrad also appealed to General Falkenhayn for two German divisions to aid his Second Army. Falkenhayn, however, did not feel any compelling reason to place German divisions into the Carpathian hell.

Repeated field commanders' pleas for rehabilitation time for their soldiers remained unanswered because of the small available troop numbers. A 65th Infantry Brigade request citing the pressing need for recuperation time for its soldiers received a terse reply: *"Aushalten"* ("hold out"). The 71st Infantry Brigade commander warned that his decimated unit contained only exhausted survivors. The negative response he received commenced with: "Experience shows that . . ."—an inappropriate reply. Many units had been in combat since the initial late January offensive. The quality of March formation troops diminished, and allegedly, some soldiers carried white flags in their knapsacks. A Russian officer prisoner of war related that on the day of his capture, some Austro-Hungarian troops raised the white flag of surrender—testimony that helps confirm the large number of soldiers listed as missing in action. In one incident, the Russians captured five officers, including two battalion commanders, and 700 soldiers.[72]

The increasing diversity of languages spoken within Habsburg combat units led to numerous difficulties on the front. March formation replacement troops were no longer conscripted exclusively from a regiment's home territory. The language barrier, combined with the arrival of inadequately trained recruits, produced chaos. Soldiers often could not communicate with one another. The practice of interspersing *kaisertreu* units with those of questionable loyalty only made matters worse. So-called minority troops accused some Hungarian officers of displaying little concern for their welfare.[73]

Seriously depleted troop stands compelled the Habsburg army to assume a defensive stance. The senior German liaison officer at Habsburg Supreme Command headquarters, General Cramon, requested that they transfer German troops to Army Group Pflanzer-Baltin to support South

Army's efforts. By 24 March, new setbacks in the Laborcz and Ondava valleys worsened Third Army's already tenuous situation. Unrelenting Russian pressure forced the army's right flank positions rearward without serious defensive resistance. That retrograde movement negatively affected the entire army defensive line, as well as Fourth Army's southern flank positions. Conrad's aide-de-camp recorded, "Nothing more can be done because the instrument fails," and "A drop of water on a hot iron always evaporates."[74] Böhm-Ermolli contemplated a Second Army retreat into the shelter of the lower valleys behind the main Carpathian ridgelines to provide his battle-weary soldiers with some long-overdue rehabilitation. A retreat would also shorten the army's supply route, improving its efficiency, while releasing significant troop numbers previously necessary to maintain the longer supply and troop traffic.

The major 24 March attack against Third Army's eastern flank positions led to a Fourth Army order to relinquish all available troops to the hard-pressed army as quickly as possible.[75] Russian assaults persisted throughout the night. Although it was imperative that III Corps resist enemy endeavors until reinforcements arrived, czarist troops broke through its 28th Infantry Division lines in hand-to-hand combat, creating a three-kilometer gap between Third and Fourth armies' inner flanks. Severe losses forced III Corps to retreat. Low battle stands, an unusually wide front, and battle-weary troops explained the setback.[76] Neighboring units joined the retrograde movement when the situation became irretrievable. Hazardous gaps appeared between the battered defensive lines. Fourth Army right flank units had to follow suit, so it could not transfer troops to Third Army because it had to defend its own positions.[77]

The enemy's rupture of Hungarian defensive lines south of Lupkov required the immediate deployment of reinforcements to halt the onslaught because it threatened that entire front. Fierce Second Army battle continued throughout the waning days of March as the enemy repeatedly attempted to smash onto the Hungarian plains.[78] The chronic shortage of troops, however, prevented the front-line breach from being sealed.[79]

Between 20 to 26 March, III Corps sacrificed 12,000 men, its regiments manned by 500 or fewer troops (a full-strength regiment consisted of 4,600 soldiers). The surviving exhausted troops actually slept through thunderous enemy fire.[80] Second Army, as its own front crumbled, received orders immediately to dispatch reinforcements to its embattled neighbor.[81] Two brigades prepared for transfer, while Conrad pressured Böhm-Ermolli to launch an attack to relieve the pressure on Third Army. Maintenance work on roadways often proved a wasted effort as rain instantly transformed them into a muddy morass. Böhm-Ermolli utilized the unfavorable terrain conditions to justify his request for an army retreat a week later.

General Falkenhayn, in evaluating his ally's situation, calculated that thirty-four Central Power divisions opposed only twenty-four czarist units. He asked his liaison to Conrad whether German divisions would make a major difference on the Carpathian front. General Cramon, the ranking German liaison officer, acknowledged that the number of divisions was accurate. However, he added that Russian divisions consisted of considerably greater numbers than Habsburg entities, and that any German divisions transferred to this front could only help to achieve local successes rather than a decisive victory.[82] Between 26 to 27 March, the Russians continued to pound Second and Third armies; they seized sizable amounts of territory but sustained severe losses for their efforts. The Russians, attacking the entire VII Corps front, tore the 20th *Honvéd* Infantry Division's right flank asunder. However, developments particularly threatened X Corps' 2nd Infantry Division. The deteriorating Habsburg situation forced Falkenhayn to transfer the weak German *Beskiden* Corps (German Reserve Corps) to the reeling X Corps' Laborcz Valley position to prevent disaster on that sector.

Meanwhile, cold-related deaths finally began to subside, but cases of intestinal illness multiplied. Numerous instances of typhus resulted in the introduction of an immunization process. IX March Battalion units would not reach the front until the end of April, but any delay in the deployment of replacement troops could spell disaster for the Habsburg military situation. This prompted an urgent appeal to transfer the replacement battalions to the front as soon as possible. The urgency of the situation resulted in an abbreviated timetable for troop training.[83]

The unraveling of the Third Army front continued to threaten Second Army's left flank positions. Böhm-Ermolli's entire frontage began to crumble, which would force the army back to the northern frontier ridges, creating an even more serious predicament. They constantly hurled auxiliary forces into battle to stem the numerically superior enemy. Second Army Command again requested permission to retreat, but Conrad replied negatively, this time because of the necessity to protect the vital Laborcz Valley. He planned to halt the Russian advance by launching a counterattack after the arrival of the reinforcing German *Beskiden* Corps.

Second Army soldiers' confidence in their commanders suffered enormously upon learning that two of its infantry brigades had to transfer to the Third Army just as their army faced a renewed Russian onslaught. Retreat provided an obvious option, but should they surrender the blood-drenched terrain? Several compelling arguments supported a withdrawal, particularly the escalating threat to Second Army's flank positions created by the progressive Third Army withdrawals. The battered army could no longer defend the Carpathian Mountain ridges without some assistance, but how much longer could the Third Army resist the intensifying and overpowering enemy pressure? The answer would prove vital to both armies. Conrad issued his standing order, *"Durchhalten!"* ("Hold out!"), to prevent the enemy from gaining additional territory, but neither army could comply with the order. Böhm-Ermolli impressed upon Conrad the danger to his forces from further Third Army retreat, but he failed to reveal his own army's horrendous condition.

Second Army's attention focused on the wretched state of its forty-eight-kilometer-long supply lines, which covered a very difficult mountain section. XVIII Corps supply trains could barely move necessities forward ten kilometers, while it required two to three days for a supply column to reach the front.[84] Efforts to maintain regular supply delivery on the overused routes by now appeared futile. So many horses died that ammunition wagons could not supply sufficient shells to the few artillery batteries at the front.[85] In addition, if Third Army utilized the Laborcz Valley road, if forced to retreat, they would have to share it with Second Army left flank units.

By 27 March, the Habsburg military mission had become to halt Russian assaults and hold present lines until German reinforcements arrived, but because the Russians still held the initiative, they could pierce Habsburg positions wherever they chose. III Corps' 28th Infantry Division would attack the enemy at Sekova because corps flank protection required occupation of the ridges. The attack soon faltered as the seriously depleted ranks attacked full-strength Russian units, resulting in retreat. On 28 March, the Russians renewed their tenacious thrusts between the Lupkov and Uzsok passes. The single traversable Habsburg supply line and Hungarian invasion route at Cisna received particular enemy attention. As artillery units directed guns to rear echelon stations for repair, they continued to return in inoperable condition.[86] Second Army sustained 47,000 casualties during the second half of March. The 37th *Honvéd* Infantry Division suffered more than 50 percent losses, while reports estimated V Corps and Group Szurmay losses as high as 7,000.[87]

Habsburg troops surrendered the blood-soaked, battle-scarred Manilova heights on 28 March. It became questionable whether any of the mauled Habsburg units could maintain their positions for much longer. IX Corps attempted to attack through deep snow, in conjunction with III Corps action, at the Third and Fourth armies' inner flanks, but strong enemy resistance halted its efforts. Aggravating the situation, Third and Fourth armies failed to agree on a mutual strategy relative to their inner flank situation, a problem detailed in numerous Fourth Army logbook entries. The Third Army crisis continued unabated while czarist assaults against the Second and Third armies' inner flanks and Third Army midfront kept them enflamed. The Carpathian front was in danger of collapsing.

During the afternoon of 28 March, the Russians smashed through Habsburg X Corps' defensive lines. The Russian strategy to seize the Homonna railroad center and then storm onto the Hungarian plains appeared to be on the verge of success. Czarist forces also pierced Group Tersztyánsky's front, forcing a swift retreat on the Baligrod and XVIII Corps fronts. The entire Second Army would soon follow suit, while the arrival of two Fourth Army divisions temporarily halted the Third Army's left flank retreat.[88]

On 29 March, the raging battle between the Lupkov and Uzsok passes spread into the Ondava and Laborcz valleys. X and XVII Corps struggled to maintain their positions until the arrival of the German *Beskiden* Corps. The rapid diminution of Third Army fighting capability raised serious questions as to whether it could persevere much longer. The chronic lack of reserves compounded the crisis as the Russians continued to receive reinforcements. A decisive enemy assault on Palm Sunday sought to bind XVIII Corps troops to deliver a fatal blow through Wola Michova. Utilizing the inclement weather conditions, Russian troops approached Habsburg forward lines undetected, smashing into the unsuspecting defenders and hurling them back five kilometers.[89] Many defending troops, too exhausted to retreat, collapsed in the snow.

On its San River front, V Corps rebuilt bridges the river had swept away, while the shortage of labor units necessitated the use of infantry troops to maintain critical supply columns and perform crucial repair work. Supply trains returning to rear echelon areas had to travel parallel to the crumbling front. Dense fog hampered V Corps' efforts to defend its positions at Polonina, which a single company could have easily accomplished under more favorable circumstances.[90] Mounting Russian pressure along the upper San River region increasingly threatened Second Army flank positions.

More than a thousand civilian workers prepared and maintained the steep approaches to Group Szurmay's positions. When the Russians launched a concentrated attack against three XIX Corps divisions in the Mikov Valley, it also threatened Army Group Pflanzer-Baltin's 42nd *Honvéd* Infantry Division's flank and rear positions.[91] Conrad ordered Second and Third armies to prepare strong reserve forces and admonished front-line officers to display greater leadership over their troops. Second Army troop strength continued to decline, exacerbated by widespread sickness and exhaustion;

consequently, it could not create the desired reserve formations. At least an entire infantry division would be necessary merely to maintain present positions. Nevertheless, Conrad claimed that his Second Army opposed equal Russian numbers and that the enemy would soon exhaust itself from its continuing offensive actions.

In view of escalating losses, Böhm-Ermolli feared that his troops would be unable to resist the persistent enemy pressure much longer. With no hope of receiving reinforcements soon, his troops' resistance power collapsed. Thus, XIX Corps requested permission to retreat when an overwhelming seven-regiment enemy force smashed into the reeling 41st *Honvéd* Infantry Division, producing over 60 percent casualties. When the division's front buckled, it also threatened neighboring X Corps positions in the Laborcz Valley.[92] The irresistible Russian pressure also forced Corps Schmidt's left flank and XIX Corps' right flank units to retreat to hastily prepared positions.[93] Casualty numbers were staggering; IV Corps' 32nd Infantry Division lost 2,300 men in battle and subsequent retreat on 27 and 28 March. V Corps' 37th *Honvéd* Infantry Division suffered 2,400 casualties, while 13th *Landwehr* Infantry Division reported 1,530 losses from the 28 March battle and retreat. The 18,000 official Second Army casualties recorded during this brief period did not include those from the decimated 34th and 41st Infantry Divisions.[94]

As Russian troops infiltrated the Dukla Pass after a series of battles, Conrad grew despondent, with his adjutant describing the situation as hopeless.[95] The Habsburg lines truly appeared to be collapsing. Meanwhile, 55,000 VIII March Battalions troops arrived to buttress the front lines. General Tersztyánsky, however, warned that his exhausted troops could not hold their positions and that the lack of reserve units assured they could not thwart any enemy breakthrough attempts. Despite Böhm-Ermolli's command to "hold your positions to the point of total sacrifice," the 13th, 32nd, and 43rd Infantry Divisions retreated.[96]

V Corps troops, meanwhile, fled their positions under no enemy pressure, assisted by the fog conditions in the higher mountain elevations. After another sound defeat, the 37th *Honvéd* Infantry Division retreated during a raging snowstorm under the cloak of darkness. Poor supply route conditions produced chaos. The Russians, again, did not press Conrad's badly beaten troops, but V Corps must regain its surrendered San River positions, and V and XVIII Corps must hold their front lines.[97] Otherwise, the Russians could attack XIX Corps' 29th Infantry Division positions and rapidly overrun the dazed 37th *Honvéd* Infantry Division. The ultimate collapse of this front and defeat of the newly deployed VIII Corps' 9th Infantry Division

finally forced a Second Army retreat. Though Conrad calculated the opposing troop numbers to be approximately equal, Second Army estimated that
its 110,000 soldiers opposed 156,000 czarist troops.[98]

An entry in the V Corps logbook observed, "It is as though Heaven is
against us. When we attack, it starts snowing and more than one meter
deep. When the Russians attack, the snow freezes and movement is possible."[99] Under favorable weather conditions, one defending regiment could
easily resist an entire enemy corps in the mountains, but dense fog and
snow enabled smaller Russian troop units to overrun Habsburg positions
with relative ease.

The increasing threat of a breakthrough of the Second Army front north
of Cisna resulted in the transfer of undermanned weary western flank infantry units to the most seriously threatened area. Unrelenting Russian attacks
on the entire Habsburg front interfered with the usual transfer of troops
from less active portions of the front to hot spots. In addition to the unavailability of reserve troop formations, the inhospitable march conditions
ensured that any reinforcements hurrying to the front arrived too late to
affect the tide of battle. Pessimistic front-line reports to army headquarters
caused Böhm-Ermolli to reflect that the commanders, not the troops, focused their attention rearward, while the neighboring Third Army continued to maintain its positions under perhaps much greater difficulties.

Böhm-Ermolli implored his field officers to inspire further effort from
his mauled army to force the enemy to pay dearly for every inch they had
conquered earlier at such great human sacrifice. Junior officers, however,
responded that the overtaxing of front-line soldiers' capabilities made
continued resistance of the enemy risky at best. The preceding week-long
sacrificial attacks caused the common soldier to further lose faith in his
commanders. Hoping that his subordinate commanders had exaggerated
their negative reports, Böhm-Ermolli took a supreme gamble by ordering
his army to continue defending its present positions for a few more days,
disregarding the fact that his officers readied themselves to retreat. Ignoring
Second Army's predicament, Conrad ordered it to attack to take pressure
off the Third Army. A General Staff officer's daily log entry summed up the
situation: "The Second Army is pitiful, the 37. *Honvéd* Infantry Division is
hurled back, the 42. *Honvéd* Division is broken through."[100]

Multiple army reports blamed weather conditions for military failures,
but Conrad's unrelenting attack orders ignored the radical weather changes.
Reports described the unfolding Carpathian tragedy as "a crazy, terrible
crime." An artillery officer complained that he was horrified at the noncha-
lance and negligence of the Habsburg Supreme Command. The inevitable

result: the poor soldiers "melted away in a shocking manner" because no one stood up to Conrad and his Operations Bureau. An example of the travesty, Field *Jäger* Battalion 11 attacked with no artillery support, sustaining over 50 percent losses.[101] Another officer complained that as frontline soldiers starved, weather conditions continued to retard supply efforts. Overnight icy conditions required that supply movement only be limited to late morning hours if the sun came out.

Commencement of the Carpathian April Easter Battle finally halted czarist efforts to break through the tenuous Habsburg positions along the lower mountain ridges at the Hungarian frontier. The hastily transferred German *Beskiden* Corps finally joined the battered Habsburg X Corps on the Laborcz Valley front and successfully reversed the unrelenting Third Army travail. Weather played a crucial role in the Easter Battle; however, this time, in a reverse of fortune, the Russians suffered more. Snowstorms followed by melting temperatures produced flooding and water-filled trenches in the valleys, with icy terrain in the higher elevations. In some lower areas, water saturated the ground to the extent that the corpses of fallen soldiers remained in an upright position. The Russians paid a heavy price for their early April successes, as growing indications suggested that the czarist esprit de corps had reached its limit. This indicated that the Russians no longer possessed adequate forces to exploit their successes. The czarist offensive halted, and they paused before preparing to launch another effort in early May. Fateful events would interfere with their plans.

One positive consequence of the severe Carpathian winter weather was the eradication of some battlefield diseases. However, rising temperatures heralded renewed widespread outbreaks of cholera. Indolence on behalf of the populace and local civil authorities exacerbated the appalling sanitary and supply situations. Oftentimes their shortsightedness hindered the implementation of preventive sanitary measures. Immunization programs often met passive resistance, and troops ignored good hygiene practices. Soldiers, out of necessity, wore the same uniforms for weeks and months at a time and rarely bathed, shaved, or cut their hair. This provided fertile ground for the spread of infectious diseases, particularly typhus, which also ran rampant on the Serbian front.[102] Before discovering the connection between the spread of disease and lice, typhus sometimes claimed as many lives as battle; however, new delousing methods rid the Carpathian armies of this devastating illness.

The Balkan theater also influenced Habsburg military calculations, while British and French landings at Gallipoli near the Dardanelles raised the specter of possible Turkish defeat. This caused General Falkenhayn to again propose a rapid crushing of Serbia to open access to Turkey, at least to seize the northeastern Njegotine corner of the country.[103] But where would Conrad find the troops for this military action? Then the failed Gallipoli campaign opened the Balkan peninsula to Central Power expansion, resulting in the fall 1915 conquest of Serbia by combined Austro-Hungarian, German, and Bulgarian forces after the Gorlice–Tarnov offensive had removed Russian pressure in the Carpathian Mountains and driven Romanov troops hundreds of miles into their own territory.

Meanwhile, in early April, Habsburg troops clung to the crests of ridges and passes against increasingly vehement Russian attacks. Conrad continued to hope that the horrendous Russian losses, particularly those suffered during the Laborcz Valley melee, would weaken czarist numbers. The arrival of Fortress Przemyśl siege divisions belied this speculation and provided renewed czarist numerical advantage. Several important questions arose, one being the critical protection of the Ung Valley heights located before the Uzsok Pass area. Could Group Szurmay defend Second Army's extreme eastern flank area and Uzsok Pass despite possessing only one usable communication line? In addition, enemy encroachment threatened South Army's left flank positions into the Ung Valley—could this key terrain be defended?

Upon its deployment behind the reeling X Corps front, the weak German *Beskiden* Corps prepared to halt the consistent czarist military successes in the Laborcz Valley and regain some terrain. Exhaustion finally overcame the Russian forces. Snow conditions caused serious delays in czarist troop movements and frequent supply stoppages. In the meantime, the Habsburg Second Army finally retreated behind the main Carpathian ridgelines to occupy much more favorable defensive positions while further complicating czarist logistical problems. The czarist Easter attack enjoyed an initial advantage of more favorable weather conditions and a lack of intact Habsburg defensive units. Thus, until mid-April, the Carpathian front remained in constant crisis as the Russians continued to batter the hapless defenders. The unfavorable Second Army preretreat positions at the last high Carpathian ridgelines unnerved the defending troops because it appeared that another major czarist thrust would easily bludgeon through their defensive cordon.

On 1 April, Conrad finally learned the true extent of the deteriorating Second Army situation. He immediately ordered the transfer of several divisions from the rupturing Third Army front with the important proviso that it occur only after the *Beskiden* Corps deployed on the X Corps front. Second Army had already reported that it could no longer maintain its ridgeline positions when another collapse of V and XVIII Corps' inner flank positions forced the army to retreat.[104] The deteriorating situation at the Cisna supply center portended its impending loss.[105] The enemy also attacked potential retreat routes, precluding an orderly rearward movement. Second Army finally received permission for its western flank to withdraw, while the middle Carpathian battlefront broke at several locations. XIX Corps initiated its retreat on 2 April.[106] Thirteen to fourteen enemy divisions opposed approximately 100,000 benumbed Second Army soldiers, but the high Carpathian ridges now posed a major hindrance to the advancing czarist forces.[107] The leisurely czarist pursuit of the retreating Habsburg forces proved beneficial.

Second Army vanguard units maintained their main Carpathian ridgeline positions during the retreat. The army's retrograde movement threatened the loss of Uzsok Pass. Group Tersztyánsky received orders to maintain its present positions until 3 April because of the pending arrival of the German *Beskiden* Corps for the Third Army. Second Army's retreat must extend only as far as necessary. Meanwhile, the enemy deployed the previous Fortress Przemyśl siege formations against the decimated Third Army X Corps troops.[108] The Russians appeared to be on the verge of invading Hungary just as the German *Beskiden* Corps arrived and deployed behind X Corps' positions.

Through the ranking German liaison officer, General Cramon, Conrad requested four additional German divisions for the Carpathian front, but suggested the Fourth Army southern flank area for their deployment. Falkenhayn replied that he had no available troops. Relative to negotiations with Italy, Habsburg leaders unanimously continued to refuse to surrender the vital Adriatic coastal areas near the major Pola naval base to the erstwhile neighbor. Conrad repeated his earlier recommendation to negotiate a separate peace agreement with Russia, so they could counter Italy.[109] Specifically, if Rome opened a third front, it meant an overextended and outnumbered Austro-Hungarian military force.

Returning to Second Army and its eastern flank retreat movement, which would compromise the vital Uzsok Pass positions, South Army Command strongly protested the possible surrender of this critical position, over which so much blood had spilled. Second Army command, citing heavy casualties and its troops' extreme fatigue, responded that Group Szurmay had no choice but to retreat.[110] South Army's General Linsingen, however, convinced Conrad to order Second Army not to evacuate the vital pass area. Eventually Conrad transferred South Army to this portion of the Second Army front, once Böhm-Ermolli's troops had retreated.[111] Conrad ordered

Group Szurmay to defend the Uzsok Pass area, where it would now join an extended South Army flank position. The group must maintain that front while shifting its left flank positions rearward to maintain contact with retreating Second Army forces. The Second Army retreat also raised the danger of enemy troops being able to maneuver behind the Beskid Mountain ridges south of Mezőlaborcz, enabling the Russians to seize the Homonna area. To avert this dangerous possibility, Conrad attempted to transfer four battered and depleted Third Army X Corps divisions (2nd, 21st, 24th, and 45th Infantry Divisions) to the Second Army, but events soon intervened to alter the situation. At the same time, Conrad transferred Group Szurmay (7th, 38th, and 40th Infantry Divisions and *Honvéd* Infantry Brigade 128) from Second to South Army to hold the Uzsok Pass.[112]

The escalating threat to Third Army's right flank lines delayed the decision of whether their units could transfer to bolster the Second Army. The German *Beskiden* Corps would eventually relieve the four decimated X Corps infantry divisions on the front lines.[113] The German corps deployed, after delays from railroad technical difficulties, at the Third Army's threatened eastern flank. Meanwhile, major battle erupted in the East Beskid region.[114] Successful enemy attacks between the Laborcz and Virava valleys against exhausted defending Habsburg troops raised the question of whether X Corps could maintain its positions until the *Beskiden* Corps arrived.

On 2 April, heavy snowfall, interlaced with freezing rain, limited events on the Second Army front. One supply route section that required constant maintenance became impassable for artillery and heavy wagons, while the slippery, frozen terrain rendered it unsuitable for large supply columns. Only lighter Polish wagons and horses could traverse the terrain. All available labor units kept the critical XIX Corps supply route open as front-line soldiers assisted in the thankless efforts.[115] A serious and perpetual shortcoming of Habsburg artillery, particularly heavy guns, during the three Carpathian Mountain campaigns resulted in the inability to counter effective Russian heavy artillery. The rapidly deteriorating military situation prompted multiple corps commanders to transfer their artillery units back from the front areas, partially because of shell shortages, the difficulties encountered in weapon emplacement, and the continued retreat movements, which worsened an already untenable situation.

Group Szurmay and V Corps now must defend Uzsok Pass and the strategic Ung Valley. When 37th *Honvéd* Infantry Division troops marched to that valley, its 2,600 soldiers desperately required rehabilitation.[116] Both V Corps divisions remained in terrible condition; in the meantime, Group Szurmay repulsed multiple enemy attacks. As the Second Army retreat commenced, enemy troops crossed the San River to attack 37th *Honvéd* Infantry Division positions, forcing it and the 31st Infantry Division to retreat.[117] The situation had become so dangerous that ammunition would only be transported to the front when absolutely necessary.[118]

Czarist forces smashed into XVIII Corps, defending a nineteen-kilometer front with 14,334 troops. Strong enemy forces then pierced the Polonina–Wetlinska defensive lines. XVIII Corps, possessing only one weak reserve battalion, had to retreat through Cisna. The Russians struck Infantry Regiment 25 during a heavy snowstorm that hindered the defenders' visibility. The 31st Infantry Division command reported that the overwhelming demands placed on its troops, the precipitous decline in troop numbers, and the lack of either reserve troops or reinforcements made it impossible to maintain its lines. Two meters of snow shrouded mountain positions, while the rocky terrain made it impossible to find shelter, resulting in further cases of frostbite. The combined troop strength of Infantry Regiments 38 and 44 and Bosnian-Herzegovinian Regiment 3 was only 1,000 soldiers. Troop conditions remained deplorable, and the constant battle since 22 January led to physical and moral depression, as well as apathy.[119]

Conrad ordered the battered XIX Corps to maintain the high terrain at Kiczera until the 29th Infantry Division could retreat. Corps artillery had to withdraw at night, making its rearward movement much more difficult. The 41st *Honvéd* Infantry Division also retreated, but it ruptured its connection to the main Beskid ridges.[120] Corps Schmidt, defending a thirteen-kilometer front with only 12,240 troops, joined the retreat movement.

An interesting sidelight to the deteriorating Habsburg situation involved the personal interchanges between the South Army commander, General Linsingen, and Second Army's Böhm-Ermolli. As the Second Army retreat commenced on 2 April, Linsingen declared that the army's retrograde movement was unnecessary. Conrad then offered Linsingen a Second Army division because he would soon extend South Army's front (Linsingen had consistently attempted to enlarge his command radius and garner additional reinforcements), but he responded that he would not accept a defeated and retreating division from another army.[121] Noting the mutual accusations exchanged between Habsburg Second and Third Army commands, Colonel Schneller, section leader of the General Staff Italian Group, scorned the helplessness of the Second Army. Each army blamed the other for its unfavorable situation, leading Schneller to write that the "Big Brother" (the Germans) would resolve the multiple military difficulties.[122]

When Conrad approved the transfer of Group Szurmay to General Linsingen's command, he ordered that it maintain its present positions and not join the Second Army retreat. This extended the South Army front from sixty to one hundred kilometers; its western flank positions now stretched from the Styr River west over Uzsok Pass. Linsingen convinced Conrad that if his left flank units retreated, the Russians could capture the important Ung Valley railroad and roadways connecting to the Uzsok Pass. Group Szurmay therefore shortened its front beside the South Army left flank positions. This specific area witnessed heavy battle during the first week of April, as the Russians' advance toward the Ung Valley seriously threatened South Army's flank units.

Böhm-Ermolli initially intended the Second Army to retreat behind the main Carpathian ridgelines to blockade the critical Ung Valley and Uzsok Pass southwest of Fenyvesvölgy. His extreme right flank positions, in that case, would anchor at the Styr River. Meanwhile, he and his chief of staff protested the transfer of Group Szurmay to the South Army and requested that they both be relieved of their commands, but Conrad flatly denied the request.[123] Another rift had occurred between Habsburg and German General Staff officers. On 2 April, the Russians unleashed another major attack against the hapless X Corps. The corps subsequently retreated an additional four kilometers, further depressing the already-low troop morale and increasing the possibility of other divisions having to follow suit.[124] The east Laborcz Valley region remained a decisive battlefront. Possessing no reserve forces, the enemy pressure continued to sap any remaining X Corps' strength; 2nd Infantry Division had again dwindled down to 2,000 men.

The *Beskiden* Corps, after its rail delays, finally arrived behind the Third Army rear echelon. The corps troops then navigated a difficult eighteen-kilometer stretch of inhospitable terrain when they approached the X Corps front. The 21st and 24th Infantry Divisions initially held their positions.[125] Its 25th Infantry Division buttressed X Corps' 2nd and 24th Infantry Division inner flanks, while its 35th Reserve and 4th Infantry Divisions assumed positions behind the battered corps to bolster the decimated Habsburg divisions. The German reinforcements thereby formed a barricade to the Beskid invasion route into Hungary. General Marwitz, its corps commander, immediately ordered X Corps to hold its present positions, while his German 25th Reserve Division launched a counterattack and quickly advanced.[126]

Meanwhile, when the enemy offensive against Third Army finally stalled then halted, Second Army had to resist Russian hammer blows for a few more days. XVIII Corps retreated south of the Wetlina Valley ridgelines without enemy pressure. Troops had to shovel snow along the retreat route while maintaining close contact with X Corps, but the enemy did not immediately cross the Wetlina River. XVIII Corps could barely delay further

Russian attacks. Deep snow made footpaths along the ridges dangerous for movement.[127] Russian failure to rapidly pursue the retreating troops spared additional serious losses. V Corps' retreat, aided by foggy conditions and no enemy interference, severed its connections to XVIII Corps.[128] Labor units and civilians hastily constructed new defensive positions and attempted to maintain traversable routes. V Corps Command meanwhile submitted inaccurate and misleading reports to army command, while its corps supply trains fled the battle area.[129]

The renewed Russian attacks against Third Army's right flank positions interfered with Second Army's urgent need for reinforcements from that army. This affected the mentioned V Corps retreat. While repulsing numerous enemy attacks, Group Szurmay also had to secure the gap between it and V Corps positions.[130] The question remained whether to transfer Third Army's battered X Corps' 2nd, 21st, 24th, and 45th Infantry Divisions to Second Army. The decision depended on whether to launch an offensive against the unrelenting enemy thrust against Third Army or support Second Army in its continuing travail. General Tersztyánsky ordered that his present positions be held as long as possible, so rear-guard units temporarily blocked his forward frontier ridgelines.[131] The rearward transfer of artillery units received priority.[132] Although more advantageous for Second Army in the present situation, the army's new resistance lines were not as formidable as the former Beskid ridge positions. The enemy meanwhile attempted to extend its previous military successes by attacking Second Army's right flank positions.

Though X Corps' situation improved somewhat on 3 April, its 21st and 24th Infantry Division positions became dangerously exposed when three-sided enemy fire forced the 2nd Infantry Division to retreat, opening a six-kilometer gap at its flank. The 81st and 82nd Russian Reserve Divisions, participants in the earlier Fortress Przemyśl siege, now compounded X Corps' desperate situation. The 21st Infantry Division, which received the order to maintain its lines until German reinforcements arrived, had its connection to X Corps severed, making it vulnerable to an enemy flank attack.[133] It retreated when the Russians attacked 2nd Infantry Division flanks; heavy losses exacerbated both divisions' depressed state.[134]

Between 1 and 3 April, Group Szurmay encountered many difficulties moving its supplies, ammunition, and, in particular, artillery to the front. The inhospitable forest terrain required significant troop numbers just to maintain the corps positions. General Szurmay's left flank units retreated with the Second Army rearward movements, but in the interim, South Army's situation had also become critical.[135] As Second Army's left flank units retreated, the Russians invaded the Ung Valley, seriously threatening both V Corps and Group Szurmay. This caused Szurmay to request reinforcements to prevent the Russians from advancing through Patakafalu in the Ung Valley.[136] The Russians also attacked neighboring VII Corps' 17th Infantry Division lines when X Corps commenced its retreat, also forcing that corps to retreat. Labor crews began to prepare a second retreat route, while just three companies of reserve troops were available to reinforce the threatened lines.[137] The Habsburg military situation had become so critical that General Bolfras of the emperor's military chancellery stated, "We are on the verge of catastrophe, the existence of the monarchy is anyone's guess."[138]

Difficult terrain conditions on its extended front also contributed to Second Army losses. Army Group Tersztyánsky protected a thirty-kilometer front with 40,000 soldiers, while 5,600 XVIII Corps troops defended a fourteen-kilometer area.[139] General Tersztyánsky estimated that his 40,000 soldiers opposed 90,000 enemy troops as battle erupted at his right flank. If his forces must retreat, it would unhinge at least an entire corps front.[140] XIX Corps' 29th, 34th, 41st, and portions of the 9th and 27th Infantry Divisions now consisted of only 25,728 soldiers, or the equivalent of one and a half full-stand divisions. Corps Schmidt's 13th, 32nd, 43rd, and portions of the 27th, 31st, and 44th Infantry Divisions numbered only 12,240 soldiers (less than one full-stand division). Battle reduced Infantry Regiments 25 and 76 to 5,083 troops on 30 March, then 2,180 by 3 April.[141] In the interim, when XIX Corps' 29th and 43rd Infantry Divisions retreated, its 13th and 41st *Honvéd* Infantry Division fronts became threatened. The Russians attacked the battle-weary XVII Corps' 1st *Landsturm* Brigade, then hurled the corps' right flank units back, recreating a gap between Third and Fourth armies' inner flanks. Third Army's right flank forces withdrew to the next Beskid ridgeline defensive positions.[142]

The excessive lack of artillery pieces through loss and damage remained persistent problems. Entire batteries fell silent, either from guns in repair or lack of shells. Ten Second Army field howitzer batteries required repair.[143] The lengthy turnaround time for such service signified that many guns remained out of action for long periods. Troops abandoned artillery during their many retreats. A Second Army advantage: after its early April retreat, it had shortened its supply and march approaches, and it could now deploy numerous additional artillery batteries in the forward front lines, at last providing adequate artillery support for the defending troops.

On 3 April an artillery captain recorded that his troops' "recent rehabilitation" lasted only one or two days. He bemoaned the enormous Russian artillery numerical superiority, and the fact that even the slightest noise led to knee-jerk reactions by his troops. He related that moving his company's artillery pieces eight kilometers required twenty-four hours, noting that the Russians were obviously cognizant of Habsburg artillery positions and concentrated their heaviest guns to counter them. This forced periodic battery position changes, which required the preparation and movement to new gun emplacements on inhospitable mountain terrain. Intermittent periods of melting temperatures worsened the situation by turning the ground into a quagmire. During his troops' short rest period, he normally placed his soldiers in an infection hospital to restore their nerves. The unit desperately needed reinforcements, and its cannons required repair.[144]

The shortage of weaponry remained a significant problem. The Austrian Steyr factory produced only 20,000 rifles during March, the lone Hungarian factory 8,000. War Minister Krobatin claimed that with an additional 200,000 weapons, he could transfer a similar number of troops to the front.[145] Artillery was also in short supply: only seventy new guns were presently available. Conrad became infuriated with Second Army leadership when repeated localized enemy breakthroughs caused some commanders to surrender entire front positions, immediately threatening neighboring units. Conrad threatened to remove any commander who surrendered his front lines without proper reason.

Second Army defended its thin lines to protect Hungary until late April. Retreating over major ridgelines during early April, the mountainous terrain separated the various units that would later reunite. When Russian assaults hurled the Third Army left flank positions rearward, only Fourth Army's right flank threat to the advancing enemy prevented catastrophe. The question remained: could Habsburg troop numbers prove sufficient to halt the unrelenting enemy onslaught? Only the last Hungarian Carpathian frontier ridges now separated Second Army from the enemy.

XVIII Corps' battlefield state was indicative of other Carpathian front units. Blizzard conditions prevented the effective corps cooperation necessary to offset Russian numerical superiority. Severe losses devastated the corps, and no hope existed for reinforcements. Deep snow provided some cover for the weary surviving troops, who remained in constant danger of a surprise enemy attack.[146] Meanwhile, the increasing emergence of nationality problems exacerbated the situation. On 3 April, Prague Infantry Regiment 28 numbered approximately 2,000 men. By the evening of 4 April, only 150 men remained. At least three companies of nonwounded soldiers surrendered to the enemy without firing a shot. This created a dangerous situation for the neighboring 8th Infantry Division, whose exposed flank sustained numerous casualties.[147] This incident became the most infamous example of reputed Czech treasonable activity and one of the first mass desertions during the war, but contrary to some historiographical accounts, the regimental band did not march across the freezing mountain terrain covered with a meter of snow! In actuality, enemy fire had almost completely decimated the regiment's officer and noncommissioned officer corps, and the unit received inadequately trained and armed troops. In addition, the *Ersatz* troops received their rifles upon arrival at the front, where they encountered bitter cold temperatures while in an indefensible position. Archduke Friedrich dissolved the regiment in this early example of mass desertion. Military High Command utilized the incident to attempt to expand its authority over the Bohemian civil administration because it had failed to halt subversive activities.

On Easter Sunday, unarmed Russian soldiers climbed out of their trenches on the Habsburg Fourth Army front and at Fortress Przemyśl's perimeter to present gifts to their opponents. The Habsburg soldiers reciprocated on the Orthodox holiday. Conversely, on the Carpathian front, savage battle continued. The case of Infantry Regiment 42 provides important insight on the constant difficulties encountered in transporting supplies, as its trains required five hours to move four kilometers on a 400-meter incline path. The snow-covered Beskid ridges disrupted all operations. By day, troops could find themselves knee-deep in water; by night, they endured bone-chilling conditions. Thousands of animals perished.

The Habsburg army needed to maintain its positions on 4 April, although Second Army surrendered additional terrain. Superior czarist numbers overpowered Second Army's vanguard units protecting the main Beskid ridgeline.[148] On 4 and 5 April, the Russians stormed the Kobila heights, initiating a week-long bloody battle over that czarist objective. During a strategy meeting to discuss cooperative V and XVIII Corps missions, V Corps commander received orders to prevent an enemy breakthrough into the Ung Valley, specifically at Patakujfalu. Group Szurmay must cooperate with V and XVIII Corps to repel the persistent Russian assaults. With its 14,000 soldiers, V Corps needed to prevent the incessant enemy attempts to break through its positions and establish a foothold in the Uzsok and Patakujfalu basins. The corps must launch counterattacks rather than just remain in a defensive mode, while corps commanders had to utilize the difficult conditions to create confusion at the enemy's flank and rear positions and drive them out of the wooded terrain.[149]

General Ludendorff wrote to Moltke, the former German chief of the General Staff, concerning the Habsburg ally, stating, "In reading the deceitful reports from the Austrian General Staff, the Austrians are not really fighting against numerical superiority. The officer corps is incapable of resistance, the Austrians retreat without battle. We will support them or be beaten; because of the Balkans we cannot allow them to be defeated."[150] This opinion was not unique to Ludendorff; many German officers shared his view.

On 5 April, Third Army's middle front suffered further severe setbacks, retreating almost ten kilometers, or half the distance to the important area of Sztropko. Simultaneously, the Russians smashed the Habsburg Third and Fourth armies' inner flank connections.[151] Thus, the overpowering czarist military successes against Third Army also threatened Second Army. The *Beskiden* Corps commander paid particular attention to the Second Army retreat movement because of its potential effect on his own flank security. All X and *Beskiden* Corps forces became engaged in battle, but once their situation stabilized, they would transfer the first available Habsburg units to Second Army.[152] The enemy progress against Second Army also forced Group Szurmay's left flank positions rearward. The Russians finally succeeded in breaking into the Ung Valley—their goal was to seize Czeremcha, which finally occurred on 11 April after fierce battle.

The terrain conditions continued to significantly influence Second Army battlefield events, limiting fighting to skirmishes or small battles. The perceived Russian objective to penetrate the army's western flank positions demanded that they deploy all available reserve forces behind the XIX Corps' right flank area to prevent local setbacks that could produce even greater crisis. XVIII Corps received the last available Habsburg reserves, so none remained for XIX Corps' extended front. The Russians expanded their attack to Kozialta, which developed into a bloody battle.[153]

A discussion relative to Group Tersztyánsky's strategy on 5 April emphasized that it must maintain and improve its positions as well as cooperate with neighboring units. It also needed to utilize terrain features to launch offensive thrusts at enemy flank positions and counterattacks. Conrad and the Second Army commander would not accept passive leadership and made the creation of reserve formations to conduct offensive operations a priority. They would transfer additional artillery units forward since the newly established Second Army defensive terrain favored the deployment of additional guns. Several approach roadways to the army's new positions became available, expediting supply and troop movement, as well as presenting far better maintenance conditions than experienced earlier along the higher mountain ridgeline elevations. The military situation demanded that the Second Army lines hold regardless of the circumstances.[154]

It was crucial that Italy remain neutral to avoid another war theater that could prove fatal to Austria-Hungary. The Habsburgs had no troops to prevent Italy and Romania from invading the Dual Monarchy to gain their perceived *irredenta*. The present Carpathian Mountain defensive lines must therefore hold, despite Second Army's crumbling front and South Army Group Szurmay's buckling defensive positions. Intelligence reports surmised that Italy probably would not declare war during the latter half of April if the present Habsburg lines held. Launching an offensive against Serbia, as suggested again by General Falkenhayn, lacked purpose, particularly in the present dire circumstances. Nor, they argued, would a Western front victory influence Romania and Italy's stance, whose rapt attention focused on the Carpathian Mountain campaign to determine their further actions.

In early April, it appeared that the enemy would finally puncture the flimsy lines of Third Army's X Corps. Between 2 and 5 April, the Russians extended their attacks against the hapless corps, but this time to no avail. Any X Corps or reinforcing *Beskiden* Corps advance required cooperation with the VII Corps right flank units, but the Russians continued to batter those positions. In addition, the enemy pierced the XIX Corps' 41st *Honvéd* Infantry Division's right flank position and broke through XVII Corps' front. Possessing no reserve troops, VII Corps could not rectify the situation after the breaching of its 1st *Landsturm* Brigade lines on 3 April during a snowstorm. The setback created far-reaching effects on the Third Army's right flank positions, including a twelve-kilometer retreat. VII Corps, although absorbing enormous losses, halted the Russian attacks, but a XVII Corps retreat forced V and VII Corps to follow suit. It became questionable whether the new Second Army defensive line would hold, and it raised the question whether the *Beskiden* Corps should halt its initial successful offensive effort because of the neighboring army's (Second) deteriorating situation. On Easter Monday, the *Beskiden* Corps conquered the eastern Laborcz Valley Kobila position. However, Army Group Tersztyánsky's repeated setbacks threatened to destabilize the entire Second Army situation. Successful operations hinged on the formation of strong reserve forces, but where would they come from?[155] All available troops and auxiliary forces struggled merely to maintain their porous defensive lines. The situation of Second Army's right flank position remained so critical that they requested replacement troops before they had completed their basic training.

On 6 April, the Russians began a major offensive against Third Army south of Mezölaborcz and also attacked the Second Army. This resulted in a request for Third Army to transfer its four combat-fatigued X Corps divisions to buttress Böhm-Ermolli's buckling lines. Meanwhile, just before the Russians seized the important Polonina-Wetlinska positions, the defending infantry received orders to hold the heights positions until the removal of supply trains.[156] Only one route existed for the retreating supply trains to Cisna. Corps Schmidt likewise initiated a retreat, while XVIII Corps left flank units retreated without enemy effect.[157] The Russians broke through defending lines between Kozialta and Nagypolany.

The Russians then unleashed a powerful attack against VII Corps positions at Sztropko. Second Army required reinforcements merely to hold its lines, so Conrad ordered Fourth Army to transfer yet another of its divisions as soon as possible. It became the 51st *Honvéd* Infantry Division.[158] In the interim, VII Corps' 1st *Landsturm* Brigade, with its lines broken through, increased the danger of a czarist envelopment. Moreover, there were still no available reserve forces.[159] Meanwhile, the *Beskiden* Corps commander ordered that X Corps' 21st Infantry Division prepare for transfer to Second Army because of its serious setbacks (General Marwitz took command of the X Corps, as well as the German *Beskiden* Corps). Combat entangled all four X Corps divisions, so none could transfer. Meanwhile, the increasingly dire Third Army situation led to a countermanding order relative to transferring any of its troops to Second Army.[160]

Russian attacks also struck the new V Corps left flank defensive positions on the dominating heights northeast of Patakafalu, intended to protect the Ung Valley railroad line and roads. The Russians fully recognized the strategic importance of the area. Meanwhile, the early arrival of the inadequately trained IX and X March Battalions (originally scheduled to arrive on 20 April) led Conrad to contemplate planning a renewed general offensive along the entire Carpathian front. Although the battered Habsburg army required reinforcements just to defend its elastic defense lines, Conrad considered attacking again.

The Russians meanwhile focused their attention on the Ung Valley, in particular between the Second and South armies' inner flanks. Enemy forces penetrated Second Army lines at three locations, and on 7, 8, and 11 April, the Russians again stormed Group Szurmay's positions. The group's situation remained critical for several days, while on 8 April the enemy launched an assault against its battered forces in the Kiczera area, where they drove the 7th Infantry Division back to the entrance of the pass. Lacking reinforcements, General Szurmay would be unable to maintain his positions much longer, particularly when his middle units retreated to the Uzsok

Pass, but the left flank held at Czeremcha.[161] Yet by mid April, despite all the repeated crises, Habsburg lines held, setting the stage for the successful early May 1915 Gorlice–Tarnov campaign. On the Russian side, they no longer possessed adequate reserves to exploit their advantageous position to invade Hungary.

At the same time, improved weather conditions led to a renewed Russian thrust against Second Army's western flank positions. The arrival of the 51st *Honvéd* Infantry Division, however, helped terminate the enemy threat by 13 April. German General Hoffmann, meanwhile, summed up the situation in the Northwest front: "We have constructed strong positions everywhere which enables us to remain on the defensive, although seven divisions have been transferred to the Austrians and we have received few reinforcements from the west."[162]

On 8 April Colonel Schneller, section chief of the "I" (Italian) Group, reported that Italy failed to respond to Vienna's recent diplomatic proposals, but that he did not consider its activity as indicating a serious escalation of the situation. Rome still awaited further Carpathian battlefield developments, such as a Russian victory, before a final decision. In an 8 April telegram to Conrad, General Falkenhayn insisted that the problematic Italian situation might still turn out favorably, and that the eastern campaign required all of the Habsburg forces for the Russian operation. However, if Italy entered the war, he insisted that its initial military efforts would be limited to attempting to occupy disputed *irredenta* areas. Therefore, there should be no diversion of significant fighting forces to the Italian theater so that they could obtain a decisive Eastern front victory before having to worry about a third Habsburg front.[163]

Conrad, on the contrary, insisted that Italy would not be content to occupy its *irredenta* objectives, reemphasizing that an Italian military intervention would decide the war. They could only prevent such a potential catastrophe by launching another major offensive against the Russians. Conrad insisted that they could not resist an Italian invasion simply because they lacked the troops necessary to counter invading Italian and Romanian forces because the majority of Habsburg troops remained occupied on the Eastern front. By the end of April, increased Italian and Romanian territorial demands made halting the czarist Carpathian threat even more imperative. As the Russians maintained their attacks, however, *k.u.k.* troops appeared increasingly incapable of maintaining an effective defense. Conrad again demanded the launching of a major offensive as early as possible and inquired about the creation of German formations as a new strategic reserve.[164] He repeated his request for additional German divisions to counter Italy and Romania if they entered the war, but Falkenhayn denied it. Citing the deteriorating military situation, Falkenhayn replied that securing the Carpathian Mountain front took precedence over the Italian or Romanian fronts. Revealing his bitterness concerning the increasing dependence on his German ally, Conrad wrote, "I cannot begin to tell you how disgusted I am with the infiltration of German troops, but the head must rule quietly over the heart."[165] Conrad telegraphed Falkenhayn on 9 April, again requesting German reinforcements so that he could delay an invading Italian force if they declared war. He insisted that the Italians, not Vienna, intentionally dragged out negotiations, intending to intervene in the war at an advantageous moment.[166] To his surprise, Falkenhayn then informed Conrad that he could transfer an additional German Corps to the Habsburg front. It would create an allied German-commanded army, but receive its orders from Habsburg Supreme Command.[167] In a 10 April telegram to Falkenhayn, Conrad accepted the fact that they must obtain an Eastern front victory before he concerned himself with a potential Italian invasion; nevertheless, he repeated his request for seven German divisions for deployment against Italy. Achieving a rapid Eastern front victory depended upon maintaining the Carpathian front defenses—a much more difficult task after the surrender of Fortress Przemyśl and release of czarist siege troops to deploy on the major battlefield.[168]

Meanwhile, as the Carpathian situation continued to deteriorate, the chief German liaison officer at Habsburg Supreme Command informed Conrad that he must maintain his present positions at all cost. General Cramon informed Falkenhayn that the Habsburg army displayed indications of imminent collapse. On the Carpathian front, the commander of a X Corps division panicked, resulting in the entire corps retreating. General Marwitz, commander of *Beskiden* Corps, relieved the commander of his position and reported to Conrad that both X Corps' and neighboring Second Army's morale remained poor because of the troops' combat fatigue. Conrad then received a welcome telegraph confirming the transfer of German troops to the Carpathian front.[169]

Incessant enemy assaults continued against the Second Army front, with some units sustaining 60 percent casualties in the weeklong battle. XIX Corps battled continually reinforced enemy contingents; thus, a counterattack failed, but troops neutralized enemy attacks against V and XVIII Corps. On 8 April, particularly adverse weather conditions intervened to affect the pace of battle.[170] A 9 April intelligence report revealed that a czarist corps previously besieging Fortress Przemyśl now fought in the Beskid ridge battle. The enemy had also fielded major reserve forces in the Lupkov area. Russian troop numbers, however, appeared to be declining. Czarist Infantry Regiment 175 reputedly numbered only 40 to 80 soldiers, Regiments 50 and 139 approximately 100 troops, and Infantry Regiment 157 had 120 troops, while Infantry Regiment 13 fielded only 390 soldiers. The czarist enemy encountered increasing difficulties transporting food supplies, artillery, and troops to the front.[171]

South Army finally achieved a significant victory after a bitter eight-week battle at the dominating Zvinin mountain range, a stark barrier to Styr River positions. Battle spread to both sides of the river, and the army repulsed additional enemy attacks. The German 1st Infantry Division defended against enemy attempts to regain the Zvinin mountain crest (an almost ten-kilometer-long barren slope) in meter-deep snow at −20°C degrees.[172] South Army Command appealed for reinforcements to buttress its battered left flank positions, as the army repulsed relentless day and night enemy attacks.[173]

Conrad repeated a threat to negotiate an agreement with the Russians so he could wage war against Italy.[174] Meanwhile, on 6 April Falkenhayn, finally switching German emphasis from the Western front, commenced planning for a major Eastern front offensive operation, emphasizing that the major allied objective must now be to settle accounts with Russia. Falkenhayn insisted that Romania would not intervene even if Italy declared war on Austria-Hungary, but Conrad disagreed. He emphasized that if Vienna surrendered any of its German or Slavic territory to Rome, it would destroy the Dual Monarchy's Great Power status. He reemphasized his request for German divisions to resist an Italian attack, but he thanked Falkenhayn for planning to transfer German troops to the Carpathian front when they became available and promised that he would maintain the present Habsburg defensive lines.[175] During early morning on 11 April, the Russians launched yet another attack in the Laborcz and Olyka valleys, and extended their breakthrough in the Ondava Valley. The enemy attack collapsed 100 paces before the defensive barbed wire. The same day, the 41st *Honvéd* and 29th Infantry Divisions retreated following a powerful enemy thrust after they had initially repulsed several enemy assaults.

On Army Group Pflanzer-Baltin's eastern flank, German General Marschall's newly formed cavalry force repulsed Russian advances. The Russians, by concentrating their military efforts on the Second Army front, ensured that the Germans' 2 May Gorlice–Tarnov offensive would succeed because they lacked sufficient reserves to defend their rear echelon areas that the offensive targeted. They lacked the reserve forces because of the creation of Ninth Army to counter Pflanzer-Baltin's success on his front. The new campaign would not commence earlier than the end of April to avoid the regional spring thaws. Replacement troops would also have replenished the severe Habsburg battlefield losses. Falkenhayn notified Conrad that he anticipated a French attack on the Western front, and thus German assistance depended on the "desperate" French offensive and threat of a major British attack. The unrelenting Second Army crisis caused Conrad to request two to three German divisions to ensure that the front held, but many more divisions could become necessary. Falkenhayn reiterated that the Carpathian Mountain situation made rapid negotiations with Italy necessary, and that if Italy declared war, Romania would not.[176]

Back on the battlefield, XIX Corps' 29th Infantry Division faced potential disaster; it possessed no reserves and experienced heavy losses when the Russians renewed their attack and hurled it back. Meanwhile, the 41st *Honvéd* Infantry Division fended off enemy storm attacks that reached within a short distance of the defenders' barbed wire. Possessing only one reserve company raised concern for a successful Habsburg defense of the Ondava Valley. Both divisions' fronts were in shambles, but the equally exhausted Russians did not press their advantage. Meanwhile, the 51st *Honvéd* Infantry Division launched a counterattack on 12 April as the Habsburg troop morale consistently declined. Nevertheless, Corps Command ordered them to defend their positions to the point of total sacrifice.[177] One can better understand the battlefield carnage by examining Second Army 11 April unit reports. By 10 April, the enormous slaughter of horses led to the deployment of cavalry troops as infantry. Infantry Regiments 81 and 88 numbers dropped 75 percent five days later. On 13 April, one *Landwehr* Infantry Regiment consisted of only three remaining officers and 340 men.[178] The steadily worsening situation only enhanced the nationality problem. Significant numbers of Slavic soldiers deserted to the enemy.

The 38th *Honvéd* Infantry Division retreated from its Styr River positions because of the unreliability of some Romanian soldiers. Czarist efforts forced South Army into a defensive stance to prevent an enemy breakthrough of their forty-kilometer front at Wyszkov Pass. The army front settled into trench warfare mainly because of insufficient troop strengths. Corps Hofmann, largely composed of exhausted Habsburg *Landsturm* troops, maintained its present positions and halted all enemy offensive efforts.[179]

Unwarranted orders to retreat resulting from localized enemy breakthroughs had already brought the removal of two Second Army corps commanders and one Divisonaire. Such actions, however, had a deleterious effect on neighboring units, producing unnecessary casualties and further retrograde movement, lowering troop morale and lessening the troops' faith in their ability to halt the enemy.[180] More modern 15- and 10.5-centimeter field howitzers began arriving at the front lines. Gun crews, while preparing to utilize the howitzers, were discouraged from adding extra gunpowder into gun tubes to increase shell range because it would cause the guns to prematurely require repair and possibly render them inoperable.[181]

On 12 April, the Russians launched further attacks, and Conrad issued the customary order to his troops to halt the enemy at any price until reinforcements arrived.[182] When Conrad could not guarantee with complete certainty that his front would hold, it convinced Falkenhayn that he had to buttress his ally. The Germans could not allow Austria-Hungary to suffer a disastrous defeat. The Habsburgs continued to deploy every possible rifle into the front lines, and they hurled supply train and ammunition column troops, even civilian wagon drivers, into front-line duty. New recruits arrived at the front after just three weeks of training. The majority of trainees for supply train duty found themselves transferred to the infantry branch—a clear indication of the seriousness of the crisis.

On 13 April, Conrad continued to ponder the ever-present Italian question. His proposed deployment of seven infantry divisions certainly could not halt an 800,000-man Italian army with half a million additional reserves (an army he misjudged as combat ready). The Carpathian situation appeared to be temporarily calm, which should assist the diplomatic problems relative to the neutrals. In the interim, Falkenhayn reiterated his opposition to Conrad's proposition to deploy German troops to fill gaps in the Carpathian front lines and kept Conrad guessing as long as possible concerning the future German offensive. He only informed his counterpart three weeks before he attacked. He designated eight German divisions to launch an offensive at the Habsburg Fourth Army Gorlice front, where Conrad had planned to launch a similar operation for some time, but lacked sufficient troop numbers. A failed small-scale effort had been launched on March 8, a continuation of previous battle at this key point. Falkenhayn conveniently ignored the crucial question of the state of Habsburg forces, almost annihilated in August–September 1914 and most recently battered in the Carpathian campaign.

Meanwhile, Second Army repulsed an early morning attack against Czeremcha in the Ung Valley. Repeated attempts to hurl the enemy from newly conquered positions provoked enemy counterattacks that the army repulsed, inflicting heavy czarist losses. Enemy assaults continued against Second Army until 20 April, but the Russian offensive had finally halted, a week earlier on the Habsburg Third Army front than on the Second. The final Russian success occurred with the seizure of the heavily contested Kozialta Mountain on 17 April. Unsuccessful Habsburg counterattacks to regain it, lasting until 20 April, produced the usual heavy losses. Then battle intensity diminished, as the opposing defensive lines solidified behind their barbed-wire entanglements.[183] Exhaustion overwhelmed both opponents. On 14 April, Conrad traveled to Berlin to negotiate the transport and utilization of the recently promised German troops.[184] Three days later, allied Railroad Bureau personnel determined transportation details. On 25 April, Conrad met the new German Eleventh Army commander, General Mackensen, setting the stage for the approaching Gorlice–Tarnov offensive. By the third week in April, Second Army had settled into a defensive posture, while Russian prisoners of war spoke of preparations for a new attack against the Habsburg army. In fact, General Ivanov planned to renew his offensive on 3 May, the day after the commencement of the Gorlice–Tarnov offensive.

On 19 April, as the threat of Italian intervention loomed, preparations intensified for the forthcoming offensive. If Habsburg Second and Third Army lines actually held and the German offensive succeeded at Gorlice, it would unhinge the four Russian armies now deeply entrapped in the Carpathian Mountains. The offensive, launched from the northern Carpathian front, would penetrate the Russian defenses and then swing north to envelop and destroy a major part of the czarist forces. The successful offensive forced the Russian armies to evacuate the mountains and retreat to the San River line within a month. By the end of May, the Russians had retreated eighty miles to the San–Dniester River line. Massed German artillery proved decisive; the nearly 1,000 guns destroyed the opposing Russian Third Army's shallow trenches; a breakthrough occurred almost immediately as fleeing Russian troops came under effective German artillery fire. The Habsburg ally accomplished its most urgent objective: neutralizing the Russian threat. However, the German General Staff had little confidence that their ally could survive without assistance, and thus they decided to continue the offensive. As in August and September 1914 and several times later in the war, Austro-Hungarian forces could not advance without German assistance.

A further German objective was to ensure that the Russian army would be incapable of launching a major offensive for some time. The dire Carpathian Mountain situation and Dardanelles Gallipoli campaign had forced Falkenhayn to launch an Eastern front offensive. As noted, the neutrals, such as Italy and Romania, were a major consideration. Diplomatic reports increasingly stressed the threat of Italy entering the war because of recurring Habsburg defeats. Particularly galling for the Habsburgs was the constant German pressure to cede territory to the perfidious ally just to assure its continued neutrality. Moreover, German High Command became concerned over the trustworthiness of Slavic units that had begun surrendering to the Russians during recent battles because it intended to retain the initiative on the Eastern front. Thus, once the advancing troops reached the San River, the fighting persisted. Falkenhayn also continued to favor launching a campaign against Serbia to relieve pressure on the Balkan front, provide armaments and weapons to the hard-pressed Turks, and assist the Austro-Hungarian army in regaining some of its lost military prestige.

The Germans would utilize battle techniques, so successfully employed in the overwhelming victory at Gorlice–Tarnov campaign, throughout the middle years of the war. The May campaign, launched with only fourteen divisions, compromised the four Russian armies entrenched in the Carpathian Mountains. The resultant victory forced Russian withdrawal from the mountains and created a large salient in Poland, Warsaw being the main feature. The offensive rescued the Austro-Hungarian army from its dire Carpathian Mountain situation and provided the Central Powers with their greatest victory of the war. The advancing German troops, meanwhile, received flank protection from the Habsburg Fourth Army on their northern flank, Third Army on the southern. This and the failure of the Gallipoli campaign would result in Bulgaria joining the Central Powers to crush Serbia in October, making 1915 a very successful year for Germany in particular. Austria-Hungary had finally been rescued from the debacle resulting from the disastrous Carpathian Mountain Winter War.

Conclusion

CONRAD VON HÖTZENDORF'S PLANS for a two-front war unraveled almost immediately upon his decision to implement a War Case Balkan mobilization. The determination to deploy 40 percent of Habsburg troops to crush Serbia and then engage the Russian colossus had serious ramifications for the *k.u.k.* army. Conrad's misjudgments resulted in defeat on both fronts and left his armies demoralized.

Political infighting between the Austrian and Hungarian parliaments allowed the empire's military standing to languish between 1867 and 1914, in comparison to its Great Power neighbors. Consequently, the Dual Monarchy found itself with insufficient troop stands, obsolete artillery, an insufficient railroad network, and an industrial base too deficient to fight a total war.

The assassination of Archduke Franz Ferdinand produced consensus among Habsburg leaders to declare war against Serbia. A war with Russia was only feasible with German military assistance, but Conrad abhorred relying on Germany. The War Case "B" mobilization assured that Conrad's armies struggled to achieve a sufficient concentration of forces against the numerically superior Russian armies. Habsburg armies received attack orders before all participating troop units arrived throughout the October and December 1914 campaigns, which resulted in excessive losses, particularly to the professional officer corps. Conrad's three Carpathian winter campaigns were no exception, but now they had the added burden of inclement weather and winter mountain-terrain conditions.

In addition to Habsburg Supreme Command's inability to achieve a sufficient concentration of force against the powerful Russian armies, it failed to provide and coordinate effective artillery support to the infantry. Obsolete equipment, a poorly functioning supply system, and a chronic shortage of artillery shells placed the Habsburg army at a further disadvantage.

By the end of 1914, only 45,000 of the initial one million Habsburg combat troops remained. The once-proud *k.u.k.* army, which had perished on the fields of Lemberg, continued bleeding in the fall campaigns until it more closely resembled a militia. At this juncture, Conrad chose the Carpathian Mountains for his next offensive operation. During the successful early December Limanova-Lapanov campaign, it became clear that Habsburg troops seriously required rehabilitation, reinforcements, weapons, and more artillery shells. Nevertheless, throughout the first half of 1915, Conrad sought a major battle of encirclement launched from Prussia and Galicia, although he lacked the necessary forces. His inability to meld his armies' capabilities with his strategic battle plans was a major flaw of Conrad's military leadership. Ignoring the admonitions of other military leaders including his German ally, Conrad pursued his Carpathian winter campaign. As we have seen, the consequences were tragic and multifold.

A staunch proponent of the cult of the offensive, Conrad ordered massive frontal attacks, producing extreme and avoidable losses. The high casualty rates resulted in a major portion of the Habsburg army being composed of replacement troops or recruits.

During October, November, and December, Austro-Hungarian and German units fought side by side in common operations. Commencing in October, General Conrad instigated a fateful process by attempting to outflank the Russians' far western flank positions from his extreme right flank. This placed the Habsburg armies squarely in the Carpathian Mountains—terrain not intended for maneuvering massive armies. Moreover, Habsburg armies relieved the antiquated, long-neglected Fortress Przemyśl (which fell to the Russians in September 1914) for a brief period in early October. Russian troops besieged the fortification again the first week in November, transforming it into the focal point of General Conrad's war planning until its surrender on 22 March 1915.

In its first significant victory of the war, the Austro-Hungarian Army soundly defeated Russian forces at the battle of Limanova-Lapanov. Meanwhile, on the Balkan front, Habsburg forces suffered three humiliating defeats. At the end of 1914, the Habsburg military faced several critical problems. To seize the initiative, General Conrad determined to attack.

The concern that the Russians would outflank Habsburg forces on their extreme right flank is understandable. Therefore, Conrad sought the initiative against a numerically superior foe possessing superior artillery, strong prepared positions on higher terrain, and, during much of the Carpathian campaign, more favorable road and railroad connections to their mountain positions.

However, in his efforts to encircle the Russians' extreme left flank positions, Conrad placed Fortress Przemyśl in the center of his strategy, resulting in the Carpathian Winter War—the first example of total warfare conducted on mountainous terrain. The horrendous losses sustained during this campaign equaled the bloodbath battles of 1916, Verdun and the

Somme. There were no historical models to use while planning for such a campaign, although indications of its potential terrible consequences were evidenced during the November–December 1914 Carpathian Mountain warfare.

The real tragedy was the mental and physical trauma on the hundreds of thousands of troops on both sides of the lines. Blizzards, freezing temperatures, intermittent sleet, wind, and snow intermixed with thawing conditions created a nightmarish existence. Enormous casualties resulted from sickness, frostbite, and the ominous White Death. Snow buried the wounded who could no longer stand. Others succumbed during the wrenching cart rides down mountain slopes. Some exhausted soldiers who dared to stop along the mountain trails froze to death. Maintaining a steady flow of supplies was almost impossible, with thousands of horses dying in the mire during the melting conditions and more succumbing to the exertion of pulling heavy loads up the snow- and ice-covered paths without sufficient feed and cover.

Austro-Hungarian soldiers invariably encountered a numerically superior enemy. Thus, as casualties mounted, and with no reserves or inadequate or no reinforcements to insert into the thinning front lines, gaps appeared that could not be closed. The soldiers could not be relieved for rehabilitation, as could their enemy.

Much of the blame for the flawed Carpathian Winter War strategy can be placed on the Habsburg Supreme Command. All three campaigns shared common characteristics: there was an obvious lack of preparation and forethought in the planning that resulted in faulty decision making; there was a general failure to concentrate troop mass at the most significant attack points; and insufficient reserve troops were available to maintain momentum if victory occurred. The customary tactic of withdrawing troops from a nonthreatened area to reinforce one under attack foundered when the Russians struck entire army fronts, as occurred three days after the initial attack when the Russians launched their counterthrust on 26 January, and again immediately after the Second Army offensive in late February 1915.

The German ally again had to rescue its floundering partner. The subsequent Gorlice–Tarnov offensive produced the greatest Central Powers victory of the war and relieved Russian pressure in the Carpathian Mountains. In addition, the success prevented czarist armies from sweeping into the Hungarian Plains, knocking Austria-Hungary out of the war and keeping neutral Romania from entering the war against the Dual Monarchy. However, just as the Gorlice victory train was gathering speed, Italy chose the inopportune moment to declare war on Austria-Hungary.

Fortress Przemyśl, a major focus of early 1915 Carpathian campaigns, surrendered on 22 March 1915. The Habsburg Army sustained at least 800,000 casualties in its futile efforts to rescue the garrison of 120,000 men. By the time the fortress finally capitulated, the once-proud *k.u.k.* army was reduced to a militia army. Germany meanwhile extended its command structure into the Dual Monarchy's military establishment, first in the creation of the South Army and then again with the deployment of the *Beskiden* Corps, which saved the Habsburg Third Army front from disaster in its extended Laborcz Valley campaign.

The Stalingrad of World War I, the Carpathian Winter War decimated the *k.u.k.* army for the third time since July 1914. Snow and mud buried the corpses of hundreds of thousands of Russian, Habsburg, and German soldiers. For their struggles, Second and Third Army troops that survived the Carpathian disaster received a special battle commendation from Habsburg Supreme Command. One of the most ill-conceived campaigns of the war, the Carpathian Winter War offers far too many examples of how *not* to conduct winter mountain battle, and provided a stark lesson about the negative effects of inadequate leadership.

NOTES

Introduction

1. Manfried Rauchensteiner, *Der Tod des Doppeladlers* (Vienna: Verlag Styria, 1993), is by far the best; cited in Holger Herwig, *The First World War: Germany and Austria-Hungary, 1914–1918* (New York: Arnold, 1997), 139.

2. Graydon A. Tunstall, "The Habsburg Command Conspiracy: The Falsification of Historiography on the Outbreak of World War I," *Austrian History Yearbook* 27 (1996): 181–198.

3. Kriegsarchiv (KA) Nachlaß (KAN), B/23, Karl Mayern, *Die k.u.k. 2. Armee in der Karpatenschlacht, 1914/15.*

4. KAN Conrad (KANC), B/13, Rudolf Kundmann, Tagebuch vom 1/1 1915–4/XI 1916; KAN, B/509, Karl Schneller; Kriegstagebücher, 1914–1918; KA Militärkanzlei Seiner Majestät (MKSM), separate fasc. No. 75, Conrad Letters to Bolfras.

5. Dave Grossman, *On Killing: The Psychological Cost of Learning to Kill in War and Society,* rev. ed. (New York: Back Bay Books, 2009).

6. Ibid., 68.

7. Ibid., 69.

8. Graf Stefan Tisza, *Briefe, 1914–1918* (Berlin: Reimer Hobbing, 1928), 50; Freiherr von Musulin, *Der Haus am Ballplatz. Erinnerungen eines österreichungarischen Diplomaten* (Munich: Verlag für Kulturpolitik, 1924), 254.

9. KA Armee Ober Kommando (AOK), Operations Abteilung, fasc. 523, Festung Przemyśl; KAN, B/1137, Hermann Kusmanek von Burgstädten, No. 2, *Przemyśl*; KA MKSM, separat fasc. 100, particularly Reserve No. 1956; a massive manuscript by Franz Stuckheil, KA MS1.Wkg., 1915, Rußland, No. 19, *Festung Przemyśl,* and his eleven-article series about the fortress in the periodical *Militärwissenschaftliche- und technische Mitteilungen* (hereafter *MTM*). Monographs include Franz Forstner's excellent *Przemyśl. Österreich-Ungarns bedeutendste Festung* (Vienna: Österreichischer Bundesverlag, 1987); Herman Heiden, *Bollwerk am San, Schicksal der Festung Przemyśl* (Berlin: Gerhard Stalling, 1946); G. M. Hans Schwalb, "Die Verteidigung von Przemyśl, 1914–1915," *Mitteilungen über Gegenstücke des Artillerie und Geniewesens* 149 (1918): 1373–1392.

10. *Österreich-Ungarns letzter Krieg* (hereafter *ÖULK*), 1914, vol. 1, *Das Kriegsjahr, 1914,* Bundesministerium für Heereswesen und vom Kriegsarchiv (Vienna: Verlag Militärwissenschaftlicher Mitteilungen, 1930).

11. KANC, B/13, Kundmann, Tagebuch.

12. Feldmarschall Franz von Hötzendorf Conrad, *Aus meiner Dienstzeit, 1906–1918* (Vienna: Rikola Verlag, 1921–1925), 520.

13. For sources on the *Ersatz* troops, see Maximilian Ehnl, "Die österreichisch-ungarische Landmacht nach Aufbau, Gliederung, Friedengarnison, Einteilung und nationaler Zusammensetzung im Sommer 1914," in *Österreich-Ungarns letzter Krieg, 1914–1918,* Bundesministerium für Heereswesen und vom Kriegsarchiv (Vienna: Verlag Militärwissenschaftlicher Mitteilungen, 1934); F. Franek, "Die Entwicklung des österreich-ungarischen Wehrmacht in den ersten zwei Kriegsjahren," *MTM* 64 (1933): 15–31, 98–111; Franek, "Probleme der Organisation im ersten Kriegsjahre," *MTM* 61 (1930): 977–994; Rudolf Hecht, *Fragen zur Heeresergänzung der Gestalten Bewaffneten Macht Österreich-Ungarns während des ersten Weltkrieges* (diss., University of Vienna, 1969); James S. Lucas, *Austro-Hungarian Infantry* (London: Almark, 1974); Wilhelm Czermak, *In deinen Lager war Österreich. Die österreichische-ungarische Armee* (Breslau: Korn Verlag, 1938).

14. *ÖULK,* vol. 2.

15. Emil Ratzenhofer, "Die Aufmarsch hinter den Karpathen im Winter 1915," *MTM* 61 (1930): 501–503.

16. For the best sources on Fortress Przemyśl, see note 9.

17. Conrad, *Aus meiner Dienstzeit,* 5:520.

1. Background to the Battles

1. Particularly valuable for this chapter were the following: Kriegsarchiv (KA) Armee Ober Kommando (AOK), fasc. 873, Evidenz der feindlichen Situation, Januar 1915; *Österreich-Ungarns letzter Krieg* (hereafter *ÖULK*), vols. 1 and 2 (Bundesministerium für Heereswesen und vom Kriegsarchiv, Vienna: Verlag Militärwissenschaftlicher Mitteilungen, 1930, 1931); KA Neue Feld Akten, 3. Armee, fasc. 42, Tagebücher; 4. Armee, fasc. 70, Tagebücher; and 7. Armee Tagebücher. Of the *Nachläße,* particularly KA Nachlaße (KAN), B/366, Karl Lauer; KAN, B/544, Gottlieb Kralowetz von Hohenrecht, Karpatenkrieg—X. Korps MS; KAN, B/557, Karl Freiherr von Pflanzer-Baltin, Tagebücher; KAN, B/600, Anton Freiherr von Lehar, No. 2 Tagebücher; KA MS1.Wkg. Rußland, 1915, No. 36, Die deutsche Südarmee von Anfang Januar bis Anfang Juli 1915; Deutsch Reichsarchiv; KA AOK, fasc. 615, Kaiserberichte Anfang Jänner bis Ende Juni; KA Nachlaß Conrad (KANC), B-13, Rudolf Kundmann, Tagebuch vom 1/1 1915–4/XI 1916. Particularly critical information was gained from reading Budapest War Archives (BWA), TGY 2819, 2:183, Kartons No. 22, 24, 143 (37, and 38 Honvéd Infantrie Divisions and Gruppe Szurmay Tagebücher).

2. KAN, B/700, Hans Mailath-Pokorny.

3. KA AOK, fasc. 512, Conrad-Falkenhayn, Rußland, Korrespondenz; KA MS1.Wkg., 1915, Rußland, No. 36, Südarmee.

4. KA AOK, fasc. 512, Conrad-Falkenhayn, Rußland, Korrespondenz; KA MS1.Wkg., 1915, Rußland, No. 36, Südarmee.

5. KA AOK, fasc. 512, Conrad-Falkenhayn, Rußland, Korrespondenz; Hermann Wendt, *Der italienische Kriegsschauplatz in europäischen Konflikten. Seine Bedeutung für die Kriegführung an Frankreichs Nordostgrenze* (Berlin: Junker und Dunnhaupt Verlag, 1936).

6. KA AOK, fasc. 512, Conrad-Falkenhayn, Rußland, Korrespondenz; Hermann Wendt, *Der italienische Kriegsschauplatz in europäischen Konflikten. Seine*

Bedeutung für die Kriegführung an Frankreichs Nordostgrenze (Berlin: Junker und Dunnhaupt Verlag, 1936).

7. Franz Forstner, *Przemyśl. Österreich-Ungarns bedeutendste Festung* (Vienna: Österreichischer Bundesverlag, 1987).

8. KA MS1.Wkg., Allgemeine, No. 4, Veith, Werdegang; ÖULK, 2:271.

9. ÖULK, 2:271.

10. KA AOK, fasc. 512, Conrad-Falkenhayn, Rußland, Korrespondenz; MS1. Wkg., 1915, Rußland, No. 36, Südarmee.

11. KA AOK, fasc. 512, Conrad-Falkenhayn, Rußland, Korrespondenz; Hermann Wendt, *Der italienische Kriegsschauplatz.*

12. KA AOK, fasc. 512, Conrad-Falkenhayn, Rußland, Korrespondenz; Hermann Wendt, *Der italienische Kriegsschauplatz.*

13. KANC, B/13, Kundmann, Tagebüch; ibid.

14. Ibid.

15. KA AOK, fasc. 512, Conrad-Falkenhayn, Rußland, Korrespondenz; KA MS1.Wkg., 1915, Rußland, No. 36, Südarmee.

16. Ibid.

17. KAN, B/726, Nowak, No. 8, Die Klammer des Reiches; Richard G. Plashka, "Zur Vorgeschichte des Übergehen von Einheiten des Infantrieregiments No. 28 an der Russiuchen Front 1915," Osterreich und Europa, Festgabe fur Hugo Hantach zum 70. Geburstag.

18. General Jury N. Danilov, *Rußland im Weltkriege, 1914–1915* (Jena: Verlag Frommann, 1925).

19. KA AOK, Ubersetzung, Nordost, No. 3.

20. Ibid., Telegram No. 7559, Ruski.

21. Ivanov, Telegram No. 387, 71; Danilov, *Rußland im Weltkriege.*

22. A. A. Brusilov, *A Soldier's Notebook, 1914–1918* (Westport, Conn.: Greenwood Press, 1930), 93.

23. KA AOK, fasc. 500, 4. Armee Etappen Kommander, Op. No. 4252, 5518 and Sanitationchefs Armee Gruppe Szurmay, Op. No. 127.

24. KAN, B/557, Pflanzer-Baltin, Tagebücher, No. 1745, 1/1, 1915; KA AOK, fasc. 500, 4. Armee, Etappen Kommander, Op. No. 13914/1.

25. KA Neue Feld Akten (NFA), 4. Armee, fasc. 70, Tagebücher, 4. Armee, Op. No. 1458, 28 November.

26. KA AOK, fasc. 615, AOK Tagebücher, AOK Op. No. 5881; ÖULK, vol. 2.

27. Emil Ratzenhofer, "Die Aufmarsch hinter den Karpathen im Winter 1915," *Militärwissenschaftliche und -technische Mitteilungen* 61 (1930).

28. KA NFA, 3. Armee, fasc. 42, Tagebücher, 3. Armee, Op. No. 2680, X Korps, Op. No. 456/10; KAN, B/554, Kralowetz, X Korps MS.

29. KAN, B/557, Pflanzer-Baltin, Tagebücher.

30. KA NFA, 3. Armee, fasc. 42, Tagebücher, 3. Armee, Op. No. 2662, 30. Dezember 1914; ÖULK, vol. 2.

31. ÖULK, 2:73, 103–104.

32. See KAN, B/557, Pflanzer-Baltin, Tagebücher.

33. ÖULK, 2:99–100; KA NFA, 4. Armee, Tagebücher; 3. Armee, fasc. 42; Tagebücher.

34. KA AOK, fasc. 14, Aus Op. No. 5501–5900; fasc. 615, AOK Tagebücher, AOK Op. No. 5984, 5997; KA NFA, XVIII Korps, Tagebücher.

35. KAN, B/713, Arthur Edler von Mecenseffy; Rudolf Hecht, *Fragen zur Heeresergänzung der Gestalten Bewaffneten Macht Österreich-Ungarns während des ersten Weltkrieges* (diss., University of Vienna, 1969); *ÖULK,* 2:107.

36. KAN, B/554, Kralowetz, X Korps Ms, X Korps, Op. No. 459/5.

37. KA NFA, 3. Armee, fasc. 42, Tagebücher, 3. Armee, Op. No. 2680; X Korps, Op. No. 456/10.

38. KAN, B/713, von Mecenseffy; Hecht, *Fragen zur Heeresergänzung.*

39. KA NFA, XVIII Korps, Tagebücher; KA AOK, fasc. 615, AOK Tagebücher; *ÖULK,* vol. 2.

40. KA NFA, 3. Armee, fasc. 42, Tagebücher; X Korps, Op. No. 460/11.

41. KA NFA, V and XVIII Korps, Tagebücher.

42. KA NFA, 64. Infantrie Brigade Gefechtsbericht, K 1825; 3. Armee, Op. No. 2714.

43. KA AOK, fasc. 615, AOK Tagebücher, AOK Op. No. 5932; *ÖULK,* 2:105; KAN, B/557, Pflanzer-Baltin, Tagebücher.

44. KA NFA, 3. Armee, fasc. 42, Tagebücher; 4. Armee, fasc. 70, Tagebücher.

45. KA AOK, fasc. 512, Conrad-Falkenhayn, Rußland, Korrespondenz, AOK Op. No. 5999.

46. KA AOK, fasc. 523, Przemyśl; KAN, B/1137, Hermann Kusmanek von Burgstädten, No. 2, *Przemyśl;* KA MS1.Wkg., Rußland, 1915, No. 19, Stuckheil, *Festung Przemyśl;* Forstner, *Przemyśl.*

47. Ibid.

48. KA NFA, V and XVIII Korps, Tagebücher; 3. Armee, fasc. 42, Tagebücher.

49. KA NFA, 3. Armee, fasc. 42, Tagebücher, 3. Armee, Op. No. 2745, 2746.

50. Ibid.; *ÖULK,* vol. 2.

51. KA AOK, fasc. 615, AOK Tagebücher; KA NFA, 3. Armee, fasc. 42, Tagebücher; XVIII Korps, Tagebücher.

52. KA NFA, 3. Armee, fasc. 42, Tagebücher; KAN, B/544, Kralowetz, X Korps MS.

53. KA AOK, fasc. 512, Conrad-Falkenhayn, Rußland, Korrespondenz; KA MS1.Wkg., 1915, Rußland, No. 36, Südarmee, *ÖULK,* vol. 2.

54. Ibid.

55. *ÖULK,* 2:101; KA NFA, 4. Armee, fasc. 70, Tagebücher; 3. Armee, fasc. 42, Tagebücher; III Korps, Tagebücher; AOK, fasc. 615, AOK Tagebücher, AOK Op. No. 5997; AOK, fasc. 500, k.u.k. Operationsabteilung R Gruppe, Jänner.

56. KA NFA, 4. Armee, fasc. 70, Tagebücher; *ÖULK,* 2:101–102.

57. KA NFA, 4. Armee, fasc. 70, Tagebücher, 4. Armee, Op. No. 2328; 3. Armee, fasc. 42, Tagebücher.

58. KA AOK, fasc. 615, AOK Tagebücher, AOK Op. No. 5965, *ÖULK,* vol. 2.

59. KAN, B/558, Aurel le von Le Beau, Tagebücher; see KA NFA, VII Korps, Tagebücher.

60. KA NFA, 3. Armee, fasc. 42, Tagebücher.

61. Ibid.; XVIII Korps, Tagebücher.

62. KA NFA, 4. Armee, fasc. 70, Tagebücher, see *ÖULK,* vol. 2.

63. KA NFA, XVIII Korps, Tagebücher, XVIII Korps, Op. No. 322.

64. KA AOK, fasc. 615, AOK Tagebücher, AOK Op. No. 6081; KA NFA, 3. Armee, fasc. 42, Tagebücher; *ÖULK*, vol. 2.

65. KA AOK, fasc. 615, AOK Tagebücher, AOK Op. No. 6093, 6154; KA NFA, 4. Armee, fasc. 70, Tagebücher; 3. Armee, fasc. 42, Tagebücher; *ÖULK*, vol. 2.

66. KA AOK, fasc. 615, AOK Tagebücher, AOK Op. No. 6514; KA NFA, XVIII Korps, Tagebücher; *ÖULK*, vol. 2.

67. KA NFA, 3. Armee, fasc. 42, Tagebücher; KA AOK, fasc. 500, Jänner; *ÖULK*, vol. 2.

68. KA MS1.Wkg., Rußland, 1915, No. 36, Südarmee MS; KANC, B/13, Kundmann, Tagebüch; Wendt, *Italienische Kriegsschauplatz*.

69. KA Militärkanzlei Seiner Majestät (MKSM), separat fasc. 78/77; KA AOK, fasc. 512, Conrad-Falkenhayn, Rußland, Korrespondenz.

70. KA NFA, 3. Armee, fasc. 42, Tagebücher, 3. Armee, Op. No. 2747; V and XVIII Korps Tagebücher. The 33. Infantrie Division was transferred to the V Korps.

71. KA AOK, fasc. 615, AOK Tagebücher; KA NFA, XIX Korps, Tagebücher; 3. Armee, fasc. 42, Tagebücher; *ÖULK*, vol. 2.

72. BWA, TGY 2819, II 143, Gruppe Szurmay, 8. Kavallrie Division.

73. KA AOK, fasc. 615, AOK Tagebücher, AOK Op. No. 6154; *ÖULK*, vol. 2.

74. KA AOK, fasc. 615, AOK Tagebücher, AOK Op. No. 6139.

75. Ibid., AOK Op. No. 6081; KA NFA, 3. Armee, fasc. 42, Tagebücher; 4. Armee, fasc. 70, Tagebücher; *ÖULK*, vol. 2.

76. KA NFA, 3. Armee, fasc. 42, Tagebücher; see V and XVIII Korps, Tagebücher.

77. KA NFA, XVIII Korps, Tagebücher; 3. Armee, fasc. 42, Tagebücher; KA MS1.Wkg., Rußland, 1915, No. 19, Stuckheil, *Festung Przemyśl*.

78. KA NFA, V Korps, Tagebücher, 3. Armee, Op. No. 2800; XVIII Korps, Tagebücher; KAN, B/557, Pflanzer-Baltin, Tagebücher.

79. KA NFA, XVIII Korps, Tagebücher; 3. Armee, fasc. 42, Tagebücher.

80. KA NFA, 3. Armee, fasc. 42, Tagebücher.

81. Ibid.; AOK Op. No. 6161, 3. Armee, Op. No. 2788/I.

82. KA NFA, XVIII Korps Tagebücher; 3. Armee, fasc. 42, Tagebücher.

83. Ibid.

84. KA AOK, fasc. 615, AOK Tagebücher, AOK Op. No. 6021, 6158.

85. KA NFA, 4. Armee, fasc. 70, Tagebücher, 4. Armee, Op. No. 2365; see also 2346; Ratzenhofer, "Aufmarsch hinter den Karpathen im Winter 1915."

86. KA Gefechtsberichte, K 1812, X Korps Kdo., Op. No. 538/6, 11 Januar–7 Februar; KAN, B/544, Kralowetz, X Korps MS; *ÖULK*, vol. 2.

87. KAN, B/544, Kralowetz, X Korps MS; see also KAN, B/713, von Mecenseffy; Hecht, *Fragen zur Heeresergänzung*.

88. August Urbanski von Ostrymiecz, *Conrad von Hötzendorf. Soldat und Mensch. Dargestellt von seinem Mitarbeiter Feldmarschalleutnant August* (Vienna: Ulrich Mosers Verlag, 1938), 312.

89. KA NFA, VII Korps, Tagebücher; KAN, B/544, Kralowetz, X Korps MS; BWA, TGY 2819, II 143, Gruppe Szurmay.

90. KA AOK, Übersetzung, Nordost, No. 3, Ivanov Telegram No. 1099.

91. BWA, TGY 935, 54. Infantrie Division, Gefechtsberichte.

92. KA NFA, 3. Armee, fasc. 42, Tagebücher.
93. KAN, B/544, Kralowetz, X Korps MS.
94. KA NFA, 3. Armee, fasc. 42, Tagebücher, 3. Armee, Op. No. 2358, 2364; KAN, B/544, Kralowetz, X Korps MS.
95. KA NFA, 3. Armee, fasc. 42, Tagebücher; KA AOK, fasc. 615, AOK Tagebücher, AOK Op. No. 2832, see *ÖULK*, vol. 2.
96. KAN, B/509, Schneller, Tagebücher.
97. KA AOK 615, AOK Tagebücher, AOK Op. No. 6091, 6093, 6124; KA NFA, XIX Korps Tagebücher.
98. KA NFA, XIX Korps, Tagebücher; *ÖULK*, vol. 2.
99. KANC, B/1450, Conrad von Hötzendorf.
100. KA AOK, fasc. 615, AOK Tagebücher, AOK Op. No. 6266; KA MS1. Wkg., 1915, Rußland, No. 36, Südarmee; *ÖULK*, vol. 2.
101. KA NFA, 3. Armee, fasc. 42, Tagebücher, 3. Armee, Op. No. 2861, AOK No. 6267; AOK, fasc. 873, Evidenz der feindlichen Situation.
102. KA NFA, XVIII Korps, Tagebücher, XVIII Korps, Op. No. 13/25; see *ÖULK*, vol. 2.
103. Urbanski, *Conrad von Hötzendorf*, 312.
104. BWA, TGY 2819, II, 143, Gruppe Szurmay.
105. KA NFA, 4. Armee, fasc. 70, Tagebücher, varia.
106. KANC, B/1450, Conrad von Hötzendorf, Tisza, letter.
107. KA NFA, V Korps, Tagebücher, V Korps, Op. No. 8/14; XVIII Korps, Tagebücher.
108. KA NFA, V Korps, Tagebücher.
109. KANC, C/6, Conrad to Burian 1/16; KA AOK 512, Conrad-Falkenhayn, Rußland, Korrespondenz; KA MKSM, separat fasc. 78/77.
110. KAN, B/1137, Kusmanek, *Przemyśl*; KA AOK, fasc. 523, Przemyśl; AOK, fasc. 615, AOK Tagebücher, AOK Op. No. 7008; Forstner, *Przemyśl*, 219.
111. KAN, B/405, K. v. Regenauer, No. 12, AOK Op. No. 6367, 6391, 6463, see B/557, Pflanzer-Baltin, Tagebücher, see *ÖULK*, vol. 2.
112. KA NFA, 3. Armee, fasc. 42, Tagebücher; KA MS1.Wkg., Rußland, 1915, No. 36, Südarmee; *ÖULK*, vol. 2.
113. KAN, B/544, Kralowetz, X Korps MS.
114. KA NFA, 3. Armee, fasc. 42, Tagebücher; KAN, B/544, Kralowetz, X Korps MS.
115. KA NFA, 4. Armee, fasc. 70, Tagebücher, 43. Landwehr Infantrie Brigade in area Zboro, 28 Januar, 4. Armee, Op. No. 2425, 2429.
116. KAN, B/713, von Mecenseffy; Hecht, *Fragen zur Heeresergänzung*.
117. BWA, TGY 2819, II, 143, Gruppe Szurmay.
118. KA NFA, XVIII Korps, Tagebücher XVIII Korps, Op. No. 13/22; see KAN, B/544, Kralowetz, X Korps MS.
119. KA NFA, Gefechtsberichte, 34. Infantrie Division, see KAN, B/544, Kralowetz, X Korps MS.
120. KAN, B/713, von Mecenseffy; AOK Op. No. 6405; Hecht, *Fragen zur Heeresergänzung*.
121. KA AOK, fasc. 512, Conrad-Falkenhayn, Rußland, Korrespondenz, AOK Op. No. 6347, 6395.

122. KA AOK, 3. Armee, fasc. 42, Tagebücher, 3. Armee, Op. No. 6404; ÖULK, vol. 2.

123. KA NFA, XVIII Korps, Tagebücher.

124. Ibid.

125. KA NFA, 3. Armee, fasc. 42, Tagebücher, 3. Armee, Op. No. 2912/I; V Korps, Tagebücher.

126. KA MS1.Wkg., 1915, Rußland, No. 23; Karl Mayern, *Die k.u.k. 2. Armee in der Karpatenschlacht, 1914/15*, 15; see ÖULK, vol. 2.

127. ÖULK, 2:107.

128. KA NFA, fasc. 70, 4. Armee Tagebücher; ÖULK, vol. 2.

129. Ratzenhofer, "Aufmarsch hinter den Karpathen im Winter 1915," 15–16.

2. The First Carpathian Offensive

1. Kriegsarchiv (KA) MS1.Wkg., Allgemeine, A-4, *Werdegang und Schicksal*, Georg Veith.

2. The main sources for this chapter include KA Neue Feld Akten (NFA), 3. Armee, fasc. 42, Tagebücher; 4. Armee, fasc. 70, Tagebücher; 7. Armee, Kriegsberichte, Tagebücher; the Austrian official history of the war, *Österreich-Ungarns letzter Krieg* (hereafter ÖULK), vol. 2; Armee Ober Kommando (AOK), fasc. 512, k.u.k. Operations Abteilung "R" Gruppe: 1915, fasc. 615, AOK Tagebücher from the Archiv Conrad, B-13, Rudolf Kundmann, Tagebüch vom 1/1 1915–4/ XI 1916. Valuable material also came from the following *Nachläße*, diaries, and manuscripts: B/366, Karl Lauer; B/544, Gottlieb Kralowetz von Hohenrecht, Manuscript—X Korps; B/557, Karl Freiherr von Pflanzer-Baltin, Tagebücher; B/600, Anton Freiherr von Lehar; as well as monographs containing pertinent information, including Rudolf Kiszling, *Österreich-Ungarns Anteil am ersten Weltkrieg* (Graz: Stiasny Verlag, 1958); Anton Pitreich, *Der österreich-ungarische Bundesgenosse im Sperrfeuer* (Klagenfurt: Arthur Killitsch, 1930); Manfried Rauchensteiner, *Der Tod des Doppeladlers* (Vienna: Verlag Styria, 1993); Norman Stone, *The Eastern Front, 1914–1917* (New York: Charles Scribner's Sons, 1975).

3. ÖULK, vol. 2; Franz Forstner, *Przemyśl. Österreich-Ungarns bedeutendste Festung* (Vienna: Österreichischer Bundesverlag, 1987), 248.

4. KA Gefechtsbericht, k.u.k. 2. I.D. Kdo., Op. No. 346/1; für die Zeit vom 23 Januar bis 29 Januar 1915, K 1802.

5. KA Nachlaß (KAN), B/600, Anton Freiherr von Lehar, No. 1 Tagebücher.

6. ÖULK, 2:126.

7. Edvard Ritter Steinitz, "Ausharren oder Ausweichen? Die Kämpfe der 2. Infantrie Division in den Karpathen Januar bis 4. Feber 1915," *Militärwissenschaftliche- und technische Mitteilungen* 61 (1930): 97–104; ÖULK, vol. 2.

8. KA MS1.Wkg., 1915, Rußland, No. 36, Südarmee MS.

9. KA AOK, fasc. 615, AOK Kaiserberichte, AOK Op. No. 6549.

10. KA NFA, 4. Armee, fasc. 70, Tagebücher, 4. Armee, Op. No. 2509; III and IX Korps, Tagebücher; ÖULK, vol. 2.

11. KA NFA, 4. Armee, fasc. 70, Tagebücher, 4. Armee, Op. No. 2328, 2443, 2475.

12. KA NFA, 3. Armee, fasc. 42, Tagebücher; Eduard Zanantoni, *Die deutsch-*

220   *Notes to Pages 74–79*

bömische 29. Infantriedivision im Kriegsjahre, 1914–15 (Reichenberg: Heimatsöhne im Weltkrieg, 1926), 177.

13. KA AOK Op. No. 3044, 3045, 3046, 3051, 3052, 3053.

14. Budapest War Archives (BWA), Tudományos Gyüjtemény (TGY) 2819, II 143, Gruppe Szurmay; KAN, B/23, Karl Mayern, *Die k.u.k. 2. Armee in der Karpatenschlacht, 1914/15*, 13–14.

15. KA NFA, 4. Armee, fasc. 70, Tagebücher, 4. Armee, Op. No. 2509; KA AOK, fasc. 615, AOK Tagebücher, AOK Op. No. 6572; *ÖULK*, vol. 2.

16. KA AOK, fasc. 615, AOK Tagebücher, AOK Op. No. 6561.

17. KAN, B/558, Aurel le von Le Beau, Tagebücher; *ÖULK*, vol. 2.

18. KA NFA, 2. Armee, fasc. 7, Tagebücher, 2. Infantrie Division Kdr., Op. No. 346/1, KA Gefechtsbericht für die Zeit vom 23 Januar bis 29 Januar 1915, K 1802; KAN, B/544, Kralowetz, X Korps MS.

19. KA NFA, 3. Armee, fasc. 42, Tagebücher; 4. Armee, fasc. 70, Tagebücher, 4. Armee, Op. No. 2509.

20. KA NFA, XVIII Korps, Tagebücher.

21. KA NFA Gefechtsberichte, 2. Infantrie Division Kdo., Op. 346/1, 2. Infantrie Division, 23/1–29/1 1915, K 1802.

22. KA NFA, Gefechtsbericht, 2. Infantrie Division, Op. No. 364/1, K 1802; see KAN, B/544, Kralowetz, X Korps MS.

23. KA NFA, VII Korps, Tagebücher; see KA NFA, Kriegsberichte, 2. Infantrie Division, Op. No. 346/1, K 1802; KAN, B/544, Kralowetz, X Korps MS.

24. KA NFA, V Korps, Tagebücher.

25. KA, NFA, 43. Infantrie Division, Gefechtsbericht über Schlacht bei Baligrod, K 1805; Steinitz, "Ausharren oder Ausweichen?"

26. KAN, B/544, Kralowetz, X Korps MS.

27. KA NFA, 4. Armee, fasc. 70, Tagebücher, 4. Armee, Op. No. 2509; III Korps, Tagebücher; *ÖULK*, vol. 2.

28. KA NFA, 3. Armee, fasc. 42, Tagebücher; KAN, B/544, Kralowetz, X Korps MS; MS1.Wkg, Rußland, 1915, No. 36, Südarmee MS.

29. KA NFA, 4. Armee, fasc. 70, Tagebücher; *ÖULK*, vol. 2.

30. KA NFA, VII Korps, Tagebücher, VII Korps, Op. No. 288/21, 27; 286/31; KA, Gefechtsbericht, 2. Infantrie Division, Op. No. 346/1, K1802; KAN, B/558, Le Beau, Tagebücher.

31. *ÖULK*, vol. 2.

32. Ibid.

33. KA NFA, 3. Armee, Op. No. 3819; AOK Op. No. 8275; KAN, B/23, Mayern, *2. Armee in der Karpatenschlacht*, 310; *ÖULK*, vol. 2.

34. BWA, TGY 2819, II 143, Gruppe Szurmay.

35. Ibid., 66. Infantrie Brigade; KAN, B/23, Mayern, *2. Armee in der Karpatenschlacht*, 3. Armee, Op. No. 3100.

36. 3. Armee, Auf. Op. No. 1915 zu AOK Op. No. 1511.

37. KAN, B/544, Kralowetz, X Korps MS.

38. KA NFA, 3. Armee, fasc. 42, Tagebücher, 3. Armee, Op. No. 2978, 3119, AOK Op. No. 8275; 3. Armee, fasc. 11, 3. Armee, Op. No. 2975.

39. KA NFA, Gefechtberichte, 2. I.D. Op. Kdo., Op. No. 346/1, K1802; XVIII Korps, Tagebücher; *ÖULK*, vol. 2.

40. KA NFA, V Korps, Tagebücher.

41. KA NFA, VII and III Korps, Tagebücher; *ÖULK*, vol. 2.

42. KA, Gefechtsberichte, 2. I.D. Op. Kdo., Op. No. 346/1, K1802; see KAN, B/544, Kralowetz, X Korps MS; *ÖULK*, vol. 2.

43. Ibid.; KA NFA, VII Korps, Tagebücher, VII Korps, Op. No. 286/31.

44. KAN, B/544, Kralowetz, X Korps MS.

45. KAN, B/23, Mayern, 2. *Armee in der Karpatenschlacht*, 16.

46. KA NFA, 3. Armee, fasc. 42, Tagebücher, 3. Armee, Op. No. 3009, 3040, 3050.

47. KA AOK, AOK 873, Evidenz der feindlichen Situation, AOK Op. No. 5865; *ÖULK*, vol. 2.

48. KA MS1.Wkg., Rußland, 1915, No. 36, Südarmee MS; see 2. Armee, fasc. 58.

49. KA NFA, VII Korps, Tagebücher; 2. Armee, fasc. 95; 2. Armee, Op. No. 286/31.

50. KA NFA, 3. Armee, fasc. 42, Tagebücher; 2. Armee, fasc. 95; Tagebücher; *ÖULK*, vol. 2.

51. Ibid., KAN, B/558, Le Beau, Tagebücher.

52. Ibid.

53. KA NFA, VII Korps, Tagebücher, VII Korps, Op. No. 289/15; *ÖULK*, vol. 2.

54. KAN, B/23, Mayern, 2. *Armee in der Karpatenschlacht*.

55. KA NFA, 2. Armee, fasc. 9, varia; *ÖULK*, vol. 2.

56. KA NFA, VII Korps, Tagebücher; 3. Armee, fasc. 42, Tagebücher; *ÖULK*, vol. 2.

57. KA, Gefechtsbericht, 43. Infantrie Division; KAN, B/23, Mayern, 2. *Armee in der Karpatenschlacht*, 134.

58. KAN, B/23, Mayern, 2. *Armee in der Karpatenschlacht*; B/544, Kralowetz, X Korps MS.

59. KA NFA, 3. Armee, fasc. 42, Tagebücher, 3. Armee, Op. No. 2997; KA MS1.Wkg., Rußland, 1915, No. 36, Südarmee MS.

60. KA MS1.Wkg., Rußland, 1915, No. 36, Südarmee MS.

61. Ibid.

62. KA NFA, VII Korps, Tagebücher, VII Korps, Op. No. 289/3,12; 2. Armee, fasc. 9.

63. Feldmarschall Erzherzog Josef, *A Világháború amilyennek én láttam* (Budapest: Ungarische Akademie Wissenschaften, 1924).

64. KA NFA, 3. Armee, fasc. 42, Tagebücher, 3. Armee, Op. No.3010/1; see KAN, B/558, Le Beau, Tagebücher; *ÖULK*, vol. 2.

65. See KA NFA, 3. Armee, fasc. 42, Tagebücher, 3. Armee, Op. No. 3060/1, 3010/1, 3018.

66. KA NFA, 3. Armee, fasc. 11, 3. Armee, Op. No. 3016.

67. *Der Weltkrieg 1914 bis 1918*, vols. 3 and 4, *Die militärischen Operationen zu Lande* (Berlin: E. S. Mittler und Sohn, 1925–1942), 86, 89; Egmont Zechlin, "Ludendorff im Jahre 1915. Unveröffentliche Briefe," *Historische Zeitschrift* 211 (1970): 316–353.

68. KA NFA, 3. Armee, fasc. 11, 3. Armee, Op. No. 3016.

69. *ÖULK*, vol. 2; Steinitz, "Ausharren oder Ausweichen?," 59.

70. KAN, B/54, Anton von Ritter Pitreich.

71. KAN, B/544, Kralowetz, X Korps MS.; KA MS1.Wkg., Rußland, 1915, No. 36, Südarmee MS.

72. KAN, B/23, Mayern, 2. *Armee in der Karpatenschlacht.*

73. Ibid.; KA NFA, Gefechtsbericht, 43. Landwehr Infantrie Division, K1824.

74. KAN, B/23, Mayern, 2. *Armee in der Karpatenschlacht;* B/544, Kralowetz, X Korps MS.; KA NFA, Gefechtsberichte, 2. Infantrie Division, Op. No. 346/1.

75. Ibid.

76. KA NFA, 4. Armee, fasc. 70, Tagebücher, 4. Armee, Op. No. 2537, 2543; *ÖULK,* vol. 2.

77. BWA, TGY 2819, II 143, Gruppe Szurmay, 8. Kavallrie Division, Op. No. 501/29.

78. KA AOK, fasc. 501, X Korps, Op. No. 518.

79. Ibid.; KAN, B/23, Mayern, 2. *Armee in der Karpatenschlacht;* Steinitz, "Ausharren oder Ausweichen?"; see KAN, B/544, Kralowetz, X Korps MS.

80. KA NFA, 3. Armee, fasc. 42, Tagebücher, 3. Armee, Op. No. 3039; KAN, B/558, Le Beau, Tagebücher; KA AOK, fasc. 615, AOK, Tagebücher; see also KA NFA, VII Korps, Tagebücher; 2. Armee, fasc. 95, Tagebücher; *ÖULK,* 2:130.

81. KA NFA, 3. Armee, fasc. 11, 3. Armee, Op. No. 3038; KAN, B/23, Mayern, 2. *Armee in der Karpatenschlacht,* 25; Stone, *Eastern Front.*

82. KA Gefechtsbericht, 2. Infantrie Division, Op. No. 346/1, K1802; KAN, B/544, Kralowetz, X Korps MS.

83. Ibid.; KA NFA, V Korps, Tagebücher, V Korps, Op. No. 290/10; 2. Armee, fasc. 9.

84. Ibid.; 7. Infantrie Division Kdo., Op. No. 101/19, 1/29.

85. KA NFA, 3. Armee, fasc. 42, Tagebücher, 3. Armee, Op. No. 3045; AOK Op. No. 6707.

86. KA NFA, 3. Armee, fasc. 11, 3. Armee, Op. No. 3051.

87. KA NFA, 3. Armee, fasc. 11, 3. Armee, Op. No. 3064; *ÖULK,* vol. 2.

88. KA AOK, fasc. 615, AOK Tagebücher; see KA NFA, 3. Armee, fasc. 42, Tagebücher, 3. Armee, Op. No. 3155.

89. KA NFA, 4. Armee, fasc. 70, Tagebücher; *ÖULK,* 2:135–137.

90. KA NFA, 3. Armee, fasc. 42, Tagebücher, 3. Armee, Op. No. 3038; see V and XVIII Korps, Tagebücher; *ÖULK,* vol. 2.

91. KA NFA, 3. Armee, fasc. 42, Tagebücher, 3. Armee, Op. No. 3055; *ÖULK,* 2:135, see also VII Korps, Tagebücher; 2. Armee, fasc. 95, Tagebücher and KAN, B/558, Le Beau, Tagebücher.

92. KA NFA, 3. Armee, fasc. 42, Tagebücher, X Korps, Op. No. 373/7; KA MS1.Wkg., Rußland, 1915, No. 36, Südarmee MS; *ÖULK,* 2:137.

93. KA MS1.Wkg., Rußland, 1915, No. 36, Südarmee MS.

94. BWA, TGY 2819, II 143, Gruppe Szurmay, 8. Kavallerie Division, 1/30 7. Infantrie Division.

95. Ibid., Op. No. 43/XIV Abschrift.

96. Ibid., Gruppe Szurmay, 66. Infantrie Brigade.

97. KAN, B/240, Albert Fiedler, No. 1, 42. Honvéd Infantrie Division; KA NFA, 3. Armee, fasc. 42, Tagebücher, 3. Armee, Op. No. 3019, 3051, 3061.

98. BWA, TGY 2819, II 143, Gruppe Szurmay; Steinitz, "Ausharren oder Ausweichen?"

99. KAN, B/23, Mayern, 2. *Armee in der Karpatenschlacht;* see *ÖULK,* vol. 2.

100. KA NFA, VII Korps, Tagebücher; 2. Armee, fasc. 95, Tagebücher, V Korps, Op. No. 630/11; Feldmarschall Erzherzog Josef, *Világháború.*

101. KA MS1.Wkg., Rußland, 1915, No. 36, Südarmee MS.

102. KA MS1.Wkg., Allgemeine, A-4, Werdegang und Shicksal, Georg Veith.

103. KAN, B/240, Fiedler, No. 1, 42. Honvéd Infantrie Division; KA NFA, 3. Armee, fasc. 11 and fasc. 42, 3. Armee, Op. No. 3051, 3061; KA AOK, fasc. 783, Evidenz der eigenen Situation.

104. KA NFA, 4. Armee, fasc. 70, Tagebücher; 3. Armee, fasc. 42, Tagebücher; *ÖULK,* 2:137.

105. *ÖULK,* 2:138.

106. KA AOK, fasc. 615, AOK Tagebücher; *ÖULK,* 2:137.

107. KA AOK, AOK Op. No. 6757; see also Rudolf Hecht, *Fragen zur Heeresergänzung der Gestalten Bewaffneten Macht Österreich-Ungarns während des ersten Weltkrieges* (diss., University of Vienna, 1969).

108. KA NFA, III Korps, Tagebücher; KAN, B/544, Kralowetz, X Korps MS; *ÖULK,* 2:137.

109. KA MS1Wkg., Rußland, 1915, No. 36, Südarmee MS.

110. KA NFA, VII Korps, Tagebücher; KAN, B/544, Kralowetz, X Korps MS; B/23, Mayern, 2. *Armee in der Karpatenschlacht; ÖULK,* vol. 2.

111. KA AOK, 3. Armee, fasc. 42, Tagebücher, 3. Armee, Op. No. 3070/11, 3079; KA AOK, fasc. 783, Evidenz der eigenen Situation; *ÖULK,* vol. 2.

112. KA NFA, 3. Armee, fasc. 42, Tagebücher, AOK Op. No. 6858; *ÖULK,* vol. 2; KAN, B/23, Mayern, 2. *Armee in der Karpatenschlacht.*

113. KAN, B/23, Mayern, 2. *Armee in der Karpatenschlacht.*

114. BWA, TGY 2819, II 143, Gruppe Szurmay, Armee Gruppe Kdo., Op. No. 46/XXXVI.

115. KAN, B/557, Pflanzer-Baltin, Tagebücher; *ÖULK,* vol. 2.

116. KA NFA, 3. Armee, fasc. 42, Tagebücher, 3. Armee, Op. No. 3102, 3109/II, AOK Op. No. 6839; V, XVIII Korps, Tagebücher; MS1.Wkg., Rußland, 1915, No. 36, Südarmee MS.

117. KA NFA, V Korps, Tagebücher.

118. KA MS1.Wkg., Rußland, 1915, No. 36, Südarmee MS.

119. KAAOK, fasc. 501, AOK Op. No. 6804 (R 1477); KA NFA, 3. Armee, fasc. 42, Tagebücher; KAN, B/23, Mayern, 2. *Armee in der Karpatenschlacht.*

120. KA NFA, 3. Armee, fasc. 42, 3. Armee, Op. No. 3081, AOK Op. No. 6770, 6804 (1477).

121. KA NFA, V Korps, Tagebücher; KAN, B/23, Mayern, 2. *Armee in der Karpatenschlacht.*

122. KA NFA, 3. Armee, fasc. 42, Tagebücher; KAN, B/544, Kralowetz, X Korps MS.

123. KAN, B/240, Fiedler, No. 1, 42. Honvéd Infantrie Division; B/557, Pflanzer-Baltin, Tagebücher; B/509, Schneller, Tagebücher.

124. KAN, B/23, Mayern, 2. *Armee in der Karpatenschlacht.*

125. KAN, B/544, Kralowetz, X Korps MS; KA NFA, 2. I.D. Gefechtsbericht, Op. No. 346/1, K 1802.

126. KA NFA, Gefechtsbericht, 2. I.D. X Korps Op. No. 574/29; Zanantoni, *Deutsch-bömische 29. Infantriedivision*, 1:183.

127. KA NFA, Gefechtsbericht 2. I.D. X Korps, Op. 574/10; see KAN, B/544, Kralowetz, X Korps MS.

128. BWA, TGY 2819, II 143, Gruppe Szurmay.

129. Ibid., Op. No. 46/XXXV, XXXVI, Op. No. 321/20.

130. Ibid., KAN, B/23, Mayern, 2. *Armee in der Karpatenschlacht.*

131. BWA, TGY 2819, II 143, Armee Gruppe Szurmay.

132. KA AOK, fasc. 523, Przemyśl, AOK Op. No. 8000; KA MS1.Wkg., Rußland, 1915, No. 19, Stuckheil, *Festung Przemyśl;* ÖULK, 2:113; Forstner, *Przemyśl.*

133. KA NFA, XVIII Korps, Tagebücher; KAN, B/23, Mayern, 2. *Armee in der Karpatenschlacht.*

134. KA NFA, 2. Armee, fasc. 58; see 3. Armee, fasc. 42, Tagebücher.

135. KA Gefechtsbericht, 2. Infantrie Division, AOK Op. No. 6814; KA NFA, III, V, and VII Korps, Tagebücher; see *ÖULK*, vol. 2.

136. KAN, B/23, Mayern, 2. *Armee in der Karpatenschlacht.*

137. KA AOK, fasc. 512, Conrad-Falkenhayn, Rußland, Korrespondenz; Rauchensteiner, *Tod des Doppeladlers*, 224.

138. KA AOK, fasc. 512, Conrad-Falkenhayn, Rußland, Korrespondenz; KA Archiv Conrad, B/13 Kundmann, Tagebüch; Hermann Wendt, *Der italienische Kriegsschauplatz in europäischen Konflikten. Seine Bedeutung für die Kriegführung an Frankreichs Nordostgrenze* (Berlin: Junker und Dunnhaupt Verlag, 1936).

139. KA NFA, 3. Armee, fasc. 11, 3. Armee, Op. No. 3086; KA AOK, fasc. 615, AOK, Tagebücher; ÖULK, vol. 2.

140. KA NFA, 3. Armee, fasc. 42, Tagebücher; see also VII and XVIII Korps, Tagebücher; KAN, B/544, Kralowetz, X Korps MS; Steinitz, "Ausharren oder Ausweichen?," 42; ÖULK, vol. 2.

141. KA NFA, V Korps, Tagebücher; 3. Armee, fasc. 42, Tagebücher.

142. KA Militärkanzlei Seiner Majestät, separate fasc. 78/17.

143. KAN, B/23, Mayern, 2. *Armee in der Karpatenschlacht.*

144. KA NFA, XIX Korps, Tagebücher; 3. Armee, fasc. 42, Tagebücher; Zanantoni, *Deutsch-bömische 29. Infantriedivision*, 29.

145. KAN, B/1137, Hermann Kusmanek von Burgstädten, No. 2, *Przemyśl;* KA MS1.Wkg., Rußland, 1915, No. 19, Stuckheil, *Festung Przemyśl;* Forstner, *Przemyśl.*

146. Ibid.; ÖULK, vol. 2.

147. KAN, B/23, Mayern, 2. *Armee in der Karpatenschlacht.*

148. Ibid.; KAN, B/554, Kralowetz, X Korps MS.

149. KA NFA, 3. Armee, fasc. 42, Tagebücher; KAN, B/23, Mayern, 2. *Armee in der Karpatenschlacht;* ÖULK, vol. 2.

150. KAN, B/23, Mayern, 2. *Armee in der Karpatenschlacht;* B/544, Kralowetz, X Korps MS.; KA NFA, 3. Armee, fasc. 42, Tagebücher; ÖULK, vol. 2.

151. KA NFA, 3. Armee, fasc. 42, Tagebücher; KAN, B/23, Mayern, 2. *Armee in der Karpatenschlacht;* ÖULK, vol. 2.

152. Ibid.

153. Ibid.

154. KAN, B/544, Kralowetz, X Korps MS.

155. KA NFA, 2. Armee, fasc. 58, VII Stand Abgänge, Infantrie Regiment 81 and 88, VII Korps, Op. No. 874/32, 2. Armee, Op. No. 3242.

156. KA NFA, XIX Korps, Tagebücher.

157. *ÖULK,* vol. 2.

158. KA NFA, XIX Korps, Tagebücher.

159. KA MS1.Wkg., Rußland, 1915, No. 36, Südarmee MS; *ÖULK,* vol. 2.

160. See *ÖULK,* vol. 2.

161. KAN, B/23, Mayern, 2. *Armee in der Karpatenschlacht;* B/544, Kralowetz, X Korps MS, *ÖULK,* vol. 2.

162. KA NFA, 3. Armee, fasc. 11, 3. Armee, Op. No. 3109/II, X Korps, Op. No. 517/33, 41; KAN, B/544, Kralowetz, X Korps, MS; *ÖULK,* vol. 2. Knauss, manuscript in private possession.

163. Knauss, manuscript in private possession.

164. KA NFA, 3. Armee, fasc. 42, Tagebücher; KA Gefechtberichte, 2 I.D., Op. No. 346/1, K 1802.

165. KAN, B/23, Mayern, 2. *Armee in der Karpatenschlacht;* see *ÖULK,* vol. 2.

166. KA NFA, VII Korps, Tagebücher; KAN, B/558, Le Beau, Tagebücher.

167. KA NFA, 3. Armee, fasc. 42, Tagebücher; see *ÖULK,* vol. 2.

168. See *ÖULK,* vol. 2.

169. Ibid.

170. Steinitz, "Ausharren oder Ausweichen?," 44; see *ÖULK,* vol. 2.

171. KA NFA, 2. Armee, fasc. 95, Tagebücher; KAN, B/23, Mayern, 2. *Armee in der Karpatenschlacht; ÖULK,* vol. 2.

172. KA NFA, 3. Armee, fasc. 11 and 42, (Tagebücher), 3. Armee, Op. No. 3110; BWA, TGY 2819, II 143, Gruppe Szurmay.

173. KA NFA, 3. Armee, fasc. 11; KAN, B/23, Mayern, 2. *Armee in der Karpatenschlacht.*

174. KAN, B/557, Pflanzer-Baltin, Tagebücher; Stone, *Eastern Front; ÖULK,* vol. 2; KA NFA, 4. Armee, fasc. 70, Tagebücher, 4. Armee, Op. No. 2597/II.

175. KA NFA, 4. Armee, fasc. 70, Tagebücher, 4. Armee, Op. No. 2597/II.

176. KA Gefechtsberichte, 2. Infantrie Division, 3 Infantrie Brigade, Op. No. 306/2, K1804.

177. KA NFA, 2. Armee, fasc. 95, Tagebücher; VII Korps, Tagebücher; KAN, B/23, Mayern, 2. *Armee in der Karpatenschlacht;* B/544, Kralowetz, X Korps, MS; *ÖULK,* vol. 2.

178. BWA TGY 2819, II 143, Gruppe Szurmay.

179. *ÖULK,* vol. 2.

180. KA MS1.Wkg., Rußland, 1915, No. 36, Südarmee MS; *ÖULK,* vol. 2.

181. Ibid.

182. Ibid.

183. KA NFA, 2. Armee, fasc. 58; *ÖULK,* vol. 2.

184. Emil Ratzenhofer, "Die Aufmarsch hinter den Karpathen im Winter 1915." *Militärwissenschaftliche und -technische Mitteilungen* 61 (1930).

185. KA NFA, 2. Armee, fasc. 58; 3. Armee, fasc. 11; see *ÖULK,* vol. 2.

186. KAN, B/557, Pflanzer-Baltin, Tagebücher; B/23, Mayern, 2. *Armee in der Karpatenschlacht.*

187. KA AOK, fasc. 501.

188. KA NFA, 2. Armee, fasc. 95, Tagebücher.

189. KAN, b/544, Kralowetz,X Korps MS; see also *ÖULK*, vol. 2.

190. KAN, B/23, Mayern, 2. *Armee in der Karpatenschlacht.*

191. KA NFA, 3. Armee, fasc. 42, Tagebücher; KAN, B/23, Mayern, 2. *Armee in der Karpatenschlacht;* *ÖULK*, vol. 2.

192. KAN, B/23, Mayern, 2. *Armee in der Karpatenschlacht;* KA NFA, 3. Armee, fasc. 4, 3. Armee, Op. No. 3167/III.

193. KAN, B/23, Mayern, 2. *Armee in der Karpatenschlacht;* KAN, B/557, Pflanzer-Baltin, Tagebücher; KA MS1Wkg., Rußland, 1915, No. 5, Paic, Die westliche Flügelgruppe der 7. Armee im Karpaten.

194. KA NFA, 3. Armee, fasc. 11, 3. Armee, Op. No. 3171; VII Korps, Tagebücher, V Korps, Op. 781/33; *ÖULK*, vol. 2.

195. *ÖULK*, vol. 2; KAN, B/23, Mayern, 2. *Armee in der Karpatenschlacht.*

196. KA NFA, 3. Armee, fasc. 11; V Korps, Tagebücher.

197. 19. Infantrie Division Kommando, report to AOK—2/8—Op. No. 418/1; KA AOK, fasc. 501, 19. Infantrie Division, Op. Zu Op. No. 418/I.

198. KAN, B/557, Pflanzer-Baltin, Tagebücher.

199. KA AOK, fasc. 615, AOK Tagebücher, AOK Op. No. 7059; KA MS1. Wkg., Rußland, 1915, No. 36, Südarmee MS; *ÖULK*, vol. 2.

200. KA NFA, 3. Armee, fasc. 42, Tagebücher, 3. Armee, Op. No. 3216, 3223; *ÖULK*, vol. 2.

201. KA NFA, 2. Armee, fasc. 58, 2. Armee, Op. No. 3242; VII Korps, Op. No. 784/32, Standabgänge Infantrie Regiment 81 + 88; *ÖULK*, vol. 2.

202. KAN, B/23, Mayern, 2. *Armee in der Karpatenschlacht.*

203. Ibid.; *ÖULK*, vol. 2.

204. KA AOK, fasc. 615, AOK Tagebücher; KA NFA, 3. Armee, fasc. 42, Tagebücher.

205. KA NFA, 3. Armee, fasc. 42, Tagebücher, 3. Armee, Op. No. 3232; KA AOK, fasc. 615, AOK Tagebücher; *ÖULK*, vol. 2.

206. KAN, B/1137, No. 2, Kusmanek, *Przemyśl;* KA MS1.Wkg., Rußland, 1915, No. 19, Stuckheil, *Festung Przemyśl;* Forstner, *Przemyśl.*

207. *ÖULK*, vol. 2.

208. KA NFA, 3. Armee, fasc. 42, Tagebücher, 3. Armee, Op. No. 3245; *ÖULK*, vol. 2; KAN, B/23, Mayern, 2. *Armee in der Karpatenschlacht.*

209. KAN, B/23, Mayern, 2. *Armee in der Karpatenschlacht.*

210. KA AOK, AOK fasc. 500, AOK Op. No. 7095.

211. KAN, B/23, Mayern, 2. *Armee in der Karpatenschlacht.*

212. Feldmarschall Erzherzog Josef, *Világháború.*

213. KAN, B/557, Pflanzer-Baltin, Tagebücher; *ÖULK*, vol. 2.

214. KA NFA, XIX Korps, Tagebücher, XIX Korps, Op. No. 335/21.

3. *The Second Carpathian Offensive*

1. Particularly valuable for this chapter is the manuscript Kriegsarchiv Nachlaß (KAN), B/23, Karl Mayern, *Die k.u.k. 2. Armee in der Karpatenschlacht, 1914/15.* Other noteworthy sources include Neue Feld Akten (NFA), 3. Armee. fasc. 11 and 42, Tagebücher. *Österreich-Ungarns letzter Krieg* (hereafter *ÖULK*) is also valuable

for battlefield events. Kriegsarchiv (KA) Armee Ober Kommando (AOK), fasc. 615, AOK Tagebücher, for major events as perceived by the Habsburg Supreme Command. For allied command relations, see KA AOK, fasc. 512, Conrad-Falkenhayn, Rußland, 1915, Korrespondenz; AOK k.u.k. Operations Abteilung "R" Gruppe. Key documents include those in fasc. 501, Februar Aus, Op. No. 6651–7620. Also worthwhile are the notes of Conrad's Flügeladjutant in KANC, Conrad, B/13, Rudolf Kundmann, Tagebüch vom 1/1 1915–4/XI 1916. *Nachläße* with interesting material include KAN, B/544, Kralowetz, X Korps MS; KAN, B/557, Pflanzer-Baltin, Tagebücher; KAN, B/600, Lehar, No. 2, Tagebücher, and KAN, B/700, Mailáth-Pokorny. Monographs of importance include Manfried Rauchensteiner, *Der Tod des Doppeladlers* (Vienna: Verlag Styria, 1993); Norman Stone, *The Eastern Front, 1914–1917* (New York: Charles Scribner's Sons, 1975); and Anton Pitreich, *Der österreich-ungarische Bundesgenosse im Sperrfeuer* (Klagenfurt: Arthur Killitsch, 1930).

2. H. Kerchnawe and E. Ottenschläger, *Ehrenbuch unserer Artillerie; Österreichs Artillerie im Weltkriege, 1914–1918* (Stockerau: Engelbert Hlavka, 1925).

3. KA NFA, V Korps, Tagebücher.

4. KAN, B/600, Lehar, No. 2, Tagebücher; *ÖULK*, 2:175–177, 186, 196; see KA NFA, 3. Armee, fasc. 42, Tagebücher; 3. Armee, Op. No. 3116, 3120; KAN, B/544, Kralowetz, X Korps MS, 241.

5. KA AOK, fasc. 615, AOK, Tagebücher, AOK Op. No. 6987.

6. KA NFA, V Korps, Tagebücher, V Korps, Op. No. 335/37, 15 Februar.

7. *ÖULK*, 2:203; see KAN, B/726, Robert Nowak, *Die Klammer des Reiches. Das Verhalten der elf Nationalitäten Österreich-Ungarns in der k.u.k Wehrmacht, 1914–1918.*

8. KAN, B/600, Lehar, No. 2, Tagebücher.

9. KA NFA, 2. Armee, fasc. 95, Tagebücher, 2. Armee, Op. No. 2272.

10. KA NFA, VII Korps, Tagebücher; 3. Armee, fasc. 42, Tagebücher; KAN, B/544, Kralowetz, X Korps MS; *ÖULK*, vol. 2.

11. KA NFA, 2. Armee, fasc. 95, Tagebücher; 3. Armee, fasc. 42, Tagebücher.

12. KAN, B/557, Pflanzer-Baltin, Tagebücher—Karpathenkrieg; *ÖULK*, vol. 2.

13. See KA NFA, 2. Armee, fasc. 95, Tagebücher; *ÖULK*, vol. 2.

14. KA NFA, 2. Armee, fasc. 95, Tagebücher, 2. Armee, Op. No. 2297; 3. Armee, fasc. 42, Tagebücher.

15. KA NFA, XIX Korps, Tagebücher; KAN, B/23, Mayern, 2. *Armee in der Karpatenschlacht.*

16. KA NFA, 2. Armee fasc. 95, Tagebücher 2. Armee, Op. No. 2396; KAN, B/23, Mayern, 2. *Armee in der Karpatenschlacht.*

17. Erich von Falkenhayn, *The German General Staff and Its Decisions, 1914–1916* (New York: Dodd, Mead and Co., 1920); Stone, *Eastern Front*; Rauchensteiner, *Tod des Doppeladler.*

18. KA NFA, XIX Korps, Tagebücher; 3. Armee, fasc. 42, Tagebücher.

19. KA NFA, XIX Korps, Tagebücher; 2. Armee, fasc. 95, 2. Armee, zu Op. No. 3304; 3. Armee, fasc. 42, Tagebücher.

20. KA NFA, XIX Korps, Tagebücher; 2. Armee, fasc. 95, Tagebücher; 2. Armee, fasc. 58.

21. KA NFA, 2. Armee, fasc. 95, Tagebücher; see *ÖULK*, vol. 2.

22. KA AOK, fasc. 501, Februar, Aus AOK Op. No. 6651–7620.

23. KAN, B/23, Mayern, 2. *Armee in der Karpatenschlacht*, 94.

24. KAN, B/544, Kralowetz, X Korps MS; *ÖULK*, vol. 2.

25. KA NFA, 4. Armee, fasc. 70, Tagebücher; KAN, B/23, Mayern, 2. *Armee in der Karpatenschlacht.*

26. Ibid.; KA NFA, Gefechtsberichte, 26. Landwehr Infantrie Division (L.I.D.), Op. No. 224/1, IX Korps Bericht über die Kampf auf der Magora, K 1810.

27. KA NFA, 3. Armee, fasc. 42, Tagebücher, 3. Armee, Op. No. 3302, 3303, 3305; KA NFA, Gefechtsberichte, 26. L.I.D., Op. No. 224/1, IX KK, Bericht über die Kampf auf der Magora, K 1810.

28. KA NFA, 2. Armee, fasc. 95, Tagebücher; *ÖULK*, vol. 2.

29. KA NFA, 3. Armee, fasc. 42, Tagebücher, 3. Armee, Op. No. 3320; XIX Korps, Tagebücher.

30. KA NFA, 3. Armee, fasc. 42, Tagebücher, 3. Armee, Op. No. 3321; KAN, B/544, Kralowetz, X Korps MS.

31. KA NFA, 4. Armee, fasc. 70, Tagebücher; KA NFA, Gefechtsberichte, 26 L.I.D., Op. No. 224/1, IX KK, Bericht über die Kampf auf der Magora, K 1810; KAN, B/23, Mayern, 2. *Armee in der Karpatenschlacht.*

32. KAN, B/1137, No. 2, Hermann Kusmanek von Burgstädten, *Przemyśl;* KA Militärkanzlei Seiner Majestät (MKSM), separat fasc. 100, Op. No. 1956; KA MS1.Wkg., Rußland, 1915, No. 19, Stuckheil, *Festung Przemyśl;* Franz Forstner, *Przemyśl. Österreich-Ungarns bedeutendste Festung* (Vienna: Österreichischer Bundesverlag, 1987).

33. KA NFA, 2. Armee, fasc. 95, Tagebücher; *ÖULK*, 2:182; KAN, B/23, Mayern, 2. *Armee in der Karpatenschlacht.*

34. Ibid.

35. Ibid.; KAN, B/23, Mayern, 2. *Armee in der Karpatenschlacht*, 111.

36. KA NFA, 2. Armee, fasc. 95, Tagebücher, 2. Armee, Op. No. 2255, 2442; *ÖULK*, vol. 2.

37. KA NFA, 4. Armee, fasc. 70, Tagebücher; KAN, B/557, Pflanzer-Baltin, Tagebücher; *ÖULK*, vol. 2.

38. KA NFA, 2. Armee, fasc. 95, Tagebücher, 2. Armee Auf Op. No. 3322; *ÖULK*, vol. 2; KAN, B/23, Mayern, 2. *Armee in der Karpatenschlacht.*

39. KA NFA, V and XVIII Korps, Tagebücher; *ÖULK*, vol. 2.

40. *ÖULK*, 2:182–183.

41. KA NFA, XVIII Korps, Tagebücher, 2. Armee, Op. No. 2259; 2. Armee, fasc. 95, Tagebücher; KAN, B/544, Kralowetz, X Korps MS.

42. KA NFA, XIX Korps, Tagebücher; 2. Armee, fasc. 95, Tagebücher; KAN, B/23, Mayern, 2. *Armee in der Karpatenschlacht; ÖULK*, vol. 2.

43. KA NFA, XVIII Korps, Tagebücher; 2. Armee, fasc. 95, Tagebücher, 2. Armee, Op. No. 2260.

44. KAN, B/544, Kralowetz, X Korps MS.

45. KA NFA, 2. Armee, fasc. 95, Tagebücher, 2. Armee, Op. No. 2272, 2320; AOK Op. No. 7397.

46. KA NFA, 2. Armee, fasc. 9, 2. Armee, Op. No. 2296; KAN, B/23, Mayern, 2. *Armee in der Karpatenschlacht.*

47. KA NFA, V Korps, Tagebücher, 2. Armee, Op. No. 2320; KAN, B/23, Mayern, 2. *Armee in der Karpatenschlacht.*

48. KA NFA, 2. Armee, fasc. 95, Tagebücher; 3. Armee, fasc. 42, Tagebücher; *ÖULK*, vol. 2.

49. KA NFA, 2. Armee, fasc. 95, Tagebücher, 2. Armee, Op. EOK No. 26700, Op. No. 2280/32; KAN, B/23, Mayern, 2. *Armee in der Karpatenschlacht.*

50. KA NFA, 2. Armee, fasc. 9, 2. Armee, Op. No. 2297.

51. KAN, B/23, Mayern, 2. *Armee in der Karpatenschlacht,* 38; KA NFA, 2. Armee, fasc. 95, Tagebücher.

52. Rudolf Hecht, *Fragen zur Heeresergänzung der Gestalten Bewaffneten Macht Österreich-Ungarns während des ersten Weltkrieges* (diss., University of Vienna, 1969).

53. KA NFA, 2. Armee, fasc. 95, Tagebücher, 2 Armee, Op. No. 2280/50; KA NFA, 3. Armee, fasc. 42, Tagebücher; KAN, B/23, Mayern, 2. *Armee in der Karpatenschlacht,* 144.

54. KAN, B/23, Mayern, 2. *Armee in der Karpatenschlacht; ÖULK,* vol. 2.

55. KA NFA, 2. Armee, fasc. 95, Tagebücher; KAN, B/23, Mayern, 2. *Armee in der Karpatenschlacht; ÖULK,* vol. 2.

56. Ibid.

57. KA NFA, V Korps, Tagebücher; KAN, B/23, Mayern, 2. *Armee in der Karpatenschlacht.*

58. KA NFA, XIX Korps, Tagebücher, XIX Korps, Op. No. 234; KA NFA, 2. Armee, fasc. 95, Tagebücher; *ÖULK,* vol. 2.

59. KA NFA, III and VII Korps Tagebücher; KAN, B/544, Kralowetz, X Korps MS; *ÖULK,* vol. 2.

60. KA NFA, 2. Armee, fasc. 58.

61. KA NFA, 2. Armee, fasc. 95, Tagebücher, 2. Armee, Op. No. 2298; KAN, B/23, Mayern, 2. *Armee in der Karpatenschlacht; ÖULK,* vol. 2.

62. Ibid.; *ÖULK,* vol. 2; KAN, B/1137, No. 2, Kusmanek, *Przemyśl;* KA MS1. Wkg., Rußland, 1915, No. 19, Stuckheil, *Festung Przemyśl;* Forstner, *Przemyśl.*

63. KA NFA, 3. Armee, fasc. 42, Tagebücher; KAN, B/23, Mayern, 2. *Armee in der Karpatenschlacht; ÖULK,* vol. 2. The 43rd Infantry Division consisted of 3,400 rifles on a 3-kilometer front; the 27th Infantry Division, 6,000 rifles on a 5.5-kilometer front; the 41st Honvéd Infantry Division, 11,900 rifles on a 5-kilometer front; the 29th Infantry Division, 5,108 rifles on a 7.5-kilometer front; and the 34th Infantry Division, 3,500 rifles on a 3-kilometer front. (Reserve Op. No. 2600.)

64. KA NFA, 2. Armee, fasc. 95, Tagebücher, 2. Armee, Op. 2317; KAN, B/23, Mayern, 2. *Armee in der Karpatenschlacht; ÖULK,* vol. 2.

65. Ibid.

66. Ibid.; 2. Armee, Op. No. 2396.

67. Ibid.; 2. Armee, Op. No. 3377, 3371/1; 3. Armee, fasc. 42, Tagebücher.

68. KA NFA, 2. Armee, fasc. 95, Tagebücher, 2. Armee, Op. No. 3375; 3. Armee, fasc. 42, Tagebücher; B/23, Mayern, 2. *Armee in der Karpatenschlacht.*

69. Ibid.; 2. Armee, Op. No. 3375.

70. Ibid.; 2. Armee, Op. 2384; 3. Armee, Op. No. 3387/1; *ÖULK,* vol. 2.

71. Ibid.; 2. Armee, Op. No. 2375/1.

72. KAN, B/23, Mayern, 2. *Armee in der Karpatenschlacht,* 159.

73. Ibid.; KA NFA, 4. Armee, fasc. 70, Tagebücher.

74. KA NFA, 2. Armee, fasc. 95, Tagebücher, 2. Armee, Op. No. 2391, 2393, 2334; KAN, B/23, Mayern, 2. *Armee in der Karpatenschlacht,* 162.

75. Ibid.; 2. Armee, fasc. 95, Tagebücher; see 2. Armee, Op. No. 2371; KA NFA, XVIII Korps, Tagebücher.

76. Ibid., 2. Armee, Op. No. 2371.

77. KA NFA, 2. Armee, fasc. 95, 2. Armee, Op. No. 2379, 2386; 3. Armee, fasc. 42, Tagebücher, 3. Armee, Op. No. 2964/1, 3404; ÖULK, vol. 2.

78. KA NFA, 2. Armee, fasc. 95, Tagebücher; 3. Armee, fasc. 42, Tagebücher, 3. Armee, Op. No. 3403.

79. Ibid.; 3. Armee, Op. No. 2964/I, 3404; 4. Armee, fasc. 70, Tagebücher; ÖULK, vol. 2; KA MS1.Wkg., Rußland, 1915, No. 36, Südarmee MS.

80. Ibid.; 3. Armee, Op. No. 3381; KA NFA, 2. Armee, fasc. 95, Tagebücher, 2. Armee, Op. No. 2330/58, 2343; ÖULK, vol. 2.

81. KA NFA, 3. Armee, fasc. 42, Tagebuch, 3. Armee, Op. No. 3385; 2. Armee, fasc. 95, Tagebücher; 2. Armee, Op. No. 2382, 2388; KAN, B/544, Kralowetz, X Korps MS.

82. KA NFA, 3. Armee, fasc. 42, Tagebücher; KAN, B/23, Mayern, 2. *Armee in der Karpatenschlacht*, 164; Hecht, *Fragen zur Heeresergänzung.*

83. Ibid., ÖULK, vol. 2.

84. KA NFA, 4. Armee, fasc. 70, Tagebücher.

85. KA NFA, 3. Armee, fasc. 42, Tagebücher, 3. Armee, Op. No. 2286; KAN, B/23, Mayern, 2. *Armee in der Karpatenschlacht*, 147; ÖULK, vol. 2.

86. KAN, B/23, Mayern, 2. *Armee in der Karpatenschlacht*, 170; ÖULK, 2:186.

87. KA NFA, 3. Armee, fasc. 42, Tagebücher; ÖULK, 2:200.

88. Ibid.; XIX Korps, Tagebücher.

89. Feldmarschall Erzherzog Josef, *A Világháború amilyennek én láttam* (Budapest: Ungarische Akademie der Wissenschaften, 1924); KAN, B/23, Mayern, 2. *Armee im der Karpatenschlacht.*

90. KA MS1.Wkg., Allgemeine, A-4, Veith, *Werdegang und Schicksal.*

91. ÖULK, 2:174, 186.

92. Ibid., 187; see KAN, B/557, Pflanzer-Baltin, Tagebücher.

93. KAN, B/600, Lehar, No. 2.

94. Ibid.

95. Ibid.

96. Ibid.

97. Ibid.

98. Feldmarschall Erzherzog Josef, *Világháború.*

99. KAN, B/557, Pflanzer-Baltin, Tagebücher; Stone, *Eastern Front.*

100. KAN, B/557, Pflanzer-Baltin, Tagebücher; Knauss, manuscript in private possession.

101. KA NFA, Gefechtsberichte, 24. Infantry Division Kdo., Op. No. 251, K 1810; see KAN, B/544, Kralowetz, X Korps MS.

102. KAN Conrad (KANC), B/13, Kundmann, Tagebüch; ÖULK, vol. 2; KAN, B/23, Mayern, 2. *Armee in der Karpatenschlacht.*

103. KA NFA, 3. Armee, fasc. 42, Tagebücher; KAN, B/544, Kralowetz, X Korps MS; KAN, B/23, Mayern, 2. *Armee in der Karpatenschlacht*, 185.

104. KA NFA, VII Korps, Tagebücher; 3. Armee, fasc. 42, Tagebücher; see KAN, B/558, Aurel le von Le Beau, Tagebücher.

105. Budapest War Archives (BWA), TGY 2819, II 143, Gruppe Szurmay MS; KAN, B/23, Mayern, 2. *Armee in der Karpatenschlacht.*

106. KAN, B/557, Pflanzer-Baltin, Tagebücher.

107. KA NFA, 2. Armee, fasc. 95, Tagebücher; 3. Armee, fasc. 42, Tagebücher; KAN, B/23, Mayern, 2. *Armee in der Karpatenschlacht.*

108. KA NFA, Gefechtsbericht, 24. I.D. Kdo., Op. No. 251, K 1810; KAN, B/544, Kralowetz, X Korps MS.

109. Ibid.; KA NFA, 3. Armee, fasc. 42, Tagebücher; KAN, B/23, Mayern, 2. *Armee in der Karpatenschlacht,* 105; see KA MS1.Wkg., Allgemeine, A-4, Veith, *Werdegang und Schicksal.*

110. KAN, B/23, Mayern, 2. *Armee in der Karpatenschlacht,* 189–90, 211; *ÖULK,* vol. 2.

111. Ibid.

112. KA NFA, 2. Armee, fasc. 95, Tagebücher, 2. Armee, Op. No. 2472.

113. KA NFA, 3. Armee, fasc. 42, Tagebücher; 2. Armee, fasc. 95, Tagebücher; 2. Armee, fasc. 58.

114. KA NFA, 4. Armee, fasc. 70, Tagebücher, see also KA NFA, 3. Armee, fasc. 42, Tagebücher; *ÖULK,* vol. 2.

115. KAN, B/23, Mayern, 2. *Armee in der Karpatenschlacht,* 206; see also KA NFA, 2. Armee, fasc. 95, Tagebücher; 2 Armee, fasc. 58; 3. Armee, fasc. 42, Tagebücher.

116. KA NFA, VII Korps, Tagebücher; KAN, B/544, Kralowetz, X Korps MS; *ÖULK,* vol. 2.

117. KAN, B/23, Mayern, 2. *Armee in der Karpatenschlacht,* 147; *ÖULK,* vol. 2.

118. KA NFA, 2. Armee, fasc. 95, Tagebücher; KAN, B/23, Mayern, 2. *Armee in der Karpatenschlacht.*

119. KAN, B/1000, Kóvess, No. 74.

120. Eduard Zanantoni, *Die deutsch-bömische 29. Infantriedivision im Kriegsjahre, 1914–15* (Reichenberg: Heimatsöhne im Weltkrieg, 1926).

121. KAN, B/23, Mayern, 2. *Armee in der Karpatenschlacht,* 196.

122. KA NFA, VII Korps, Tagebücher; KAN, B/23, Mayern, 2. *Armee im der Karpatenschlacht;* B/544, Kralowetz, X Korps MS; *ÖULK,* vol. 2.

123. KA MS1.Wkg., 1915, Rußland, No. 36, Südarmee MS.

124. KANC, B/13, Kundmann, Tagebüch.

125. KAN, B/557, Pflanzer-Baltin, Tagebücher; see *ÖULK,* vol. 2.

126. KA NFA, 4. Armee, fasc. 70, Tagebücher; see 3. Armee, fasc. 42, Tagebücher; *ÖULK,* vol. 2.

127. KAN, B/1137, No. 2, Kusmanek, *Przemyśl;* KA MS1.Wkg., Rußland, 1915, No. 19, Stuckheil, *Festung Przemyśl;* Forstner, *Przemyśl; ÖULK,* vol. 2.

128. KA NFA, 2. Armee, fasc. 95, Tagebücher; VII, XIX Korps, Tagebücher; KAN, B/23, Mayern, 2. *Armee in der Karpatenschlacht;* KAN, B/544, Kralowetz, X Korps MS; *ÖULK,* vol. 2.

129. KA NFA, V and XVIII Korps, Tagebücher; BWA, TGY 2819, II 143, Gruppe Szurmay.

130. See KA NFA, 2. Armee, fasc. 58; 2. Armee, fasc. 95, Tagebücher ; 3. Armee, fasc. 42, Tagebücher, 3. Armee, Op. No. 3457; KAN, B/544, Kralowetz, X Korps MS.

131. KA NFA, 3. Armee, fasc. 42, Tagebücher; KA MS1.Wkg., Allgemeine, A-4, Veith, *Werdegang und Schicksal;* KAN, B/23, Mayern, 2. *Armee in der Karpatenschlacht,* 220; Forstner, *Przemyśl,* 244.

132. Feldmarschall Erzherzog Josef, *Világháború.*

133. See KA AOK, fasc. 512, Conrad-Falkenhayn, Rußland, Korrespondenz; fasc. 551, Balkan, Korrespondenz; KANC, B/13, Kundmann, Tagebüch.

134. KAN, B/23, Mayern, 2. *Armee in der Karpatenschlacht*, 220–221; KA NFA, 3. Armee, fasc. 42, Tagebücher, 3. Armee, Op. No. 3457.

135. KA MKSM, separat fasc. 100, Res. No. 144, Zur Lage auf dem Kriegschauplatz.

136. KA AOK, fasc. 512, Conrad-Falkenhayn, Rußland, Korrespondenz; Hermann Wendt, *Der italienische Kriegsschauplatz in europäischen Konflikten. Seine Bedeutung für die Kriegführung an Frankreichs Nordostgrenze* (Berlin: Junker und Dunnhaupt Verlag, 1936).

137. KAN, B/557, Pflanzer-Baltin, Tagebücher; B/23, Mayern, 2. *Armee in der Karpatenschlacht*; *ÖULK*, vol. 2.

138. KA AOK, fasc. 512, Conrad-Falkenhayn, Rußland, Korrespondenz; KA NFA, 2. Armee, fasc. 95, Tagebücher; 4. Armee, fasc. 70, Tagebücher; V and XVIII Korps, Tagebücher; *ÖULK*, vol. 2; KAN, B/23, Mayern, 2. *Armee in der Karpatenschlacht*.

139. KAN, B/23, Mayern, 2. *Armee in der Karpatenschlacht*; *ÖULK*, vol. 2.

140. KA NFA, VII Korps, Tagebücher; 2. Armee, fasc. 95, Tagebücher; 3. Armee, fasc. 42, Tagebücher; *ÖULK*, vol. 2; KAN, B/23, Mayern, 2. *Armee in der Karpatenschlacht*.

141. KA NFA, 2. Armee, fasc. 95, Tagebücher; 3. Armee, fasc. 42, Tagebücher; *ÖULK*, 2:202.

142. KA NFA, 2. Armee, fasc. 95, Tagebücher; XIX Korps, Tagebücher; *ÖULK*, vol. 2.

143. KA NFA, 2. Armee, fasc. 95, Tagebücher; *ÖULK*, vol. 2.

144. KAN, B/23, Mayern, 2. *Armee in der Karpatenschlacht*, 238.

145. KA NFA, 2. Armee, fasc. 95, Tagebücher; KAN, B/557, Pflanzer-Baltin, Tagebücher; *ÖULK*, 2:202.

146. KA NFA, 3. Armee, fasc. 42, Tagebücher; 4. Armee, fasc. 70, Tagebücher; *ÖULK*, 2:203; KAN, B/23, Mayern, 2. *Armee in der Karpatenschlacht*.

147. KA NFA, XIX Korps, Tagebücher; KAN, B/557, Pflanzer-Baltin, Tagebücher; *ÖULK*, vol. 2.

148. Ibid.; KA NFA, 2. Armee, fasc. 95, Tagebücher; KAN, B/23, Mayern, 2. *Armee in der Karpatenschlacht*.

149. KA NFA, V Korps, Tagebücher.

150. KA NFA, 4. Armee, fasc. 70, Tagebücher; KA AOK, fasc. 615, AOK Tagebücher.

151. KAN, B/23, Mayern, 2. *Armee in der Karpatenschlacht*.

152. KA MS1.Wkg., Rußland, 1915, No. 36, Südarmee MS; *ÖULK*, vol. 2.

153. Ibid.

154. KA NFA, 3. Armee, fasc. 42, Tagebücher; III Korps, Tagebücher; KAN, B/544, Kralowetz, X Korps MS; B/23, Mayern, 2. *Armee in der Karpatenschlacht*, 240.

155. KANC, B/13, Kundmann, Tagebuch; KAN, B/23, Mayern, 2. *Armee in der Karpatenschlacht*, 255–256.

156. BWA, TGY 2819, II 143, Gruppe Szurmay; KA NFA, 3. Armee, fasc. 42, Tagebücher; V Korps, Tagebücher; see also KAN, B/23, Mayern, 2. *Armee in der Karpatenschlacht*, 263; 2. Armee, fasc. 58.

157. KAN, B/23, Mayern, 2. *Armee in der Karpatenschlacht.*

158. KA NFA, 2. Armee, fasc. 95, Tagebücher; XIX Korps, Tagebücher; *ÖULK,* vol. 2.

159. Ibid.

160. KA NFA, V Korps, Tagebücher; see BWA, TGY 2819, II 143, Gruppe Szurmay; KAN, B/23, Mayern, 2. *Armee in der Karpatenschlacht.*

161. Ibid.; *ÖULK,* vol. 2.

162. KA NFA, 2. Armee, fasc. 95, Tagebücher; 3. Armee, fasc. 42, Tagebücher; V and XVIII Korps, Tagebücher; BWA, TGY 2819, II 143, Gruppe Szurmay.

163. KA NFA, 2. Armee, fasc. 7; KAN, B/23, Mayern, 2. *Armee in der Karpatenschlacht.*

164. KAN, B/23, Mayern, 2. *Armee in der Karpatenschlacht.*

165. KANC, B/13, Kundmann, Tagebüch; Wendt, *Italienische Kriegsschauplatz.*

166. KA NFA, 3. Armee, fasc. 42, Tagebücher; 4. Armee, fasc. 70, Tagebücher; KAN, B/23, Mayern, 2. *Armee in der Karpatenschlacht.*

167. KAN, B/600, Lehar, No. 2.

168. Ibid.

169. See *ÖULK,* vol. 2; KAN, B/23, Mayern, 2. *Armee in der Karpatenschlacht.*

170. KA NFA, XIX Korps, Tagebücher; 2. Armee, fasc. 95, Tagebücher, 2. Armee, Op. No. 2560; KAN, B/23, Mayern, 2. *Armee in der Karpatenschlacht,* 253.

171. KA NFA, 2. Armee, fasc. 95, Tagebücher; V, XVIII and XIX Korps, Tagebücher; *ÖULK,* 2:203; KAN, B/23, Mayern, 2. *Armee in der Karpatenschlacht;* Forstner, *Przemyśl,* 244.

172. KAN, B/23, Mayern, 2. *Armee in der Karpatenschlacht.*

173. Ibid.; KA NFA, 2. Armee, fasc. 95, Tagebücher; XIX Korps, Tagebücher; *ÖULK,* vol. 2; Steinitz, "Ausharren oder Ausweichen," 101.

174. KA NFA, 3. Armee, fasc. 42, Tagebücher; 4. Armee, fasc. 70, Tagebücher; *ÖULK,* vol. 2.

175. BWA, TGY 2819, II 143, Gruppe Szurmay; KAN, B/23, Mayern, 2. *Armee in der Karpatenschlacht.*

176. KA MS1.Wkg., Allgemeine, A-4, Veith, *Werdegang und Schicksal; ÖULK,* vol. 2.

177. KA AOK, fasc. 512, Conrad-Falkenhayn, Rußland, Korrespondenz; fasc. 561, Conrad-Falkenhayn, Italien, Korrespondenz; KANC, B/13, Kundmann, Tagebüch; KAN, B/23, Mayern, 2. *Armee in der Karpatenschlacht; ÖULK,* vol. 2; Wendt, *Italienische Kriegsschauplatz.*

178. KA MS1.Wkg., Allgemeine, A-4, Veith, *Werdegang und Schicksal;* KAN, B/23, Mayern, 2. *Armee in der Karpatenschlacht; ÖULK,* vol. 2.

179. Ibid.

180. KAN, B/600, Lehar, No. 2, Tagebücher.

181. KA NFA, 4. Armee, fasc. 70, Tagebücher; *ÖULK,* vol. 2; KAN, B/23, Mayern, 2. *Armee in der Karpatenschlacht.*

182. KAN, B/23, Mayern, 2. *Armee in der Karpatenschlacht.*

183. Feldmarschall Erzherzog Josef, *Világháború.*

184. KAN, B/23, Mayern, 2. *Armee in der Karpatenschlacht,* 304; *ÖULK,* vol. 2.

185. Ibid.; KAN, B/1137, No. 2, Kusmanek, *Przemyśl*; KA MS1.Wkg., Rußland, 1915, No. 19, Stuckheil, *Festung Przemyśl*; Forstner, *Przemyśl*.

186. KA NFA, 2. Armee, fasc. 95, Tagebücher; KAN, B/23, Mayern, 2. *Armee in der Karpatenschlacht*; ÖULK, vol. 2.

187. Stone, *Eastern Front*.

188. KANC, B/13, Kundmann, Tagebüch.

189. See KA NFA, 2. Armee, fasc. 95, Tagebücher; KAN, B/23, Mayern, 2. *Armee in der Karpatenschlacht*.

190. Ibid.

191. KAN, B/700, Pokorny.

192. KA NFA, 4. Armee, fasc. 70, Tagebücher; KAN, B/23, Mayern, 2. *Armee in der Karpatenschlacht*.

193. KA AOK Op. No. 7947; KAN, B/23, Mayern, 2. *Armee in der Karpatenschlacht*.

194. KAN, B/23, Mayern, 2. *Armee in der Karpatenschlacht*.

195. KA NFA, 3. Armee, fasc. 42, Tagebücher.

196. Ibid.; KA AOK, fasc. 512, Conrad-Falkenhayn, Rußland, Korrespondenz; fasc. 561, Italien Korrespondenz; KANC, B/13, Kundmann, Tagebüch.

197. ÖULK, vol. 2; KAN, B/23, Mayern, 2. *Armee in der Karpatenschlacht*.

198. KA NFA, XIX Korps, Tagebücher; 2. Armee fasc. 95, Tagebücher.

199. KA NFA, 2. Armee, fasc. 58.

200. KAN, B/23, Mayern, 2. *Armee in der Karpatenschlacht*, 313.

201. Ibid.; KA NFA, V, XVIII and XIX Korps, Tagebücher.

202. KAN, B/23, Mayern, 2. *Armee in der Karpatenschlacht*.

203. See KAN, B/557, Pflanzer-Baltin, Tagebücher; KA MS1.Wkg., Rußland, 1915, No. 5, Paic, *Die westliche Flügelgruppe der 7. Armee im Karpaten*.

204. KA AOK Op. No. 8008–R1672; ÖULK, vol. 2, Forstner, *Przemyśl*.

205. KA NFA, 2. Armee, fasc. 95, Tagebücher, 2. Armee, Op. No. 2643.

206. KA MKSM, separat fasc. 100; ÖULK, vol. 2; KA NFA, 2. Armee, fasc. 58.

207. KAN, B/1137, No. 2, Kusmanek, *Przemyśl*; KA MS1.Wkg., Rußland, 1915, No. 19, Stuckheil, *Festung Przemyśl*; Forstner, *Przemyśl*; ÖULK, vol. 2.

208. KANC, B/13, Kundmann, Tagebüch; ÖULK, vol. 2.

209. Ibid.

4. The Third Offensive and Easter Battle

1. Kriegsarchiv (KA) Armee Ober Kommando (AOK), fasc. 512, Conrad-Falkenhayn, Rußland, Korrespondenz; KA Nachlaß Conrad (KANC), B/13, Rudolf Kundmann, Tagebüch vom 1/1 1915–4/XI 1916; *Der Weltkrieg 1914 bis 1918* (Berlin: E. S. Mittler und Sohn, 1925–1942), 8:121–122.

2. KANC, B/13, Kundmann, Tagebüch.

3. KANC, B/1450, Conrad von Hötzendorf; Hermann Wendt, *Der italienische Kriegsschauplatz in europäischen Konflikten. Seine Bedeutung für die Kriegführung an Frankreichs Nordostgrenze* (Berlin: Junker und Dunnhaupt Verlag, 1936).

4. KA Militärkanzlei Seiner Majestät (MKSM), separat fasc. 78/17; AOK, fasc. 512, Conrad-Falkenhayn, Korrespondenz, Rußland; fasc. 561, Conrad-Falkenhayn, Korrespondenz, Italien; Wendt, *Italienische Kriegsschauplatz*.

5. KANC, B/13, Kundmann, Tagebüch.

6. Ibid.; KA Neue Feld Akten (NFA), 2. Armee, fasc. 58; V and XVIII Korps, Tagebücher; Budapest War Archives (BWA), TGY 2819, II 143, Gruppe Szurmay, 7. Infantrie Division MS.

7. KA MKSM, separat fasc. 78/17, Conrad to Bolfras.

8. KA NFA, 2. Armee, fasc. 95, Tagebücher; V Korps, Tagebücher; BWA, TGY 2819, II 143, Gruppe Szurmay; Kriegsarchiv Nachlaß (KAN), B/557, Pflanzer-Baltin, Tagebücher; B/558, Aurel le von Le Beau, Tagebücher.

9. KA AOK, fasc. 512, Conrad-Falkenhayn, Korrespondenz, Rußland; Wendt, *Italienische Kriegsschauplatz.*

10. KA MKSM, separat fasc. 78/77, Conrad to Bolfras.

11. KAN, B/23, Karl Mayern, 2. *Armee in der Karpatenschlacht, 1914/15; Österreich-Ungarns letzter Krieg* (hereafter ÖULK), 2.

12. Manfried Rauchensteiner, *Der Tod des Doppeladlers* (Vienna: Verlag Styria, 1993).

13. KAN, B/1137, No. 2, Hermann Kusmanek von Burgstädten, *Przemyśl;* KA MS1.Wkg., Rußland, 1915, No. 19, Stuckheil, *Festung Przemyśl;* Franz Forstner, *Przemyśl. Österreich-Ungarns bedeutendste Festung* (Vienna: Österreichischer Bundesverlag, 1987).

14. Ibid.

15. Ibid.

16. Ibid.

17. Ibid.

18. See Rauchensteiner, *Tod des Doppeladlers;* ÖULK, vol. 2; Kriegsarchiv (KA) Neue Feld Akten (NFA) 3. Armee, fasc. 42., Tagebücher.

19. KA NFA, V Korps, Tagebücher; ÖULK, vol. 2; KAN, B/23, Mayern, 2. *Armee in der Karpatenschlacht.*

20. KA NFA, 4. Armee, fasc. 70, Tagebücher; ÖULK, vol. 2.

21. Ibid.; KAN, B/23, Mayern, 2. *Armee in der Karpatenschlacht.*

22. ÖULK, vol. 2; Rauchensteiner, *Tod des Doppeladlers.*

23. ÖULK, vol. 2; KA NFA, 3. and 2. Armee, Tagebücher.

24. KA NFA, V Korps, Tagebücher; 2. Armee, fasc. 95, Tagebücher.

25. KA NFA, V Korps, Tagebücher; ÖULK, vol. 2.

26. KA MS1.Wkg., Allgemeine, A-4, Veith, *Werdegang und Schicksal.*

27. KAN, B/23, Mayern, 2. *Armee in der Karpatenschlacht;* Rauchensteiner, *Tod des Doppeladlers.*

28. Rauchensteiner, *Tod des Doppeladlers.*

29. KAN, B/600, Lehar, No. 2; KA NFA, V Korps, Tagebücher; KAN, B/23, Mayern, 2. *Armee in der Karpatenschlacht, 139.*

30. ÖULK, vol. 2; KAN, B/23, Mayern, 2. *Armee in der Karpatenschlacht, 431.*

31. KA NFA, 2. Armee, fasc. 95, Tagebücher; see ÖULK, vol. 2, and KAN, B/23, Mayern, 2. *Armee in der Karpatenschlacht.*

32. Ibid.

33. KAN, B/23, Mayern, 2. *Armee in der Karpatenschlacht;* see also ÖULK, vol. 2.

34. KA NFA, V Korps, Tagebücher; sec KAN, B/23, Mayern, 2. *Armee in der Karpatenschlacht;* ÖULK, vol. 2.

35. KA NFA, V Korps, Tagebücher; see KAN, B/23, Mayern, 2. *Armee in der Karpatenschlacht.*
36. KA NFA, 2. Armee, fasc. 95, Tagebücher, 2. Armee Op. No. 2773; V Korps, Tagebücher; KAN, B/23, Mayern, 2. *Armee in der Karpatenschlacht.*
37. Ibid.; also see *ÖULK*, vol. 2.
38. KAN, B/23, Mayern, 2. *Armee in der Karpatenschlacht.*
39. KA NFA, 2. Armee, fasc. 95, Tagebücher, 2. Armee Op. No. 2712; see KAN, B/23, Mayern, 2. *Armee in der Karpatenschlacht; ÖULK*, vol. 2.
40. KA NFA, V Korps, Tagebücher, V Korps Op. No. 820/2, 3, 13; KAN, B/23, Mayern, 2. *Armee in der Karpatenschlacht.*
41. *ÖULK*, vol. 2; KAN, B/23, Mayern, 2. *Armee in der Karpatenschlacht.*
42. KA NFA, XVIII Korps, Tagebücher; *ÖULK*, vol. 2.
43. *ÖULK*, vol. 2.
44. KA MS1.Wkg., Rußland, 1915, No. 36, Südarmee MS; see *ÖULK*, vol. 2.
45. KAN, B/1137, No. 2, Kusmanek, *Przemyśl*; KA AOK, fasc. 523, Przemyśl; KA MS1.Wkg., Rußland, 1915, No. 19, Stuckheil, *Festung Przemyśl*; Forstner, *Przemyśl*; Rauchensteiner, *Tod des Doppeladlers.*
46. KA AOK, fasc. 551, Conrad-Falkenhayn, Korrespondenz, Balkan.
47. KANC, B/1450, Conrad; KAN, B/23, Mayern, 2. *Armee in der Karpatenschlacht.*
48. KAN, B/23, Mayern, 2. *Armee in der Karpatenschlacht.*
49. Ibid.; see *ÖULK*, vol. 2.
50. Ibid.; KA AOK, AOK Op. No. 8245; see KAN FA, 2. Armee, fasc. 95, Tagebücher.
51. KA NFA, VII Korps, Tagebücher, 2. Armee Op. No. 2748/12; 2. Armee, fasc. 95, Tagebücher; fasc. 12, 2. Armee Op. No. 2939; KAN, B/544, Kralowetz, X Korps MS.
52. KA NFA, 4. Armee, fasc. 70, Tagebücher; *ÖULK*, vol. 2; KAN, B/23, Mayern, 2. *Armee in der Karpatenschlacht.*
53. KAN, B/23, Mayern, 2. *Armee in der Karpatenschlacht*; KA NFA, V and XIX Korps, Tagebücher; see *ÖULK*, vol. 2.
54. KA NFA, V Korps, Tagebücher; see KAN, B/23, Mayern, 2. *Armee in der Karpatenschlacht; ÖULK*, vol. 2.
55. KA Verbingdungs Officier (VO), Übersetzungen, No. 3, 17; see *ÖULK*, vol. 2.
56. KA NFA, 2. Armee, fasc. 95, Tagebücher; see *ÖULK*, vol. 2 and KAN, B/23, Mayern, 2. *Armee in der Karpatenschlacht.*
57. KA NFA, 3. Armee, fasc. 42, Tagebücher.
58. *ÖULK*, vol. 2.
59. KAN, B/600, No. 2, Lehar, Tagebücher.
60. KA NFA, V and XVIII Korps, Tagebücher; KAN, B/544, Kralowetz, X Korps MS; *ÖULK*, vol. 2.
61. Rauchensteiner, *Tod des Doppeladlers.*
62. KA NFA, 2. Armee, fasc. 95, Tagebücher; see also KA AOK, fasc. 615, AOK Tagebücher; *ÖULK*, vol. 2.
63. KAN, B/23, Mayern, 2. *Armee in der Karpatenschlacht.*
64. *ÖULK*, vol. 2.
65. KAN, B/557, Pflanzer-Baltin, Tagebücher.

66. KA NFA, 3. Armee, fasc. 42, Tagebücher, 3. Armee Op. No. 3000/9; III Korps, Op. No. 257/4.
67. *ÖULK,* vol. 2.
68. KA NFA, 4. Armee, fasc. 70, Tagebücher; KAN, B/23, Mayern, 2. *Armee in der Karpatenschlacht.*
69. KA NFA, 2. Armee, fasc. 95, Tagebücher; 3. Armee, fasc. 42, Tagebücher; V, VII, and XVIII Korps, Tagebücher; KAN, B/544, Kralowetz, X Korps, MS; B/23, Mayern, 2. *Armee in der Karpatenschlacht.*
70. KA MS1.Wkg., Rußland, 1915, No. 36, Südarmee MS; *ÖULK,* vol. 2.
71. KA NFA, 3. Armee, fasc. 42, Tagebücher; KAN, B/544, Kralowetz, X Korps MS; *ÖULK,* vol. 2.
72. KAN, B/23, Mayern, 2. *Armee in der Karpatenschlacht.*
73. Ibid.
74. KANC, B/13, Kundmann, Tagebüch.
75. KA AOK, Op. No. 8525; KA NFA, 3. Armee, fasc. 42, Tagebücher; 4. Armee, fasc. 70, Tagebücher; *ÖULK,* vol. 2; KAN, B/23, Mayern, 2. *Armee in der Karpatenschlacht.*
76. KA NFA, III Korps, Tagebücher; 3. Armee, fasc. 42, Tagebücher; KA Gefechtsberichten, 28. Infantrie Division, Res. No. 359, Gefechtsbericht über den 25 März 1915; KA AOK, AOK Op. No. 8347.
77. KA NFA, 3. Armee, fasc. 11, 3. Armee, Op. No. 3100/12 (Zu Op. 3032); KAN, B/23, Mayern, 2. *Armee in der Karpatenschlacht.*
78. KAN, B/23, Mayern, 2. *Armee in der Karpatenschlacht; ÖULK,* vol. 2.
79. KA NFA, 3. Armee, fasc. 42, Tagebücher; see also *ÖULK,* vol. 2; KAN, B/23, Mayern, 2. *Armee in der Karpatenschlacht.*
80. KAN, B/23, Mayern, 2. *Armee in der Karpatenschlacht;* KA NFA, 3. Armee, fasc. 11.
81. KA NFA, 2. Armee, fasc. 95, Tagebücher; KAN, B/23, Mayern, 2. *Armee in der Karpatenschlacht.*
82. KA AOK, fasc. 607, Cramon.
83. KANC, B/13, Kundmann, Tagebüch, Op. No. 2858/25; KAN, B/23, Mayern, 2. *Armee in der Karpatenschlacht.*
84. *ÖULK,* vol. 2.
85. KA NFA, III, V, and XVIII Korps, Tagebücher; 2. Armee, fasc. 95, Tagebücher; KAN, B/544, Kralowetz, X Korps MS.
86. KAN, B/23, Mayern, 2. *Armee in der Karpatenschlacht.*
87. KA NFA, V Korps, Tagebücher; BWA, TGY 2819, II 143, Gruppe Szurmay, Tagebücher; *ÖULK,* vol. 2.
88. KA NFA, V Korps, Tagebücher; 2. Armee, fasc. 95, Tagebücher; KAN, B/544, Kralowetz, X Korps MS; *ÖULK,* vol. 2.
89. Ibid.
90. KA NFA, V Korps, Tagebücher; KAN, B/23, Mayern, 2. *Armee in der Karpatenschlacht; ÖULK,* vol. 2.
91. KA NFA, XIX Korps, Tagebücher; BWA, TGY 2819, II 143, Gruppe Szurmay, Tagebücher; *ÖULK,* vol. 2.
92. KA NFA, V Korps, Tagebücher; 2. Armee, fasc. 95, Tagebücher; KAN, B/544, Kralowetz, X Korps MS; *ÖULK,* vol. 2.

93. *ÖULK*, vol. 2; KAN, B/23, Mayern, 2. *Armee in der Karpatenschlacht.*
94. KA NFA, 2. Armee, fasc. 58.
95. KANC, B/13, Kundmann, Tagebüch.
96. See KAN, B/23, Mayern, 2. *Armee in der Karpatenschlacht.*
97. KA NFA, V and XVIII Korps, Tagebücher; KANC, B/13, Tagebücher.
98. KA NFA, V Korps, Tagebücher; see *ÖULK*, vol. 2.
99. Ibid.
100. KAN, B/509, Schneller, Tagebücher.
101. KAN, B/600, Lehar, No. 2, Tagebücher.
102. KA MS1.Wkg., Allgemeine, A-4, Veith, *Werdegang und Schicksal.*
103. KA AOK, fasc. 512, Conrad-Falkenhayn, Korrespondenz, Rußland; fasc. 551, Conrad-Falkenhayn, Korrespondenz, Balkan; KAN, B/509, Schneller, Tagebücher; KANC, B/13, Kundmann, Tagebüch.
104. KA AOK, fasc. 615, AOK Tagebücher.
105. KAN, B/23, Mayern, 2. *Armee in der Karpatenschlacht*, 362–363.
106. KA NFA, 2. Armee, fasc. 95, Tagebücher, varia; see KAN, B/23, Mayern, 2. *Armee in der Karpatenschlacht; ÖULK*, vol. 2.
107. Ibid.
108. KA NFA, 3. Armee, fasc. 42, Tagebücher; KAN, B/544, Kralowetz, X Korps MS; AOK, Op. No. 8624; KAN, B/23, Mayern, 2. *Armee in der Karpatenschlacht.*
109. KA AOK, fasc. 607, Cramon; August Cramon, *Unser österreich-ungarischen Bundesgenosse im Weltkriege: Erinnerungen aus meiner vierjährigen Tätigkeit als bevollmächtigter deutscher General beim k.u.k. Armeeoberkommando* (Berlin: E. S. Mittler & Sohn, 1920), 11–12.
110. KA AOK, fasc. 615, AOK, Tagebücher; *ÖULK*, vol. 2.
111. KA MS1.Wkg., Rußland, 1915, No. 36, Südarmee MS; KA NFA, 2. Armee, fasc. 95, Tagebücher.
112. KA AOK, fasc. 615, AOK Tagebücher, AOK Op. No. 8665; KA NFA; 2. Armee, fasc. 95, Tagebücher; 3. Armee, fasc. 42, Tagebücher; KAN, B/544, Kralowetz, X Korps MS; KA MS1.Wkg., Rußland, 1915, No. 36, Südarmee MS, 127; KAN, B/23, Mayern, 2. *Armee in der Karpatenschlacht.*
113. KA NFA, 3. Armee, fasc. 42, Tagebücher, 3. Armee Op. No. 3723.
114. *ÖULK*, vol. 2.
115. KA NFA, 2. Armee, fasc. 12, 2. Armee, Op. No. 2948; XIX and XVIII Korps, Tagebücher; BWA, TGY 2819, II 143, Armee Gruppe Szurmay, 7. Infantrie Division MS.
116. KAN, B/23, Mayern, 2. *Armee in der Karpatenschlacht.*
117. KA NFA, V Korps, Tagebücher; KAN, B/23, Mayern, 2. *Armee im der Karpatenschlacht*, 420.
118. KAN, B/23, Mayern, 2. *Armee in der Karpatenschlacht*, 665.
119. Ibid.; KA NFA, V Korps, Tagebücher.
120. KAN, B/23, Mayern, 2. *Armee in der Karpatenschlacht.*
121. KAN, B/23, Mayern, 2. *Armee in der Karpatenschlacht; ÖULK*, vol. 2; KA AOK, fasc. 615, AOK Tagebücher, AOK Op. No. 8703; KA NFA, 2. Armee fasc. 12, 2. Armee, Op. No. 2927; KA MS1.Wkg., Rußland, 1915, No. 36, Südarmee MS.
122. KAN, B/509, Schneller, Tagebücher.

123. KA MS1.Wkg., Rußland, 1915, No. 36, Südarmee MS.
124. Ibid.; KAN, B/23, Mayern, 2. *Armee in der Karpatenschlacht*; KA NFA, 2. Armee, fasc. 95, Tagebücher; KAN, B/509 Schneller.
125. Ibid.; *ÖULK*, vol. 2.
126. KA NFA, 3. Armee, fasc. 42, Tagebücher; XVIII Korps, Tagebücher; KAN, B/544, Kralowetz, X Korps MS; E. von Tschischwitz, *General von Marwitz: Weltkriegsbriefe* (Berlin: Steiniger Verlag, 1940); see also *ÖULK*, vol. 2.
127. KAN, B/23, Mayern, 2. *Armee in der Karpatenschlacht*.
128. Ibid.
129. Ibid.
130. KAN, B/544, Kralowetz, X Korps, MS; B/23 Mayern, 2. *Armee in der Karpatenschlacht*.
131. KAN, B/23 Mayern, 2. *Armee in der Karpatenschlacht*.
132. Ibid.
133. KA NFA, 3. Armee, fasc. 42, Tagebücher; KAN, B/544, Kralowetz, X Korps MS; B/23 Mayern, 2. *Armee in der Karpatenschlacht*; *ÖULK*, vol. 2.
134. Ibid.
135. KA NFA, 2. Armee, fasc. 12, 2. Armee Op. No. 2960 (AOK Op. No. 8665); BWA, TGY 2819, II 143, Gruppe Szurmay, Tagebücher; KAN, B/23, Mayern, 2. *Armee in der Karpatenschlacht*; B/405, Regenauer, No. 13.
136. KAN, B/23, Mayern, 2. *Armee in der Karpatenschlacht*.
137. Ibid., see *ÖULK*, vol. 2.
138. KA MKSM, separat fasc. 78/77.
139. See *ÖULK*, vol. 2; KAN, B/23, Mayern, 2. *Armee in der Karpatenschlacht*.
140. Ibid.
141. KA NFA, 2. Armee, fasc. 58.
142. KAN, B/23 Mayern, 2. *Armee in der Karpatenschlacht*; *ÖULK*, vol. 2.
143. KAN, B/23 Mayern, 2. *Armee in der Karpatenschlacht*.
144. KAN, B/600, Lehar, No. 2, Tagebücher.
145. *ÖULK*, vol. 2; see Rudolf Hecht, *Fragen zur Heeresergänzung der Gestalten Bewaffneten Macht Österreich-Ungarns während des ersten Weltkrieges* (diss., University of Vienna, 1969).
146. KA NFA, 3. Armee, fasc. 42, Tagebücher; *ÖULK*, vol. 2.
147. *ÖULK*, vol. 2.
148. Ibid.
149. Discussion on 4 Avril 1915, handwritten notes relative to the mission of V Corps, KA AOK, fasc. 503.
150. Egmont Zechlin, "Ludendorff im Jahre 1915. Unveröffentliche Briefe," *Historische Zeitschrift* 211 (1970).
151. KA NFA, 3. Armee, fasc. 11; *ÖULK*, vol. 2.
152. KAN, B/23, Mayern, 2. *Armee in der Karpatenschlacht*, 639–640.
153. KAN, B/23, Mayern, 2. *Armee in der Karpatenschlacht*; KA NFA 2. Armee, fasc. 95, Tagebücher; AOK Op. Nr. 8791, 8813; *ÖULK*, vol. 2.
154. *ÖULK*, vol. 2; KAN, B/23, Mayern, 2. *Armee in der Karpatenschlacht*.
155. Ibid.
156. Ibid.
157. Ibid.

158. *ÖULK*, vol. 2.

159. KAN, B/23, Mayern, 2. *Armee in der Karpatenschlacht.*

160. Ibid.

161. Ibid.

162. General Max Hoffmann (not to be confused with Habsburg Corps commander Hofmann), *War Diaries and Other Papers*, trans. Eric Sutton (London: M. Seeker, 1926), 56–57.

163. KA AOK, fasc. 615, AOK Tagebücher, AOK 8894/1; fasc. 512, Conrad-Falkenhayn, Korrespondenz, Rußland; KANC, B/13; Kundmann, Tagebüch.

164. KA AOK, fasc. 512, Conrad-Falkenhayn, Korrespondenz, Rußland.

165. KAN, B/607, Cramon; KAN, B/23, Mayern, 2. *Armee in der Karpatenschlacht*; KA MKSM, separat fasc. 78/77, Bolfras.

166. KA AOK, fasc. 512, Conrad-Falkenhayn, Korrespondenz, Rußland.

167. Ibid.

168. Ibid.

169. Ibid.; KA AOK, fasc. 607, Cramon.

170. KAN, B/23, Mayern, 2. *Armee in der Karpatenschlacht*, 855; *ÖULK*, vol. 2.

171. Ibid.

172. KAN, B/23, Mayern, 2. *Armee in der Karpatenschlacht*, 855; *ÖULK*, vol. 2.

173. Ibid.

174. KA MKSM, separat fasc. 78/77, Bolfras.

175. KA AOK, fasc. 512, Conrad-Falkenhayn, Korrespondenz, Rußland; KAN, B/23, Mayern, 2. *Armee in der Karpatenschlacht.*

176. Ibid.

177. *ÖULK*, vol. 2; KA NFA, V Korps, Tagebücher; 3. Armee fasc. 42, Tagebücher, 3. Armee, Op. No. 3138/25.

178. *ÖULK*, vol. 2; KA NFA, 2. Armee, fasc. 58; 2. Armee, fasc. 95, Tagebücher.

179. KAN, B/23, Mayern, 2. *Armee in der Karpatenschlacht*; *ÖULK*, vol. 2.

180. KAN, B/23, Mayern, 2. *Armee in der Karpatenschlacht.*

181. KA NFA, 2. Armee, fasc. 12, 2. Army Op. No. 3128, 3122; 2. Armee Kdo., Res. No. 4616.

182. KAN, B/23, Mayern, 2. *Armee in der Karpatenschlacht*; KA AOK, fasc. 503, AOK Op. No. 9030; KAN, B/509, Schneller, Tagebücher.

183. Ibid.; *ÖULK*, vol. 2.

184. KA AOK fasc. 512, Conrad-Falkenhayn, Korrespondenz, Rußland; *ÖULK*, vol. 2.

BIBLIOGRAPHY

Unpublished Documents

VIENNA WAR ARCHIVES

Armee Ober Kommando
Conrad-Falkenhayn

Fasc. 512   Conrad-Falkenhayn—Rußland Korrespondenz
Fasc. 551   Conrad-Falkenhayn—Balkan Korrespondenz
Fasc. 560   Conrad-Falkenhayn—Italien Korrespondenz

ARMEE OBER KOMMANDO (AOK)

Fasc. 10–15 Aus Op. No. 4801–5200

AOK OPERATIONS ABTEILUNG

Fasc. 22–29 Aus Op. No. 7301–7700

K.U.K. OPERATIONS ABTEILUNG "R" GRUPPE: 1915

Fasc. 497–503, 523, 607, 614–615
Juni

AOK TAGEBÜCHER

Fasc. 679–682   1914 7/23–11/29
Fasc. 796   12/16–12/31 1914
Fasc. 797   Februar 1915
Fasc. 799   März 1915
Fasz. 800   April 1915 Evidenz der feindlichen Situation
Fasc. 873   Jänner 1915
Fasc. 874   Februar 1915
Fasc. 875   März 1915
Fasc. 876   Avril 1915

ARCHIV CONRAD

A-6   Varia
A-7   Varia
B-7   Januar 1915 bis Avril 1915
B-12   Rudolf Kundmann Tagebüch 23 Juli–31 Dezember
B-13   Rudolf Kundmann Tagebüch vom 1/1 1915–4/XI 1916

NEUE FELD AKTEN

2. Op. Armee Kdo.
Fasc. 15–21, 46–53, 66, 95

3. Op. Armee Kdo.
Fasc. 10–15, 27–35, 42, 48–51
4. Armee
Fasc. 14–15, 70, 73, 78–81

7. Armee 1915: Armee Gruppe Pflanzer-Baltin
Fasc. 4   Januar 1915
Fasc. 9   April
Fasc. 10   Mai
Fasc. 11   Mai
Fasc. 21   Tagebücher
Fasc. 29   Operativen Akten general Januar–Juni

MILITÄR KANZLEI SEINER MAJESTÄT (MKSM)
Separate Fasc. 78/77   Korrespondenz Conrad-Bolfras, 1914, 1915
Separate Fasc. 79/42
Separate Fasc. 79/53
Separate Fasc. 84
Separate Fasc. 100
1915 MKSM 69-8 Standesbewegung Juni 1915 (Document)

NACHLÄSSE
B/4   Svetozar von Bonya Boroević
B/8   Eduard Fischer
B/16   Ferdinand Freiherr von Marterer
B/23   Karl Mayern
B/45   Georg Veith
B/58   August Urbanski von Ostrymiecz No. 3: Generaloberst Karl Freiherr von Pflanzer-Baltin. Das Lebensbild eines österreichisch-ungarischen Heerführers
B/75   Arthur Freiherr Bolfras von Ahnenberg
B/151   Theodor Ritter von Zeynek
B/203   Otto Ritter von Berndt No. 2, 3, Tagebücher
B/366   Karl Lauer
B/405   K. V. Regenauer
B/509   Karl Schneller No. 2: Kriegstagebuch
B/544   Gottlieb Kralowetz von Hohenrecht Karpatenkrieg—X. Korps—Manuskript
B/557   Karl Freiherr von Pflanzer-BaltinTagebücher—Karpathenkrieg
B/558   Aurel le von Le Beau
B/589   August von Pitreich
B/600   Anton Freiherr von Lehar, No. 2 Tagebücher
B/700   Hans Mailath-Pokorny
B/726   Robert Nowak No. 8: Die Klammer des Reiches. Das Verhalten der elf Nationalitäten Österreich-Ungarns in der k.u.k Wehrmacht, 1914–1918
B/800   Rudolf Kiszling Die k.u.k. 2. Armee vom 10. November 1914 bis zum Jahresschluss
B/844   Waltern Heyendorff, Tagebücher

B/1000 Hermann Baron Kövess von Kövessháza
B/1041 Karl Bornemann Kriegsgeschichte-Vortragsentwürfe Weltkrieg, 1914–1918
B/1063 Johann von Burgauhof Straub No. 6: Auskünfte über Eisenbahn technische Fragen
B/1137 Hermann Kusmanek von Burgstädten, No. 2, Przemyśl

MANUSKRIPTE
Manuskripte 1. Weltkrieg 1914: Balkan
No. 12 Österreich-Ungarn Krieg gegen Serbien-Montenegro, Woinewich
No. 13 Tageweise Zusammenstellung der Ereignisse am Balkan Kriegschauplatz 9/1–12/31 1914, AOK
No. 15 Der Herbstfeldzug 1914 gegen Serbien und Montenegro Anfang September–15 November 1914—Karl Mayern
No. 16 Der Herbstfeldzug 1914 gegen Serbien und Montenegro 16 November–Ende Dezember—Karl Mayern
No. 18 Zusammenfassung des Herbstfeldzugen 1914 gegen Serbien und Montenegro—Karl Mayern
No. 23 Die OHL und Balkan-Regenauer

Manuskripte 1. Weltkrieg 1915: Rußland
No. 1   Die k.u.k. 2. Armee in der Karpatenschlacht 1914/15. Karl Mayern
No. 2   Die Karpatenschlacht Mitte Jänner bis Ende April 1915. Karl Mayern
No. 3   Kriegserrinerungen aus den Karpaten. Sturm in Gebirge März, 1915
No. 5   Die westliche Flügelgruppe der 7. Armee in Karpaten. Paic
No. 6   Der Winterfeldzug in Polen und Galizien. 18/12. 1914–Anfang Jänner 1915. Holy
No. 19 Festung Przemyśl, Stuckheil
No. 26 Zur Vorgeschichte der deutschen Südarmee
No. 32 Die Winterschlacht in den Karpaten 1915—Obstlt. M. Schwarz
No. 36 Die deutsche Südarmee von Anfang Januar bis Anfang Juli 1915. Deutsch Reichsarchiv

Übersetzung Nordost
No. 2   Strategische Skizzen des Krieges der Jahre 1914–1918. Periode vom 12 (25) Nov. 1914–15 (28) Feb. 1915. A. Nesmanow
No. 3   Unser Verlust von Galizien im Jahre 1915. M Bontsch—Brujewitsch
No. 8   Das militärische Ubereinkommen Rußlands
No. 10 Strategische Studie über den Weltkrieg, 1914–1918 (14 Sept. bis 20 Nov. 1914). G. Korolkow
No. 14 Der Sturm auf Przemyśl 7.10.1914. Peter Wladimirowitsch Tscherkassow
No. 28 Von Lodz bis Gorlice Jänner–März 1915. A. M. Zajonstschowskij

Manuskripte 1. Wkg.—Allgemeine
A-4   Werdegang und Schicksal—Georg Veith
A-9   Statische Übersicht d. Verluste in Weltkrieg bis Juni 1915—Obstlt. Waschutz
A-70   Die österreich-ungarische Heereskavallerie Nordost Front—Oberst Alfred von Dragoni

A-75   Militärgeographische und operative Betrachtungen über die Karpaten—
Emil Ratzenhofer

BUDAPEST WAR ARCHIVES

Manuscript Pamperl
TGY, II 143 Armee Gruppe Szurmay
7. Infantrie Division
40. Honvéd Infantrie Division
38. Honvéd Infantrie Division
54. Infantrie Division
8. Kavallerie Division

Published Sources

Afflerbach, Holger. *Falkenhayn. Politsches Denken und Handeln im Kaisserreich.* Munich: R. Oldenbourg Verlag, 1994.

Arz, Generaloberst von Straussenburg. *Zur Geschichte des Großen Krieges, 1914–1918. Aufzeichnungen.* Vienna: Rikola Verlag, 1924.

Bardolff, Carl Freiherr von. *Soldat im alten Österreich. Erinnerungen aus meinem Leben.* Jena: E. Diederichs Verlag, 1943.

Beck, Ludwig. "West- oder Ost-Offensive 1914?" In *Studien,* 141–185. Edited by Hans Speidel. Stuttgart, 1955.

Broucek, Peter. "Taktische Erkenntnisse aus dem russish-japanischen Krieg und deren Beachtung in Österreich-Ungarn." *Mitteilung des Österreichischen Staatsarchiv* 30 (1977): 191–220.

Brusilov, A. A. *A Soldier's Notebook, 1914–1918.* Westport, Conn.: Greenwood Press, 1930.

Churchill, Winston. *The Unknown War: The Eastern Front.* New York: Charles Scribner's Sons, 1931.

Conrad, Feldmarschall Franz von Hötzendorf. *Aus meiner Dienstzeit, 1906–1918.* 5 vols. Vienna: Rikola Verlag, 1921–1925.

Cramon, August. *Unser österreich-ungarischen Bundesgenosse im Weltkriege: Erinnerungen aus meiner vierjährigen Tätigkeit als bevollmächtigter deutscher General beim k.u.k. Armeeoberkommando.* Berlin: E. S. Mittler & Sohn, 1920.

Czermak, Wilhelm. *In deinen Lager war Österreich. Die österreichische-ungarische Armee.* Breslau: Korn Verlag, 1938.

Danilov, General Jury N. *Rußland im Weltkriege, 1914–1915.* Jena: Verlag Frommann, 1925.

Ehnl, Maximilian. "Die österreichisch-ungarische Landmacht nach Aufbau, Gliederung, Friedengarnison, Einteilung und nationaler Zusammensetzung im Sommer 1914." Ergänzungsheft 9 zum *Österreich-Ungarns letzter Krieg, 1914–1918.* Bundesministerium für Heereswesen und vom Kriegsarchiv. Vienna: Verlag Militärwissenschaftlicher Mitteilungen, 1934.

Enderes, Bruno. "Die österreichischen Eisenbahnen." *Verkehrswesen im Kriege. Die österreichischen Eisenbahnen.* Wirtschafts- und Sozialgeschichte des Weltkrieges. Vienna: Holder-Pichler-Tempsky, 1931.

Falkenhayn, Erich von. *The German General Staff and Its Decisions, 1914–1916.* New York: Dodd, Mead and Co., 1920.

Ferenc, Julies. *1914–1918: A világháboru magyar szemmel.* Budapest: Magyar Szemle Tarasog, 1933.

Fischer, Dr. Eduard. *Krieg ohne Heer, Meine Verteidigung der Bukowina gegen die Russen.* Vienna: Franz Schubert, 1935.

Forstner, Franz. *Przemyśl. Österreich-Ungarns bedeutendste Festung.* Vienna: Österreichischer Bundesverlag, 1987.

Franek, Major Dr. Fritz. "Die Entwicklung des österreich-ungarischen Wehrmacht in den ersten zwei Kriegsjahren." *Militärwissenschaftliche und -technische Mitteilungen* 64 (1933): 15–31, 98–111.

———. "Probleme der Organisation im ersten Kriegsjahre." *Militärwissenschaftliche und -technische Mitteilungen* 61 (1930): 977–990.

Freytag-Loringhoven, Freiherr Hugo von. *Menschen und Dinge, wie ich sie in meinem Leben sah.* Berlin: E. S. Mittler & Sohn, 1923.

Gabriel, F. "Wichtigste Waffen." *Österreichische Militärische Zeitung,* 1968, 436–438.

Glaise-Horstenau, Edmund von. *Ein General im Zwielicht: Die Erinnerungen Edmund Glaises von Horstenau.* Edited by Peter Broucek. Vol. 1. Vienna: Böhlau, 1980.

Goiginger, Feldmarschalleutnant. "Betrachtungen über die anfänglichen Operationspläne der Mittelmächte." *Militärwissenschaftliche und -technische Mitteilungen* 58 (1927): 171–181.

———. *The Russian Campaign of 1914: The Beginning of the War and Operations in East Prussia.* Translated by A. G. S. Muntz. Carlisle, Pa.: The Command and General Staff School Press, 1933.

Golovine, Nikolai. *The Russian Army in the World War.* New Haven, Conn.: Yale UniversityPress, 1931.

Gomoll, Wilhelm Conrad. *Im Kampf gegen Rußland und Serbien.* Leipzig: A. Brockhaus, 1916.

Grossman, Dave. *On Killing: The Psychological Cost of Learning to Kill in War and Society.* Revised edition. New York: Back Bay Books, 2009.

Hecht, Rudolf. *Fragen zur Heeresergänzung der Gestalten Bewaffneten Macht Österreich-Ungarns während des ersten Weltkrieges.* Diss., University of Vienna, 1969.

Heiden, Herman. *Bollwerk am San, Schicksal der Festung Przemyśl.* Berlin: Gerhard Stalling, 1946.

Herwig, Holger. *The First World War: Germany and Austria-Hungary, 1914–1918.* New York: Arnold, 1997.

Höbelt, Lothar. "Schlieffen, Beck, Potiorek und das Ende der gemeinsamen deutsch-österreichisch-ungarischen Aufmarschpläne im Osten." *Militärgeschichtliche Mitteilungen* 36 (1984): 7–30.

Hoffmann, General Max. *War Diaries and Other Papers.* Translated by Eric Sutton. London: M. Seeker, 1926.

Jerábek, Rudolf. *Die Brussilowoffensive. 1916. Ein Wendepunkt der Koalitionskriegfuhrung der Mittelmächte.* Vienna: PHD, 1982.

Josef, Feldmarschall Erzherzog. *A Világháború amilyennek én láttam.* Budapest: Ungarische Akademie der Wissenschaften, 1926–1931.

Kerchnahwe, Hugo. "Der Karpatenfeldzüge 1914/15." *Militärwissenschaftliche und -technische Mitteilungen* (1922): 594–604.

———. "Die unzureichende Kriegsrüstung der Mittelmächte als Hauptursache ihrer Niederlage." Vienna: Verlag der militarwissenschaftlichen, 1933.

Kerchnawe, H., and E. Ottenschläger. *Ehrenbuch unserer Artillerie; Österreichs Artillerie im Weltkriege, 1914–1918.* Stockerau, Austria: Engelbert Hlavka, 1925.

Kiszling, Rudolf. *Die Hohe Führung der Heere Habsburg im Ersten Weltkrieg.* Vienna: Bundesministerium für Landesverteidigung: Büro für Wehrpolitik, 1984.

——. "Das Nationalitätproblem in Habsburgs Wehrmacht, 1848–1918." *Der Donauraum* 4 (1959): 82–92.

——. *Österreich-Ungarns Anteil am ersten Weltkrieg.* Graz: Stiasny Verlag, 1958.

——. "Österreich-Ungarns Kriegsvorbereitungen. Mobilisierung, Aufmarsch und Operationspläne im Sommer 1914." *Militärwissenschaftliche und -technische Mitteilungen* 53 (1922): 273–288.

Lengyel, Bela von. "Die Heerführung des Feldmarschall Conrad im Jahre 1914." *Allgemeine Schweizerische Militärische Zeitschrift* 102 (1956): 679–689, 756–789.

Lincoln, W. Bruce. *Passage through Armageddon. The Russians in War and Revolution, 1914–1918.* New York: Simon & Schuster, 1986.

Lucas, James S. *Austro-Hungarian Infantry.* London: Almarck, 1974.

Ludendorff, General Erich von. *Meine Kriegserinnerungen, 1914–1918.* Berlin: E. S. Mittler & Sohn, 1921.

Matthes, Kurt. *Die 9. Armee im Weichselfeldzug, 1914.* Berlin: Junker & Dunnhaupt, 1936.

Mátyás, Rákosi. *Visszaemlékezések, 1892–1925.* Budapest: Napvilag Kiade, 2002.

Mayern, Karl. "Die Karpatenschlacht Jänner–April 1915." *Militärwissenschaftliche und -technische Mitteilungen* 54 (1923): 354–364.

Moltke, Generaloberst Helmuth Graf von. *Erinnerungen, Briefe, Dokumente, 1877–1916. Ein Bild vom Kriegsausbruch, erster Kriegsführung und Persönlichkeit des ersten militärischen Führers.* Stuttgart: Der Kommende Tag A.G. Verlag, 1922.

Moran, Lord. *The Anatomy of Courage.* 1945; New York: Carrol & Graf, 2007.

Musulin, Freiherr von. *Der Haus am Ballplatz. Erinnerungen eines österreichungarischen Diplomaten.* Munich: Verlag für Kulturpolitik, 1924.

Nónay, Dezsö. *A volt. m. kir. szegedi 5. Honvéd gyalogezred a világháborúban.* Budapest, 1931.

Österreich-Ungarns letzter Krieg, 1914–1918. Vol. 1, *Das Kriegsjahr, 1914. Vom Kriegsausbruch bis zum Ausgang der Schlacht bei Limanowa-Lapanów.* Bundesministerium für Heereswesen und vom Kriegsarchiv. Vienna: Verlag Militärwissenschaftlicher Mitteilungen, 1930, 1931.

Österreich-Ungarns letzter Krieg, 1914–1918. Vol. 2, *Das Kriegsjahr, 1915.* Bundesministerium für Heereswesen und vom Kriegsarchiv. Vienna: Verlag Militärwissenschaftlicher Mitteilungen, 1931.

Peball, Kurt. *Conrad von Hötzendorf. Private Aufzeichnungen, Erste Veröffentlichungen aus den Papieren des k.u.k. Generalstabchefs.* Vienna: Amalthea Verlag, 1977.

Pitreich, Anton. *Der österreich-ungarische Bundesgenosse im Sperrfeuer.* Klagenfurt: Arthur Killitsch, 1930.

Pitreich, Max Freiherr von. *Lemberg, 1914.* Vienna: Verlag von Adolf Holzhausens Nachfolger Universitätsbuchdrucker, 1929.

————. *1914: Die militärischen Probleme unseres Kriegsbeginnes. Ideen, Gründe und Zusammenhänge.* Vienna: Selbstverlag, 1934.

Plaschka, Richard G. "Zur Vorgeschichte des Übergangen von Einheiten des Infantrieregiments No. 28 an der russischen Front 1915." *Österreich und Europa. Festgabe fur Hugo Hantsch zum 70. Geburtstag.* Graz: Verlag Styria, 1965.

Ratzenhofer, Emil. "Die Aufmarsch hinter den Karpathen im Winter 1915." *Militärwissenschaftliche und -technische Mitteilungen* 61 (1930): 499–513.

————. "Truppentransporte beim Winterfeldzug in den Karpaten." *Wissen und Wehr* 10 (1929): 231–244.

————. "Verlust Kakül für den Karpatenwinter 1915." In *Österreich-Ungarns letzter Krieg, 1914–1918.* Bundesministerium für Heereswesen und vom Kriegsarchiv. Vienna: Verlag Militärwissenschaftlicher Mitteilungen, 1930.

Rauchensteiner, Manfried. *Der Tod des Doppeladlers.* Vienna: Verlag Styria, 1993.

Regele, Oskar. *Feldmarschall Conrad. Auftrag und Erfüllung, 1906–1918.* Vienna: Verlag Herold, 1955.

Ronge, Max. *Kriegs- und Industriespionage. Zwölf Jahre Kundschaftsdienst.* Vienna: Amalthea Verlag, 1930.

Rothenburg, Gunther E. "The Habsburg Army in the First World War: 1914–1918." In *The Habsburg Empire in World War I,* edited by Robert A. Kann, Béla K. Kiraly, and Paula S. Fichter, 73–86. Boulder, Colo.: East European Quarterly Press, 1976.

Rutherford, Ward. *The Russian Army in World War I.* London: Gordon Cremonesi, 1975.

Schafer, Theobald von. "Die militärische Zusammenwirken der Mittelmächte im Herbst 1914." *Wissen und Wehr* 7 (1926): 215–234.

————. "Operationen gegen Übermacht, dargestellt an den Ostfeldzügen des Jahres 1914." *Wissen und Wehr* 7 (1926): 257–276.

Schwalb, Hans G. M. "Die Verteidigung von Przemyśl, 1914–1915." *Mitteilungen über Gegenstücke des Artillerie und Geniewesens* 149 (1918): 1373–1392.

Schwarte, Max. *Der große Krieg, 1914–1918.* Vol. 5: *Der österreichisch-ungarische Krieg.* Leipzig: Barth in Ausgl., 1922.

Silberstein, Gerard E. *The Troubled Alliance: German–Austrian Relations, 1914 to 1917.* Lexington: University Press of Kentucky, 1970.

Sondhaus, Lawrence. *Franz Conrad von Hötzendorf: Architect of the Apocalypse.* Boston: Humanities Press, 2000.

Steinitz, Edvard Ritter. "Ausharren oder Ausweichen? Die Kämpfe der 2. Infantrie Division in den Karpathen Januar bis 4. Feber 1915." *Militärwissenschaftliche-und-technische Mitteilungen* 61 (1930): 97–104.

————. "Die Reichsbefestigung: Österreich-Ungarns zur Zeit Conrads von Hötzendorf." In *Österreich-Ungarns letzter Krieg, 1914–1918.* Bundesministerium für Heereswesen und vom Kriegsarchiv. Vienna: Verlag Militärwissenschaftlicher Mitteilungen, 1930.

Stöckelle, Gustav. "Der Feldzug von Limanowa-Lapanów 1.–20. Dezember 1914. Abschluss der Herbstkämpfe gegen Rußland." *Österreichische Militärische Zeitschrift* 1 (1965): 39–46.

Stone, Norman. "Austria-Hungary." In *Knowing One's Enemies,* edited by Ernest R. May, 37–61. Princeton, N.J.: Princeton University Press, 1988.

————. *The Eastern Front, 1914–1917.* New York: Charles Scribner's Sons, 1975.

Straube, Wolfgang Berhard. *Przemyśl, 1914/15.* Vienna: Payer, 1936.

Stuckheil, Franz. "Die Festung Przemyśl in der Ausrustüngszeit." *Militärwissenschaftliche und -technische Mitteilungen* 55 (1924): 200–230.

———. "Die strategische Rolle Przemyśl auf dem ostlichen Kriegschauplatz." *Militärwissenschaftliche und -technische Mitteilungen* 54 (1923): 60–78, 132–146.

———. "Die zweite Einschließung der Festung Przemyśl. II. *Abschnitt Zeiten des Niederganges.*" *Militärwissenschaftliche und -technische Mitteilungen* 55 (1924): 226–231.

———. "Die zweite Enschließung der Festung Przemyśl. III. *Abschnitt das Ende.*" *Militärwissenschaftliche und -technische Mitteilungen* 55 (1924): 289–309, 395–417; 56 (1925): 110–133, 222–236, 346–367; 57 (1926): 162–173, 286–296, 405–410, 530–535.

Stürgkh, Graf Joseph von. *Im deutschen Großen Hauptquartier.* Leipzig: Paul List Verlag, 1921.

Szabó, Laszló. *A nagy temetö (Przemyśl ostroma, 1914–1915).* Budapest: Nepszerü Törtenelem, 1982.

Tisza, Stephan Count. *Briefe, 1914–1918.* 2 vols. Berlin: Reimer Hobbing, 1928.

Tschischwitz, E. von. *General von Marwitz: Weltkriegsbriefe.* Berlin: Steiniger Verlag, 1940.

Tunstall, Graydon A. "Die Karpatenschlachten 1915" (two-part series). *Truppendienst* 2 and 3, (1990): 132–137, 226–231.

———. "The Habsburg Command Conspiracy." *Austrian History Yearbook* 27 (1996): 181–198.

———. *Planning for War against Russia and Serbia. Austro-Hungarian and German Military Strategies, 1871–1914.* New York: Columbia University Press, 1993.

Urbanski von Ostrymiecz, August. *Conrad von Hötzendorf. Soldat und Mensch. Dargestellt von seinem Mitarbeiter Feldmarschalleutnant August.* Vienna: Ulrich Mosers Verlag, 1938.

Wegs, J. Robert. "Transportation: The Achilles' Heel of the Habsburg War Effort." In *The Habsburg Empire in World War I.* Edited by Robert A. Kann, Béla K. Kiraly, and Paula S. Fichter, 121–134. Boulder, Colo.: East European Quarterly Press, 1976.

Der Weltkrieg 1914 bis 1918. Vols. 3 and 4. *Die militärischen Operationen zu Lande* (RAWK). Berlin: E. S. Mittler und Sohn, 1925–1942.

Wendt, Hermann. *Der italienische Kriegsschauplatz in europäischen Konflikten. Seine Bedeutung für die Kriegführung an Frankreichs Nordostgrenze.* Berlin: Junker und Dunnhaupt Verlag, 1936.

Wisshaupt, Ernst. *Die Tiroler Kaiserjäger im Weltkriege, 1914–1918.* Vienna: Verlagsanstalt Amon Fran Göth, 1935.

Zanantoni, Eduard. *Die deutsch-bömische 29. Infantriedivision im Kriegsjahre, 1914–15.* Vol. 1, *Vom Juli 1914 bis Juli 1915.* Reichenberg: Heimatsöhne im Weltkrieg, 1926.

Zechlin, Egmont. "Ludendorff im Jahre 1915. Unveröffentliche Briefe." *Historische Zeitschrift* 211 (1970): 316–353.

INDEX